Professional
WPF Programming:
.NET Development with the Windows® Presentation Foundation

Professional
WPF Programming:
.NET Development with the
Windows® Presentation
Foundation

Chris Andrade,
Shawn Livermore,
Mike Meyers,
Scott Van Vliet

Wiley Publishing, Inc.

Professional WPF Programming: .NET Development with the Windows® Presentation Foundation

Published by
Wiley Publishing, Inc.
10475 Crosspoint Boulevard
Indianapolis, IN 46256
www.wiley.com

Copyright © 2007 by Wiley Publishing, Inc., Indianapolis, Indiana

Published simultaneously in Canada

ISBN: 978-0-470-04180-2

Manufactured in the United States of America

10 9 8 7 6 5 4 3 2 1

Library of Congress Cataloging-in-Publication Data is available from the publisher.

For general information on our other products and services please contact our Customer Care Department within the United States at (800) 762-2974, outside the United States at (317) 572-3993 or fax (317) 572-4002.

Trademarks: Wiley, the Wiley logo, Wrox, the Wrox logo, Programmer to Programmer, and related trade dress are trademarks or registered trademarks of John Wiley & Sons, Inc. and/or its affiliates, in the United States and other countries, and may not be used without written permission. All other trademarks are the property of their respective owners. Wiley Publishing, Inc., is not associated with any product or vendor mentioned in this book.

Wiley also publishes its books in a variety of electronic formats. Some content that appears in print may not be available in electronic books.

About the Authors

Chris Andrade is a Principal with Novera Consulting, a Microsoft Certified Partner specializing in enterprise architecture and development with .NET and Microsoft server technology. Chris devotes most of his time to assisting companies in applying Microsoft technologies to improve their business processes and operations. Chris has worked within a diverse range of business verticals, including automotive, healthcare, and mortgage. Chris also takes active participation within the local developer community, speaking and presenting along the west coast whenever possible.

Shawn Livermore (MCAD, MCSD, PMP) [shawnlivermore.blogspot.com] has been architecting and developing Microsoft-based solutions for nearly a decade. Shawn has been consulting as an enterprise and solutions architect for Fortune 500 clientele within highly visible enterprise implementations. His range of technical competence stretches across platforms and lines of business, but he specializes in Microsoft .NET enterprise application architectures and Microsoft server-based product integrations. Shawn lives in the Southern California area with his beautiful wife Shantell and amazing daughter Elexzandreia. Shawn also enjoys beating his friend Jason at air hockey, basketball, baseball, football, arcade games, cards, billiards, ping pong, shuffleboard, trivia, golf, racquetball, dirt bike races, cross-country skiing... and pretty much any other sport in existence. Shawn would like to once again remind Jason, "Who's your daddy?"

Mike Meyers is president of Novera Consulting Inc, a software development and consulting firm specializing in custom application development utilizing the .NET platform and Microsoft server technology. Based in Orange County, California, Mike's company is focused on providing solutions based on Microsoft platforms and technology to companies spanning multiple industries. Mike has worked in a number of industries, including mortgage, healthcare, and various ecommerce ventures as developer, architect, and project manager. When he's not writing code, Mike is active mountain biking in southern California, hiking with his four-legged Labrador Dakota or playing music with friends.

Scott Van Vliet is an accomplished Solutions Architect who has spent the past decade delivering successful Microsoft-based solutions to his clients. Currently a Senior Manager with Capgemini, a worldwide leader in technology consulting services, Scott has managed, architected, and developed solutions for companies across the globe. He is also the Microsoft Delivery Leader for Capgemini's Telecom, Media & Entertainment practice, providing technical and engagement leadership on all Microsoft-based projects. Scott can be reached via his Web site at http://www.scottvanvliet.com/.

To my wife Sena and son Ethan: for their patience, love, and understanding during the process of writing this book. I love you both so much.

—Chris Andrade

To my best friend and life companion, Shantell, who has stuck around with me through it all and never once doubted me. You've believed in me from the beginning when we had nothing. I appreciate your friendship and your love, and look forward to getting old and wrinkled together. Thank you for supporting this book and the time it required.

And, of course, I am so thankful for my daughter Elexzandreia, who has taught me so many things. Thanks for letting daddy type on the laptop while you write me little cards and "projects." We must have gone through thousands of tape dispensers and construction paper packages over these last few years. You're an angel, and my greatest accomplishment in this life would be to see your life flourish and grow into the woman God has designed you to be.

—Shawn Livermore

To my parents, Richard and Linda, who have always supported my entrepreneurial spirit, helping me to become who I am today. In particular, I dedicate this to my father for spending 30 years with I.B.M. to support his family and foster my interest in computers, and to my mother for raising a handful and teaching me an appreciation for writing and the arts. I would also like to dedicate this book to my brother Nick. No one could ask for a better brother or friend.

—Mike Meyers

Credits

Senior Acquisitions Editor
Jim Minatel

Development Editor
John Sleeva

Technical Editor
Carl Daniel

Production Editor
Christine O'Connor

Copy Editor
Nancy Rapoport

Editorial Manager
Mary Beth Wakefield

Production Manager
Tim Tate

Vice President and Executive Group Publisher
Richard Swadley

Vice President and Executive Publisher
Joseph B. Wikert

Graphics and Production Specialists
Brooke Graczyk
Denny Hager
Jennifer Mayberry
Barbara Moore
Alicia B. South

Quality Control Technicians
Cynthia Fields
Brian H. Walls

Project Coordinator
Adrienne Martinez

Proofreading and Indexing
Aptara

Anniversary Logo Design
Richard Pacifico

Acknowledgments

Many thanks to the many colleagues and friends I have worked with who have contributed so much to my life and professional development. I would especially like to thank my partner Mike Meyers for his accountability and support, and Mickey Williams, who inspires me to never stop learning and give back as much as I can to the community.

—Chris Andrade

I must acknowledge the Lord Jesus. My life would be a hopeless recursion without Him in charge. For all you computer geeks out there reading these books, be advised: your search for information and advancement in technology and science will not have any significance if your search for the Savior has not been fulfilled. This life means nothing without a Savior, and the only true Savior is Jesus Christ. If your logical approach to life has somehow given into the false "scientific" explanations for our existence, then I appeal to your spirit. Be a searcher for truth in your spirit and do not stop until you fill that gaping hole in your spirit. It is a need placed deep within you that only Jesus Christ can satisfy.

—Shawn Livermore

I would like to thank the members of the WPF development team who took time out of their busy day to provide me with insight into the internals of the .NET 3.0 platform. I would like to personally thank each of the developers who work with me on a daily basis. In particular, I would like to thank Daniel Kesler, who gave me numerous opportunities to lead projects early in my career, and Anthony Dulkis, for taking the leap with me into the once unfamiliar world of software consulting. I would especially like to thank Chris Andrade for asking me to participate in the writing of this book and for working tirelessly with me on numerous projects over the years.

—Mike Meyers

First and foremost, I'd like to thank my wife, Sebrina, for her love, friendship, and unwavering support. I must also thank my wonderful children, Chloe, Aidan, and Gabriella—your smiles help get me through those long nights of writing and coding. I'd also like to thank my father, Tom, for his infinite wisdom and unimpeded confidence in me; my best friend Anthony Valentino, always my partner in crime; and my mentor Mark Borao for his guidance and leadership. Finally, a very big thank you to the Wrox team for their understanding and support!

—Scott Van Vliet

Contents

Acknowledgments ix

Introduction xix

Chapter 1: Overview of Windows Presentation Foundation 1

A Brief History of the Windows API 2

Platform Evolution 2

Introducing .NET Framework 3.0 3

Meet Windows Presentation Foundation 3

Guiding Design Principles 3

Architecture 5

XAML 15

Declarative vs. Imperative 15

Visual Design Tools 18

XamlPad 18

Microsoft Expression Blend 19

Visual Designer for Windows Presentation Foundation 20

Electric Rain ZAM 3D 21

Mobiform Aurora 22

Summary 23

Chapter 2: WPF and .NET Programming 25

Getting Started 26

Required Installations 26

Types of WPF Applications 26

My First WPF Application 27

WPF Development Concepts 29

XAML 29

The Application Object 30

Creating the User Interface 32

Handling Events 35

Working with Controls 41

Triggers 51

Language Support 58

Deployment 61

Summary 61

Contents

Chapter 3: Anatomy of a WPF-Enabled Application   **63**

Project Composition   **63**

App.Manifest   66

AssemblyInfo.cs   66

Resources.resx   68

Settings.settings   68

MyApp.xaml   70

.NET Framework 3.0 Windows Application   **71**

Window1.xaml   72

XAML Browser Application   **73**

Page1.xaml   73

WCF Service Library   **75**

Class1.cs   75

WPF Custom Control Library   **78**

UserControl1.xaml   79

Summary   **82**

Chapter 4: Building a Rich UI with Microsoft Expression Blend — Part I   **83**

Overview   **84**

The Design Environment   **85**

Workspace Panels   86

The Artboard   87

Configuring the Environment   88

Project Structure   **90**

Adding a New Project File   90

Building and Deploying a Project   91

Creating Vector Objects   **91**

Shapes   92

Paths   93

Manipulating Objects with the Properties Panel   **94**

The Transform Panel   94

The Brushes Panel   95

Opacity, Transparency, and Visibility   97

Manipulating Text   **98**

Managing Layouts   **99**

UI Layout Panels   100

Other Layout Controls   103

Nesting Layout Panels   103

Animation **104**
Timeline Sub-Panel 104
Keyframes 105
Animate an Object's Property 106
Motion Paths 106
Triggers 107
Creating Controls 108
Templates 110
Styles 111
States 112
Importing Audio/Video Media 113
Summary **113**

Chapter 5: Building a Rich UI with Microsoft Expression Blend — Part II **115**

Expression Blend Workflow **116**
Code Editing with Visual Studio 2005 117
Handling User Input **118**
Keyboard and Mouse Classes 118
Events and Event Handling 118
Positioning 120
Hit Testing 124
The WPF Animation API **135**
Animation Classes 135
Creating a Dynamic Animation Procedurally with Code 135
Programmatic Animation 139
Interacting with Storyboards **143**
WPF Drawing API **145**
Geometry 145
Shapes 146
Brushes 149
Summary **153**

Chapter 6: Special Effects **155**

Brushes **156**
SolidColorBrush 156
GradientBrush 162
ImageBrush 165
DrawingBrush 167
VisualBrush 169

Contents

Bitmap Effects **171**
Transformations **175**
    TranslateTransform 178
    ScaleTransform 180
    SkewTransform 183
    RotateTransform 186
    Opacity Masks 188
Putting It All Together — Combining Effects **191**
    Bouncing Ball with Reflection Example 191
    Animated Image Viewer Example 197
Summary **203**

Chapter 7: Custom Controls **205**

Overview **206**
Control Base Classes **207**
    The UserControl Class 207
    Creating a User Control 207
Data Binding in WPF **217**
    Binding Markup Extensions 217
    Binding Modes 217
    Data Templates 219
    Data Conversions 221
Creating and Editing Styles **222**
    Specifying a Style's Target Type 223
    Inheriting and Overriding Styles 224
    Style Triggers 226
Customizing Existing Controls with Templates **228**
Summary **231**

Chapter 8: Using WPF in the Enterprise **233**

WPF Application Models **234**
    Standalone Applications 235
    Browser-Based Applications 238
    Security Considerations 247
State Management **248**
    Application Object 248
    Isolated Storage 250
    State Management Example 252

Contents

Navigation   **258**
   Elements of Navigation   258
   Structured Navigation   259
   Navigation Topologies   269
Application Localization   **286**
   Automatic Layout Guidelines   287
   Using Grids for Flexibility   289
   Localization Attributes and Comments   290
WPF Deployment Models   **291**
   Building Applications   292
   Deploying Standalone Windows Applications   294
   Deploying XAML Browser Applications   295
   Deploying the .NET Framework 3.0 Runtime   296
Summary   **298**

Chapter 9: Security   **299**

WPF Security Model   **299**
Trusted Versus Express Applications   **300**
Core OS Security   **300**
   LUA   301
   Virtualization   301
   Sandboxing   301
   Cryptography Next Generation   302
CLR Security   **302**
   Code Access Security   303
   The Critical Code Methodology   311
   Verification   313
Microsoft Internet Explorer Security   **313**
   Zone Restrictions   313
   XBAP Sandbox Workarounds   314
   XAML Browser Application Security   315
ClickOnce Security   **323**
   Trusted Publishers   323
   Personal Certificate File   324
.NET 3.0 Security Utilities   **327**
Summary   **328**

Contents

Chapter 10: WPF and Win32 Interop   **329**

Win32 User Interface Overview   **330**
How WPF and HWNDs Interoperate   **330**
Using Win32 HWNDs Inside of WPF   **331**
Hosting a Win32 Button in WPF   332
Using WPF in Win32 Applications   **335**
Adding Windows Forms Controls to WPF   **337**
Adding Your WindowsFormsHost in Code   337
Adding Your HwndHost in XAML   339
Adding ActiveX Controls to WPF   339
Adding the ActiveX Control in XAML   344
Adding WPF Controls to Windows Forms   345
Affecting Control Properties   349
Summary   **351**

Chapter 11: Advanced Development Concepts   **353**

WPF Architecture   **354**
Core Subsystems   356
WPF Threading Model   359
Desktop Window Manager   360
The WPF Framework   **361**
Dispatcher Object   362
DependencyObject/DependencyProperty   362
Application   363
Freezable   364
Visual   364
UIElement   370
FrameworkElement   371
Control   371
A Deeper Look at XAML   **373**
XAML Under the Hood   373
Manipulating XAML On-the-Fly   378
Deconstructing Window1.xaml   382
x:Class   383
XAML Markup Extensions   385
XAML and Custom Types   386

Contents

WPF Multithreading   **388**

    Single-Threaded Application Model   388

    Thread Affinity and DispatcherObject   389

    WPF Dispatcher   390

    Working with Single-Threaded Applications   391

    Asynchronous Threading   393

Windows Communication Foundation   **397**

    Service Orientation   397

    WCF Architecture   398

    WCF Fundamentals   399

    Building a WCF Service   402

Windows Workflow Foundation   **409**

    Workflow Defined   410

    WF Architecture   411

    WF Fundamentals   411

Summary   **427**

Index   **429**

Introduction

This is an exciting time for developers using Microsoft technologies. A seemingly endless array of new platforms, techniques, and tools is now available or will soon be released. The developer's playground is growing fast. One of the new platforms emerging from the think-tank at Microsoft is the .NET Framework 3.0, a key component of which (and the subject of this book) is the Windows Presentation Foundation (WPF). WPF provides both developers and designers with a unified platform for creating rich-media applications that take full advantage of the graphics capabilities of modern PC hardware.

We've come a long way from the command-line interfaces of decades past. Today's application user expects a visually engaging and streamlined interactive experience due in part to their exposure to rich media and content found on the Internet. WPF is all about creating a rich user interface that meets these expectations, incorporating media of all types, such as animation, video, and audio. Furthermore, through the use of a new markup syntax called XAML and a new suite of design tools called Microsoft Expression Blend, developers and designers can now collaborate on projects seamlessly as never before. Prior to WPF, designers would create graphical elements for applications and hand those elements off to developers in the form of image files. Developers would then have to model a user interface (UI) around them. Designers can now model UI using Expression Blend, save the design as a XAML file, and simply hand the file off to a developer to code against in Visual Studio using WPF.

This book covers the concepts and components that make up the Windows Presentation Foundation. You learn how to create a rich UI, exploring the various controls now available to you, and how to leverage the new content model that WPF provides. You explore the WPF object model as well as the new subsystems offered in WPF, such as the dependency property system and the routed event model. You learn how to develop and deploy WPF applications targeting both the desktop and the browser. This book also covers the new XAML syntax, which is a markup language used to define UI in your WPF applications, regardless of whether you are developing for a standalone Windows-based environment or targeting the web. Additionally, you learn the basics of working with Expression Blend, the new graphical design tool offered by Microsoft.

WPF is a large platform, and we've tried to cover a wide range of topics in this book. Our intent is to touch on a bit of everything WPF has to offer, so you know not only what's provided by the platform, but also how to utilize it. Of course, because it's a large platform, we won't be able to cover everything, but we've tried to pick the essential concepts you'll need to get started. We hope you find it both fun and educational and that it provides a solid foundation for you as you venture in to the new world of rich UI development using Windows Presentation Foundation.

Whom This Book Is For

This book is aimed primarily at .NET Framework developers who want to learn how to develop applications using Microsoft's new presentation framework, WPF. Designers who may consider using the new Expression Blend suite of design tools and who are seeking to understand how these tools will enhance collaboration with developers will also find this book to be a good introduction. For new developers, there is some value in learning the new XAML syntax, but most concepts will be too advanced. For these readers, we suggest learning .NET 2.0 as a positive first step toward WPF.

Readers who will find this book useful include:

❑ Microsoft .NET application developers looking to learn about the new WPF platform

❑ Designers looking to gain insight into Microsoft Expression Blend and the collaboration capabilities offered by WPF and the tools that support it

In addition, familiarity with the following related technologies is a strong indicator that this book is for you:

❑ Microsoft .NET Framework

❑ C#

❑ Web Services

❑ HTML

❑ CSS

Of the preceding list, a basic understanding of the .NET Framework and C# is essential. Familiarity with Web Services, HTML markup, and CSS concepts would be beneficial, but is not required to understand the content of this book. Those readers without at least .NET Framework and C# knowledge should instead refer to books such as *Professional .NET Framework 2.0* (ISBN 978-0-7645-7135-0) and *Professional C# 2005* (ISBN 978-0-7645-7534-1).

Reading this book from cover to cover, in sequence, is not a requirement. We suggest reading Chapters 1 through 3 initially, to get a basic understanding of WPF and XAML. After that, skipping around through the chapters, as interest or needs dictate, should be fine.

What This Book Covers

Professional WPF Programming provides a developer-level tutorial of WPF programming techniques, patterns, and use cases.

The book begins with an overview of WPF. Questions such as "What is WPF?", "How do I start using WPF?" and "What does WPF have to offer me?" are answered early in the first chapter, followed swiftly by a detailed look at the subsystems and graphical features offered by the platform.

Following the overview, you dive right into the programming techniques you need for WPF. Using Visual Studio to create some examples, you get up-to-speed fast and start creating applications right away. Also, you are introduced to XAML, the new markup syntax for creating a UI. XAML is actually a separate technology from WPF, but WPF uses it extensively.

With the basic concepts and programming techniques of WPF under your belt, you take a brief journey into the world of design tools. Microsoft now offers its own suite of compelling design tools, and you'll get some firsthand experience with the new Microsoft Expression Blend. Using Expression Blend, you create advanced UI and learn to implement styling, layout, and animation. You also see how easy it is to save your design in XAML and then use that very same markup in Visual Studio to begin coding application logic.

Next, you learn how to create special effects in WPF, including bitmap effects, transformations, and the use of brush objects to get glass or reflection effects. The book demonstrates these techniques and provides a foundation for creating visually stunning elements in your applications.

Following special effects, you are introduced to custom control authoring in WPF. WPF provides a very customizable object model that allows you to apply styles and templates to existing elements. A new content model allows you to place almost any element inside of another element. Given these new capabilities, you're unlikely to encounter many scenarios where you need to create a custom control. However, we "never say never," and there may be some scenarios in which a custom control is the way to go. This book covers the topics you should take into consideration when deciding whether to create a custom control, as well as how to build a custom control when necessary.

Next, the book dives into developing WPF applications for the enterprise. WPF offers two flavors of application that you can create: standalone Windows-based, or web-based. The key thing to understand is that both models utilize the same code-base, XAML, and .NET. This means that specifying your target hosting environment is really just a matter of tweaking project file settings and then managing deployment. This is extremely powerful stuff, and it is all covered within the enterprise topics discussed in this book.

After you gain a good understanding of application models and deployment, you will want to understand security. Security in WPF is based on the .NET 2.0 CAS security model. Security is also based on the application model you choose and where the application will be hosted. If it is hosted in a browser, you will need to understand the Internet Zone permission set. These topics are covered in depth.

With the basics of WPF application development, deployment, and security fully explored, the book then dives into some more advanced concepts. One of those concepts is how to mix Win32 and WPF code. Interoperation considerations will be covered. Hosting Win32 in WPF and the reverse is possible, and you'll learn how to implement this feature so that you can start incorporating WPF into your Win32 applications right away.

The book finishes with a WPF deep dive into architecture, WPF framework, XAML, and threading considerations. In addition, the book covers the basics of both Windows Workflow Foundation (WF) and Windows Communication Foundation (WCF) so that you can become familiar with the other components of the .NET Framework 3.0. To round out your understanding of these important components, you will build a sample WCF service and a simple WF workflow application.

How This Book Is Structured

Professional WPF Programming begins by providing some background on how and why Microsoft is shifting away from the long-standing Win32 platform in the direction of WPF. This is followed by an overview of WPF and the core components and subsystems of the platform. Next, a tour of Expression Blend is offered, and we provide examples to show you how to build rich UI. The remaining chapters then focus on individual topics related to WPF development. The book ends with a brief introduction to two other components that, along with WPF, make the .NET Framework 3.0 such an important and powerful platform.

Introduction

The chapter-level breakdown is as follows:

- ❑ **Chapter 1, "Overview of Windows Presentation Foundation"**—This chapter explores the evolution of the Windows API over the years and how this paved the way for a new platform, WPF. You will then take a high-level tour of the WPF architecture, including the new graphics capabilities and subsystems that are introduced by the platform. Additional development tools are also introduced.

- ❑ **Chapter 2, "WPF and .NET Programming"**—This chapter walks you through the requirements for building and running WPF applications. You also learn about the various subsystems, such as the dependency property and routed event systems. Furthermore, you are introduced to the controls offered by WPF, and you learn how you can modify and extend these controls using the new constructs provided by the platform.

- ❑ **Chapter 3, Anatomy of a WPF-Enabled Application**—This chapter introduces the various application models you can use in WPF, such as those for standalone and browser-based applications. The anatomy, which includes the files and configuration settings, will also be explored so that you are able to get up and running quickly developing WPF applications.

- ❑ **Chapter 4, "Building a Rich UI with Microsoft Expression Blend: Part I"**—This chapter introduces the new tools for designers working with WPF, specifically, Microsoft Expression Blend. You take a tour of the design environment provided by Expression Blend and look at the project file structure. The chapter also covers creating vector graphics, layouts, animation, and controls.

- ❑ **Chapter 5, "Building a Rich UI with Microsoft Expression Blend: Part II"**—This chapter builds on the concepts introduced in Chapter 4. You learn about how to add interactivity to your projects to handle user input, events, and hit testing. The chapter also provides a series of animation examples and you are introduced to the WPF drawing API. This chapter also illustrates the collaboration features provided between Expression Blend and Visual Studio 2005.

- ❑ **Chapter 6, "Special Effects"**—This chapter explores the rich capabilities and special effects offered in WPF. Brushes, bitmap effects, and transformations are all covered extensively. Using these concepts, you can create rich UI both easily and quickly in WPF.

- ❑ **Chapter 7, "Custom Controls"**—This chapter tackles custom control development in WPF. Because of the extensive support for templates and styles in WPF, you will likely find that your need for custom controls will be slim. However, there are times you will need or want to create a custom control. This chapter covers not just how to create custom controls, but also how to determine if you can get by with using the built-in support for templates and styles because they are such powerful tools.

- ❑ **Chapter 8, "Using WPF in the Enterprise"**—This chapter explores the many factors to consider when building an enterprise-level application with WPF. Application models, deployment, hosting environment, security considerations, navigation, state management, and localization are covered thoroughly in this chapter.

- ❑ **Chapter 9, "Security"**—This chapter explores the security features of WPF. Security in WPF is primarily based on the application model you choose and where your application is hosted. This chapter covers OS security, CAS security, the Internet security sandbox, and ClickOnce security.

- ❑ **Chapter 10, "WPF and Win32 Interop"**—This chapter focuses on how your WPF application can interoperate with existing Win32 applications. The question "Can I host my WPF application in a Win32 application?" and vice versa will be answered. You will learn about how HWNDS differ in WPF from Win32-based applications.

❑ **Chapter 11, "Advanced Development Concepts"**—This chapter dives deeper into many concepts introduced throughout the book. You get a thorough look at WPF architecture and what makes WPF tick. You take a tour through the important classes in the WPF framework, such as the `Application` and `DependencyObject` classes. The chapter covers XAML syntax and structure in great depth. Threading in WPF applications is explored. Finally, this chapter takes a high-level look at two other components of the .NET 3.0 Framework: Windows Workflow Foundation and Windows Communication Foundation.

What You Need to Use This Book

To develop WPF applications and create the examples in this book, you must have the following installed:

❑ Windows SDK

❑ .NET Framework 3.0 Runtime Components

❑ Visual Studio 2005 with Visual Studio codename "Orcas" CTP WinFX Development Tools or the Orcas release of Visual Studio 2005

Chapter 2 outlines these requirements in more detail as well as where and how to obtain the necessary components.

Conventions

To help you get the most from the text and keep track of what's happening, we've used a number of conventions throughout the book.

> **Boxes like this one hold important, not-to-be forgotten information that is directly relevant to the surrounding text.**

Tips, hints, tricks, and asides to the current discussion are offset and placed in italics like this.

As for styles in the text:

❑ We *highlight* new terms and important words when we introduce them.

❑ We show keyboard strokes like this: Ctrl+A.

❑ We show filenames, URLs, and code within the text like so: `persistence.properties`.

❑ We present code in two different ways:

```
In code examples we highlight new and important code with a gray background.
```

```
The gray highlighting is not used for code that's less important in the present
context, or has been shown before.
```

Source Code

As you work through the examples in this book, you may choose either to type in all the code manually or to use the source code files that accompany the book. All of the source code used in this book is available for download at `http://www.wrox.com`. Once at the site, simply locate the book's title (either by using the Search box or by using one of the title lists) and click the Download Code link on the book's detail page to obtain all the source code for the book.

> *Because many books have similar titles, you may find it easiest to search by ISBN; this book's ISBN is 978-0-470-04180-2.*

Once you download the code, just decompress it with your favorite compression tool. Alternately, you can go to the main Wrox code download page at `http://www.wrox.com/dynamic/books/download.aspx` to see the code available for this book and all other Wrox books.

Errata

We make every effort to ensure that there are no errors in the text or in the code. However, no one is perfect, and mistakes do occur. If you find an error in one of our books, such as a spelling mistake or faulty piece of code, we would be very grateful for your feedback. By sending in errata you may save another reader hours of frustration and at the same time you will be helping us provide even higher quality information.

To find the errata page for this book, go to `http://www.wrox.com` and locate the title using the Search box or one of the title lists. Then, on the book details page, click the Book Errata link. On this page you can view all errata that has been submitted for this book and posted by Wrox editors. A complete book list including links to each book's errata is also available at `www.wrox.com/misc-pages/booklist.shtml`.

If you don't spot "your" error on the Book Errata page, go to `www.wrox.com/contact/techsupport.shtml` and complete the form there to send us the error you have found. We'll check the information and, if appropriate, post a message to the book's errata page and fix the problem in subsequent editions of the book.

p2p.wrox.com

For author and peer discussion, join the P2P forums at `p2p.wrox.com`. The forums are a Web-based system for you to post messages relating to Wrox books and related technologies and interact with other readers and technology users. The forums offer a subscription feature to e-mail you topics of interest of your choosing when new posts are made to the forums. Wrox authors, editors, other industry experts, and your fellow readers are present on these forums.

At http://p2p.wrox.com you will find a number of different forums that will help you not only as you read this book, but also as you develop your own applications. To join the forums, just follow these steps:

1. Go to p2p.wrox.com and click the Register link.

2. Read the terms of use and click Agree.

3. Complete the required information to join as well as any optional information you wish to provide and click Submit.

4. You will receive an e-mail with information describing how to verify your account and complete the joining process.

You can read messages in the forums without joining P2P but in order to post your own messages, you must join.

Once you join, you can post new messages and respond to messages other users post. You can read messages at any time on the Web. If you would like to have new messages from a particular forum e-mailed to you, click the Subscribe to this Forum icon by the forum name in the forum listing.

For more information about how to use the Wrox P2P, be sure to read the P2P FAQs for answers to questions about how the forum software works as well as many common questions specific to P2P and Wrox books. To read the FAQs, click the FAQ link on any P2P page.

Overview of Windows Presentation Foundation

For those of us who have been developing applications to run on the Windows platform, the topic of this book presents a compelling and exciting wave of change to how such applications can be built. In addition, for those of us who have been developing web-based applications, an even more exciting shift is approaching.

Windows Presentation Foundation, also known as *WPF*, is the next-generation graphics platform on which both Windows- and web-based applications can be built to run on Windows Vista, the latest evolutionary release of the Windows operating system. WPF provides the foundation for introducing an elegant and high fidelity User Experience (UX) by juxtaposition of user interface, application logic, documents, and media content.

> *Although originally targeted solely for Windows Vista, WPF will be made available for Windows XP and Windows Server 2003 as part of the .NET Framework 3.0 (formerly WinFX) developer platform.*

This coalescence of form and function is further empowered by tools such as XAML and the Microsoft Expression Designers, which allow designers and developers to work in parallel on the user interface and the application logic, coming together to provide a seamless UX.

This chapter provides an overview of WPF, including the following key topics:

❑   Evolution of the Windows API

❑   .NET Framework 3.0, the next-generation APIs for Windows-based development

❑   WPF architecture and development model

❑   XAML, the new declarative language backing WPF

❑   Tools to develop WPF applications

A Brief History of the Windows API

The Windows API exposes the core set of functionality provided by the Windows operating system for use in applications. Primarily designed for C/C++ development, the Windows API has been the most direct mechanism with which an application can interact with Windows.

The Windows API comprises the following functional groups:

❑ **Base Services** — Provides access to the core resources of the computer, such as memory, filesystems, devices, processes, and threads

❑ **Common Control Library** — A collection of common control windows used throughout the Windows operating system, providing the distinctive Windows look and feel

❑ **Common Dialog Box Library** — A collection of dialog boxes used to execute common tasks, including file opening, saving, and printing

❑ **Graphics Device Interface (GDI)** — Provides the facilities for an application to generate graphical output to displays, printers, and other devices

❑ **Network Services** — Provides access to various networking capabilities of the Windows operating system, including RPC and NetBIOS

❑ **User Interface (UI)** — Provides the mechanism for managing windows and controls in an application and input from devices such as the mouse and keyboard

❑ **Windows Shell** — The container that organizes and presents the entire Windows UI, including the desktop, taskbar, and Windows Explorer

Through these services, developers have had significant flexibility in creating powerful applications for the Windows operating system. However, this flexibility also bore the responsibility of handling low-level and often tedious operations.

With each new release of the Windows operating system, additions and updates to the Windows API were almost always included. Yet with each release, Microsoft strived to support backwards compatibility. Thus, many functions included in the original Windows API still exist today in Windows XP and Windows Server 2003.

The following list includes major versions of the Windows API:

❑ **Win16** — The API for the first 16-bit versions of Windows

❑ **Win32** — Introduced in Windows NT, the API for 32-bit versions of Windows

❑ **Win32 for 64-bit Windows** — Formerly known as Win64, the API for 64-bit versions of Windows XP and Windows Server 2003

Platform Evolution

Since the release of Windows 1.0 more than 20 years ago, the GDI and the UI services of the Windows API have provided a reliable graphics platform for Windows applications. Many applications we use on a day-to-day basis, including the Microsoft Office suite and Internet Explorer, are built on this foundation.

Although this graphics platform has seen many successes, fundamental changes have occurred in technology since its initial appearance more than two decades ago. With the proliferation of the personal computer and the increasing availability of broadband Internet access, the demand for rich visual experiences has dramatically increased. Moreover, advancements in graphics hardware technology have paved the way for astounding digital media and interactive entertainment products. Facing this new demand for a rich visual experience, Microsoft has invested heavily in providing such an experience as part of the next-generation Windows API — .NET Framework 3.0.

Introducing .NET Framework 3.0

.NET Framework 3.0 is a revolutionary milestone for developing applications on the Windows operating system. Built atop the .NET Framework 2.0, .NET Framework 3.0 is a set of managed APIs that provide enhanced functionality for messaging, workflow, and presentation.

Key components of .NET Framework 3.0 include:

- ❑ **Windows Presentation Foundation (WPF)** — The graphical subsystem for all things related to the UI

- ❑ **Windows Communication Foundation (WCF)** — The messaging subsystem of .NET Framework 3.0, securing program communication through a single API

- ❑ **Windows Workflow Foundation (WF)** — Provides workflow services for applications built to run on Windows

As the new programming model for Windows Vista, .NET Framework 3.0 fuses the Windows platform with applications developed using Visual Studio 2005. With direct access to low-level services of the operating system and hardware surface, .NET Framework 3.0 provides a compelling solution for creating applications with a rich UX.

Although WCF and WF are equally important components of .NET Framework 3.0, they are beyond the scope of this book. For more information on WCF and WF, visit the .NET Framework Developer Center on MSDN (http://msdn2.microsoft.com/en-us/netframework).

Meet Windows Presentation Foundation

Formerly known as *Avalon*, Windows Presentation Foundation (WPF) is the new graphical subsystem in Windows Vista that provides a holistic means for combining user interface, 2D and 3D graphics, documents, and digital media. Built on the .NET Framework, WPF provides a managed environment for development with the Windows operating system. This takes advantage of the existing investment made by Microsoft in the .NET Framework, and allows developers familiar with .NET technologies to rapidly begin developing applications that leverage WPF.

Guiding Design Principles

To enhance UX and empower both designers and developers, WPF has been built under the following design principles:

- ❑ Integration
- ❑ Vector graphics
- ❑ Declarative programming
- ❑ Simplified deployment
- ❑ Document portability

Integration

In today's world, developing a Windows application may require the use of any number of different technologies, ranging from GDI/GDI+ for 2D graphics, UI services (User32 or WinForms), or Direct3D or OpenGL for 3D graphics. On the contrary, WPF was designed as a single model for application development, providing seamless integration between such services within an application. Similar constructs can be used for developing storyboard animation, data bound forms, and 3D models.

Vector Graphics

To take advantage of new powerful graphics hardware, WPF implements a vector-based composition engine. This allows for graphics to scale based on screen-specific resolution without loss of quality, something nearly impossible with fixed-size raster graphics. WPF leverages Direct3D for vector-based rendering, and will utilize the graphics processing unit (GPU) on any video card implementing DirectX 7 or later in hardware. In anticipation of future technology, such as high-resolution displays and unknown form factors, WPF implements a floating-point logical pixel system and supports 32-bit ARGB colors.

Declarative Programming

WPF introduces a new XML-based language to represent UI and user interaction, known as *XAML* (eXtensible Application Markup Language — pronounced "zammel"). Similar to Macromedia's MXML specification, within XAML elements from the UI are represented as XML tags. Thus, XAML allows applications to dynamically parse and manipulate UI elements at either compile-time or runtime, providing a flexible model for UI composition.

Following the success of ASP.NET, XAML follows the code-behind model, allowing designers and developers to work in parallel and seamlessly combine their work to create a compelling UX. With the aid of design-time tools such as the Visual Designer for Windows Presentation Foundation add-in for Visual Studio 2005, the experience of developing XAML-based applications resembles that of WinForms development. Moreover, designers accustomed to visual tools such as Macromedia Flash 8 Professional can quickly ramp-up to building XAML-based solutions using visual design tools such as Microsoft Expression Blend. These tools are covered later in this chapter and throughout this book.

Simplified Deployment

WPF applications can be deployed as standalone applications or as web-based applications hosted in Internet Explorer. As with smart client applications, web-based WPF applications operate in a partial-trust sandbox, which protects the client computer against applications with malicious purpose.

Furthermore, WPF applications hosted in Internet Explorer can exploit the capabilities of local client hardware, providing a rich web experience with 3D, digital media, and more, which is the best argument for web-based applications available today.

Document Portability

Included in WPF is an exciting new set of document and printing technologies. In conjunction with the release of Microsoft Office 12, WPF utilizes Open Packaging Conventions, which supports compression, custom metadata, digital signatures, and rights management. Similar to the Portable Document Format (PDF), the XML Paper Specification (XPS), which allows for documents to be shared across computers without requiring that the originating application be installed, is included in WPF.

Architecture

The anatomy of WPF consists of unmanaged services, managed subsystems, and a managed API available for consumption by WPF applications, known as the *presentation framework*.

Figure 1-1 outlines the general underlying architecture of WPF, with each major component detailed in the sections that follow.

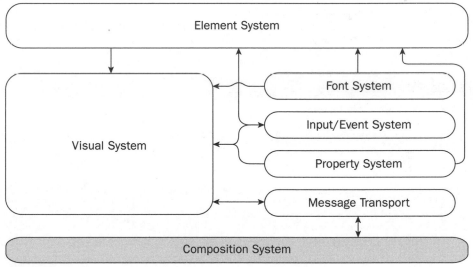

Figure 1-1

Element System

The *element system* represents the surface of WPF with which developers will interact. Contained within the element system are the core components making up the UI, such as styles, layout, controls, binding, and text layout.

Almost all the components in the element system derive from the all-important `System.Windows` `.FrameworkElement` class. This class provides the base functionality required to interact with WPF core presentation service, and implements key members of its parent class, `System.Windows.UIElement`, which provides functionality for all visual elements within WPF for layout, eventing, and input. The `UIElement` class can be compared to `HWND` in Win32, and is the starting point for input-specific functionality within the WPF inheritance hierarchy. The `FrameworkElement` and related classes are discussed further in Chapter 2.

Most of the topics covered within this book related to WPF application development pertain to components and features of the element system. However, the underlying subsystems are indeed used extensively by WPF applications, and will be noted where appropriate.

Element Trees

An important concept to grasp in WPF is the notion of element trees, which represent the visual elements of which a WPF application is comprised. Two element trees exist within a WPF application: the logical tree and the visual tree.

Logical Tree

The *logical tree* is the hierarchical structure containing the exact elements of your WPF application as defined either declaratively within a XAML file, or imperatively in code. Consider the following XAML code snippet:

```
<Window x:Class="ElementTrees.Sample"
  xmlns="http://schemas.microsoft.com/winfx/2006/xaml/presentation"
  xmlns:x="http://schemas.microsoft.com/winfx/2006/xaml"
  Title="ElementTrees" Height="300" Width="300"
  >
  <StackPanel Name="drawingCanvas">
    <Label Name="nameLabel">Please Enter Your Name:</Label>
    <TextBox Name="nameTextBox" Margin="2px"></TextBox>
    <Button Name="submitButton" Margin="2px"
            Click="submitButton_Click">Submit</Button>
  </StackPanel>
</Window>
```

When compiled for or parsed under WPF, this code snippet would yield a logical tree like that depicted in Figure 1-2.

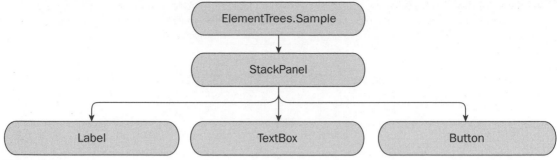

Figure 1-2

The logical tree outlines the 1:1 mapping of the nested XAML elements declared in the code snippet to their appropriate classes in the WPF API. The top-level element is `ElementTrees.Sample`, which derives from `System.Windows.Window`, the top-most, non-navigable container for a WPF application.

The `Window` class itself derives from `System.Windows.Controls.ContentControl`, which is the base class for all controls containing a single piece of content within WPF. To provide support for context-aware layout, the `System.Windows.Controls.Panel` class is available and includes functionality to arrange and lay out elements in WPF. The next element in the logical tree for the preceding code snippet is `System.Windows.Controls.StackPanel`, which derives from `Panel`. `StackPanel` arranges all client elements of the control in a single line, oriented either horizontally or vertically. This control behaves similarly to an HTML table with a single column or row, depending on orientation.

Contained within the `StackPanel` instance are the controls visible to the user: `System.Windows.Controls.TextBox`, `System.Windows.Controls.Button`, and `System.Windows.Controls.Label`. Although ubiquitous, these controls are unique implementations created from the ground up for WPF. Although they may behave in much the same way as their counterparts in WinForms from a user's perspective, their composition and behavior within the programming model and the visual tree are quite different.

Visual Tree

As its name implies, the logical tree makes sense — each element in the application is represented by a corresponding instance created by WPF. Under the hood, however, much more is taking place.

For each element in the logical tree, additional elements may be created to represent visual aspects required by the element. The combination of application elements and the elements created for visualization support is known as the *visual tree*. Considering the previous code snippet, the visual tree shown in Figure 1-3 would result.

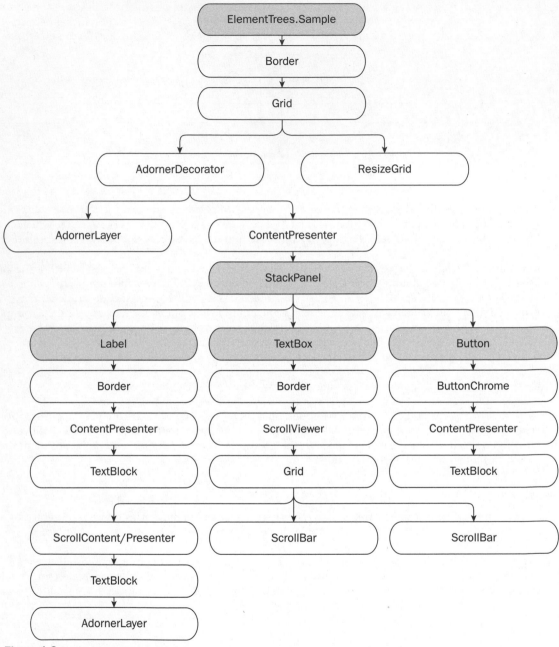

Figure 1-3

Okay, take a moment to catch your breath. WPF does a lot of work under the hood to support the flexible visual model implemented therein. In addition to the elements of the application included in the logical tree, 20 additional elements are created to support visualization. The following are some of these elements created for the `ElementTrees.Sample` element:

❑ `System.Windows.Controls.Border` — This control will draw a border and/or background surrounding its nested elements. The Border control is commonly found in many default controls, such as `System.Windows.Controls.Canvas`, `System.Windows.Controls.Label`, and `System.Windows.Controls.TextBox`.

❑ `System.Windows.Controls.Grid` — Similar to an HTML table, the Grid control provides a flexible area for content layout and positioning using rows and columns. Note, however, that there is a distinct Table control, `System.Windows.Documents.Table`, which provides block-level content flow also based on rows and columns and derives from a different class than `Grid`, which derives from `System.Windows.Controls.Panel`.

❑ `System.Windows.Documents.AdornerDecorator` — This control is used for styling of the control to which the element belongs. Adorners are discussed further in Chapter 10.

    ❑ `System.Windows.Documents.AdornerLayer` — The AdornerLayer control represents the surface for rendering adorners.

    ❑ `System.Windows.Controls.ContentPresenter` — This control is used to specify the location in the visual tree wherein content should be loaded for a specific control. In this case, the ContentPresenter control will specify where the contents of `ElementTrees.Sample` will be located.

❑ `System.Windows.Controls.Primitives.ResizeGrip` — This control enables the `Window` to have a resize grip within the visual tree. Thus, interaction with the host window of the WPF application will be captured by ResizeGrip such that the application can respond accordingly (for example, layout changes with a new surface area caused by the expansion or contraction of a host window).

Although many more elements have been created in the visual tree for this example, the preceding list should provide a basic understanding of their purpose and importance.

Although you can access both the logical and visual trees from code, you will spend most of your time developing WPF applications using the logical tree to interact with controls, their properties, methods, and events.

Visual System

The *visual system* is the subsystem through which applications access the core presentation services available through WPF. This subsystem examines the components within an application (labels, buttons, text, 2D and 3D graphics, animations) and will communicate with the underlying composition system (via the message transport) to generate the rendered result to the screen.

Although the concept of the visual system is key to the architecture of WPF, much of the heavy lifting is done in the underlying composition system.

Font System

The font system was completely rewritten for WPF to provide a superior font and text engine over that of the systems previously available in Windows. The two font engines available in Windows today, GDI and Uniscribe, have significant drawbacks that do not make them suitable for WPF.

The new font system provides a unique mechanism for creating and caching information about fonts in WPF, including TrueType and Adobe OpenType fonts. The metrics, glyphs, and paths that make up a particular typeface are calculated by the font system, cached, and made available for use by WPF. This process is expensive, and using this caching technique significantly improves the performance of text layout and rendering in WPF.

> *Note that the font system is the only managed component outlined in Figure 1-1 that runs out-of-process, and communicates directly with WPF through interprocess communication to share font data from the cache.*

As outlined in Figure 1-1, the font system interacts with two main subsystems — the element system and the visual system — each for a different purpose:

❑ The font system interacts with the element system's Page and Table Service (PTS). PTS is responsible for the organization and layout of text within the UI. This includes paragraphs, tables, and blocks of text.

❑ The visual system leverages the font system for text layout services within a single line of text, such as kerning, leading, and spacing.

Input/Event System

The input/event system in WPF introduces significant advancements for input and user interaction over that of previous systems available in Windows, such as Win32. Messages evoked by Win32 for device-based user input, such as WM_* messages, provide a verbose mechanism for input and lack enhanced support for modern devices, such as a stylus.

As such, WPF sports a succinct input/event system that provides streamlined integration of user input with the visual tree. Through commands, WPF provides an advanced mechanism with which an application can discover and respond to user input.

Consider the following chain of events:

1. The user clicks his or her mouse.

2. User32 receives the device input message.

3. WPF receives the raw message and converts it into an input report (a WPF wrapper surrounding device input).

4. The application distinguishes the type of input report received from WPF and performs structural and geometric hit tests to determine the click target.

5. After validating the click target, the input report is converted into one or more events. For each event discovered, an event route is created, based on the composition of the hit area.

6. Each discovered event is raised by the input/event system.

As just outlined, WPF bears the responsibility of receiving the device input gesture and determining the appropriate course of action based on the type of input received and events exposed by elements within an application. Furthermore, WPF supports routed events, which allow for elements within the visual tree to listen and respond to events of parent and nested elements through tunneling and bubbling. Event routing is an important concept to understand when developing WPF applications. To learn more, see Chapter 2.

When implementing a pure delegate model for user input and device interaction, consider a number of issues. Given the complexity of the visual tree, implementing instance-based delegation through routed events can incur serious performance and storage overhead. As such, WPF implements class handlers as part of the input/event system. Class handlers provide static event listeners for any instance to respond to user input, such as text being typed on a keyboard.

Property System

The property system is integral to core data-related functions within WPF. It comprises the following three main components:

❏ Change notification

❏ Storage

❏ Expressions

Change Notification

The change notification system is the basis for many aspects of WPF. All data within WPF is exposed through properties; as such, changes to these properties are integral to interaction with the elements within a WPF application.

In .NET 2.0, change notification is achieved by implementing the System.ComponentModel .INotifyPropertyChanged interface. This interface defines only one member, the PropertyChanged event, which will notify listeners when a property of the implementing class is changed. Although this mechanism works well, it leaves much to be desired. When implementing this interface, it is the responsibility of the derived class to set up the necessary plumbing required to raise the PropertyChanged event for each property to be monitored. The following code snippet depicts a typical implementation of this interface:

```
public class MyTextBox : System.ComponentModel.INotifyPropertyChanged
{
  //
  // Private storage for Text property
  //
  private string _text;

  //
  // Change-aware property
  //
  public string Text
  {
    get { return _text; }
    set
    {
```

```
      _text = value;
      OnPropertyChanged("Text");
    }
  }

  //
  // INotifyPropertyChanged.PropertyChanged
  //
  public event System.ComponentModel.PropertyChangedEventHandler PropertyChanged;

  //
  // Method to raise PropertyChanged event
  //
  private void OnPropertyChanged(string propertyName)
  {
    if (PropertyChanged != null)
    {
      PropertyChanged(
          this,
          new System.ComponentModel.PropertyChangedEventArgs(propertyName));
    }
  }
}
```

As evident in this snippet, there are several common areas of plumbing to be inserted into any class wanting to implement this change notification mechanism. Although this example may seem trivial, consider the scale of change notification if this object implemented 40 change-aware methods. Moreover, consider the situation in which a property's value is set to the same value currently held. If your requirements distinguished this to be a non-change, then additional logic would need to be included in each property to first test the equality of the property's current and specified changed values and raise the PropertyChanged event only when these values were different.

Enter the notion of dependency properties in WPF. *Dependency properties* represent properties registered with the WPF property system that implement value expressions, styling, data binding, change notification, and more. Considering the preceding code snippet, the following revised snippet depicts the same functionality using a dependency property:

```
public class MyTextBox : DependencyObject
{
  //
  // Dependency property for Text
  //
  public static readonly DependencyProperty TextProperty =
    DependencyProperty.Register(
        "Text",
         typeof(string),
         typeof(MyTextBox));

  //
  // Change-aware property
  //
  public string Text
  {
```

```
      get { return base.GetValue(TextProperty) as string; }
      set { base.SetValue(TextProperty, value); }
   }
}
```

Immediately apparent is the sheer reduction in code required to implement a dependency property. Let's dissect this to understand the difference between this snippet and the previous listing.

For the Text property of the MyTextBox class, we've removed the private _text variable used to store the value for that instance, and we've replaced the get and set functions with calls to methods included in the base class, DependencyObject. The GetValue and SetValue methods work within the dependency property system to store and retrieve property values, and trigger notification when such properties change. In order for this class to participate in the dependency property system, it must define static DependencyProperty members for each property to be included. In the case of the Text property, a TextProperty member was created and registered to the Text property using the DependencyProperty.Register method. This method creates an entry in the dependency property system for the MyTextBox class and will be responsible for change notification.

Storage

As noted earlier, properties are the main data element of WPF. Properties provide the foundation upon which a declarative model can be supported, and enable many of the key features included in WPF, such as styling, data binding, animation, and more.

This extensive coupling to properties is not without drawbacks, however. Supporting extensive properties within WPF elements can create a massive storage overhead because each element can contain many properties. Using instance-based property storage, WPF elements would be too bloated to support the ambitious goals for runtime performance and visual appeal. Thus, the dependency property system, as mentioned previously, provides support for streamlined property storage. Leveraging helper methods, classes can easily access properties and partake in change notification, data binding, styling, and other features available in this system.

Expressions

Expressions within WPF provide the extensibility required to successfully implement a declarative model. Features of WPF, such as styling, inheritance, and data binding, rely on expressions to dynamically evaluate and move data around the system.

Consider the following code snippet:

```
<Window x:Class="XamlExpressions.Window1"
  xmlns="http://schemas.microsoft.com/winfx/2006/xaml/presentation"
  xmlns:x="http://schemas.microsoft.com/winfx/2006/xaml"
  Title="XamlExpressions" Height="300" Width="300"

  <Window.Resources>
    <Style TargetType="{x:Type Button}">
      <Setter Property="FontFamily" Value="Segoe Black" />
      <Setter Property="FontSize" Value="12pt" />
      <Setter Property="Foreground" Value="#777777" />
      <Setter Property="HorizontalAlignment" Value="Center" />
    </Style>
```

```
    </Window.Resources>
    <Grid>
      <Grid.RowDefinitions>
        <RowDefinition Height="50px" />
        <RowDefinition Height="*" />
      </Grid.RowDefinitions>
      <Button Grid.Column="0" Grid.Row="0">Click Me!</Button>
    </Grid>
  </Window>
```

In this example, we've created a rather simple WPF application containing a `Grid` and `Button` control. This should not be new, as we've touched on these controls and seen their declaration earlier in this chapter. However, points of interest are the elements under the `Window.Resources` element.

The `Style` element provides the mechanism for creating custom styles for controls within WPF. If you use expressions, styles can be applied to elements within a WPF application in one of two ways: through the `TargetType` attribute or through a unique style identified and stored in the `x:Key` attribute of the `Style` element. The previous listing demonstrated the former method by assigning an expression distinguishing the type of element to which this style should apply.

Although we cover styling later in this book, it's important to note here that you can apply styles to elements within a WPF application through the use of expressions.

Expressions are not limited to styling; they are used extensively throughout WPF. The concept of expressions is embedded in almost every subsequent chapter of this book, and we'll dive deeper as needed.

Message Transport System

The message transport service is a key component of the WPF architecture that ties the visual system to the composition system. As mentioned previously, the visual system provides a managed interface through which all other managed subsystems within WPF provide instructions on what elements need to be represented on the screen. Although the visual system provides this hook, it doesn't perform the work itself; rather, it offloads such tasks to the composition system.

For such offloading to take place, the message transport system provides communication channels between the visual system and the composition system. These channels implement a .NET Remoting protocol that creates an efficient mechanism through which data structures can be passed. Moreover, leveraging a Remoting protocol allows WPF to transfer data structures across boundaries, thus providing the possibility of offloading the rendering of UI elements to an entirely different machine. This concept is very compelling for terminal client scenarios, such as Remote Desktop or Citrix MetaFrame, where graphics processing of applications executing remotely can be offloaded from the server to the terminal client.

Composition System

As we have alluded to throughout this section, the composition system really provides the internal combustion of the WPF architecture. The composition system is an unmanaged subsystem that receives instructions from the managed visual system and turns such instructions into graphics that appear on the screen.

The composition system provides the functionality to visualize the seemingly nebulous elements within a WPF application. This includes the functionality to calculate pixels for a particular element, and generates triangle geometries for visual elements, which, in turn, are sent directly to the GPU for output to the display. This process of hardware-based rendering — through Direct3D — frees up the CPU to perform other operations, improving the overall success of WPF applications. Moreover, the quality of onscreen graphics is significantly higher through the use of hardware-based rendering.

Although WPF has been built to leverage the GPU for hardware-based rendering, software-based rendering is available as a fallback.

XAML

Now that you have a good understanding of the underlying plumbing of WPF, let's take a closer look at XAML. As noted earlier in this chapter, XAML is the new declarative language for use in developing WPF applications. As a declarative language, XAML introduces significant flexibility in the way WPF applications can be developed. Such flexibility is examined in the following section.

Declarative vs. Imperative

The recent history of developing a UI for a typical Windows-based application encompasses the following general tasks (in no particular):

❑ **Layout UI** — Define and set up controls on a form, typically with the aid of a visual designer (for example, Visual Basic 6 or Visual Studio 2005).

❑ **Create bindings** — Hook data-bound controls to data sources, typically a database or related data access objects.

❑ **Wire up user interaction** — Configure control events so that user interaction triggers application logic to manipulate data and/or the UI.

Although overly simplistic, this covers most of the things that must occur to develop a UI. What's important to realize is that almost all of the plumbing required to achieve the tasks in the preceding list is imperative — that is, the definition of controls, their binding, and user interaction is included as statements within code. These imperative statements modify the state of the application, and are typically compiled directly into an executable format. For example, the WinForms Visual Design in Visual Studio 2005 generates code for every control dragged onto the design surface, which in turn is compiled with the rest of the application code into an executable .NET assembly.

So what's wrong with this approach? In fact, nothing is wrong with this approach. Although XAML provides a declarative model for developing WPF applications, you can achieve any task possible in XAML purely in code. However, there are benefits of the declarative model that make XAML such a compelling solution.

To see one benefit of leveraging the declarative model of XAML, consider the following code snippet:

```
<Window x:Class="XamlXample.Window1"
  xmlns="http://schemas.microsoft.com/winfx/2006/xaml/presentation"
  xmlns:x="http://schemas.microsoft.com/winfx/2006/xaml"
  Title=" XamlXample" Height="300" Width="300"
  >
  <Grid>
    <Grid.RowDefinitions>
      <RowDefinition Height="50px" />
      <RowDefinition Height="*" />
    </Grid.RowDefinitions>
    <Label Grid.Column="0" Grid.Row="0">Click This Button:</Label>
    <Button Grid.Column="0" Grid.Row="1"
        DockPanel.Dock="Top" Name="clickButton">Click Me!</Button>
  </Grid>
</Window>
```

Although this is yet another simple example, this code snippet depicts a very simple example of the straightforward approach implemented by XAML. In this example, we've defined a `Window` element containing a Grid control for content containment. The Grid defines some properties about itself and contains two simple controls: a Label and TextBox. Seems simple enough, right?

Now, let's examine the code necessary to generate the same elements as outlined in the preceding XAML code snippet:

```
class ImperativeWindow : Window
{
  public ImperativeWindow()
  {
    InitializeComponent();
  }

  private void InitializeComponent()
  {
    this.Title = "XamlXample";
    this.Height = 300;
    this.Width = 300;

    Grid grid = new Grid();

    RowDefinition row1 = new RowDefinition();
    row1.Height = new GridLength(50);
    grid.RowDefinitions.Add(row1);

    RowDefinition row2 = new RowDefinition();
    row2.Height = GridLength.Auto;
    grid.RowDefinitions.Add(row2);

    Label label = new Label();
    label.Content = "Click This Button:";

    grid.Children.Add(label);
```

```
        Grid.SetColumn(label, 0);
        Grid.SetRow(label, 0);

        Button button = new Button();
        button.Name = "clickButton";
        button.Content = "Click Me!";

        DockPanel.SetDock(button, Dock.Top);

        grid.Children.Add(button);
        Grid.SetColumn(button, 0);
        Grid.SetRow(button, 1);
    }
}
```

As you can see, creating the exact same application using code requires a significantly greater amount of statements than its XAML counterpart. It is important to note that under the hood, WPF will actually create a source file at compile time for each XAML file in your application. The code that's generated will be very similar to the preceding code; however, the source of your application remains as a XAML file.

XAML Runtime Support

The benefit we've covered thus far pertains simply to preference and convenience. We have not yet dived into some of the additional features of a declarative model. So far, we've discussed XAML as a language that's interpreted at compile time and, when combined with code-behind files and other resources, is included in a distributable executable. In addition to this method, WPF provides runtime support for dynamic parsing of XAML files. This exciting feature of WPF creates many new possibilities for applications.

To further appreciate the power of a dynamic declarative model, consider the following scenario.

> **You've been tasked with developing a kiosk-style application for your customer, a global record store chain. This application will allow their customers to browse the entire catalog of music available throughout all stores, listen to song previews, view album artwork and artist photographs, and even watch video clips. The look and feel for this application must be avant-garde, and the application must include animation and sync up with the visual identity of this edgy corporate brand. Moreover, the style and layout of the application must be dynamic so that each store can present a localized interface on a seasonal basis.**

This scenario provides a not-so-extreme example of what many companies might seek within a consumer-facing application. While many of the requirements make for a great case to use WPF (animation, images, audio, and video integration), a few stand out.

Dynamic styling and layout for localized applications is a very non-trivial feat accomplished only by the most skilled developers. To achieve this using current technology, developers have limited support out-of-the-box, and have to rely on third-party and custom solutions to create dynamic interfaces. On the contrary, with WPF, developers are empowered with foundational support to create declarative UIs that can be interpreted dynamically. Moreover, enhanced support for localization in WPF makes developing global applications much easier to develop.

Designer and Developer Collaboration

In the example scenario, the customer desires a visually aesthetic application that will wow customers and represent the avant-garde visual identity of their edgy corporate brand. Although some developers might consider themselves astute graphic designers, odds are you're more focused on function than form.

With current technologies, developing such an application would require a large team of developers to build out services available out-of-the-box with WPF, such as digital media integration and animation. Moreover, the visual design of the application would be limited to such developed services and would most likely be an adaptation of design compositions provided by a graphic designer. This doesn't provide the customer with a best-of-breed solution and is not only quite limited to the services available, but is also constrained by time to integrate the visual design and the translation of the designers' vision into the application by the development team.

Thankfully, this problem has, in fact, been solved with WPF. Through the use of XAML, designers and developers have a unified platform on which visual design and application logic can be seamlessly integrated. Visual designers available for XAML, including Microsoft Expression Blend, further support this notion by providing designers with a familiar interface for design, typesetting, and illustration, all while generating XAML under the hood. The resultant XAML can then be handed off to a developer for integration with business logic and other application-specific features. Never has the designer and developer experience been so tightly integrated.

Visual Design Tools

As mentioned throughout this chapter, several visual design tools are available for WPF. These tools can provide a familiar interface for both designers and developers to create WPF applications. Moreover, these tools support the notion of designer and developer collaboration.

XamlPad

Provided with the Windows SDK, XamlPad is a basic visual editor for XAML. Similar to the ubiquitous Notepad, XamlPad will be used by almost all WPF developers for quick and easy editing of XAML files. XamlPad provides real-time visualization of XAML code, allowing developers to author, test, and validate XAML code on-the-fly. Furthermore, XamlPad features XAML syntax validation, making it easy to troubleshoot errors in a XAML file.

Figure 1-4 illustrates the XamlPad user interface.

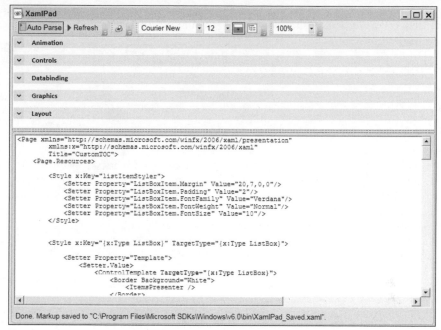

Figure 1-4

Microsoft Expression Blend

As illustrated in Figure 1-5, Microsoft Expression Blend (formerly "Expression Interactive Designer") is Microsoft's flagship tool for designing WPF applications. A full-featured design tool, Expression Blend provides a truly usable authoring environment for designers to create sophisticated designs for WPF applications.

Some of the key features in Expression Blend include:

❑   Vector drawing tools

❑   Timeline-based animation support, media integration, and 3D authoring

❑   Robust integration with data sources and seamless integration with Visual Studio 2005

For a detailed discussion of Expression Blend, please see Chapters 4 and 5.

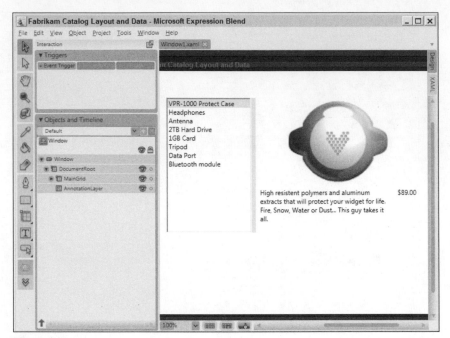

Figure 1-5

Visual Designer for Windows Presentation Foundation

Code-named *Cider*, the visual designer for WPF provides a visual authoring environment for WPF applications in Visual Studio 2005. As illustrated in Figure 1-6, Cider provides a design experience familiar to those who have developed WinForms applications using Visual Studio 2005.

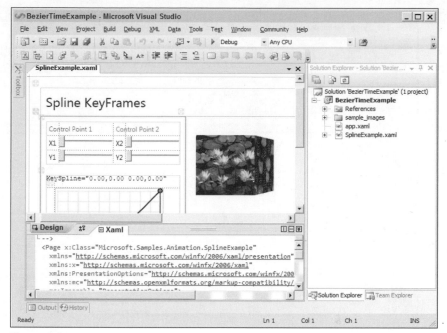

Figure 1-6

Electric Rain ZAM 3D

From Electric Rain (www.erain.com), the creators of the excellent Flash 3D plug-in Swift3D, comes ZAM 3D, a 3D modeling and animation application based on WPF. Touted as a developer productivity tool, ZAM 3D offers a robust environment for modeling and animating 3D graphics, while automatically generating the XAML markup representing such models.

If have experience with Swift3D (or any other 3D authoring environment, such as 3D Studio Max), you'll find the UI very familiar. It features dual viewports, which provide instant gratification for animations, as well as model and environment effects. Under the hood, ZAM 3D creates XAML files containing the ViewPort3D element to draw and animate models and scenes created within the tool. One really nifty feature is the Copy XAML command, which will generate the appropriate XAML for your current model and place this text on the clipboard. This is extremely handy if you want to test your model in XamlPad.

Figure 1-7 depicts the ZAM 3D user interface.

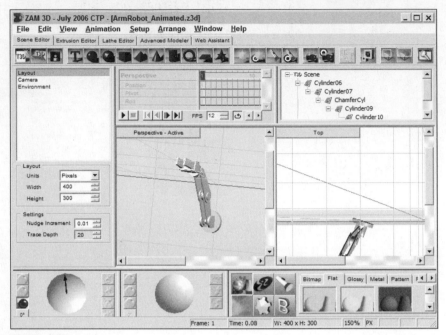

Figure 1-7

Mobiform Aurora

At the forefront of WPF, Mobiform Software, Inc. (www.mobiform.com) has created a very compelling visual designer: Aurora. Aurora is itself a WPF application that provides a design experience similar to EID, generating XAML documents. Documents created in Aurora are pure XAML and can be used interchangeably with other designers, including Visual Studio 2005 and EID.

In addition to providing a design experience for functionality available in WPF, Aurora includes custom controls developed by Mobiform for use your applications, such as Pie Chart and File Control.

Figure 1-8 illustrates Aurora's clean WPF-based user interface.

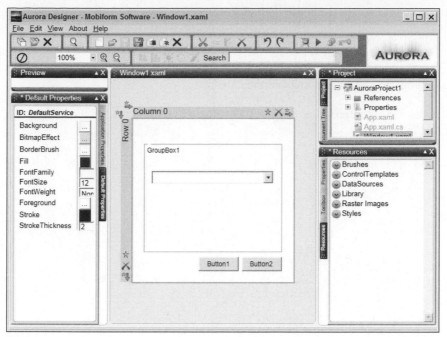

Figure 1-8

Summary

In this chapter, we've merely peeked into the exciting new world of application development with WPF. We started by reviewing the evolution of the Windows platform and how WPF empowers developers to create Windows- and web-based applications with a superior User Experience. This chapter also outlined some key areas of the WPF architecture, including:

- ❑ Element system and element trees (visual and logical)
- ❑ Visual system
- ❑ Font system
- ❑ Input/event system
- ❑ Property system (change notification, storage, and expressions)
- ❑ Message transport system
- ❑ Composition system

You learned about the new declarative language of WPF and XAML, and how this language introduces greater flexibility in application development and deployment. You also learned that the XAML provides a unified platform for design and development collaboration.

Finally, you caught a glimpse of the visual design tools with which WPF applications can be developed, including XamlPad and Microsoft Expression Blend.

The following chapters expand on what you've learned and provide a detailed look at .NET programming with WPF.

2

WPF and .NET Programming

In pursuit of a greater visual experience for your user audience, you're venturing into a wondrous land of vector graphics and animated .NET assemblies. For some time now, roughly 4–5 years and running, Microsoft has been tirelessly working to bring us a presentation framework that supports something more impressive than the GDI and GDI+ graphics being drawn to the screen. As a result of their labor, and mainly at their expense, the .NET developers of the planet are now able to leverage this foundational layer to bring to life all that runs on a computer processing unit.

Commonly misunderstood, Windows Presentation Foundation (WPF) is not just a layered representation of objects in XAML markup; it also maintains an extensive and robust development model. There are numerous changes in the development process that a .NET programmer will need to learn in order to properly convert to being a WPF programmer. And, yes, there is a difference. WPF applications (aka .NET Framework 3.0 applications) are built with the presentation layer in mind and structured to support multiple deployment possibilities within the same code base.

This chapter discusses the building blocks that make up WPF as it pertains to a programmatic approach. It provides an in-depth look at .NET development concepts and processes specific to the new WPF framework. The goal of the chapter is to provide a clear and detailed analysis of each major area within WPF, and how the developer interacts or consumes it in real-world scenarios. In particular, this chapter covers:

- ❏ The application model
- ❏ The object model
- ❏ Logical and visual trees
- ❏ User interface elements
- ❏ Events
- ❏ Commands
- ❏ Navigation

Getting Started

This section describes the necessary installs you will need to run WPF applications, and then provides a primer for those of you just getting your feet wet in WPF.

Required Installations

To create .NET Framework 3.0 applications — that is, applications that use WPF — you must have the following installed:

❑ Visual Studio 2005

❑ Windows SDK

❑ .NET Framework 3.0 Development Tools, or the "Orcas" release of Visual Studio 2005

❑ Windows Vista or Windows XP (with the .NET Framework 3.0)

A downloadable limited version of Visual Studio 2005 is available at `http://msdn.microsoft.com/vstudio/products/trial/`, but you probably already have it installed and running given that you're reading a Wrox Professional book, and you are ready to skip to the meat of WPF.

Once the installations are complete, you should be ready to develop applications using the WPF platform. The next section walks you through the basic operations of creating an application and rendering graphics with WPF.

Types of WPF Applications

The following four types of WPF applications are available through .NET Framework 3.0 within Visual Studio 2005:

❑ **.NET Framework 3.0 Windows Application** — The .NET Framework 3.0 Windows Application is essentially the equivalent of a .NET Windows Forms project with all the perks of the WPF API.

❑ **.NET Framework 3.0 XAML Browser Application** — The .NET Framework 3.0 XAML Browser Application (XBAP) is the WPF version of an ASP.NET web application, with a limited amount of WPF namespaces and functionality available to it, because of the browser's security access limitations on the client.

❑ **.NET Framework 3.0 Service Library Project** — The .NET Framework 3.0 Service Library is a Windows Communication Foundation project type and is not held within its sibling WPF platform. This project type is outside of the scope of this book and largely ignored throughout. This book does, however, touch upon some aspects of the WCF technology, including services, in a later chapter.

❑ **.NET Framework 3.0 Custom Control Library Project** — The .NET Framework 3.0 Custom Control Library is a project designed to output a reusable control that can be redistributed to a .NET application in the form of a dynamic-link library (DLL) .NET assembly.

Figure 2-1 depicts the Visual Studio .NET selection of these projects:

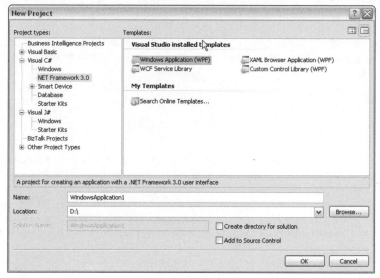

Figure 2-1

Although each project type uses nearly the same structural and referenced components, each provides different deployable units intended for different audiences and purposes.

My First WPF Application

Without further delay, it's time to get your fingers on the keyboard. Start by opening Visual Studio 2005, and then perform the following steps:

1. Select File ➪ New Project. From the Project Types tree view, select the Visual C# Node, and then click the .NET Framework 3.0 Windows Application icon from the list. Name your project **MyFirstWPFApp**, and click OK. This new project should create a Window1.xaml file and a MyApp.xaml file. Both of these will have corresponding code-behind files, which may or may not be visible within the Solution Explorer.

2. From the toolbar, click the Button within the Common Controls group. With the mouse cursor set to crosshairs, click and drag a small section on your form window. A new Button control should appear in the area you drew. Select the Button in the designer and open the Properties window. Change the Name property to **btnGo** and the Content property to **Go**.

3. From the Window1.xaml file, click the Xaml tab in the IDE to view its XAML code contents. Look for the XML button declaration within the XAML code. The section to be edited should look similar to the following excerpt:

```
<Button VerticalAlignment="Top" HorizontalAlignment="Stretch" Grid.Column="0"
Grid.ColumnSpan="1" Grid.Row="0" Grid.RowSpan="1" Margin="28,16,462,0" Width="Auto"
Height="34" Name="btnGo">
    Go
</Button>
```

Find the `<Button` opening tag, insert the mouse cursor, and type the following into the tag:

```
Click="MyClickEvent"
```

This attribute added to the declaration of a Button control would generate an event handler within the automatically generated (hidden) code-behind partial classes for this window. The XAML syntax for this button would now be similar to the following:

```
<Button Click="MyClickEvent" VerticalAlignment="Top" HorizontalAlignment="Stretch"
Grid.Column="0" Grid.ColumnSpan="1" Grid.Row="0" Grid.RowSpan="1"
Margin="28,16,462,0" Width="Auto" Height="34" Name="btnGo">
    Go
</Button>
```

At the time of this writing, creating events for user interface (UI) controls from the designer interface is not a working feature of Visual Studio 2005 with WPF. Steps 3 and 4 could be performed in the production release simply by double-clicking the button from the window designer.

4. Because there is now a control with a declared event handler, you can create the event itself within the code-behind file. Double-click the Window1.xaml.cs file in the Solution Explorer to view its contents. Manually type in the event anywhere within the class definition, after or before the constructor. The syntax to be added to the class would be as follows:

```
private void MyClickEvent(object sender, RoutedEventArgs e) {}
```

5. Within the contents of the event handler, add some actions for the application to perform. A simple starting point would be to add a message box to the application. Type in the following to provide this message box:

```
MessageBox.Show("Elexzandreia the beautiful!", "Message", MessageBoxButton.OK,
        MessageBoxImage.Hand);
```

The code-behind file should then have the following logic:

```
using System;
using System.Windows;
using System.Windows.Controls;
using System.Windows.Data;
using System.Windows.Documents;
using System.Windows.Media;
using System.Windows.Media.Imaging;
using System.Windows.Shapes;

namespace MyFirstWPFApp
{
    // <summary>
    // Interaction logic for Window1.xaml
    // </summary>

    public partial class Window1 : Window
    {
        private void MyClickEvent(object sender, RoutedEventArgs e) {
            MessageBox.Show("Elexzandreia the beautiful!", "Message",
MessageBoxButton.OK,
            MessageBoxImage.Hand);
```

```
        }

        public Window1()
        {
            InitializeComponent();
        }
    }
}
```

6. Click F5 to run the application, which will provide a simple button that displays a message box when clicked (see Figure 2-2).

Figure 2-2

> **WPF requires Single Threaded Apartment (STA) threading, so you must apply a** `[System.STAThread()]` **attribute to your** `Main` **method.**

WPF Development Concepts

This section dives into some of the basic platform-level WPF subjects, such as the `Application` object, XAML, WPF project types, and some important WPF development concepts.

XAML

Perhaps the most obvious new feature of WPF is the fuel of its rendering engine: the newly developed XAML markup language. XAML (eXtensible Application Markup Language) is the declarative language that is used to compose an application made up of XML elements, which are designed to represent a structured set of .NET classes. Each element of a XAML file represents a class in .NET, and each attribute within a XAML file represents a property, method, or event within a .NET class. Because a XAML file is a textual or serialized form of a .NET class, it leverages all the tools and firepower of the .NET Framework. XAML files are designed to be mapped to a code-behind file, named with a .xaml.cs extension. These code-behind partial classes contain the events, methods, and properties that the XAML presentation layer can use to provide a powerful user experience.

The vision of WPF involves XAML for many architectural goals. In order to provide a flexible and extensible structure for .NET applications, XAML was invented with many possible development perspectives in mind. One such perspective is that of the GUI-minded developer. The WPF graphics engine is vector-based, allowing for specific coordinate-based positioning of elements. If positioning of elements is not specific to a set of coordinates, the use of a hierarchical model between XAML entries provides a "nested" relationship for positioning elements on the screen. Each window item can be dependent upon another to be positioned properly on the screen. Another strategic reason for XML-based design markup involves a transparent use of XAML between web applications and desktop installations. XAML that is designed for a web application can be slightly modified to fit within a desktop application very easily. In addition, third-party tools (not to mention, ahem, "Sparkle") can allow for externally designed UIs to be pasted into a XAML file and immediately developed against within Visual Studio.NET with the WPF framework.

The following is a very basic XAML file structure containing only one button:

```
<Window Title="VeryBasicXAMLfile">
    <Grid>
        <Button Width="134" Height="27" Name="button1"
            Margin="73,53,0,0" Grid.RowSpan="1" Grid.Row="0"
                VerticalAlignment="Top" HorizontalAlignment="Left"
                Grid.Column="0" Grid.ColumnSpan="1">Button
        </Button>
    </Grid>
</Window>
```

You may have noticed the use of the xmlns (XML namespace) attribute of the window element. This allows the application to reference the XAML namespace and the WPF namespace for using class objects within them.

The Application Object

The Application object is accessible from within all WPF .NET projects and provides an interface between your application and the system. It is the entry point of a WPF application, where initialization and information preparation can take place. This feature works the same way in both WPF XBAPs and WPF Windows Applications. It acts similar to how the global.asax file manages contextual session and application information for ASP.NET applications. It gives you the opportunity to hook into events and override virtual methods for your application. Specifically, each virtual method corresponds to an event by the same name. For example, the OnActivated virtual method raises the Activated event within the Application object. You can either override the OnActivated method or create an event handler for the Activated event to insert functionality at that point shortly after. The following table lists these methods and their corresponding events.

Events	Methods	Description
Activated	OnActivated	A window activated by the system
Deactivated	OnDeactivated	A window deactivated by the system
SessionEnding	OnSessionEnding	Raised when a user session ends or the operating system terminates (i.e., logoff or shutdown)
Exit	OnExit	Raised after all windows are destroyed
Startup	OnStartup	Occurs prior to any windows being created or navigations being performed

Within Visual Studio .NET, the Application object is defined by the MyApp.xaml file and its corresponding code-behind file. The method and event hooks are implemented within these files and can be used for various startup and shutdown routines.

Typically, developers would tap into this type of control system to manage initialization and termination of the site-wide settings or shared resources, connections, and so on. The following section illustrates how you can override one of these methods or hook into one of the events within this Application object.

Obtaining a Reference to the Application Object

The Application object wraps a set of XAML files and creates a shared data environment between the pages. The Application object loads with the initial load and provides shared variables at that time. The following example obtains a reference to the Application object:

```
Application myApp;
myApp = System.Windows.Application.Current;
```

Now you can access non-static methods contained within this Application object.

Sharing Information

The use of the Application object to share variables across pages is fundamental to its purpose. XAML pages and their classes can store variables of any type within the Application object's Properties collection. All pages within this project can access these properties at any point within your application only by adding the data using a string key value. The following example shows how to store a class variable object within your Application object using a string key value of Book:

```
public class Book
{
    public decimal price;
    public string title;
    public string author;
}

class Window1
{
        public Window1()
```

```
        {
            InitializeComponent();

            //Create a variable
            Book x = new Book();
            x.author = "Shawn Livermore";
            x.title = "Professional WPF Programming";
            x.price = (decimal)49.99;

            //Store the variable in the application
            Application.Current.Properties["Book"] = x;
        }

        // ...
    }
```

When you need to extract this variable later, simply access it the same way, as a property of the
`Application` object.

```
private void MyClickEvent(object sender, RoutedEventArgs e)
{
    //Extract a reference to the stored variable
    Book y = (Book)Application.Current.Properties["Book"];
    MessageBox.Show(y.title, y.author, MessageBoxButton.OK,
            MessageBoxImage.Hand);
}
```

Creating the User Interface

Designing a UI in WPF is slightly different from the traditional Windows Forms or ASP.NET development process.

Screen Design

All the controls available to the developer are brand new native .NET controls built to render in the new
graphics platform. It is possible to host Windows Forms controls within the WPF environment, as well
as to host WPF controls within the Windows Forms environment.

Before you start designing your XAML window (where are my manners?), I must first mention the
designer. The designer provides robust tools for creating vector-based UI elements. The drag-and-drop
technique of the old world (Windows Forms and ASP.NET) simply places a new instance of the control
onto the design interface. Drawing is now more precise, using crosshairs and drawing motions instead
of the old archaic "drag, drop, and pray" style of design and development.

The Window, NavigationWindow, and Page Objects

In the WPF world, there are some different uses and perspectives of the various building blocks of a user
interface. XAML-based Windows are the first on the list, and are somewhat more capable as compared
to their Win32 WinForm predecessor. WPF Windows are used within WPF as containers of controls and
content. Essentially, as with other XAML objects, the `Window` base class object is a transferable piece of
XAML that can be moved among applications relatively easily. That is, if you have a WPF Windows

Application with a XAML file containing a `Window` object, you can copy and paste the XAML markup from this application to an XBAP without a single change to the syntax.

Although the XAML is interchangeable between application types, some features of WPF are not permissible by default for XBAPs because of security constraints.

The window objects used within WPF are threefold:

❑   `Window`

❑   `NavigationWindow`

❑   `Page`

The `Window` object provides properties, methods, and events that allow the application to respond and handle interaction with the user, and so on. In many cases, this is your typical layout area of development. Each WPF application has a reference to a window that is designated to be the "main window." You can control this by setting the `MainWindow` property of the `Application` object.

In order to access the `Window` object, you must first obtain a reference to the application's `MainWindow` object, as follows:

```
NavigationWindow navWindow = (NavigationWindow) MyApplication.MainWindow;
```

Once this is established, you can access its members and properties in order to customize the user experience or provide meaningful workflow between screens of an application, as displayed in the following table.

Event	Description
Activated	A window has been activated.
Closed	A window has been closed.
Closing	A window is closing.
ContentRendered	A window's content has been rendered. The event is not raised if there is no content within the window.
Deactivated	A window has been deactivated.
LocationChanged	A window's location has changed.
StateChanged	A window's state has been changed between maximized, minimized, and normal.

The collection of windows held within the `Application` *object contains only windows created on the same thread as the* `Application` *object. If a window is created via another thread, it is not added to the collection of windows, and cannot be accessed via the* `Application` *object.*

The `NavigationWindow` object is specifically designed for navigation applications, and inherits from the `Window` base class. It provides the following:

❑ Navigation between XAML pages

❑ A journal-tracking mechanism to store and manage navigation history

❑ Programmatic access to the various members of the window via the `Navigation` object

The navigation window is accessible via programmatic, object-level commands, such as the following:

```
myFrame.Navigate(new System.Uri("MyXAMLpage.xaml", UriKind.RelativeOrAbsolute));
```

By referencing the `Navigate` method of the `Frame` object, the page can navigate to other pages within the navigation project.

The basic steps involved with a `Navigate` method are strikingly similar to an ASP.NET page request:

1. Locate the next page.

2. Download the page.

3. Download any related resources, such as images.

4. Parse the page and construct the visual tree.

5. Render the page.

Because the WPF platform is based on an asynchronous execution model, the `Navigate` method will return to the caller the moment it initiates the navigation process. From this point, the state of events that fire as stated in the preceding list will be managed by the `NavigationService` object. Specifically, the events of a navigation process are listed in the following table.

Event	Description
Navigating	The process has been started. To halt the rest of navigation, you can cancel this event.
NavigationProgress	An event that provides the status of the navigation completion process. Hook into this event to provide the application a status of navigation in progress.
Navigated	The navigation target has been identified and requested for download, and the download has begun. Some portion of the XAML page's logical tree has been parsed through and potentially is attached to the page.
LoadCompleted	The page has been fully loaded and parsed, and can be rendered accordingly.

The `Page` object is used as an alternative means by which to access the `Navigation` object. `Page` inherits from `FrameworkElement` and is normally seen in use within a XAML page's markup. This is because the programmatic access (code-behind file) is provided by the `NavigationWindow` object.

The Page object exposes the following:

❑ Events raised by the FrameworkElement class, such as Loaded

❑ Properties that are specific to a window's dimensions

❑ Properties dictating a window's appearance, such as captions, title fonts, background color, transparency, and so on

Handling Events

Events are defined as isolated occurrences to which applications can respond. Common events include button clicks, keyboard key presses, or mouse actions, but can also include environmental events or programmatically created events.

To handle events within WPF, you have two options:

❑ XAML event handlers

❑ Programmatic event handlers

The XAML event handlers are probably the fastest way to go, but rely on the designer to specify events. This is not always a recommended approach, as the developer may be better equipped to create events programmatically instead of inline XAML markup events. In this method, the designer would insert the event handler assignment as an attribute to the specific XAML element that acts as the event *listener*. The event attribute value will become the name of the new event handler the developer creates.

Window Events

The events specific to the Window object as it changes state are considered *window events* and are described in the following table.

Events	Description
Activated	The window has been activated.
Closed	The window has been closed.
Closing	The window has been closing.
ContentRendered	Window content has been rendered.
Deactivated	The window has been deactivated.
LocationChanged	The location or source for the window has been changed.
StateChanged	The state of the window has been changed. The three window states available are maximized, minimized, and normal.

One of the most useful events to attach a handler to is the ContentRendered event. The following example displays the two areas to modify within a page in order to capture the ContentRendered event:

1. In the XAML page, named Page1.xaml in this case, within the <window> element, add a ContentRendered attribute, as follows:

```
<Window xmlns="http://schemas.microsoft.com/winfx/2006/xaml/presentation"
        xmlns:x="http://schemas.microsoft.com/winfx/2006/xaml"
        x:Class="Window_API.Page1"
        ContentRendered="OnContentRendered">

</Window>
```

2. In the code-behind file of this same page, named Page1.xaml.cs, add an event handler method with the appropriate arguments:

```
private void OnContentRendered(object sender, EventArgs e)
{
    //Here you handle the ContentRendered event
    MessageBox.Show("Content Rendered Event Fired!");
}
```

The events within the content of a window are a little more interesting and are outlined in the next section.

Routed Events

Raising and handling events within WPF is based on the new XAML markup structures and how events are routed through a tree of elements. When a XAML page contains nested controls, there are interactive complexities that never before existed in the typical .NET UI environment. As mentioned in Chapter 1, "nested" controls create what is known as a *logical tree* and a *visual tree*. Application developers have been required in times past to "walk the tree" by raising events and/or calling methods for each logical "node" within a nested hierarchy. Events in WPF are called *routed* because there is a brand new process to handle these events. This ordered, or routed, list of events will fire in a controlled fashion, providing a full view of even the most complex visual trees. With the advent of routed events in WPF, the complications involved with capturing a series of hierarchical events are encapsulated and simplified. Routed events are a pipeline of event handlers that are automatically fired for a control when any of its nested controls' events fire. This means that it performs as a self-aware component, knowing when its members are being interacted with, and providing handler logic to respond to user- or system-related interactions.

A FrameworkElement could possibly contain other sibling and child elements, thereby forming a tree of elements. In WPF, the parent element can provide information to child elements, providing usage, customization, and visibility to the potentially smaller, nested objects. "Control Composition" is a term used to describe the creation or design concepts used when creating controls. It leads developers to create better structure for controls to control and direct the logical flow of events for the tree and its members.

There are three types of routed events:

❑   Tunneling

❑   Bubbling

❑   Direct

Bubbling and Tunneling Events

A bubbling event is the first place we will start, as it provides event handling from the originating element of a visual tree to the root of the tree. Tunneling events, on the other hand, fire in the opposite direction and are used to hook into the pre-condition of the controls within the visual tree, from the top of the visual tree down.

Consider the following XAML syntax, which declaratively creates a `TextBox` control within a `Button` control within a `Grid` control:

```xaml
<Window x:Class="TunnelingBubbling.Window1"
      xmlns="http://schemas.microsoft.com/winfx/2006/xaml/presentation"
      xmlns:x="http://schemas.microsoft.com/winfx/2006/xaml"
      Title="TunnelingBubbling"
      >
      <Grid       MouseLeftButtonDown="MouseDownGrid"
                  PreviewMouseLeftButtonDown="PreviewMouseDownGrid"
                  Width="313"
                  Height="271">

          <Button PreviewMouseLeftButtonDown="PreviewMouseDownButton"
                  MouseLeftButtonDown="MouseDownButton"
                  Click="MyClickEvent"
                  Name="btnGo">

              <TextBox MouseLeftButtonDown="MouseLeftButtonDown"
                      PreviewMouseLeftButtonDown=
                          "PreviewMouseLeftButtonDown"
                      Width="173"
                      Height="27"
                      Name="textBox1">
              </TextBox>

          </Button>

      </Grid>
</Window>
```

The structure of the tree is such that the Grid control contains a Button control, which contains a TextBox control. The nested controls create a visual tree, which exposes events in a tunneling and bubbling process. When a user clicks in the TextBox control, an event fires in a tunneling process and launches a series of events that are managed by WPF. The following code-behind illustrates the capturing of events from the beginning of the tunneling activity:

```csharp
using System;
using System.Windows;
using System.Windows.Controls;
using System.Windows.Data;
using System.Windows.Documents;
using System.Windows.Media;
using System.Windows.Media.Imaging;
using System.Windows.Shapes;
using System.Diagnostics;

namespace TunnelingBubbling
```

```
{
    // <summary>
    // Interaction logic for Window1.xaml
    // </summary>

    public partial class Window1 : Window
    {

        public Window1()
        {
            InitializeComponent();
        }
        private void PreviewMouseDownGrid(object sender, RoutedEventArgs e)
        {
            Debug.WriteLine("PreviewMouseDownGrid");
        }
        private void PreviewMouseDownButton(object sender, RoutedEventArgs e)
        {
            Debug.WriteLine("PreviewMouseDownButton");
        }
        private void PreviewMouseLeftButtonDown(object sender, RoutedEventArgs e)
        {
            Debug.WriteLine("PreviewMouseLeftButtonDown");
        }
        private void MyClickEvent(object sender, RoutedEventArgs e)
        {
            Debug.WriteLine("MyClickEvent");
        }
        private void MouseLeftButtonDown(object sender, RoutedEventArgs e)
        {
            Debug.WriteLine("MouseLeftButtonDown");
        }
        private void MouseDownButton(object sender, RoutedEventArgs e)
        {
            Debug.WriteLine("MouseDownButton");
        }
        private void MouseDownGrid(object sender, RoutedEventArgs e)
        {
            Debug.WriteLine("MouseDownGrid");
        }
    }
}
```

From the preceding code-behind, the application would hook into the various events declared from the XAML page, allowing interactivity to any level for these nested controls.

Figure 2-3 shows the chronological order of events to be called within this nested group of controls. The figure is numbered from the Grid down through the TextBox on the left in order to demonstrate the sequence of event actions from a click on the Grid to the end resulting event. Once the TextBox is clicked by the mouse, the `PreviewMouseLeftButtonDown` event within the Grid is raised by the tunneling event handler written within the XAML markup. The "Preview" prefix in the event name denotes that the event is a part of the tunneling model, and fires in order, travelling down the tree to the base control that was the source of the original click event. Because there are other events attached within the visual tree, they each will fire in order. The following table displays the chronological order of events as used in the example.

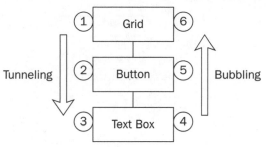

Figure 2-3

Order	Control	Event	Type of Event
1	Grid	PreviewMouseDownGrid	Tunneling
2	Button	PreviewMouseDownButton	Tunneling
3	TextBox	PreviewMouseLeftButtonDown	Tunneling
4	TextBox	MouseLeftButtonDown	Bubbling
5	Button	MouseDownButton	Bubbling
6	Grid	MouseDownGrid	Bubbling

Tunneling and *bubbling* event models assist in the complicated logic associated with events raised from/by controls within other controls. Developers can hook into an action before or after it occurs in context to its parent and child controls. Figure 2-4 further demonstrates the tunneling and bubbling process.

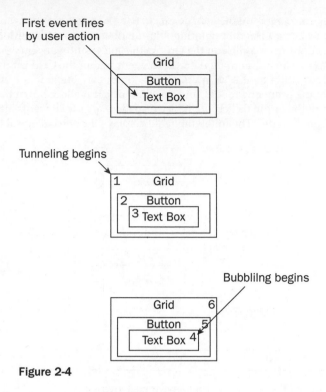

Figure 2-4

Figure 2-4 captures the chronological order of the routed events in WPF when using nested controls. Note that the order of the events flows downward into the nested controls for the tunneling events, whereas the order flows upward through to the outer container controls for the bubbling events.

Only the events explicitly cited within the markup of a visual tree of controls will be included in the ordered list of events to be raised. All ommitted event handlers represent missed opportunities to handle events.

Direct Events

Direct events represent the typical approach to which .NET programmers have become accustomed. When an event handler is created (programmatically or via XAML markup), the system will provide the same event handler/delegate operations as previous .NET development provides. That is, the only event handlers that are notified of the raised event are the ones attached to the originating element of the visual tree.

Suppressing the Event Handling

To suppress the handling of an event, you need to set that `Handled` property of the `RoutedEventArgs` parameter, as follows:

```
private void PreviewMouseDownButton(object sender, RoutedEventArgs e){
    Debug.WriteLine("PreviewMouseDownButton");
    e.Handled = true;
}
```

As displayed in the preceding code-behind file excerpt, the e.handled = true; syntax represents the series of routed events being hooked into within the visual tree of nested controls. Hooking into the event and then setting the Handled property to True is what suppresses the event in this case.

Find the Source Element in an Event Handler

In order to find a source control within a window that originated a raised event, you need to access the Source property of the RoutedEventArgs parameter, as displayed in the following excerpt:

```
private void PreviewMouseDownButton(object sender, RoutedEventArgs e){
    Button myButton = e.Source as Button;
    Debug.WriteLine(myButton.Name);
}
```

The e.Source passes in an actual object instance of the control that you can cast to System.Windows.Controls.Button. From this variable, you can access all the native properties, methods, and events that this control has to offer.

Working with Controls

Controls are the foundational elements for building a UI in WPF. Since Microsoft went back to the drawing board on all the WPF controls, (building them 100 percent natively as managed code in the form of .NET classes), there have been some dramatic areas of improvement and rearchitecture. The two base classes that a WPF control uses are the FrameworkElement class and the Control class. The changes in conceptual and physical design to a control are as follows and have additional implications that are explained within this section.

❑   Controls have nested controls, allowing the idea of a visual tree. The previous section touched on the use of controls as it depicted the general process for routed events within a visual tree of controls.

❑   Controls that have visual trees can raise numerous events for each control within the tree, providing a much more extensible and flexible event-processing model, called *event routing*. In this new model, events raised within the visual tree are *routed* to provide the automated calling of event handlers attached to any of the nodes within the visual tree. Thus, a small control can be infinitely complex and provide its own intrinsic behaviors and functionality, all without creating any custom user controls or pre-built and compiled assemblies beforehand.

❑   Controls can use routed commands to invoke shared functionality between controls and UI elements.

❑   Routed commands are able to provide a single invokable action that can be accessed once to execute numerous different functions or capabilities.

Because this topic of events within the UI can often be the area of focus for application developers, this section will dive into the usage scenarios for each of the preceding areas of interest.

WPF Controls

When developing controls for WPF, Microsoft did not provide 100 percent of the Windows Forms controls as corresponding WPF controls. This is not a problem, as you can utilize the concept of interoperation to host Windows Forms controls where a corresponding WPF control does not exist.

❑ Button

❑ CheckBox

❑ ComboBox

❑ ContextMenu

❑ DockPanel

❑ Expander

❑ Grid

❑ GridSplitter

❑ GroupBox

❑ HorizontalScrollBar

❑ Image

❑ Label

❑ ListBox

❑ ListView

❑ MediaPlayer

❑ Menu

❑ MonthCalendar

❑ OpenFileDialog

❑ PageSetupDialog

❑ PasswordBox

❑ Pointer

❑ PrintDialog

❑ ProgressBar

❑ RadioButton

❑ RichTextBox

❑ SaveFileDialog

❑ ScrollViewer

❑ Slider

- ❑ StatusBar

- ❑ TabControl

- ❑ TabItem

- ❑ TextBox

- ❑ ToolBar

- ❑ ToolTip

- ❑ TreeView

- ❑ UserControl

- ❑ VerticalScrollBar

- ❑ Window

- ❑ WrapPanel

Before walking through some of these controls, you need to understand how controls generally operate within the application. The next few sections describe their functions and usage scenarios.

Control Types

The following four types of controls are used within WPF:

- ❑ **Content controls** — Content controls are basically limited-scope controls, allowing for what is known as *singular content*. That is, a content control provides only basic data elements, such as strings, integers, or image content, unless a panel control is used as its main child element. If a panel is used, any nested content below the panel can exist, although the panel control itself remains the sole child element of the content control. Examples of content controls include Button, CheckBox, and RadioButton. Content controls do not contain header properties or items collections.

- ❑ **Items controls** — Items controls are used to contain lists of values or elements. These include ComboBox, ContextMenu, ListBox, Menu, and TabControl. They expose items collections but do not possess a `Content` property or any `Header` property.

- ❑ **Headered items controls** — Headered items controls are used to show a main, parent-level control or object, along with its needed child controls. Menu items are perfect examples of headered items controls.

- ❑ **Headered content controls** — Headered content controls are controls that contain a unique `Header` property and a `Content` property. The `Header` property consists of a text value, and the `Content` property consists of just one content item. Example `Content` property settings include specific instances of Expander or TabItem controls.

Dependency Property System

The dependency property system is based on the concept of inherited property values, and allows cascading changes to various UI element properties. Dependency properties provide support for animation, value expressions, dependent-value coercion, default values, inheritance, property change notification, data binding, property invalidation, and content styling.

Dependency Properties

Dependency properties establish the styling, data binding, animation, and other advanced graphics behaviors for WPF applications. These properties are registered with the WPF dependency property system. More specifically, dependency properties provide:

❑ The ability for controls to inherit their container element's properties (such as coordinates, size, and so on)

❑ Object-independent storage

❑ Tracking the changes made to elements in order to control the state of a control or element for undo commands to be used

❑ Complex data binding

❑ Constructs for animation routines for a control

Examples of dependency properties include the `Width`, `Background`, and `Text`. Each of these has a corresponding static `DependencyProperty` field. Parent elements can automatically propagate their dependency properties to their child elements.

Attached Properties

Attached properties are used to maintain values that are needed by child or nested elements. For example, a DockPanel control maintains the `Dock` property as an attached property, registered within the dependency property system. In this way, the child elements of the DockPanel control properly calculate their positioning. These properties can be set on any controls that are eligible to use attached properties.

Control Composition

Controls are made up of XAML markup and code-behind programmatic logic. They are the displayed components of a UI that designers manipulate to perfection. Although Web applications and desktop applications require the use of very different controls, WPF unifies the design experience to one set of controls for both locally installed .NET Framework 3.0 Windows Applications as well as .NET Framework 3.0 XBAPs. Using the same controls means the controls generate the same XAML in both uses. This is ideal, providing a flexible implementation of screens for the web and for windows, with very little, if any, rework. Both deployments have some developmental limitations, however, because the Internet zoning permissions system restricts access to a few areas of the WPF API from browser-based code on a client. This is not a major problem, however, because most of the API is usable at this level.

Styles

To establish a solid architectural model for designers (remember that WPF is mainly about the visuals), a flexible and reusable design has been implemented. UI designers can create presentation-layer patterns for controls and enforce those patterns intrinsically for all controls within specific portions of applications. To learn more about styles, see Chapter 4.

Control Templates

The visual portions of the controls are controlled by templates instead of the forced, designer-level properties of a control's XAML markup. That is, unlike .NET Windows Forms or ASP.NET development, WPF provides the format settings of a control as intrinsic class object references to themes and control templates, completely disconnected from the traditional graphic-designed display of the control. *Control templates* are essentially sets of elements, storyboards, and triggers that ultimately provide the visual appearance of one or more controls. This is also documented in greater detail in Chapter 4.

Control Styles

Control styles are used to share and structure the reusable formatting guides for the XAML page to use. Once entered into the `<Window>` node of the XAML, control styles can be referenced by any control that consumes their entries as attributes. Control styles contain the control's visual formatting information for showing the control to the outside world.

The following is an example of a XAML page with two control styles declared and a button assigned to one of them:

```
<Window x:Class="ControlStyles.Window1"
    xmlns="http://schemas.microsoft.com/winfx/2006/xaml/presentation"
    xmlns:x="http://schemas.microsoft.com/winfx/2006/xaml"
    Title="ControlStyles"
    >
    <Window.Resources>
        <Style x:Key="BigLettersStyle">
            <Setter Property="Control.FontSize" Value="20" />
            <Setter Property="Control.FontWeight" Value="Bold" />
            <Setter Property="Control.BorderThickness" Value="2" />
        </Style>
        <Style x:Key="SmallLettersStyle">
            <Setter Property="Control.FontSize" Value="10" />
            <Setter Property="Control.FontWeight" Value="Normal" />
            <Setter Property="Control.BorderThickness" Value="1" />
        </Style>
    </Window.Resources>
    <Grid>
        <Button Click="MyClickEvent"
            Style="{StaticResource SmallLettersStyle}"
            VerticalAlignment="Top"
            HorizontalAlignment="Left"
            Grid.Column="0"
            Grid.ColumnSpan="1"
            Grid.Row="0"
            Grid.RowSpan="1"
            Margin="43,61,0,0"
            Width="75"
            Height="23"
            Name="btnGo">Go
        </Button>
    </Grid>
</Window>
```

The preceding excerpt demonstrates the possible application of a `<Style>` to the XAML page and how it can be easily assigned to a control.

The `<Window.Resources>` XML element contains a `<Style>` XML element, which contains three `<Setter>` XML elements. These are the defining XML entries for establishing a page-level UI control formatting guide ("guide" meaning a catalog of styles to be applied at will to the controls on a page). The `<Button>` control has an attribute set aside for assigning a style to it, which is the obvious `Style` attribute. It is set to `Style="{StaticResource SmallLettersStyle}"` in order to provide the necessary pointer back to the page-level format "style." This is the assignment of the afore-named style to the control itself. This is obviously an evolution of a CSS of sorts, but it allows the application's presentation layer to remain abstracted from the complex code implementation that may exist behind the scenes.

You can also set styles programmatically by specifying a `Style` property of a control, as displayed in the following sample:

```
private void MyClickEvent(object sender, RoutedEventArgs e)
{
    btnGo.Style = (Style)FindResource("BigLettersStyle");
}
```

The assignment of a style to the control demonstrates the programmatic assignments that are possible within the WPF API.

Visual Tree

In the same way that a logical tree provides a view into the structure and nodes of a control, the concept of a visual tree, also introduced within WPF, is based on the physical and controllable components of a set of nested controls. It includes the created hierarchy of a set of nested controls at various levels with any number of attributes (properties) or members (triggers, events, and so on). Visual trees can be interactively used and parsed to capture information or specific session data from a user experience. These structured hierarchical models are of great assistance when exercising control over drawing and user interactivity for optimization and/or performance purposes. The `LogicalTreeHelper` class provides methods such as `GetChildren` and `GetParent` for querying the tree object to extract a list of child collections of elements from the tree of object elements.

The following XAML excerpt defines a control with nested child controls, forming a visual tree.

```
<Grid Width="313" Height="271">
    <Button Click="MyClickEvent" Name="btnGo">
        <TextBox Width="173" Height="27" Name="txt">
        </TextBox>
    </Button>
</Grid>
```

The Grid contains the button, which also contains a text box. The example is simple, but the implications are significant to the application developer, who has to account for the often complex and dynamic interactions within controls of a window.

To access an element within the tree, the following logic could be used:

```
void MyClickEvent(object sender, RoutedEventArgs e)
{
    object desiredNode = btnGo.FindName("txt");
    if (desiredNode is TextBox)
```

```
    {
        //If the text box was identified from the logic above...
        TextBox desiredChild = desiredNode as TextBox;
        desiredChild.Background = Brushes.Green;
    }
}
```

The preceding logic allows a node of the tree to be identified and accessed programmatically.

Commands

Essentially, *commands* are a means by which shared actions can be grouped and invoked in several different ways within an application. In most WPF applications, you will find numerous commonly needed features that can be called at any point from menu items with shortcut keys, buttons, miscellaneous controls on a window, or programming logic. Each of these items can be associated with execution logic in order to perform these common activities. To reduce redundancy, WPF provides commands to the developer. Uses of these commands would include the ability to select Edit ⇨ Cut from the Windows menu or to press Control+X from the keyboard. Either process would cut the selected text from the currently used application and add it to the Windows Clipboard. This centralization of logic using commands is essential to a thorough approach with an application interface design effort.

Commands are considered "routed" in part because they follow the same line of tunneling and bubbling as events do in WPF. Each time the command is executed, the capability of hooking into its tunneling and bubbling events exists. When the RoutedCommand class is invoked by your application, it raises the PreviewExecuteEvent and the ExecuteEvent events. PreviewExecuteEvent provides a tunneling event to proactively handle the upcoming event, whereas ExecuteEvent provides the associated bubbling event to access logic that should exist directly after the event fires. In addition, the RoutedCommand class also provides an overloaded Execute method that can be utilized, passing in as a parameter a specific target element to provide context.

The following table describes the four different classes for routed commands built into WPF.

Class	Description
ApplicationCommands	Includes common Clipboard and file-level commands available, such as File ⇨ Open, File ⇨ New, and so on.
ComponentCommands	Allows you to scroll up or scroll down, or move to the front of a section of text or move to the end of a section of text.
EditCommands	Provides editing capabilities such as the formatting of fonts, and so on.
MediaCommands	Provides multimedia-related operations such as play, pause, stop, and so on.

Most of the commands used by different controls within a typical application would reside within the ApplicationCommands class. TextBox controls utilize valuable ApplicationCommands class functionalities such as cut, copy, paste, and so on.

Declaring Commands

A fundamental difference between commands and events is that commands do not exist in relation to controls, as there are many elements that will call them. In addition, commands run in the context of a single instance within the application runtime. Whenever an application invokes a command, tunneling and bubbling events are raised. As commands can be executed from anywhere within the application or programmatic logic, there should be some provision of context for which a command is executed in order to be self-aware and understand the nature of the requested operation. A CommandBinding class is used to provide UI element-specific context to the execution of commands within a window or area of an application. The CommandBinding class connects an event handler within a UI control with a RoutedCommand object. Then, the CommandBinding class object raises the PreviewExecute and Execute events to allow for event handlers on the established command. The CommandBinding class actually offers a total of four events: Execute, PreviewExecute, QueryEnabled, and PreviewQueryEnabled.

The following example demonstrates how to invoke a Paste command when the focus of the cursor is within the area of the designated control.

XAML markup:

```xml
<Window x:Class="Commands.Window1"
xmlns="http://schemas.microsoft.com/winfx/2006/xaml/presentation"
xmlns:x="http://schemas.microsoft.com/winfx/2006/xaml"
Title="Commands">
<Grid>
    <StackPanel>
        <StackPanel.CommandBindings>
            <CommandBinding Command="ApplicationCommands.Paste"
                    Executed="InvokeApplicationCommand"/>
        </StackPanel.CommandBindings>
        <Button Command="ApplicationCommands.Paste">
            Paste something (Control + V) when I have the focus!"
        </Button>
    </StackPanel>

</Grid>
</Window>
```

C# code-behind:

```csharp
using System;
using System.Windows;
using System.Windows.Controls;
using System.Windows.Input;

namespace Commands
{
    public partial class Window1 : Window
    {
        static Window1()
        {

        }
        void InvokeApplicationCommand(object target, ExecutedRoutedEventArgs args)
        {
```

```
                    MessageBox.Show("The ApplicationCommands has been invoked.");
            }
        }
    }
```

The following steps take place in order to invoke `ApplicationCommands` using the preceding code excerpts:

1. A `StackPanel` control contains a `CommandBinding` XML entry. This entry allows the generic paste command within the `ApplicationCommand` class to be bound to this control and execute a method within the Executed bubbled event.

2. Within the `StackPanel` control is a Button control with the command attribute set to the `ApplicationCommands.Paste` value. This identifies the paste command as being the specifically desired command to be executed when this control has the focus.

3. The Button control within the window accepts the focus as the user tabs through the controls. While the focus is on this control, the Application command is executed by pressing Ctrl+V from the keyboard.

4. `CommandBinding` is now going to allow the application to handle the specified tunneling event called Executed. Because the command binding contained a user-defined method entitled `InvokeApplicationCommand`, the page's code-behind logic will execute this method, performing whatever user-defined functionality may exist.

So now you have fully handled an existing application command. But what if you need to find your own command? The next section addresses this in detail.

Defining New Commands

You can define commands easily by using the following four steps:

1. Declare the static command object:

```
public static RoutedCommand myCmd;
```

2. Create an `InputGestureCollection`:

```
static Window1()
{
    InputGestureCollection myInputs = new InputGestureCollection();
```

3. Add input gesture items:

```
myInputs.Add(new KeyGesture(Key.G, ModifierKeys.Control | ModifierKeys.Shift));
```

4. Create the routed command with the name, type, and the `InputGestureCollection` variable you created:

```
myCmd = new RoutedCommand("Go", typeof(Window1), myInputs);
```

The entire set of code would then be:

```
public static RoutedCommand myCmd;

static Window1()
{
    InputGestureCollection myInputs = new InputGestureCollection();
    myInputs.Add(new KeyGesture(Key.G, ModifierKeys.Control | ModifierKeys.Shift));
    myCmd = new RoutedCommand("Go", typeof(Window1), myInputs);
}
```

The resulting application logic would allow the user to press Ctrl+Shift+G to invoke the custom command. In this case, you can use the same sort of command binding as in the previous example to provide raised events to accompany this command execution. Although you have learned how to handle a command and how to create a custom command, you still need to invoke the command from the application logic.

Invoking Commands

Invoking a command simply requires making a call to the WPF runtime, asking for this predefined, globally registered execution call. More specifically, there is one command class object that provides all the command execution functionality to the application. Commands are invoked using the notion of input gestures. Two input gesture types are supported: MouseGesture and KeyGesture. These represent the potential activating invocations from a keyboard shortcut or a drag-drop-drawing event. Ctrl+V is a standard keyboard shortcut used to perform Paste operations. But this shortcut is actually an input gesture and performs the call to the application host with the user's focus in order to invoke the ApplicationCommands class object's paste command.

The InputGestureCollection class is used to house all the input gestures that can invoke a command. Once you have added the desired input gestures to the InputGestureCollection, your command can be accessed through any of the key combinations entered.

Alternatively, because the command classes in use are static, you can access them as a utility call passing in the control for the context of the execution as an optional parameter. In this way, you can invoke a command programmatically by calling its Execute method, as follows:

```
using System;
using System.Windows;
using System.Windows.Controls;
using System.Windows.Input;

namespace Commands
{
    public partial class Window1 : Window
    {

        public static RoutedCommand myCmd;

        static Window1()
        {
            InputGestureCollection myInputs =
```

```
                 new InputGestureCollection();
         myInputs.Add(new KeyGesture(Key.G,
             ModifierKeys.Control | ModifierKeys.Shift));
         myCmd = new RoutedCommand("Go",
             typeof(Window1), myInputs);
     }

     private void ExecuteCommandClickEvent(object sender,
         RoutedEventArgs e)
     {
         myCmd.Execute(sender,null);
     }
   }
 }
```

Triggers

So far this chapter has outlined the use of control styles and the setter elements within a style. WPF provides a new concept to the UI development effort: the trigger. *Triggers* are used to control and manipulate the visual representation of a control's style elements within a window. Numerous different types of triggers are in use:

- ❑ Property triggers
- ❑ Event triggers
- ❑ Data triggers
- ❑ Multi-condition data triggers
- ❑ Multiple triggers
- ❑ Multi-condition triggers

The following sections explain each type of trigger and walk you through examples for a better understanding of their real-world usage.

Property triggers check WPF dependency property values in order to provide conditional execution, whereas data triggers are based on CLR property values.

Property Triggers

These are the most common and basic types of triggers within the WPF programmatic model. They are basically XAML condition statements that check the state of a property to determine whether to use a specific style/setter value within the style of the element.

The following are the basic steps for creating a property trigger:

1. Create a top-level `<Style>` XML element in your XAML page and set the `TargetType` of the `<Style>` XML element to `{x:Type Button}`:

```
<Style TargetType="{x:Type Button}">
```

2. Within the <Style> entries, define the <Style.Trigger> element:

```
<Style.Triggers>
```

3. Within the <Style.Triggers> XML element, create a <Trigger> XML element with the property to check and the value to compare it to set as attributes for this class:

```
<Trigger Property="IsMouseOver" Value="True">
</Trigger>
```

4. Enter the <Setter> XML element to designate the actual property value of the Button control(s) that will need to be rendered. In this case, the developer can set the property to be modified in the trigger's condition routine.

```
<Setter Property="Background" Value="Orange" />
```

5. Add a button to the XAML page, with no special settings needed:

```
<Button VerticalAlignment="Top"
        HorizontalAlignment="Stretch"
        Height="46"
        Name="button1">Button
</Button>
```

The final syntax should resemble the following:

```
<Window x:Class="PropertyTrigger.Window1"
xmlns="http://schemas.microsoft.com/winfx/2006/xaml/presentation"
xmlns:x="http://schemas.microsoft.com/winfx/2006/xaml"
Title="PropertyTrigger"
>
<Window.Resources>
  <Style TargetType="{x:Type Button}">
      <Style.Triggers>
            <Trigger Property="IsMouseOver" Value="True">
                    <Setter Property="Background" Value="Orange" />
            </Trigger>
      </Style.Triggers>
  </Style>
</Window.Resources>

<Grid>
        <Button VerticalAlignment="Top"
            HorizontalAlignment="Stretch"
            Height="46"
            Name="button1">Button
        </Button>
</Grid>
</Window>
```

As displayed, the setter property would apply only when the trigger is evaluated to be a True condition. If the trigger is evaluated to a False value, it will not fire.

Multiple Triggers

You can provide multiple triggers within one style element if there are different possible conditions that would constitute a style change. The different triggers are evaluated chronologically from the first to the last. If more than one trigger's condition statement evaluates to `True`, the XAML renders only the final trigger's property change.

The following example demonstrates multiple triggers within one style element:

```
<Window.Resources>

    <Style TargetType="{x:Type Button}">
        <Style.Triggers>
            <Trigger Property="IsMouseOver" Value="True">
                <Setter Property="Background" Value="Orange" />
            </Trigger>
            <Trigger Property="IsFocused" Value="True">
                <Setter Property="Background" Value="Red" />
            </Trigger>
        </Style.Triggers>
    </Style>

</Window.Resources>
```

The `IsMouseOver` condition within the first trigger will cause the button to turn orange, but when the button is clicked, the `IsFocused` property changes to `True`, which in turns causes the second trigger to fire, turning the button red.

Multi-Condition Triggers

When a style requires multiple conditional evaluations, you must use the `MultiTrigger.Conditions` XML element. This element provides a check constraint for all of the conditional statements to be evaluated to `True` in order for it to take effect. For example, a conditional set could require that the mouse be over a button and the displayed content of the button to be "Go." For this requirement to be set within a `MultiTrigger`, the following syntax would be required:

```
<Window.Resources>

<Style TargetType="{x:Type Button}">
  <Style.Triggers>
      <MultiTrigger>
        <MultiTrigger.Conditions>
            <Condition Property="IsMouseOver" Value="True" />
            <Condition Property="Content" Value="Go" />
        </MultiTrigger.Conditions>
      <Setter Property="Background" Value="Green" />
      </MultiTrigger>
  </Style.Triggers>
</Style>

</Window.Resources>
```

So you've learned how to use the various application triggers in order to provide event-driven application flow logic within an XAML file of the UI. The next section will provide insight to working with data triggers, an important area when designing and developing data-intensive UIs.

Data Triggers

Data triggers are used to check the values within non-visual and/or non-WPF control elements. That is, data triggers are designed to work outside of the WPF dependency property system, accessing CLR properties or non-visual objects such as form content or variable values. You can use data triggers for numerous application functions, including:

❑ Checking the value of a field or calculation

❑ Controlling behaviors based on a variable in memory

❑ Checking a non-visual data element

❑ Checking a field within a bound control

The basic WPF pattern for style manipulation becomes well rounded using these data triggers, as they extend the style-changing powers into the "old world" of .NET control values and variables.

The following example depicts the application of a DataTrigger and a MultiDataTrigger within a window, bound to a set of Person custom class objects:

XAML:

```
<?Mapping XmlNamespace="MyMappingNamespace" ClrNamespace="DataTriggerSample" ?>
<Window Background="LightGray"
  xmlns="http://schemas.microsoft.com/winfx/2006/xaml/presentation"
  xmlns:x="http://schemas.microsoft.com/winfx/2006/xaml"
  xmlns:c="MyMappingNamespace"
  x:Class="DataTriggerSample.Window1"
  Title="DataTrigger"
  Width = "320"
  Height = "300"
  >
<Window.Resources>
  <c:People x:Key="PeopleData"/>

  <Style TargetType="{x:Type ListBoxItem}">
    <Style.Triggers>
  <DataTrigger Binding="{Binding Path=RelationshipType}"
          Value="Pastor">
        <Setter Property="Background" Value="Yellow" />
      </DataTrigger>
        <DataTrigger Binding="{Binding Path=RelationshipType}"
          Value="Brother">
          <Setter Property="Background" Value="Pink" />
        </DataTrigger>
    </Style.Triggers>
  </Style>

  <DataTemplate DataType="{x:Type c:Person}">
    <Canvas Width="260" Height="20">
```

```xml
            <TextBlock FontSize="12" Width="130" Canvas.Left="0"
                       Text="{Binding Path=Name}"/>
          <TextBlock FontSize="12" Width="130"  Canvas.Left="130"
                          Text="{Binding Path=RelationshipType}"/>
      </Canvas>
    </DataTemplate>
  </Window.Resources>

  <StackPanel>
    <TextBlock FontSize="18" Margin="5" FontWeight="Bold"
      HorizontalAlignment="Center">Data Trigger Sample</TextBlock>
    <ListBox Width="250" HorizontalAlignment="Center" Background="White"
      ItemsSource="{Binding Source={StaticResource PeopleData}}"/>
  </StackPanel>

</Window>
```

C# code-behind file:

```csharp
using System;
using System.ComponentModel;
using System.Windows;
using System.Windows.Controls;
using System.Windows.Documents;
using System.Windows.Navigation;
using System.Windows.Shapes;
using System.Windows.Data;
using System.Collections.ObjectModel;

namespace DataTriggerSample
{
  public partial class Window1 : Window
  {
    public Window1()
    {
      InitializeComponent();
    }
  }

  public class Person
  {
    private string _name;
    private string _relationshipType;

    public string Name
    {
      get { return _name; }
      set { _name = value; }
    }

    public string RelationshipType
    {
      get { return _relationshipType; }
      set { _relationshipType = value; }
```

```
        }

    public Person(string name, string relationshiptype)
    {
        this._name = name;
        this._relationshipType = relationshiptype;
    }
}

public class People : ObservableCollection<Person>
{
    public People()
    {
        Add(new Person("Shantell", "Best Friend"));
        Add(new Person("Bill", "Pastor"));
        Add(new Person("Keith", "Friend"));
        Add(new Person("Jason", "Friend"));
        Add(new Person("Sean", "Friend"));
        Add(new Person("Chris", "Friend"));
        Add(new Person("Peter", "Brother"));
        Add(new Person("Jeremy", "Brother"));
        Add(new Person("Kevin", "Brother"));
    }
}
}
```

The preceding code-behind would produce the screenshot displayed in Figure 2-5. The shaded items are based on the values of the relationship column.

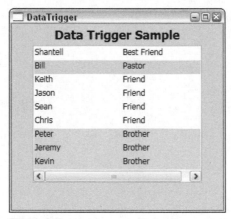

Figure 2-5

Each data trigger uses a `Binding` attribute, allowing expressions or objects to be used as the established bound fields for the events to fire under. The following excerpt shows this in action:

```
<DataTrigger Binding="{Binding Path=RelationshipType}" Value="Pastor">
    <Setter Property="Background" Value="Yellow" />
</DataTrigger>
```

Note the `Path` variable within the `Binding` attribute has a value of `RelationshipType`. This is a pointer through the `DataTemplate` element, shown here:

```
<DataTemplate DataType="{x:Type c:Person}">
    <Canvas Width="260" Height="20">
        <TextBlock FontSize="12" Width="130" Canvas.Left="0"
                       Text="{Binding Path=Name}"/>
      <TextBlock FontSize="12" Width="130"  Canvas.Left="130"
                        Text="{Binding Path=RelationshipType}"/>
    </Canvas>
  </DataTemplate>
```

By referencing the `Person` class within the `DataTemplate`, you set the type of the data. The `Person` type contains values such as `Name` and `RelationshipType`, as set within the code-behind file (a section of which is listed here):

```
public class People : ObservableCollection<Person>
{
  public People()
  {
    Add(new Person("Shantell", "Treasured Friend"));
    Add(new Person("Elexzandreia", "Daughter"));
    Add(new Person("Bill", "Pastor"));
    Add(new Person("Keith", "Friend"));
    Add(new Person("Jason", "Friend"));
    Add(new Person("Sean", "Friend"));
    Add(new Person("Chris", "Friend"));
    Add(new Person("Peter", "Brother"));
    Add(new Person("Jeremy", "Brother"));
    Add(new Person("Kevin", "Brother"));

  }
 }
}
```

The preceding section of the code-behind file demonstrates the use of generics, as the `People` class is exposed to the application as a public class made up of a collection of the `Person` type. Generics classes are based on custom types, and this class possesses a list of a custom type. Each `Person` class object is added to the class collection within the constructor. This class represents bindable data to the ListView control because it inherits from the .NET `ObservableCollection` base class.

Multi-Condition Data Triggers

The previous sample provided insight into checking a set of data for a single condition, and responding within the UI for such a condition. But what if your interface needs to check for the existence of multiple possible conditions and provide a response mechanism for cases when all conditions exist? You would need to employ a multi-condition data trigger. The example application could be modified within its style tags to include the multi-condition data trigger, as the following code demonstrates:

```
<MultiDataTrigger>
   <MultiDataTrigger.Conditions>
       <Condition Binding="{Binding Path=Name}" Value="Shantell" />
       <Condition Binding="{Binding Path=RelationshipType}"
```

```
                    Value="Best Friend" />
        </MultiDataTrigger.Conditions>
        <MultiDataTrigger.Setters>
            <Setter Property="Background" Value="LightGreen" />
        </MultiDataTrigger.Setters>
    </MultiDataTrigger>
```

This markup contains a multi-condition data trigger with two condition elements. The first condition element creates a requirement that the Name field of the bound data be the text "Shantell," and the RelationshipType field of the bound data be the text "Best Friend." If both conditions evaluate to True, then the Setter property element below these conditions will be applied, setting the background of the data row to LightGreen. Figure 2-6 represents the modified application with both individual data triggers and the multi-condition data trigger working simultaneously.

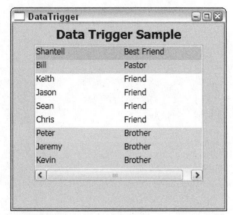

Figure 2-6

Notice in the figure that the first row is now highlighted because both conditions of the multi-condition data trigger evaluated to True for that record. The other data triggers still apply.

Now that you have a good grasp of the concepts involved with property and data triggers, let's tackle a slightly different angle with event triggers.

Event Triggers

Event triggers are very different from property and data triggers in that they are based solely on events fired within the application. These triggers are designed to hook into events and set off animations within a storyboard. This is based on a design concept, covered in greater detail in Chapter 4.

Language Support

WPF has built-in support for creating applications that can be modified to meet the expectations of target audiences in various different languages. The concepts of globalization and localization are central to this effort with provisions for the following:

- ❑ Multilingual User Interface (MUI)
- ❑ Flow direction
- ❑ Encoding
- ❑ Characters
- ❑ Unicode
- ❑ Satellite assemblies

The following sections explain globalization and localization, and provide tips on how to create a flexible application for deployment in any language.

Globalization

Multilingual User Interface (MUI) is Microsoft's model for moving between different languages within a single UI. A WPF application uses an "assembly model" to provide the MUI. The concept of MUI and globally aware application development models has been around for some time but has recently taken a newer definition. *Globalization* in the WPF platform means that the application should be developed with globally universal control references, and should not require recompilation in order to accommodate different languages. That is, recompilation has been the defining aspect of whether an application is considered "globalized," as it is an architectural negative to perform recompilation under this basic premise alone.

Globalization is achieved in WPF through the use of the `ResourceManager` class. This system for managing data and content is independent of the build itself, pointing to external resource files as needed. The `ResourceManager` class is used to provide culture-specific resource files and content at runtime. It provides a fallback resource embedded within it when a localized version of a resource does not exist under its expected location within the file-folder structure.

The concept of resources represents embedded content (images, strings, or binary data), which can be retrieved at runtime by the `ResourceManager` and rendered to the presentation layer. The `ResourceManager` class retrieves specific resources for the application, which exist in external files. Before it can determine which folder to look in for the resource, it must know the desired culture. A *culture* is defined as being a language and a location. Commonly used cultures include en-US, en-GB, and en-CA, which represent the English language within the United States, Great Britain, and Canada, respectively. These are used specifically for those regions, as there are plenty of instances where phrases and terminology are used differently between the regions. If `ResourceManager` determines that the culture is en-US, it will look in the en-US folder under the en folder within the application's localized folder repository.

Once an application has created satellite assembly files, it can access them when the `CurrentUICulture` property is specified from either the configuration file or via a programmatic reference. Satellite assembly files are essentially .NET projects compiled and deployed as DLL files. Each DLL may contain content such as images, text, or other resources. You can use the following syntax to set the `CurrentUICulture` property within an application's runtime:

```
Thread.CurrentThread.CurrentUICulture = new CultureInfo("en-US");
```

The system-set culture uses the `GetUserDefaultUILanguage` method within Windows 2000 and Windows XP MUI editions since the user can set the culture upon install. If the culture is not specified, it refers to the language of the operating system.

Localization

When a XAML file is compiled, it creates a BAML file, which can be accessed by the `ResourceManager` class. BAML files are compiled and deployable XAML applications that run under various .NET Framework deployment environments. BAML files are able to be accessed at runtime as a resource and utilized as content or functionality. To enable localized content support in your application, you must include localizable embedded resources within a separate "resource" assembly. This separate DLL file is created specific to a language, with the main content to be referenced from the .proj project file.

Creating resources is made simpler by the use of the Visual Studio 2005 design interface. You can expose the tool by double-clicking the Properties folder of a .NET Framework 3.0 project. Figure 2-7 shows the tool in its default load mode for maintaining string values.

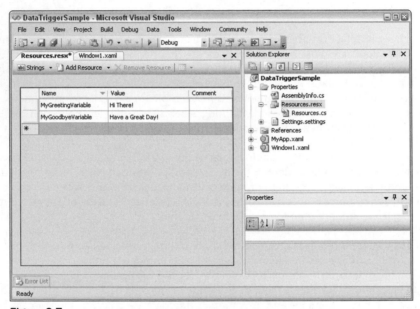

Figure 2-7

The top bar area of the tool allows you to select from the available file or content types to manage. You can choose to create and embed strings, images, icons, audio files, or other file types within your assembly.

Throughout your development, you can refer to strings and content that have been entered into the embedded resources files of your assembly by referencing the `ResourceManager` class. The following sample shows how you would retrieve a specific textual value from your resource repository:

```
ResourceManager rm = new
ResourceManager("YourApplicationName.data.stringtable",
Assembly.GetExecutingAssembly());
String x = rm.GetString("SpecificStringNameHere");
```

Thus, any of the files or string values entered proactively into the resource file management interface can be effectively retrieved and used throughout your development process. These resource files are duplicated for the various cultures, within separate projects. Once compiled, projects with resource files can be used as the satellite assemblies for the localization process to occur.

When the XAML markup is compiled, it generates a BAML file, which, along with other images and content, is ultimately embedded into the satellite assembly. When the XAML file is tokenized, embedded logic is removed out of the XAML page and compiled into one or more different DLL assemblies.

Deployment

Deployment within WPF is based on the current .NET deployment models, including the setup project, web-setup project, or a ClickOnce deployment package. This topic is outside of the scope of this book, but worth mentioning nonetheless.

Summary

This chapter introduced the majority of core development concepts you need to create a WPF application. You learned about windows, navigation, events, commands, styles, controls, triggers, and localization. Specifically, you should be able to:

❑ Create a new WPF application, selecting either an XBAP, Desktop, Service, Navigation, or a Custom Control

❑ Design user-friendly interfaces with a consistent style and user experience across the board

❑ Create interactive control elements in XAML, embedding triggers and other response mechanisms directly within the XAML markup

❑ Hook into events exposed at the control level, including multiple levels of nested controls (via tunneling and bubbling events), providing meaningful and managed activities at all interaction points between the control and the user

❑ Create property or data triggers to handle contextual information on bound and non-bound controls

❑ Programmatically access all the window, control, and visual design elements on the XAML page using the WPF object model

The next chapter highlights the basic anatomy of a WPF-enabled application, as it walks you through each file in detail, explaining its usage within the application.

Anatomy of a WPF-Enabled Application

The file structure of WPF applications is relatively similar across all four of the .NET 3.0 project types:

❑ .NET Framework 3.0 Windows Application

❑ .NET Framework 3.0 XAML Browser Application (XBAP)

❑ .NET Framework 3.0 Custom Control Library Project

❑ .NET Framework 3.0 Service Library Project

This chapter will walk you through each file of each project, outlining its usage and purpose. It will provide you with a solid understanding of how the project types compare to one another, what their compilation lifespan looks like, and how you can expect to work with them within your project.

Project Composition

This section will identify the shared files of each of the projects, highlighting those that exist only in certain projects. The referenced assemblies provided by default for these four application types are different for each one, but are listed here along with a brief description.

Referenced Assembly	Description
PresentationCore	Provides direct graphics manipulation (visuals, geometry, model3D, imaging, and so on)
PresentationFramework	Used to provide graphics processing for applications, controls, and styling, which in turn can host a layout, data, content, and actions
ReachFramework	Provides XPS document and printing capabilities, among others
System	Contains classes that define commonly used value and reference data types, events and event handlers, interfaces, attributes, and processing exceptions
System.Data	Provides access to classes that represent the ADO.NET architecture
System.Printing	Provides all classes for printing and formatting
System.Runtime.Serialization	Contains classes that can be used for serializing and de-serializing objects
System.Security.Authorization	Provides security functionality within the .NET Framework 3.0
System.ServiceModel	Handles foundational communications and messaging for .NET Framework 3.0
System.Xml	Exists as the core XML functionality class used in .NET
UIAutomationProvider	Provides programmatic access to the UI
UIAutomationTypes	Provides UI automation type classes
WindowsBase	Exists as one of the foundational classes for .NET Framework 3.0 applications, and allows some visibility into the shared events and functionalities of Windows

Figure 3-1 illustrates a logical technology stack of the classes as they pertain to the overall WPF engine.

The PresentationFramework, PresentationCore, and milcore are the foundational development pieces that make up most of WPF. Of these components, only milcore is unmanaged code. Milcore is written in unmanaged code for the sole purpose of enhancing its integration capabilities with DirectX, the underlying graphics and rendering model. All rendering is performed via DirectX, which enhances the hardware and software display capabilities. In addition, in order to give the WPF system strong control over memory and execution, milcore was built to be extremely "performance-aware," and the development team on the WPF left many advantages of the CLR behind for the benefit of raw horsepower in terms of rendering performance on both hardware and software levels.

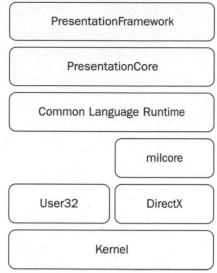

Figure 3-1

The following table portrays the actual project files, along with an indicator as to whether they are provided by default within each of the applications.

Filename	XAML Browser Application	Service Library Project	Custom Control Library Project	Windows Application
Properties\app.manifest	X			
Properties\AssemblyInfo.cs	X	X	X	X
Properties\Resources.resx	X		X	X
Properties\Settings.settings	X		X	X
MyApp.xaml	X			X
Page1.xaml	X			
Class1.cs		X		
UserControl1.xaml			X	
Window1.xaml				X

As displayed in the table, many of the files listed are common across .NET Framework 3.0 projects. Some of them are new in the .NET Framework 3.0 platform, whereas others have been in use since .NET 1.1.

The following subsections explore each project in greater detail, explaining the purpose and usage of each file.

App.Manifest

The App.Manifest file is used primarily for deployment, and is an XML-based document that lists the composite elements of an application, including specifying its identity, dependency files, and level of trust the application requires. The manifest is "signed" in order to guarantee application integrity. Although the details of configuring and mastering the App.Manifest file are beyond the scope of this book, the following is a sample file:

```xml
<?xml version="1.0" encoding="utf-8"?>
<asmv1:assembly manifestVersion="1.0" xmlns="urn:schemas-microsoft-com:asm.v1"
xmlns:asmv1="urn:schemas-microsoft-com:asm.v1" xmlns:asmv2="urn:schemas-microsoft-
com:asm.v2" xmlns:xsi="http://www.w3.org/2001/XMLSchema-instance">
  <trustInfo xmlns="urn:schemas-microsoft-com:asm.v2">
    <security>
      <applicationRequestMinimum>
        <defaultAssemblyRequest permissionSetReference="Custom" />
        <PermissionSet class="System.Security.PermissionSet" version="1"
ID="Custom" SameSite="site" />
      </applicationRequestMinimum>
    </security>
  </trustInfo>
</asmv1:assembly>
```

AssemblyInfo.cs

Known and loved by all, the AssemblyInfo.cs file is used as a repository for storing an assembly's authorship, security, localization, and version settings.

```csharp
#region Using directives

using System.Reflection;
using System.Runtime.CompilerServices;
using System.Resources;
using System.Globalization;
using System.Windows;
using System.Runtime.InteropServices;

#endregion

// General information about an assembly is controlled through the following
// set of attributes. Change these attribute values to modify the information
// associated with an assembly.
[assembly: AssemblyTitle("WPFWindowsAppBreakdown")]
[assembly: AssemblyDescription("")]
[assembly: AssemblyConfiguration("")]
[assembly: AssemblyCompany("kbb")]
[assembly: AssemblyProduct("WPFWindowsAppBreakdown")]
[assembly: AssemblyCopyright("Copyright @ kbb 2006")]
[assembly: AssemblyTrademark("")]
[assembly: AssemblyCulture("")]
[assembly: ComVisible(false)]

//In order to begin building localizable applications, set
```

```
//<UICulture>CultureYouAreCodingWith</UICulture> in your .csproj file
//inside a <PropertyGroup>.  For example, if you are using US English
//in your source files, set the <UICulture> to en-US.  Then uncomment
//the NeutralResourceLanguage attribute below.  Update the "en-US" in
//the line below to match the UICulture setting in the project file.

//[assembly: NeutralResourcesLanguage("en-US",
UltimateResourceFallbackLocation.Satellite)]


[assembly: ThemeInfo(
    ResourceDictionaryLocation.None, //where theme specific resource dictionaries
are located
    //(used if a resource is not found in the page
    // or application resource dictionaries)
    ResourceDictionaryLocation.SourceAssembly //where the generic resource
dictionary is located
    //(used if a resource is not found in the page,
    // app, or any theme specific resource dictionaries)
)]


// Version information for an assembly consists of the following four values:
//
//      Major Version
//      Minor Version
//      Build Number
//      Revision
//
// You can specify all the values or you can default the Revision and Build Numbers
// by using the '*' as shown below:
[assembly: AssemblyVersion("1.0.*")]
```

Among the new additions to this file in .NET Framework 3.0 projects is the UICulture setting, which enables you to set the language to provide localized support for your application. The following line sets the localized culture to be US-English:

```
[assembly: NeutralResourcesLanguage("en-US",
    UltimateResourceFallbackLocation.Satellite)]
```

The UltimateResourceFallbackLocation enumeration provides the assembly information needed by the ResourceManager class to retrieve the appropriate local resources. The two possible values are MainAssembly and Satellite. MainAssembly would provide the resources embedded within the same assembly, whereas Satellite would require an external file(s) used to store the localization resources.

Also appearing with .NET Framework 3.0 projects is the ThemeInfo entry, which identifies the location of the resource dictionaries used to index the resources needed for a particular project.

Resources.resx

The Resources.resx file is used to store all sorts of resource files to be embedded within the assembly itself. The following types of data can be stored within their resource file:

❑   Files

❑   Strings

❑   Images

❑   Icons

❑   Text files

.NET Framework 3.0 provides a clever interface for adding different sorts of resource files to the assembly at design time.

Settings.settings

The Settings.settings file is used to specify the project's application or user settings. If a user prefers certain color schemes or configuration settings, the application can intuitively save those light pieces of information context outside of a database, and retrieve them as needed. .NET Framework 3.0 within Visual Studio 2005 has a settings designer window that generates values as strongly typed class entries in a code-behind supportive file. The following is the default contents of Settings.settings in the code-behind file:

```
//------------------------------------------------------------------------
// <auto-generated>
//      This code was generated by a tool.
//      Runtime Version:2.0.50727.42
//
//      Changes to this file may cause incorrect behavior and will be lost if
//      the code is regenerated.
// </auto-generated>
//------------------------------------------------------------------------

namespace WPFWindowsAppBreakdown.Properties {


    [global::System.Runtime.CompilerServices.CompilerGeneratedAttribute()]

[global::System.CodeDom.Compiler.GeneratedCodeAttribute("Microsoft.VisualStudio.Edi
tors.SettingsDesigner.SettingsSingleFileGenerator", "8.0.0.0")]
    internal sealed partial class Settings :
global::System.Configuration.ApplicationSettingsBase {

        private static Settings defaultInstance =
((Settings)(global::System.Configuration.ApplicationSettingsBase.Synchronized(new
Settings())));

        public static Settings Default {
            get {
```

```
                    return defaultInstance;
            }
        }
    }
}
```

If a setting value is actually added to the design time user interface, the system would create several entries into the code-behind file. For two settings entered (firstname, lastname), the following code would be inserted into the code-behind file automatically by the IDE:

```
[global::System.Configuration.UserScopedSettingAttribute()]
    [global::System.Diagnostics.DebuggerNonUserCodeAttribute()]
    [global::System.Configuration.DefaultSettingValueAttribute("firstname")]
    public string Setting {
        get {
            return ((string)(this["Setting"]));
        }
        set {
            this["Setting"] = value;
        }
    }

    [global::System.Configuration.UserScopedSettingAttribute()]
    [global::System.Diagnostics.DebuggerNonUserCodeAttribute()]
    [global::System.Configuration.DefaultSettingValueAttribute("lastname")]
    public string Setting1 {
        get {
            return ((string)(this["Setting1"]));
        }
        set {
            this["Setting1"] = value;
        }
    }
```

As mentioned, Visual Studio includes a settings configuration utility. When the settings utility is used, it also creates organized entries in the App.config file automatically. The following excerpt is from an App.config file in the given example of the firstname, lastname entries.

```
<?xml version="1.0" encoding="utf-8" ?>
<configuration>
    <configSections>
        <sectionGroup name="userSettings"
type="System.Configuration.UserSettingsGroup, System, Version=2.0.0.0,
Culture=neutral, PublicKeyToken=b77a5c561934e089" >
            <section name="WPFWindowsAppBreakdown.Properties.Settings"
type="System.Configuration.ClientSettingsSection, System, Version=2.0.0.0,
Culture=neutral, PublicKeyToken=b77a5c561934e089"
allowExeDefinition="MachineToLocalUser" requirePermission="false" />
        </sectionGroup>
    </configSections>
    <userSettings>
        <WPFWindowsAppBreakdown.Properties.Settings>
            <setting name="Setting" serializeAs="String">
                <value>firstname</value>
```

```
            </setting>
            <setting name="Setting1" serializeAs="String">
                <value>lastname</value>
            </setting>
        </WPFWindowsAppBreakdown.Properties.Settings>
    </userSettings>
</configuration>
```

MyApp.xaml

MyApp.xaml is the primary XAML file that comes with your application. The `Application` object is loaded and controlled from this XAML file, which is the successor for the global.asax from older .NET platform versions 1.0 and 1.1. As mentioned in Chapter 2, the use of the `Application` object to share variables across pages is fundamental to its purpose. XAML pages and their classes can store variables of any type within the `Application` object's `Properties` collection.

The contents of the MyApp.xaml file begin with the standard XAML that it needs to establish the namespace of the project and the .NET Framework 3.0 XAML markup. The following excerpt is from the MyApp.xaml file:

```
<Application x:Class="WPFWindowsAppBreakdown.MyApp"
    xmlns="http://schemas.microsoft.com/winfx/2006/xaml/presentation"
    xmlns:x="http://schemas.microsoft.com/winfx/2006/xaml"
    StartupUri="Window1.xaml"
    >
    <Application.Resources>

    </Application.Resources>
</Application>
```

The entries added within your XAML file will allow any number or combination of application-level steps and processes to be hooked into your application.

As stated in Chapter 2, the `Application` object is used within all WPF projects and provides the following for your application:

❑   An interface between your application and the system

❑   An entry point of a WPF application, so initialization of variables can take place

❑   Functions the same for both WPF XBAP and WPF Window Applications

❑   The ability to hook into events and override virtual methods for your application

In order to tie into this `Application` object, you have to hook into an event. To pull information out of it, you can obtain a reference to the `Application` object and access its `Current` class member.

The following example overrides an application event:

```
protected override void OnActivated(System.EventArgs e)
{
    System.Console.WriteLine("starting up!");
}
```

By overriding, you can insert event logic for this application event such as storing variables or setting up a session with data.

The following example obtains a reference to the `Application` object:

```
Application myApp;
myApp = System.Windows.Application.Current;
```

Now you can access application-based, non-static methods or session-based information contained within this `Application` object.

.NET Framework 3.0 Windows Application

The files within this project type are actually quite different from the old world of .NET, within a WinForms development effort. In this .NET Framework 3.0 Windows Application, you'll notice the brand-new and ever prominent use of XAML files.

Figure 3-2 displays the project tree for a .NET Framework 3.0 Windows Application.

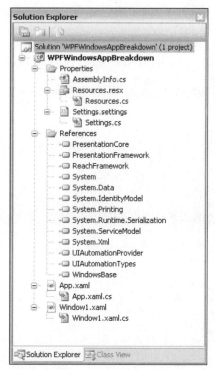

Figure 3-2

For most Windows desktop applications, the Window1.xaml file would be the place to begin writing logic. The following section outlines this file in detail.

Window1.xaml

This window is the visible interface of the initial screen of your application. Previously known as WinForms, WPF Windows objects are the new concept of the normal design plane for a Windows application. The XAML markup is the composite structure of this window object, and has corresponding .NET Window class representations within the .NET runtime.

In this new .NET Framework 3.0 platform, the XAML file takes over, and Windows Forms, Web Forms, and other form elements or concepts become less relevant for the next generation of development starting on Windows Vista.

The `Window` object behind the Window1.xaml file provides properties, methods, and events that allow the application to respond and handle interaction with the user. The following excerpt is from the default Window1.xaml file:

```
<Window x:Class="WPFWindowsAppBreakdown.Window1"
    xmlns="http://schemas.microsoft.com/winfx/2006/xaml/presentation"
    xmlns:x="http://schemas.microsoft.com/winfx/2006/xaml"
    Title="WPFWindowsAppBreakdown" Height="300" Width="300"
    >
<Grid>

</Grid>
</Window>
```

The preceding window XAML is essentially an XML representation of a .NET `Window` class, with some specific markup representing child nodes and elements of that class.

The following is the code-behind file for this XAML page:

```
using System;
using System.Collections.Generic;
using System.Windows;
using System.Windows.Controls;
using System.Windows.Data;
using System.Windows.Documents;
using System.Windows.Input;
using System.Windows.Media;
using System.Windows.Media.Imaging;
using System.Windows.Shapes;

namespace WPFWindowsAppBreakdown
{
    /// <summary>
    /// Interaction logic for Window1.xaml
    /// </summary>

    public partial class Window1 : Window
    {
        public Window1()
        {
            InitializeComponent();
```

```
        }
    }
}
```

In summary, this Window1.xaml file is the visual representation for an instance of a `Window` class.

XAML Browser Application

Figure 3-3 displays the project tree for an XBAP.

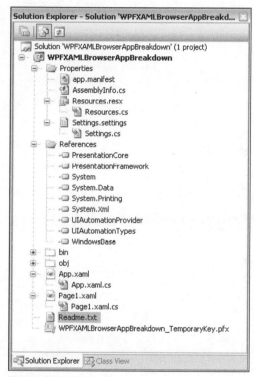

Figure 3-3

One of the most important files within this application is the Page1.xaml file.

Page1.xaml

Page1.xaml is the default XAML page provided with your XBAP. It is the designer interface for the website application, replacing the ASP.NET WebForm concept. As with the MyApp.xaml file, the contents of this file begin with the standard declarative attributes used to establish the WPF and .NET Framework 3.0 namespaces for purposes of identifying IntelliSense tags within the markup of the page, among others. The following excerpt is from the Page1.xaml file:

```
<Page x:Class="WPFWebBrowserAppBreakdown.Page1"
    xmlns="http://schemas.microsoft.com/winfx/2006/xaml/presentation"
    xmlns:x="http://schemas.microsoft.com/winfx/2006/xaml"
    Title="Page1"
    >
    <Grid>

    </Grid>
</Page>
```

The underlying file in support of this presentation layer is the Page1.xaml.cs code-behind file. This file acts as the replacement for the code-behind files of the ASP.NET Web-Form world. It contains all the needed "interaction logic" for the XAML page, providing a managed code environment from which the developer can work. Dynamic content, interactive functionality, custom logic, and other desired functionality could be achieved from the code-behind file as a supportive element to the outwardly visible XAML page.

The following code sample is taken from the code-behind file for the Page1.xaml file:

```
using System;
using System.Collections.Generic;
using System.Windows;
using System.Windows.Controls;
using System.Windows.Data;
using System.Windows.Documents;
using System.Windows.Input;
using System.Windows.Media;
using System.Windows.Media.Imaging;
using System.Windows.Navigation;
using System.Windows.Shapes;

namespace WPFWebBrowserAppBreakdown
{
    /// <summary>
    /// Interaction logic for Page1.xaml
    /// </summary>

    public partial class Page1 : Page
    {

        public Page1()
        {
            InitializeComponent();
        }

    }
}
```

From within this web page's code-behind file (Page1.xaml.cs), you can plug into events and create functionality in the same way you would for a typical ASP.NET webform.

WCF Service Library

Figure 3-4 displays the project tree for a WCF Service Library.

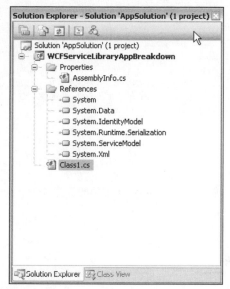

Figure 3-4

Although the Service Library is a Windows Communication Foundation project type, not under the WPF umbrella, we will explain it in this chapter at a high level.

While the other WPF projects utilize XAML as the basis in their "presentation" layers of their applications, this project is actually a WCF project, focused on the processing of logic, rather than the markup and display of visual elements. The main file of note in this project type is the Class1.cs, documented in the following section.

Class1.cs

The Class1.cs file contained within the Service Library project is unique in its purpose and content. It is the engine for creating a Windows Service that can be hosted and managed from another application. .NET Framework 3.0 Service Library applications are not within the scope of WPF specifically, falling instead under the realm of Windows Communication Foundation (WCF), formerly known as Indigo. Although WCF and WPF are both under the .NET Framework 3.0 umbrella, the focus of this book is on WPF, so the scope of content is limited to the basic description of this project type.

The following are the contents of the Class1.cs file:

```
using System;
using System.Collections.Generic;
using System.Text;
using System.ServiceModel;
```

```
using System.Runtime.Serialization;

/*

    HOW TO HOST THE WCF SERVICE IN THIS LIBRARY IN ANOTHER PROJECT
    You will need to do the following things:
    1)    Add a Host project to your solution
          a.    Right click on your solution
          b.    Select Add
          c.    Select New Project
          d.    Choose an appropriate Host project type (e.g. Console Application)
    2)    Add a new source file to your Host project
          a.    Right click on your Host project
          b.    Select Add
          c.    Select New Item
          d.    Select "Code File"
    3)    Paste the contents of the "MyServiceHost" class below into the new Code
File
    4)    Add an "Application Configuration File" to your Host project
          a.    Right click on your Host project
          b.    Select Add
          c.    Select New Item
          d.    Select "Application Configuration File"
    5)    Paste the contents of the App.Config below that defines your service
endpoints into the new Config File
    6)    Add the code that will host, start and stop the service
          a.    Call MyServiceHost.StartService() to start the service and
MyServiceHost.EndService() to end the service
    7)    Add a Reference to System.ServiceModel.dll
          a.    Right click on your Host Project
          b.    Select "Add Reference"
          c.    Select "System.ServiceModel.dll"
    8)    Add a Reference from your Host project to your Service Library project
          a.    Right click on your Host Project
          b.    Select "Add Reference"
          c.    Select the "Projects" tab
    9)    Set the Host project as the "StartUp" project for the solution
          a.    Right click on your Host Project
          b.    Select "Set as StartUp Project"

    ################# START MyServiceHost.cs #################

    using System;
    using System.ServiceModel;

    // A WCF service consists of a contract (defined below),
    // a class which implements that interface, and configuration
    // entries that specify behaviors and endpoints associated with
    // that implementation (see <system.serviceModel> in your application
    // configuration file).

    internal class MyServiceHost
    {
```

```csharp
        internal static ServiceHost myServiceHost = null;

        internal static void StartService()
        {
            //Consider putting the baseAddress in the configuration system
            //and getting it here with AppSettings
            Uri baseAddress = new Uri("http://localhost:8080/service1");

            //Instantiate new ServiceHost
            myServiceHost = new
ServiceHost(typeof(WCFServiceLibraryAppBreakdown.service1), baseAddress);

            //Open myServiceHost
            myServiceHost.Open();
        }

        internal static void StopService()
        {
            //Call StopService from your shutdown logic (i.e. dispose method)
            if (myServiceHost.State != CommunicationState.Closed)
                myServiceHost.Close();
        }
    }

    ################# END MyServiceHost.cs #################
    ################# START App.config or Web.config #################

    <system.serviceModel>
    <services>
        <service name="WCFServiceLibraryAppBreakdown.service1">
          <endpoint contract="WCFServiceLibraryAppBreakdown.IService1"
binding="wsHttpBinding"/>
        </service>
      </services>
    </system.serviceModel>

    ################# END App.config or Web.config #################

*/
namespace WCFServiceLibraryAppBreakdown
{
    // You have created a class library to define and implement your WCF service.
    // You will need to add a reference to this library from another project and add
    // the code to that project to host the service as described below.  Another way
    // to create and host a WCF service is by using the Add New Item, WCF Service
    // template within an existing project such as a Console Application or a Windows
    // Application.

    [ServiceContract()]
    public interface IService1
```

```
{
    [OperationContract]
    string MyOperation1(string myValue);
    [OperationContract]
    string MyOperation2(DataContract1 dataContractValue);
}

public class service1 : IService1
{
    public string MyOperation1(string myValue)
    {
        return "Hello: " + myValue;
    }
    public string MyOperation2(DataContract1 dataContractValue)
    {
        return "Hello: " + dataContractValue.FirstName;
    }
}

[DataContract]
public class DataContract1
{
    string firstName;
    string lastName;

    [DataMember]
    public string FirstName
    {
        get { return firstName; }
        set { firstName = value; }
    }
    [DataMember]
    public string LastName
    {
        get { return lastName; }
        set { lastName = value; }
    }
}
}
```

Although heavily documented within itself, this file contains a slightly more complicated approach for .NET application developers. It requires a developer to perform several steps in order to create, compile, deploy, and utilize it as a hosted and managed service.

WPF Custom Control Library

The actual usage of this Custom Control Library project is to create a custom control for use within WPF that can be used by consuming applications as a dynamic-link library (DLL) file. The project essentially serves as a template for creating your own reusable control.

The next WPF application, the Custom Control Library, utilizes many of the same files as seen in the other project tree structures (see Figure 3-5).

Figure 3-5

The primary file of merit within this application is the UserControl1.xaml file, documented in the following section.

UserControl1.xaml

The UserControl1.xaml file is a part of the Custom Control project, providing the rendered area or visual portion of the actual control.

The following are the contents of the UserControl1.xaml file:

```
<UserControl x:Class="WPFCustomControlLibraryAppBreakdown.UserControl1"
    xmlns="http://schemas.microsoft.com/winfx/2006/xaml/presentation"
    xmlns:x="http://schemas.microsoft.com/winfx/2006/xaml"
    >
    <Grid>

    </Grid>
</UserControl>
```

In this code, the XAML could be expanded to include other visual elements such as buttons, text boxes, labels, and so on. Any valid XAML markup would be allowed in this file, and parsed by the compiler.

As with the Page1.xaml file, this XAML file also has an associated code-behind file, UserControl1 .xaml.cs, the contents of which are as follows:

```
using System;
using System.Collections.Generic;
using System.Windows;
using System.Windows.Controls;
using System.Windows.Data;
using System.Windows.Documents;
using System.Windows.Input;
using System.Windows.Media;
using System.Windows.Media.Imaging;
using System.Windows.Navigation;
using System.Windows.Shapes;

namespace WPFCustomControlLibraryAppBreakdown
{
    /// <summary>
    /// Interaction logic for UserControl1.xaml
    /// </summary>

    public partial class UserControl1 : UserControl
    {

        public UserControl1()
        {
            InitializeComponent();
        }

    }
}
```

By default, this UserControl1.xaml and its code-behind file are relatively useless. The best practice in creating custom controls would be to delete these files, and add a new .NET Framework 3.0 Custom Control class to the project. By doing this, your project's main custom control file will be set up properly for you, with commented instructions on how to create and deploy the control.

The following excerpt is taken from a newly added .NET Framework 3.0 Custom Control class:

```
using System;
using System.Windows;
using System.Windows.Controls;
using System.Windows.Controls.Primitives;
using System.Windows.Data;
using System.Windows.Documents;
using System.Windows.Media;
using System.Windows.Media.Imaging;
using System.Windows.Shapes;

namespace WPFCustomControlLibraryAppBreakdown
{
```

```
/// <summary>
/// A custom control.
///
/// To use this custom control from a XAML file,
/// do 1a or 1b, and then 2.
///
/// Step 1a)
/// To use this custom control from a XAML file
/// in this project, add this mapping PI before
/// the root element in the markup file:
/// <?Mapping XmlNamespace="controls"
ClrNamespace="WPFCustomControlLibraryAppBreakdown" ?>
///
/// If you want to do this, in this build, you'll
/// also need to set <UICulture>en-US</UICulture> in
/// your project file. (or some other value).
/// This will start building your application with a
/// satellite assembly, which enables this feature.
///
/// Step 1b)
/// To use this custom control from a XAML file in
/// another project, add this mapping PI before the
/// root element in the markup file:
/// <?Mapping XmlNamespace="controls"
///          ClrNamespace="WPFCustomControlLibraryAppBreakdown"
///          Assembly="WPFCustomControlLibraryAppBreakdown"?>
/// From the project where the XAML file lives, you'll
/// need to do add a project reference to this project:
///     [Add Reference/Projects/ThisProject]
/// Note: You may need to use Rebuild to avoid compilation errors.

/// Step 2)
/// In the root tag of the .xaml, define a new namespace
/// prefix.  The uri inside must match the value for the
/// XmlNamespace attribute in the mapping PI:
///     <Window xmlns:cc="controls" ... >
/// Then go ahead and use your control in the .xaml somewhere.
///     <cc:MyCustomControl />
/// Note1: IntelliSense in the xml editor won't currently
/// work on your custom control.
/// </summary>

public class MyCustomControl : Control
{
    static MyCustomControl()
    {
        // This OverrideMetadata call tells the system that
        // this element wants to provide a style that is different
        // than its base class.
        // This style is defined in themes\generic.xaml
        DefaultStyleKeyProperty.OverrideMetadata(typeof(MyCustomControl), new
FrameworkPropertyMetadata(typeof(MyCustomControl)));
    }
}
}
```

The preceding code represents the foundation of your Custom Control Library project. It is the user control class file, with helper comments from Visual Studio. The idea is to provide you, the developer, with the basic shell structure of the user control, and explain in the comments of this file where to begin making changes. The complexity of building a user control is mostly surrounding the configuration and deployment of the control, and then in the usage of the control in another project. This is complicated because of the namespace usage and XML namespace terminology that many developers are not yet accustomed to.

From this file's instructions, you can deduce the steps that must take place in order to consume your new custom WPF control.

Summary

In this chapter you learned about the following types of projects that exist under the .NET 3.0 project list, along with the specific files in each of the projects.

❑ Windows Application

❑ XAML Browser Application

❑ Custom Control Library Project

❑ Service Library Project

You reviewed the dissected files, markup, code-behind, and supporting files in order to understand their background and purposes. You followed along as each of the supporting files were explained, including the XAML markup and code-behind files.

You also reviewed the internal core assemblies of WPF, including the key engine files required for rendering and processing WPF-based application commands.

In the next chapter, you will learn about designing and developing WPF-based applications within a new tool from Microsoft, Expression Blend. This revolutionary IDE provides a whole new way to design, develop, and animate your WPF objects.

4

Building a Rich UI with Microsoft Expression Blend — Part I

The Microsoft Expression suite of design tools provides graphic and interactive designers with the power to leverage the rich content provided by the .NET Framework 3.0 runtime. The suite provides easy-to-use tools designed to both increase productivity and streamline workflow between designers and developers.

Specifically, Expression Blend was created to provide designers with the ability to create WPF application interfaces and interactive media. Designers are presented with an intuitive workflow that provides a level of abstraction above the lower level APIs required for creating WPF applications. Designers are also able to design free from the need to understand the XAML syntax since the tools emit markup for all graphical elements.

Expression Blend is more than just an animation and online media tool. Designers can build powerful and intuitive application UIs to create a richer and far more engaging user experience. Expression Blend and Visual Studio 2005 share the same project formats so that code, components, and controls can be created and shared between environments. This allows designers and developers to collaborate effectively when creating WPF applications.

In this chapter, we will explore Expression Blend and get acquainted with its design environment, workflow, and toolset.

> **The description of Expression Blend's features is based on the January 2007 beta 1 release. There may be some significant changes in the final release.**

Overview

There are two different tools you can use to build WPF applications, Expression Blend or Visual Studio 2005, each of which is suited to the particular needs and experience of either developer or designer. The goal of Expression Blend is to provide an environment where graphic and interactive designers can create WPF applications using tools and concepts common to design applications they already use. This enables a designer to get up-to-speed and working efficiently in the shortest time possible.

The output of the Expression design suite is XAML, which facilitates collaboration between designers and developers. Designers can use the Expression design tools to create graphics, UI elements, and controls. The generated XAML can then be shared between application tools. Developers using Visual Studio 2005 can open Expression Blend projects in order to utilize the visual elements and begin coding their applications. C# and Visual Basic .NET code-behind files can also be generated, coded, and shared between applications.

Figure 4-1 represents the collaborative flow between the Expression suite of design applications and Visual Studio.

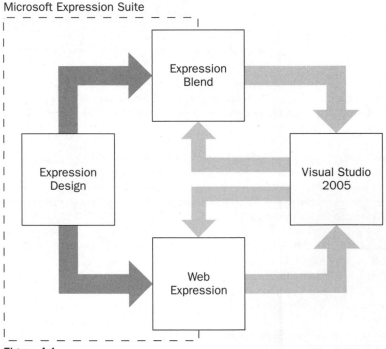

Figure 4-1

Expression Blend also represents a paradigm shift in the way that user interfaces are created. Both designers and developers can work independently in their core competency while still collaborating in a synchronized and concerted effort.

In addition to collaboration features, Expression Blend's versatility can handle the tasks of creating rich media and animation as well as complex application UIs. For example, data-bound controls that require a custom look and feel or perhaps a richer display can be created. You will explore these features throughout this chapter and the next.

The Design Environment

Every project consists of one or more file types that are common to a WPF application. The file types that are common to each application are Windows, Pages, User Controls, and Resource Libraries. The environment provides two application views for authoring scenes. First is the design view where you can visually create and manipulate elements using tools and controls in the panels and the artboard. The second is the XAML code view where you can edit XAML directly in order to create visual elements. This system is synonymous with the Visual Studio .NET code and design view. The majority of your time will probably be spent in the visual design mode, and you'll use the XAML code view for any elements that require manual editing.

Figure 4-2 illustrates Expression Blend's workspace, which is comprised of tools and panels designed to enhance the workflow of creating media and interface elements.

Figure 4-2

The design environment offers two different workspace orientations that are tailored for authoring in two different modes: design and animation. The environment defaults to the design orientation for authoring application elements. The animation workspace orientation docks the animation timeline panel to the bottom of the designer in order to provide better visibility when creating animations.

You can change the workspace orientation by selecting the window item in the main menu. Alternatively, you can toggle between both orientations by pressing the F6 key for design and F7 for animation.

Workspace Panels

The workspace panels enable you to manage tools, assets, and context-specific information about objects on the artboard. Different panels provide control over the properties and cosmetic appearance of elements on the screen. Each panel has a set of subpanels that logically categorize the functions they perform.

You can show or hide each of the panels to provide a customized orientation within the workspace by accessing the Window menu item. The workspace can return to the default orientation by selecting Window ⇨ Reset Active Workspace.

The workspace panels are all docked by default and are arranged according to which workspace orientation you have selected. A panel can be undocked to float independently of the workspace. Figure 4-3 shows an example of two panels.

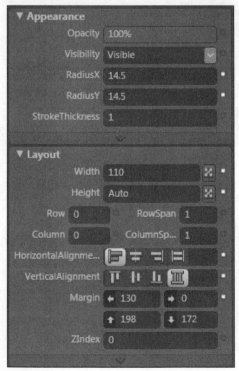

Figure 4-3

The following is a list of the workspace panels and their descriptions.

- ❑ **Toolbox** — Contains a list of available tools that you can use to create and manipulate elements on the artboard. The tools enable you to visually create, paint, and translate vector objects.

- ❑ **Project** — Contains a list of components, controls, and assets local to the project or imported from external library references.

- ❑ **Properties** — Enables you to alter the visual and positional properties of an element in the artboard, including opacity, stroke, and fill color.

- ❑ **Resources** — Contains a list of all available resources in the current project such as styles, templates, and brushes.

- ❑ **Interaction** — Contains subpanels where the designer can create triggers and the timeline subpanel for authoring animations.

The Artboard

The artboard is the main composition area for each expression project and serves as the viewing space for the interface or media that you create. Using the artboard composition area, interactions and animations can be orchestrated and laid out for each scene that you create in your project. This is the area in which controls and objects are both added and animated.

The artboard enables you to transition between a XAML code view and graphic design view. Most of your time will be spent in the design view as the lower-level details of XAML markup are generated for you by the designer.

Figure 4-4 shows the artboard in action as the elements and background of a scene are manipulated.

Figure 4-4

Configuring the Environment

All the panels in the Expression Blend design environment are resizable, removable, and collapsible, and can be docked. As such, the panels give the designer control over what visual configuration of the Expression Blend tool is best suited to their needs and workflow.

A unique feature of the designer is the ability to zoom in and out of the workspace, enabling the designer to modify the display sizes of each section of the workspace. Figure 4-5 shows the effect of zooming into the workspace, which brings the artboard into focus.

Figure 4-5

The workspace options panel, accessed by selecting Tools ➪ Options, provides control over the zoom ratio. Figure 4-6 shows the workspace zoom control in the options panel in detail.

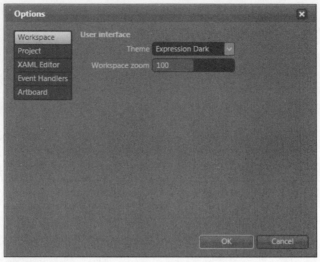

Figure 4-6

Project Structure

The structure of each Expression Blend project is organized similar to a Visual Studio 2005 project. In fact, both applications utilize the same project file type so that a project can be opened up in either environment allowing side-by-side development. All the files associated with a project can be efficiently organized into multiple project folders. The only difference is that when adding a new folder, the designer will not modify the namespace to incorporate the subfolder name. All working files are kept within the main project namespace.

Each screen in an Expression Blend project can be created using individual pages. Each page is encapsulated and declared as one XAML file. The XAML file is nothing more than a serialized representation of a scene and all its child elements in XML. Each page also has an associated code-behind file that controls any event handling or other programmatic features in your application

Adding a New Project File

There are four different file types that can be added to your Blend project. The following steps describe the process of creating and adding a new file type to the project:

1. Select File ➪ New Item. You are then prompted to choose one of the following:

   ❑ **Window** — Creates a new top-level window for the project or a new dialog window.

   ❑ **Page** — Creates a new page within your application that can be reached by navigation.

   ❑ **UserControl** — Creates a new user control that will serve as a UI component that facilitates a certain UI function.

   ❑ **Resource Dictionary** — Creates a XAML file that contains reusable resources such as styles and control templates that can be shared across projects.

2. Provide a name for the new project file.

3. If you select a Window, Page, or UserControl, you can also optionally select to include a code-behind file where you will place any additional procedural logic.

Figure 4-7 illustrates the Add New Item dialog box and its available options.

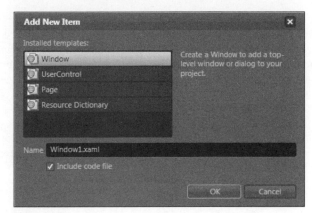

Figure 4-7

Building and Deploying a Project

Expression Blend provides the designer with a very basic set of options when building a project. From the Project item in the main menu, the designer can build, clean, and test the project. Selecting Project ⇨ Test Project or pressing the F5 key will build and launch the project in a window for visual testing.

Because Blend is primarily a design tool, it defers managing the details of deployment to Visual Studio 2005 — an environment much more suited to handling the process and details of deployment.

The following steps describe the process to follow when you're ready to deploy your Blend project:

1. Right-click the project folder within the project panel. Select Edit Externally from the context menu. If you have Visual Studio 2005 installed, the project automatically opens up in Visual Studio.

2. Right-click the project icon in Visual Studio and select properties. From there, select the desired security and publish options.

Because a Blend project is essentially just a WPF application, the methods for deploying and securing the application are the same as if you created it in Visual Studio.

Creating Vector Objects

Expression Blend provides the designer with a variety of tools for creating intricate vector drawings and objects for application UIs and interactive media projects. Vector images are preferable to raster graphics for building UI elements.

A raster image is a data file or structure representing an image as a grid or collection of pixels on a computer monitor. Raster images are highly resolution dependent and can become visually coarse-grained if resized beyond their original dimensions.

With vector graphics, shapes and paths are represented as a series of geometric primitives such as points, lines, and curves, which can be recalculated to scale while retaining a smoothly rendered appearance.

Designing UIs with a flexible layout using vector graphics offers many advantages—one of which is that content scales predictably without compromising the visual fidelity of the supporting graphics. Raster images must remain at a static size or suffer the cost of becoming pixilated as the image size increases. Rather than creating multiple bitmaps to support multiple resolution scenarios (a good example of this is icons), vector objects will always resize elegantly to different dimensions. This consistency of layout makes the user experience much more predictable across machines with different graphics hardware and monitors with higher resolution displays.

Vector objects in Expression Blend can be lines, shapes, or controls. Each vector object can easily be modified and manipulated by moving, rotating, skewing, mirroring, or resizing them.

Shapes

Expression Blend provides tools to create primitive vector shapes. These shapes can be modified or edited to make custom shapes. The following list describes the three primitive vector shapes:

❑ **Rectangle**—Draws rectangles and squares with or without rounded corners

❑ **Ellipse**—Draws circles and ellipses

❑ **Line**—Draws a straight line between two points

Editing Shapes

You can edit shapes in different ways. For instance, the corner radius of a rectangle can be modified by dragging the handles on the upper-left corner of the rectangle that appear after it is selected. Figure 4-8 shows the corner radius handles in the upper-left corner.

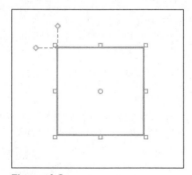

Figure 4-8

Editing other shapes involves breaking down and converting the shapes into paths for the creation of custom shapes. To edit a shape as a path, select Object ⇨ Path ⇨ Convert to Path from the main menu. Once converted, the sub-selection tool can be used to modify the points or control vertices of a path. Once a shape is converted to a path, it will not retain the ability to edit any of the properties it had as a shape.

Paths

Vector shapes are composed of individual paths. They are very flexible and can be used to create any shape specific to your needs. Paths are made up of connected points, lines, and/or curves. Paths can be created to define custom shapes for controls or graphics. They can also be used to define motion paths for objects in animation.

The Pen, Pencil, and Line tools in the Toolbox panel are used to draw paths. Those paths can then be manipulated by the selection and direct selection tools.

Paths can be broken up into three general categories:

❑ **Straight Lines** — Straight segments created by either using the Pen or Line tool.

❑ **Curves** — Curved path segments have control handles that define the properties of the curve. The handles are defined for either their beginning or ending node. The control handle represents the tangent of a line at the node.

❑ **Freeform** — Freeform paths are created using the Pencil tool. This emulates a natural drawing action. Freeform paths can be any shape.

Compound Paths

You also can combine two or more paths to create a compound path. With a compound path, any areas that intersect between both of the paths are removed from the result. The final resulting path that is produced takes on the visual properties of the bottom-most path.

In order to create a compound path, you must select two or more path objects. If you have shapes on the artboard that you would like to include as part of the compound path, they must be converted to paths first by selecting the shape and choosing Object ⇨ Path ⇨ Convert to Path command from the main menu.

The following example demonstrates the basic process of creating a compound path from two shape objects on the artboard:

1. From the Toolbox, select the Ellipse tool and create a circle. In order to create a perfect circle, click and drag with the Ellipse tool and simultaneously press and hold the Shift key. Once the circle is created, make sure it is the active selection and select Object ⇨ Path ⇨ Convert to Path from the main menu.

2. Copy and paste the circle path you just created in step one and place the second circle so that it overlaps somewhere on the first.

3. Select both circle paths and select Object ⇨ Path ⇨ Make Compound Path from the main menu.

Figure 4-9 illustrates a possible outcome from compounding two overlapping circle paths.

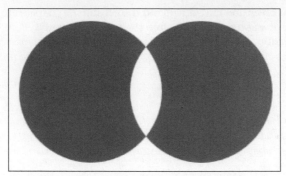

Figure 4-9

Any compound path that is created can be deconstructed to its individual paths by selecting Object ⇨ Path ⇨ Release Compound Path.

Manipulating Objects with the Properties Panel

Expression Blend provides a set of panels that gives the designer a fine-grained level of control over customizing the look and feel of an application and its visual components. Within the properties panel are a set of subpanels that provide control over color, layout, typographical, contextual, and positional properties of a selected object.

The Transform Panel

The Transform panel provides tools to position, scale, rotate, shear, and mirror objects. The following list outlines the effect of each transformation.

❑ **Position**—Alters the x and y position of the object on the artboard.

❑ **Rotation**—Rotates an object by an angle in degrees.

❑ **Scale**—Resizes the height and width of an object.

❑ **Skew**—Skews or distorts an object's width or height.

❑ **Flip**—Mirrors an object either vertically or horizontally.

These options are also available to you in a much more generalized manner when you select an object from the artboard. Around the bounding box for the selected object you will see handles that provide the ability to transform your object. Hovering over the corner nodes will provide handles to scale uniformly and rotate the selected object. The midpoint node handles enable you to shear or scale the object. Holding down the Shift key will constrain the manipulations to either vertical and horizontal position changes or uniform changes to the object.

In the Transform panel you can transform your objects with more precision using values to two decimal places if you require greater control over your object transformations.

The Brushes Panel

The Brushes panel enables you to manipulate the color of an objects background, foreground, opacity mask, and stroke.

Selecting Colors

The Expression Blend color editing panel supports depicting colors with either a set of RGB values or its corresponding hexadecimal value. Within the color subpanel is a color selection tool for selecting a color visually. The eyedropper in the bottom-right corner of the color selector can also be used to sample a color from an existing object in the artboard. Figure 4-10 shows the color selection tools in the brushes subpanel.

Figure 4-10

Applying Fills

Fills are used to change the color of an object. You can apply fills to objects either as a solid color, a gradient to produce a smooth color gradation, or a tiled pattern. The fill type can be selected from the horizontal list of buttons above the color selector in the Brushes panel. When applied appropriately, gradients can give visual objects the illusion of depth on what would otherwise be perceived as flat and two-dimensional. Figure 4-11 illustrates the gradient slider control in the Appearance panel.

Figure 4-11

Gradients stops are the controls on the Gradient slider that mark a change in color. There is virtually no limit to how many stops can be applied to a gradient. To add another stop, simply click on the gradient slider. Stops can be removed by dragging them off of the gradient slider. Figure 4-12 illustrates the gradient fill applied to a square.

Figure 4-12

Strokes

The borders surrounding the perimeter of objects are called *strokes*. The color of strokes can be modified through the Brushes subpanel. The thickness of a stroke can be altered through the Appearance panel. When strokes are applied to an object, they are always applied on top of a fill.

Opacity Masks

An opacity mask is a path or shape that is applied to another object. The transparent parts of the opacity mask represent areas where the underlying object is hidden. The opaque portions represent the area where the underlying object will show through.

An opacity mask can be created as a gradient that shows or hides portions of an object based on transparency. Figure 4-13 illustrates the effect of a gradient opacity mask where portions of the underlying shape are masked by a rectangle containing a gradient fill with a gradient stop having zero alpha value.

Figure 4-13

Opacity, Transparency, and Visibility

The Appearance subpanel's Opacity item controls the total transparency of an object and its visibility. Adjusting the opacity slider will give you varying percentages of transparency for an object. The transparency information for an object, gradient, or opacity mask is controlled and stored in an alpha channel.

Opacity affects the entire object's transparency. Alternatively, modifying the alpha channel of an individual element within an object will affect only its transparency while keeping other object transparency values intact. For example, a rectangle object can have a fill that is slightly transparent while the stroke on the rectangle retains its transparency at 100 percent.

The Appearance subpanel's Visibility drop-down affects whether an object on the scene is hidden or shown. This may be useful during scene transitions where certain objects need to be hidden from screen-to-screen but still need to remain on the artboard.

Putting It All Together

You will now put together a basic project and scene combining all the topics covered thus far. This project will form the basis of each subsequent example as you proceed through the details of the environment:

1. From the menu, select File ➪ New Project. From the Create New Project prompt, select the Standard Application (.exe) project type, assign it the project name of Workspace, and then click OK.

2. Select and activate the Layout Root from the objects category in the interaction panel. The Layout Root is a Grid panel that is created by default with each new page. Bring up the brushes category by selecting the properties panel.

3. From the brushes category, select the Background item from the list box. From the brush types below, select the gradient brush. This should apply a default black-to-white gradient fill. Modify the gradient by adding another black gradient stop from the gradient slider. Position the gradient stops so that the right and left are black and the middle is white.

4. Select the Brush Transform tool from the Toolbox panel. Mouse over the feather end of the arrow on the artboard, and then click and drag the arrows to adjust the brush 90 degrees. This will adjust the gradient to a vertical position.

5. Select the Rectangle tool from the Tools panel and then create a square by clicking and dragging the corner handle until both the height and width dimensions equal 80. Alternatively, you can select the Layout category of the properties panel and adjust the width and height. Apply a fill or gradient to the rectangle from the appearance panel using the same procedure as the Layout Root. Select the Stroke property from the Brush subpanel and apply a stroke color of your choosing.

6. Select the Rectangle to activate it and notice the corner radius adjustment handle on the upper-left corner of the rectangle. Click and drag to any random corner radius adjustment.

Pressing F5 debugs the application, and displays our workspace application (see Figure 4-14).

Figure 4-14

Manipulating Text

Text in Expression Blend is in many ways similar to other visual elements. The size, layout, and visual appearance of text can be accessed and altered using the properties panel. Within the properties panel you can alter text in the following ways:

❏ Brushes can be applied to the background, foreground, and border of the text control.

❏ The typographic properties of the text can be set such as the font, font size, font weight, and alignment. The Text category of the properties panel provides access to the designer to alter these properties

❏ Transformations can be applied to text control such as scale, rotation, and skew.

Text is created through a set of distinct controls designed for encasing and displaying text. The following text controls are available through the design interface:

❏ **Text Box** — A region of text that is designed to accept user text input.

❏ **Rich Text Box** — A region of text that accepts user input with the additional ability of containing other objects such as shapes and images.

❏ **TextBlock** — A non-editable region of text that is meant to present a static text display to the user. The TextBlock control can also contain objects such as shapes, paths, and images.

❏ **PasswordBox** — An editable region of text that is designed to mask user text input with a character. The character can be changed based on preference.

❏ **Label** — A non-editable region of text that is used for labeling controls and objects within the UI.

❏ **FlowDocumentScrollViewer** — A scrollable region of text that can contain other objects such as images, shapes, and paths.

Managing Layouts

Layout is a concept in WPF that describes the process of arranging and positioning elements onscreen. The WPF layout system controls three different properties in regards to the positioning of a control's child elements. Each layout panel controls alignment, margins, and padding. These properties are manipulated to produce the desired look and feel of an application or one of its components.

❏ **Alignment** — This describes a child element's position in relation to its parent element. For example, a button can be aligned to the right, center, or left of a container.

❏ **Margin** — This describes the amount of space around the perimeter of a control. Margin can be thought of as padding around the outside of a control.

❏ **Padding** — This describes the amount of space between the parent element's bounding border and each child element.

Figure 4-15 illustrates the alignment, margin, and padding properties.

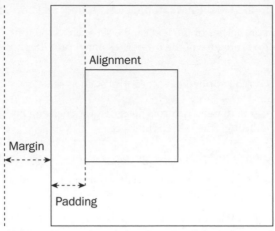

Figure 4-15

WPF provides a set of layout containers for use in your applications. These containers determine the position, size, and arrangement of the elements they hold. Layout panels automatically manage the position and placement of the child elements they contain relative to their position in the panel.

Layout panels can be implemented implicitly or explicitly. Implicit means that a layout panel will resize automatically in relation to its parent container. This is useful when the UI layout must accommodate varying resolutions and screen sizes. "Explicitly" means that a layout panel's width and height are fixed to set values so that they maintain their size and appearance when a window is resized.

Layout panels should be used judiciously and the selection of a panel should be appropriate for the UI functionality required. At runtime, the position of each child control within a layout panel is calculated as each panel is resized. The complexity of the calculation increases in relation to the quantity of child objects onscreen. As such, if a UI element can be positioned correctly using a simple canvas panel, you will find that it yields better runtime performance than a complex grid panel.

UI Layout Panels

The WPF Presentation Framework class library contains a variety of panels and controls that manage the layout of child elements, but five primary panels are optimized for the specific purpose of UI layout.

Canvas

A Canvas panel is the simplest and most flexible layout panel in the Presentation Framework. Each of the child elements is absolutely positioned relative to the local coordinate space of the Canvas (see Figure 4-16).

Figure 4-16

Elements within the same canvas that overlap will be layered based on the order in which they are declared. The ordering of overlapping elements is expressed as a property of each element called ZIndex.

Grid

The Grid panel manages the layout of child elements in a tabular format similar to a table. A grid can be positioned to span multiple rows and columns. Child elements within each cell of the Grid panel can be absolutely positioned within the local coordinate space of the cell. Grid cells also support the encasing of multiple child elements.

An important detail about Grid panels is that its cells can be accessed by index. Child elements can be added to a specific cell within a Grid defined by its row and column position.

Stack

A Stack panel arranges elements sequentially, either horizontally or vertically, as shown in Figure 4-17.

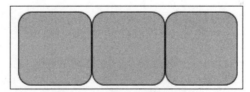

Figure 4-17

Stack panels are ideally suited for lists of elements such as thumbnails or list box selections.

Wrap

The Wrap panel arranges the position of elements to flow in sequential order from left to right. When a child element's position reaches the edge of the container, its position will wrap to the next line (see Figure 4-18). Additional child elements that are added to the Wrap will continue to be positioned in a similar fashion until all the available area has been filled.

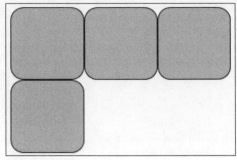

Figure 4-18

As with the Stack panel, the Wrap can be oriented to display elements vertically or horizontally.

Dock

The Dock panel manages the layout of child elements by positioning them along the edges of the container. A child element can be positioned at the top, bottom, left, or right. This panel works well for controls that need to be grouped together within some common area or for application UIs that require panes to separate workflow elements.

If no docking position is assigned to a child element, the Dock panel will automatically position it to the left of the panel.

When adding child elements to a dock layout panel, the artboard will prompt you with a compass type control where you can select what side of the panel to dock to. This is very similar in function to docking panels in Visual Studio 2005. Figure 4-19 shows the compass prompt.

Figure 4-19

The Dock panel also contains a unique Boolean property called LastChildFill. When true, the panel will fill the remaining space left within the layout with the last control or element added to the Dock panel.

Creating a Simple Dock Layout

Using the Workspace project we created earlier we will now show you how to construct a basic dock layout:

1. Select the Dock Panel control from the Toolbox and draw the panel anywhere on the scene. For the purpose of this example, alter the dimensions of the panel to accommodate four instances of the square in the project.

2. Select the Rectangle created earlier in the Workspace and drag it over the Dock panel. The Dock panel will form a dashed line around itself with a tooltip indicating you must press the Alt key to dock the rectangle in the panel.

3. While pressing the Alt key and dragging the rectangle over the panel, you will notice a set of arrows pointing to each side for docking. Select the left arrow to dock the rectangle to the left.

4. Activate the docked rectangle by double-clicking on it. Open the properties panel and scroll to the Layout. Set the height property to Auto by typing it in the Height text field (case sensitive) or by clicking the Set To Auto button next to it. The rectangle's height will now scale automatically to the size of the docking panel.

Other Layout Controls

There are additional layout panels that control how child elements are displayed. The purpose of these layout controls is more specific than the primary panels that manage overall scene or UI layout. The following is a list of each element and its corresponding description.

❑ Border — A container that draws a border and/or background around a single child element.

❑ BulletPanel — An element that can take only two child elements, which are typically a text string and a glyph (which represents a control such as a checkbox).

❑ Popup — A window that renders above all other content in an application but relative to another element. You can use a pop-up menu to provide additional information and options to users who interact with the primary piece of UI that it is relative to. It takes a single child element and positions itself based on a target element.

❑ ScrollViewer — Creates a scrollable area for any child element within it.

❑ ToolbarOverflowPanel — Manages the layout of content in a toolbar control.

❑ UniformGrid — Arranges child elements within equal, or *uniform*, grid regions.

❑ Viewbox — Scales all its child elements similar to a zoom control.

Nesting Layout Panels

Intricate UI designs often require a much more flexible and complex layout structure than those provided by the primary layout containers. To accommodate for these scenarios, layout panels can be nested to create complex layouts. Many of the layout panels that allow for only a single child element can be combined with a primary layout container to support multiple child elements.

For example, you can embed a Stack panel within a scrollable view to create a control that is a series of scrollable elements, such as news, headlines, or stock quotes.

Adding Child Elements to Layout Panels

By default, Expression Blend adds all elements to the layout root. In the Timeline panel, the root is the top-most element of the scene. The root itself is a panel that can be changed to any layout type. It is a grid by default. To change the root layout type, you simply select the type in the Layout panel.

You can easily change a child element's parent container by selecting the object, pressing the Alt key, and then dragging the object to its new parent — or by changing the focus of the active element by double-clicking the panel you want to change focus to. The selected panel will be highlighted yellow to indicate that it is the selected element.

Animation

Expression Blend provides all the tools necessary for creating animations. The details of XAML markup and API level details of creating animation are abstracted by the design environment through the artboard and Timeline subpanels, which are located within the Interaction panel. Animation is created by marking specific points in time, called *keyframes*, and manipulating object properties at each keyframe. Expression Blend handles work of interpolating the property changes in time between keyframes for you. Expression Blend also provides you with control over how the interpolation is calculated.

Expression Blend, in tandem with the .NET Framework 3.0 runtime, introduces a new concept: the storyboard animation model. A *storyboard* provides targeting information for the timelines it contains. Storyboards enable you to combine timelines into a single timeline tree, allowing you to organize and control complex timing behaviors. Each set of actions is coordinated in a time-dependent fashion.

The goal of the model is to separate a scene into two distinct parts. The storyboard represents the animation, triggers, events, and interactivity and is separated from the layout elements and rendering structure. The separation of these elements allows animations to become more componentized where they can be marked up independently of the objects they act upon.

Timeline Sub-Panel

Expression Blend animations are created using timelines. Timelines are organized and orchestrated in the Timeline panel. Timelines are segments of time on which animation occurs. Each animation represents a series of property changes on an object.

Multiple timelines can be added to a scene, each representing another set of unique property changes for any object in the scene. Timelines work independently of one another. They can be initialized by any arrangement of events using the Trigger sub-panel in the Interaction panel. All available timelines are represented in a drop-down list in the Timeline category.

When a new page or window is created, a default timeline is created where property values for objects on the artboard can be edited without recording keyframes.

When a new timeline is created, a trigger is automatically generated that will cause the animation to begin playback once the application is loaded. To change the behavior of the trigger, you can either change the event that triggers the animation or delete the trigger altogether.

Timeline Control

The Timeline subpanel (see Figure 4-20) enables you to select and manipulate objects you want to animate in what is referred to as the *structure view*. The structure view displays a visual tree of all the objects in a scene. Objects scopes can be brought into focus or drilled into so that their child elements are accessible in the structure view.

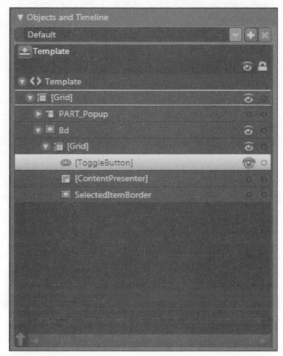

Figure 4-20

Layers can be created within the Timeline panel that allow you to group sets of objects independently from one another on a single timeline. Layering allows the designer to group together related elements such as a group of controls into a single area where they can modified, hidden or locked.

The Timeline panel also works in concert with the artboard. Items can be brought into focus or the scope of the items in a scene can be changed.

Timing adjustments can be made at detailed levels by using the Zoom Tool in the Timeline panel. By using the Zoom tool, time duration between keyframes can be adjusted to fine-grained increments of less than a tenth of a second.

Keyframes

Keyframes represent points in time where property changes occur and animation takes place. Keyframes are added to the timeline in one of two ways:

❑ You can create new keyframes using the Create Keyframe control.

❑ Expression Blend automatically inserts a keyframe whenever a property change occurs between two points in time.

Interpolation

Expression Blend interpolates property changes as they occur between keyframes on the timeline. The method by which Blend interpolates each transition can be selected by right-clicking the keyframe to be altered and selecting the value for the interpolation method. The interpolation methods offered are:

❑ In linear interpolation, property changes are interpolated between keyframes in equal increments.

❑ The ease-in value modifies how the property value changes as time approaches the keyframe. You can set the ease value from 0 to 100 percent in 25 percent increments.

❑ The ease-out value modifies how the property values change as time moves away from the keyframe. You can set the ease value from 0 to 100 percent in 25 percent increments.

The Hold Out method isn't an interpolation method. Rather than interpolate changes over time, it makes an abrupt change to the new property value when the playhead reaches the keyframe where the change occurs.

Animate an Object's Property

In this next example, we take our Workspace rectangle and animate some basic properties:

1. Create a new timeline by clicking the Create New Timeline control (the plus sign) in the Timeline panel. Give the new timeline the name of *Motion* and press OK.

2. From the existing project, select the rectangle box.

3. Click the Record Keyframe control in the Timeline panel. A new keyframe will be created at zero in the timeline.

4. Advance the playhead to five seconds and move the object across the scene to any distance of your choosing. A keyframe will automatically be created at the five second mark in the timeline for the rectangle object.

5. Drag the playhead back to zero and select the keyframe at zero. Right-click on the selected keyframe to bring up the keyframe context menu, and adjust the Ease-In and Ease-Out values to 100 percent.

6. Press the play button in the Timeline panel to preview the animation.

7. Click and drag the keyframe at the five second mark and adjust its position to three seconds and preview the animation again.

Motion Paths

Motion paths enable you to have an object follow a set path on the artboard. Figure 4-21 shows a rectangle object animated along a curve. Motion paths can be useful when objects need to be animated along curves or circular objects.

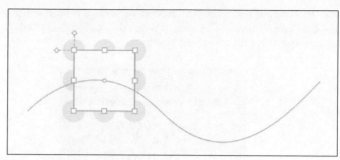

Figure 4-21

Animate Along a Motion Path

The next example walks you through creating a motion path animation in the sample Workspace project:

1. In the Toolbox panel, select the Ellipse tool, and then draw an elongated ellipse that stretches from one side of the artboard to the other.

2. In the Appearance panel, make sure that the Fill property is set to No Brush and the Stroke property is set to a Solid Color Brush so that you can see the outline of the ellipse.

3. Select the Rectangle object and make a copy of it by cutting and pasting onto the artboard.

4. In the Toolbox panel, click Selection, and then on the artboard, click the large ellipse.

5. On the Object menu, select Path ➪ Convert to Motion Path, and then in the Choose target for Motion Path dialog box, select the name of the copied Rectangle (by default it should be Rectangle_Copy) you want to be the target. Click OK.

6. Expand the Rectangle_Copy ➪ Render Transform ➪ Translation node in the Structure View. Right-click the Motion Path node and select Edit Repeat Count. Set the repeat to Forever and click OK.

7. Test your scene by clicking Test Project on the Project menu. Notice that the copied rectangle moves along the outline of the large ellipse.

Triggers

You will use triggers to control timeline playback based on events when building animations. Triggers are added to a scene visually without the need to write any code by using the Triggers subpanel located within the Interaction panel. Within the Triggers subpanel, three components must be selected to create a trigger:

❑ The object that fires the event.

❑ The specific event that fires the trigger.

❑ The timeline action to take when the trigger fires. The timeline playback can Begin, End, Pause, or Resume.

Figure 4-22 illustrates the Trigger setup process. In this instance, a button control named "Button" on the scene will fire off the timeline "Timeline1" to begin when the button is clicked. New triggers can simply be added or deleted through the Add and Delete buttons.

Figure 4-22

Conceptually, triggers are very similar to event handlers in that they both respond to events. However, triggers are represented declaratively through XAML with no need for procedural code.

Creating a Basic Trigger

In the next example, we create a trigger that fires off the basic animation we created earlier:

1. In the Library panel, select and create a button control on the scene. Position it in the bottom-right corner of the scene.

2. Select the Motion timeline from the drop-down list of available timelines in the Timeline sub-panel.

3. Click the +Event Trigger button to add a new trigger to the scene.

4. In the bottom section of the Trigger subpanel, select the When drop-down box and choose Button. This specifies the object that will fire the trigger.

5. Select Click from the drop-down box to the right of the previous step. This is the event that will fire the trigger.

6. Now press the plus sign to reveal a third drop-down box. Select Motion timeline from the third drop-down box and select Begin from the fourth drop-down box. This is the playhead action that will occur when the trigger is fired.

7. Press F5 to test the project. Click the button and view the animation.

Creating Controls

Controls are the basic components of the UI that handle user input and interaction in your WPF application. Examples of some of the basic common controls you will frequently use are text boxes, buttons, checkboxes, and lists.

Expression Blend provides all the standard WPF controls in the Library panel of the designer. Creating an instance of a control is done in two ways:

❏ Selecting the control in the Library panel and drawing it to the desired size and location on the artboard.

❏ Double-clicking the control in the Library to create the instance and inserting it into the currently active element at its default size.

The key thing to remember about controls in Expression Blend is that they are visually customizable. Creating custom controls in Expression Blend can be thought of as a composition of visual elements and existing controls.

Controls differ from vector elements in that they are typically comprised of child elements or other controls, templates, styles, and a set of behaviors they support.

You can place controls, layout panels, and custom vector shapes within controls to create custom controls. For example, to create an icon button, you would create a new instance of the button and place a layout panel in the content of the button. You could then add the image to the layout panel within the button.

Control Inheritance

Some controls act as containers with one or many child elements, whereas some controls do not support any child elements at all. For example, a ScrollViewer control accepts only one nested child element, whereas a StackPanel can contain many nested child elements. To overcome situations in which you require a single-child element control to support multiple child elements you can use control composition. For example, if you require a ScrollViewer to scroll through multiple instances of a control or visual element, you can place a StackPanel within a ScrollViewer and add your child elements to the nested StackPanel.

When you add new controls in a scene Expression Blend attempts to add the control to the layout root by default. To place a child control within another control you must first make the other control active by double-clicking it. A yellow border is placed around the control to indicate that it is now active. Double-clicking a control in the library will nest the control in the active parent control.

Blend supports four different types of controls with varying inheritance, as described in the following list:

❏ **Simple controls** — These controls consist of the control itself and its properties. Simple controls do not host content. In other words, they cannot have child elements within them. Examples are an Image and ScrollBar.

❏ **Content controls** — Content controls can host another element (or can show a string as text for simple scenarios). Content controls have a `Content` property. This means that they can contain a single content item such as a string. Content controls can also contain another element, such as a layout panel. Examples are a CheckBox and RadioButton.

❏ **Items controls** — Items controls can host a collection of child elements. Items controls expose items collections and have no `Content` property and no `Header` property. Examples are a ComboBox, ListBox, and ContextMenu.

❏ **Headered items controls** — Headered items controls host a header child element and content that may or may not be a collection. The control's Header property labels the items of the control and the items collection contains the items themselves. The Header property specifies the label for the entire MenuItem and the individual items are the child elements. Examples are a MenuItem, TabItem, and ListItem.

Editing and Styling Controls

The style and visual structure of a control is made up of two primary parts: templates and styles. Templates represent the element tree of child controls, text, and shapes used to build a control. Styles determine how properties are defined for a control. You can customize both default and custom controls in one of two ways:

❏ Modify a control's default template and styles to the desired appearance.

❏ Create new templates and styles and apply them to existing controls.

Rather than constructing new controls from scratch, you can stylize and customize a control's look and feel by defining styles and/or swapping out control templates.

Templates

Every control in WPF is built using templates. A template represents the elements used to build the control. A control template can be edited so that the visual properties and behavior of the control can be set. Templates can also contain styles for further standardization of the look and feel of control elements.

Editing a Template

You can modify the combo box template to change the look of each child element from the button to the actual list of items. Here's a quick example of editing the template.

1. In the Presentation Framework library, double-click the ComboBox control to place an instance of the control on the artboard.

2. Right-click the combo box and select Edit Control Parts(Template) ⇨ Edit Copy from the context menu. Select the default options from the resource pop-up box.

3. In the structure view, drill down the Grid element tree and activate the [ToggleButton] template. Right-click the template and select the same edit options.

4. Drill down the element tree and activate the Arrow graphic. Rotate the graphic by 90 degrees and align it to the right using the Layout ⇨ Margin panel option.

This process yields a new template resource, which that instance of the combo box is now bound to. The template resource can be bound to any other instance of a combo box by selecting Edit Template ⇨ Apply Resource and selecting the desired template to apply. This process can be performed for any standard Presentation Framework control.

Common Elements Inside a Template

Because templates define the structure of a control rather than specific styles of individual attributes, the list of controls illustrates what can commonly be found or used in template construction. These elements include the following:

❏ **Border** — A simple panel that shows a border. It accepts a single child element. If you want to change the background of control, then rather than removing the Border and creating a new panel like a Grid, just set the Background of the Border.

❏ **Grid** — A layout panel that can hold multiple child elements. Make it the active element to view rows and columns and element.

❏ **Pop-Up** — A layout panel that is used to show a panel above any existing windows or elements. It accepts a single child element.

❏ **Dock** — A layout panel that arranges controls around its edges.

❏ **Stack** — A layout panel that takes multiple child elements and arranges them horizontally or vertically.

❏ **ScrollViewer** — Provides scrollbars and scrolling support.

❏ **ContentPresenter** — Used within a Content control such as button to show child elements that are outside of the template.

❏ **ItemsPresenter** — Used in an items control (for example, ListBox) to show a set a collection of child elements.

❏ **HeaderPanel** — Used in a headered items control (for example, Menu) to show the `Header` element.

Styles

Styles are often used in one form or another to create a standardized look and feel for an application UI or document. In Expression Blend, styles can be easily created and applied to objects. A style sets how a control's default property values are defined.

You can create, copy, edit, and apply styles by right-clicking the control to be styled and selecting Edit Style from the context menu.

Working with Styles

In WPF styles are applied to controls similar to how CSS is applied to HTML elements. In CSS, styles such as font properties, background color, and dimensions are defined by a single class (or assigned by an element ID to be specific). To apply a style to particular page element, the element need only inherit from the class in order for the style to be applied to it. Style definitions are located in one file so style changes need only occur in one location where they are cascaded to all elements that inherit the style. Inherited elements can also override specific attributes for individual situations. In WPF, styles are applied using the same concepts as CSS. Styles can be created and applied to individual elements as local resources.

There are several ways to extend styles to controls:

❏ Use the default style of a control. The style typically maps to the Microsoft Windows system style definition.

❏ Extend a style from a parent element so that child elements inherit the style.

❏ Copy the default style and save it as a resource. It can then be modified and applied to an element on the scene. The system style is brought locally to the project.

❏ Create an empty style and save it as a resource. The empty style represents a fresh style free of any default system style properties.

❏ Define an explicit style that overrides any other style that may be applied through inheritance or binding.

The Apply Resource command on the Style context menu enables you to change the style of a control to another style that exists in the scene.

Common Styles in an Element

Three common styles are found in an element. These include:

❏ Style—Represents the style of the control itself. This will typically set default attributes such as background color and foreground color.

❏ ItemContentStyle—Used for item controls (for example, ListBox) to set the style and template used for each item within the control. This is useful for binding data to a control where you draw elements into the template within the ItemContentStyle and then bind each to a field in the DataSource.

❏ FocusVisualStyle—Used to set the look of focus for the control.

States

States are the visual representations of a control whenever certain conditions are true. For example, the button control by default has a state, or different visual appearance, for mouse over and press events. Controls are the only objects that can have states.

States are added or edited through the Triggers panel. For each event in the Triggers panel, properties of the control can be modified uniquely for each state change. Animations can also be triggered to fire for each state change.

Creating and Styling a Basic Button Control

Without further delay, let's get your fingers on the keyboard. Start by opening Blend, and then perform the following steps:

1. Select the Rectangle to make it active.

2. Select Tools ⇨ Make Button from the main menu.

3. Select the default options from the Create Style Resource popup box.

4. Right-click on the newly created button and select Edit Control Parts(Template) ⇨ Edit Template from the context menu.

5. From the Triggers subpanel, select the IsMouseOver event.

6. Adjust the fill color of the rectangle to unique color from the Appearance panel.

7. Select the IsPressed event from the Triggers subpanel and repeat the same process.

8. Click F5 to preview the project. Click and mouse-over the button to see the property changes.

Importing Audio/Video Media

Expression Blend offers you the ability to add audio and video to your project and then insert it into a scene. The audio or video clip can then be controlled within the Timeline panel.

To add a new video item to a scene, perform the following steps:

1. Select Project ⇨ Add Existing Item from the main menu. The video item will appear in the Project panel when complete.

2. Right-click the video item in the Project panel and select Insert from the context menu.

The inserted media will display on the timeline as another layer in the structure view. If you expand the media node, a gray bar will appear representing the duration of playing time. You can manipulate the bar and offset its play time by expanding the inserted audio/video object node in the structure view of the Timeline panel until you see a Media Time property.

Summary

Expression Blend is designed to abstract the XAML and API level details of creating WPF applications. It offers you the ability to rapidly create:

❑ Custom vector graphic elements

❑ Custom animation

❑ UI screens and controls

The next chapter builds on what you have learned here as we begin programming with EID and explore its programmatic capabilities.

5

Building a Rich UI with Microsoft Expression Blend — Part II

Macromedia Flash has long been the standard by which designers have created rich media online. However, the demand for a more complex and interactive UI continues to grow. To meet this demand, the Flash scripting environment requires modification and extension in order for designers to provide their audience with the capabilities they desire. Furthermore, designers must cross the skills boundary from designer to developer in order to perform the basic programming required within the Flash environment to transform simple animations into interactive and responsive media.

Enter Microsoft Expression Blend. Expression Blend allows designers to develop rich interactive online media that meets the needs of today's audience. Within the Expression Blend development environment, the designer can easily create vector-based imagery, animations, and custom controls visually through a WYSIWYG interface. At the same time, the designer can quickly change to a supplementary coding environment, such as Visual Studio 2005, that supports coding features and workflow as well as allows for fine-grained programmatic control over the visual elements. More likely however, the designer will be able to excel in the designer role, and then hand the project off to a developer who will implement the programming requirements through Visual Studio. The ability for designers and developers to collaborate with one another eliminates the need for the designer to cross skill boundaries. Expression Blend offers the flexibility of switching between design and programming while enabling you to leverage the power of the .NET 3.0 runtime, a significantly more powerful platform than Flash.

In this chapter, we cover programming with Expression Blend as well as tackling some common situations for creating interaction and media elements programmatically. The key topics in the chapter are:

❑   Workflow design and coding

❑   Handling user input and events

❑   Programming animation

❑   The .NET 3.0 2D Graphics API

Expression Blend Workflow

Expression Blend is a development tool that allows designers to create rich UI for Windows applications. Expression Blend focuses on the visual design aspects of WPF, such as creating custom vector geometry, layout, and animations. The tool's WYSIWYG-style development environment offers the designer a flexible workflow for performing what can often be tedious tasks in XAML (such as property settings, gradient fills, and storyboards) easily and efficiently.

The WYSIWYG designer provides support for editing visual elements through two distinct views: a design view and an associated XAML view. The Artboard panel of the Expression Blend interface provides two buttons that allow you to toggle between the design view and the XAML view. The design view supports editing of objects using visual tools and auxiliary panels for altering properties. The XAML view provides fine-grained control over the generated XAML where designers can freely edit the text to hand-tweak attributes and nodes of the visual tree. Toggling between these two views enables the designer to view changes in real time (see Figure 5-1).

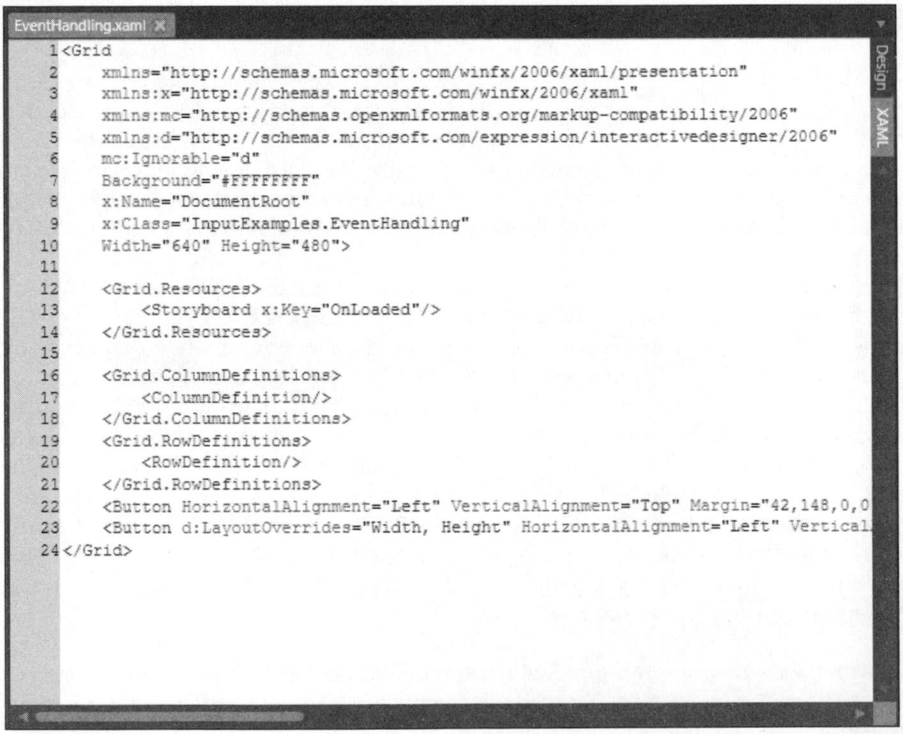

```
EventHandling.xaml  ✕
1 <Grid
2     xmlns="http://schemas.microsoft.com/winfx/2006/xaml/presentation"
3     xmlns:x="http://schemas.microsoft.com/winfx/2006/xaml"
4     xmlns:mc="http://schemas.openxmlformats.org/markup-compatibility/2006"
5     xmlns:d="http://schemas.microsoft.com/expression/interactivedesigner/2006"
6     mc:Ignorable="d"
7     Background="#FFFFFFFF"
8     x:Name="DocumentRoot"
9     x:Class="InputExamples.EventHandling"
10    Width="640" Height="480">
11
12    <Grid.Resources>
13        <Storyboard x:Key="OnLoaded"/>
14    </Grid.Resources>
15
16    <Grid.ColumnDefinitions>
17        <ColumnDefinition/>
18    </Grid.ColumnDefinitions>
19    <Grid.RowDefinitions>
20        <RowDefinition/>
21    </Grid.RowDefinitions>
22    <Button HorizontalAlignment="Left" VerticalAlignment="Top" Margin="42,148,0,0
23    <Button d:LayoutOverrides="Width, Height" HorizontalAlignment="Left" Vertical
24 </Grid>
```

Figure 5-1

Each Expression Blend project that you create will contain files that represent common WPF types you will use in your application. You can easily add a new item to your project by right-clicking the project node in the project panel and selecting Add New Item. The following table provides a description for each type.

File Type	Purpose
Page	Creates a new `Page` class. Pages can be navigated and displayed within your application.
Window	Creates a new `Window` class. Can only be used within a WPF standalone Windows-based application.
UserControl	Creates a new `UserControl` class. A custom user control encapsulates a piece of UI functionality.
ResourceDictionary	Creates a new `ResourceDictionary` for the project. A `ResourceDictionary` is a hash table optimized for loading resources in the project.

You can generate a code-behind file for each item by selecting the Include code file checkbox in the Add New Item dialog box (see Figure 5-2).

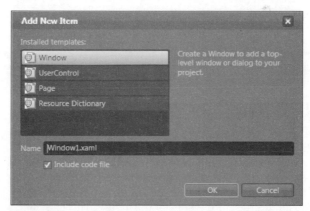

Figure 5-2

For programmatic control and editing of the code-behind files for each file type, Expression Blend interoperates with Visual Studio 2005.

Code Editing with Visual Studio 2005

Expression Blend is geared toward design professionals and aims to provide them with a set of tools common to other design applications with which they are already familiar. The goal is to provide an easy transition to Expression Blend and preserve the workflow to which they are accustomed.

A primary principle underlying Expression Blend is to provide collaboration between the designer and developer working in a team environment. To support this collaboration, Expression Blend interoperates with Visual Studio 2005 for the editing of code via a shared project file format. Expression Blend supports the creation of code-behind files for each page, window, or user control you add to your Expression Blend project as well as the creation of event handling method stubs for any elements in your composition.

This interoperability provides enormous benefits and flexibility when creating code-driven functionality within your WPF application. On the visual side, Expression Blend provides you with all of the design tools you will need, making the process of creating visual elements such as shapes and animations both quick and easy. For development, you get the benefit of using the same rich set of code creation and editing features provided in Visual Studio 2005, such as IntelliSense and line-by-line debugging capabilities.

A project can be open in both Visual Studio and Expression Blend at the same time, allowing you to make changes to your project files in both environments.

Handling User Input

WPF uses object-oriented design principles to model user input. In WPF, the input API primarily resides within the `FrameworkElement` and `FrameworkContentElement` classes. Each class exposes all input events, enabling you to capture events and attach handlers to them:

```
// Assign event handlers for mouse events
MyWPFControl.MouseUp += new MouseButtonEventHandler(MouseUpHandler);
MyWPFControl.MouseDown += new MouseButtonEventHandler(MouseDownHandler);
```

Keyboard and Mouse Classes

The `System.Media.Input` namespace provides two classes with static methods for accessing the current state of the keyboard and mouse input devices: these are the `Keyboard` and `Mouse` classes, respectively. Each class provides static methods for attaching event handlers for their respective events. Of course, each class also provides properties to determine the current state of the device.

The `Mouse` class encapsulates the current state of the mouse. This class will be a key focus in this chapter because it provides a means of finding the mouse position relative to a specified element. In further examples we will use this method to specify points for hit tests.

Events and Event Handling

Rich client applications can provide highly responsive, interactive applications. For a rich client, this usually implies a lot of event handling procedures to coordinate complex workflows and interactivity. A user interface may have a series of actions that must occur once a user input action takes place.

Event handling methods can be added to any event for any element easily through the use of the Properties palette in the Expression Blend interface.

Adding Event Handlers in the Properties Palette

The Properties palette enables the designer to easily attach event handlers to events raised by UI element within the page or window. The steps to assign an event handler to a UI element event are as follows:

1. Select the element to which an event handler will be attached.

2. Select the Properties palette. This palette allows you to toggle between two views: the Properties view and the Events view. Toggle to the Events view by clicking the Events button (the button with the lightning bolt icon, as shown in Figure 5-3).

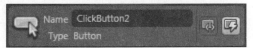

Figure 5-3

3. The Events panel will display a list of events for the selected element. Type in the event handling method you want to attach that corresponds to the event within the Events panel. If the method does not exist within the code-behind file, Expression Blend will perform one of two actions depending on whether or not you have Visual Studio 2005 installed. If you do not have Visual Studio 2005 installed, Expression Blend will create a method stub for the event handling method and add it to the Clipboard for you to paste into your code-behind file (see Figure 5-4). If you have Visual Studio 2005 installed, it will automate this process for you.

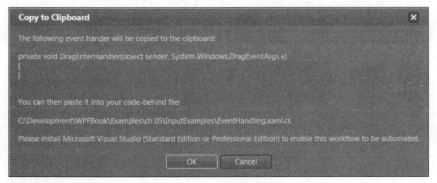

Figure 5-4

For example, the following code block defines an event handling method for the click event of a button.

```
private void ClickHandler(object sender, RoutedEventArgs e)
{
  Button clicked = e.Source as Button;
  MessageBox.Show(String.Format("{0} was clicked!", clicked.Name));
}
```

In the Design mode within Expression Blend, you assign the method by finding the Click event within the Events view of the property panel and typing the name of the method you wish to use. Figure 5-5 illustrates this example.

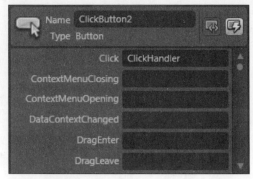

Figure 5-5

Expression Blend associates event handlers declaratively in the XAML definition of the element rather than procedurally in the code-behind file, adding attributes to each element for their respective events. The following code fragment is an example of what's produced from Expression Blend:

```
<Button Click="ClickHandler" PreviewMouseUp="ButtonMouseUpHandler" .... />
```

Deleting an event handler in the Properties palette will remove the event-handling assignment in the XAML but will not delete the event handler method in the code-behind. This is because one or more elements may exist in the visual tree that are dependent on the event-handling method.

Positioning

Layout flexibility is a core concept in WPF. The flexible layout model provides designers and developers with a consistent mechanism for developing UIs that are resolution independent.

Designers and developers often run into problems with layout that stem from the positioning of elements in an absolute manner. For many designers coming from the Flash Platform, not doing this may take some getting used to. In Flash, graphical elements, such as buttons and MovieClips, are positioned absolutely with x and y coordinates on the stage (equivalent of the Artboard in Expression Blend). There is the notion of relative coordinate systems within MovieClip instances, but you can still absolutely position to a specific (x,y) coordinate pair.

In WPF, you must remember that the position of an element, or even a mouse click, is relative to the containing element within which they reside. When you use the `Mouse.GetPosition` method to retrieve the coordinates of the mouse, you must specify the element to which the position will be relative.

The preceding statement doesn't take into account the Canvas container control. We will cover absolute positioning with the Canvas in the next section.

To illustrate how the WPF Input API returns coordinate information based on relative coordinate spaces, we will build a small example that contains four individual elements, and we will output the values of `Mouse.GetPosition()` on all of them.

The following XAML file contains a page definition that specifies four ellipses positioned at the four corners of a rectangle. A label is placed at each of the four corners, next to the Ellipse, which you will use to display the output. The scene also contains another Ellipse that will follow the mouse position in order to visualize the mouse movement:

1. In Expression Blend, select File ⇨ New Project from the menu. In the Create New Project dialog box, select Standard Application (.exe) and name the project **Input Examples**.

2. Right-click on your project and select Add New Item from the menu. In the Add New Item dialog box, select Page and name your page **Mouse Position**.

3. In the designer, switch to XAML view and modify the MousePosition XAML as follows:

```
<Page
    xmlns="http://schemas.microsoft.com/winfx/2006/xaml/presentation"
    xmlns:x="http://schemas.microsoft.com/winfx/2006/xaml"
    xmlns:mc="http://schemas.openxmlformats.org/markup-compatibility/2006"
    xmlns:d="http://schemas.microsoft.com/expression/interactivedesigner/2006"
    mc:Ignorable="d"
    x:Class="InputExamples.MousePosition"
    x:Name="Page"
    WindowTitle="Page"
    FlowDirection="LeftToRight"
    Width="640"
    Height="480"
    WindowWidth="640"
    WindowHeight="480"
    >
    <Grid
        Background="#FFFFFFFF"
        x:Name="DocumentRoot"
        Width="640"
        Height="480"
        >
    <Label d:LayoutOverrides="Height" HorizontalAlignment="Left"
        VerticalAlignment="Top" Margin="193,140,0,0" Width="66" Height="22"
            x:Name="firstCoordinates"/>

    <Rectangle Stroke="#FF000000" Fill="#FFFFFFFF" HorizontalAlignment="Stretch"
        VerticalAlignment="Stretch" Margin="228,177,264,162" Width="Auto" Height="Auto"
            x:Name="Rectangle" StrokeDashCap="Square" StrokeDashOffset="3"/>

    <Ellipse Stroke="#FF000000" Fill="#FFFFFFFF" HorizontalAlignment="Right"
        VerticalAlignment="Top" Margin="0,171,258,0" Width="14" Height="14"
            x:Name="secondEllipse"/>

    <Ellipse d:LayoutOverrides="Height" Stroke="#FF000000" Fill="#FFFFFFFF"
        HorizontalAlignment="Left" VerticalAlignment="Top" Margin="221,171,0,0"
            Width="14" Height="14" x:Name="firstEllipse"/>

    <Ellipse d:LayoutOverrides="Width" Stroke="#FF000000" Fill="#FFFFFFFF"
        HorizontalAlignment="Right" VerticalAlignment="Bottom" Margin="0,0,258,155"
```

```
                Width="14" Height="14" x:Name="fourthEllipse"/>

  <Ellipse d:LayoutOverrides="Width" Stroke="#FF000000" Fill="#FFFFFFFF"
    HorizontalAlignment="Left" VerticalAlignment="Bottom" Margin="221,0,0,155"
      Width="14" Height="14" x:Name="thirdEllipse"/>

  <Label d:LayoutOverrides="Width, Height" HorizontalAlignment="Right"
    VerticalAlignment="Top" Margin="0,140,201,0" Width="66" Height="22"
      x:Name="secondCoordinates"/>

  <Label d:LayoutOverrides="Width, Height" HorizontalAlignment="Left"
    VerticalAlignment="Bottom" Margin="193,0,0,123" Width="66" Height="22"
      x:Name="thirdCoordinates"/>

  <Label d:LayoutOverrides="Width, Height" HorizontalAlignment="Right"
    VerticalAlignment="Bottom" Margin="0,0,201,123" Width="66" Height="22"
      x:Name="fourthCoordinates"/>

  <Ellipse Fill="sc#1, 0, 0, 0" HorizontalAlignment="Right" VerticalAlignment="Top"
    Margin="0,158,149,0" Width="16" Height="16" x:Name="DragEllipse"/>

</Grid>

</Page>
```

In the code-behind file, you retrieve the mouse position relative to each element, frame-by-frame, as the page is rendered to the screen. Once the position is retrieved, you display the results in each of the corresponding labels that are assigned to each point. Calling the `ToString()` method on a `Point` class will output the coordinate relation as x-position, y-position.

4. Open the MousePosition.xaml.cs code-behind file and modify as follows:

```
using System;
using System.Windows;
using System.Windows.Input;
using System.Windows.Media;

namespace InputExamples
{
  public partial class MousePosition
  {
    private TranslateTransform ellipseTransform = new TranslateTransform();

    public MousePosition()
    {
      this.InitializeComponent();
    }

    protected override void OnInitialized(EventArgs e)
    {
      base.OnInitialized(e);

      DragEllipse.RenderTransform = ellipseTransform;
      CompositionTarget.Rendering += this.CompositionTarget_Rendering;
```

```
    }

    private void CompositionTarget_Rendering(object sender, EventArgs e)
    {
      Point mouse1 = Mouse.GetPosition(firstEllipse);
      Point mouse2 = Mouse.GetPosition(secondEllipse);
      Point mouse3 = Mouse.GetPosition(thirdEllipse);
      Point mouse4 = Mouse.GetPosition(fourthEllipse);

      firstCoordinates.Content = mouse1.ToString();
      secondCoordinates.Content = mouse2.ToString();
      thirdCoordinates.Content = mouse3.ToString();
      fourthCoordinates.Content = mouse4.ToString();

      Point position = Mouse.GetPosition(DragEllipse);
      ellipseTransform.X += position.X - (DragEllipse.Width / 2);
      ellipseTransform.Y += position.Y - (DragEllipse.Height / 2);
    }
  }
}
```

5. Select Project ➪ Test Project from the Expression Blend menu to run the application.

Figure 5-6 shows the compiled result. The origin of each relative coordinate space for the elements begins at the top-left corner. You can see that the mouse position's x and y coordinates reflect their position relative to each shape.

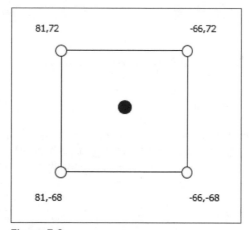

Figure 5-6

Absolute Positioning with the Canvas

If precise control over the x and y position of each element is desired, you can use the Canvas container control as it supports the absolute positioning of elements. The Canvas class itself contains a set of static methods that enable the developer to precisely position each child element in the relative coordinate system of the Canvas. The following table describes the fundamental positioning methods.

Name	Behavior
SetLeft	Sets the left coordinate for a specified UIElement child control to a given value.
SetTop	Sets the top coordinate for a specified UIElement child control to a given value.
SetRight	Sets the right coordinate for a specified UIElement child control to a given value.
SetBottom	Sets the bottom coordinate for a specified UIElement child control to a given value.
GetLeft	Retrieves the left coordinate for a given UIElement child control.
GetTop	Retrieves the top coordinate for a given UIElement child control.
GetRight	Retrieves the right coordinate for a given UIElement child control.
GetBottom	Retrieves the bottom coordinate for a given UIElement child control.

Margins for Positioning

The Margin property of UI elements within a container can also provide a means of positioning elements that is relative to absolute positioning. Margins define the amount of space between a control and its adjacent sibling within a container. As a matter of fact, when moving elements around in the design view, Expression Blend is simply modifying the Margin property of the positioned element.

If you need a certain degree of control over the positioning of your elements, but would prefer using a container control other than a canvas, modifying the margins on elements may be an adequate solution to your problem.

Hit Testing

The hit testing capabilities of WPF allow you to receive notification when one or more objects (framework elements or user input such as mouse clicks) collide. The UIElement class (which is the base class from which FrameworkElement derives) contains a method called InputHitTest that allows you to perform hit testing on elements relative to a coordinate point.

The InputHitTest method limits the developer to hit testing against a single element and a single point on the screen. It does not support more complex scenarios such as determining when objects collide with the actual geometry of an object or if many objects collide at once. To support more complex hit testing scenarios, one must use the VisualTreeHelper class.

The VisualTreeHelper Class

The VisualTreeHelper class in the System.Windows.Media namespace contains static utility methods for tasks that involve inspecting the nodes of a visual tree. The method of importance for us is HitTest.

The HitTest method (and its overloads) is meant to determine whether or not a point or geometrical object is within the boundary at any point of a specified element. The method supports hit testing at a specific point or geometry.

The following table specifies each of the method signatures and their behaviors.

Method Signature	Behavior
`HitTest(Visual, Point)`	Performs a hit test on the specified Visual object and returns the top-most (highest z-index) element.
`HitTest(Visual, HitTestFilterCallback, HitTestResultCallback, HitTestParameters)`	Performs a hit test on the specified Visual object and calls the specified `HitTestFilterCallback` and `HitTestResultCallback` on each hit.
`HitTest(Visual3D, HitTestFilterCallback, HitTestResultCallback, HitTestParameters3D)`	Performs a hit test on the specified Visual3D object and calls the specified `HitTestFilterCallback` and `HitTestResultCallback` on each hit.

For each of the overloaded methods listed, it's important to note that the Visual argument of the method always specifies the portion of the visual tree against which the hit test will be performed. The hit test will be performed on the Visual specified as well as any child element.

The following example shows how to use the `VisualTreeHelper` to determine if one object has collided with another:

```
public void PerformHitTest()
{
  // Retrieve the coordinate of the mouse position
  // relative to my control
  Point position = Mouse.GetPosition(firstElement);

  // Perform the hit test against another element
  HitTestResult result = VisualTreeHelper.HitTest(secondElement, position);

  if (result != null)
  {
    MessageBox.Show("Collision detected");
  }
}
```

Each `HitTest` method returns an instance of the `HitTestResult` and also allows you to specify a delegate to be called whenever a collision occurs. The `HitTestResult` class provides the Visual that was hit during the test. The following code illustrates an example of accessing the `VisualHit` property of the `HitTestResult` class.

```
  // Perform the hit test against another element
  HitTestResult result = VisualTreeHelper.HitTest(secondElement, position);

  if (result != null)
  {
    Visual hitVisual = hitResult.VisualHit;

    // If Visual is a Rectangle shape, do some
    // additional work
    if (hitVisual.GetType() == typeof(Rectangle))
```

```
    {
      // Do additional processing
      ...
    }
  }
}
```

The HitTestResultCallback Delegate

Performing a hit test using the `VisualTreeHelper` class also allows you to iterate through each object that is affected by the hit test, regardless of the object's z-index. This provides you with an opportunity to define custom actions to be executed each time a specific object is the result of a particular hit test. You may also want to collect all of the objects that are a result of the hit test and perform some additional processing.

In order to iterate through each object identified by a hit test, you use the `HitTestResultCallback` delegate. This delegate is called each time the system identifies an element whose coordinates or geometry collide within a specified part of the visual tree.

The `HitTestResultBehavior` argument defined by the `HitTestResultCallback` delegate is an enumeration that defines the action to be performed on subsequent hit test result callbacks. The enumeration has the following two values:

❑   `Stop`—Exits out of any further hit testing.

❑   `Continue`—Signals to proceed hit testing on the next element in the visual tree.

To assign the `HitTestResultCallback` delegate, use the overloaded version of the `VisualTreeHelper.HitTest` method, which enables you to pass an instance of the delegate. The following code example illustrates assigning the delegate in the `HitTest` method call:

```
public void PerformHitTest()
{
  // Retrieve the coordinate of the mouse position
  // relative to my control
  Point position = e.GetPosition((UIElement)sender);

  // Perform the hit test
  VisualTreeHelper.HitTest(
    myContainer,
    null,
    new HitTestResultHandler(MyHitTestResult),
    new PointHitTestParameters(position));

  // Perform next actions on the hit test results.
  ....
}
```

In the `MyHitTestResult` method, you place any logic that you want to execute on each hit test that returns. You then determine whether to stop hit testing or to continue to the next element in the z-index stack.

```
public HitTestResultBehavior MyHitTestResult (HitTestResult result)
{
  // Get the object that was hit
  Visual element = result.VisualHit;

  // If the element that was hit is the one
  // I'm looking for, stop. Else, continue
  if (element == myObject)
    return HitTestResultBehavior.Stop;
  else
    return HitTestResultBehavior.Continue;
}
```

Filtering the Hit Test

You can pre-filter elements from the hit test before the `HitTestResultCallback` is executed by using the `HitTestFilterCallback` delegate. Within this method, you can perform filtering logic that determines whether the element should be filtered from the result as well as how to proceed to the next elements in the hit test.

Performance can also be improved by filtering objects that aren't of interest in the hit test. So filtering elements with many children that you know in advance should be excluded from the hit test is a good idea.

The `HitTestFilterCallback` delegate returns a `HitTestFilterBehavior` enumeration to specify the course of action to take in proceeding with the hit test. The behaviors within the enumeration are as follows:

- ❑   `Continue` — Proceed to hit test the current visual element and any of its child elements.

- ❑   `ContinueSkipChildren` — Proceed to hit test the current visual element but skip any of its child elements.

- ❑   `ContinueSkipSelf` — Bypass hit testing the current visual element but proceed to hit test any of its child elements.

- ❑   `ContinueSkipSelfAndChildren` — Bypass hit testing the current visual and any of its child elements.

- ❑   `Stop` — Stop hit testing at the current Visual element.

The following code block provides a sample method declaration for hit test filtering. Based on the type of the object that is returned, it determines the next course of filtering.

```
public HitTestFilterBehavior MyHitTestFilter(DependencyObject objectToFilter)
{
  // Test for the object value you want to filter.
  if (objectToFilter.GetType() == typeof(Shape))
  {
    return HitTestFilterBehavior.ContinueSkipSelf;
  }
  else
  {
    return HitTestFilterBehavior.Continue;
  }
}
```

Detecting a Hit Test to a Point

This example covers the basic steps of hit testing to a point while implementing a custom `HitTestResultCallback` delegate to output the results of the hit test.

1. In Expression Blend, open the InputExamples project you created earlier or create a new Standard Application (.exe) project and name it **InputExamples**.

2. Add a new page to the project by selecting File ⇨ New Item and choosing Page from the list of installed templates. Name the file **PointHitTest.xaml** and click OK.

3. Double-click your new XAML page and create a new Rectangle shape on the drawing area. With the rectangle selected, choose the Properties tab. Alter the fill and stroke properties to your liking. Set the name property for the rectangle instance to `RectangleArea`. Next, add a Label control to the scene and place it below the rectangle (you may have to select the double down-facing arrow at the bottom of the toolbox to find the Label control). In the properties panel, modify the Width property to 400 and set the name value to **HitLabel**. This label will output the result of the hit test.

Or, copy the following markup into the file through the XAML view.

```xml
<Page
  xmlns="http://schemas.microsoft.com/winfx/2006/xaml/presentation"
  xmlns:x="http://schemas.microsoft.com/winfx/2006/xaml"
  xmlns:mc="http://schemas.openxmlformats.org/markup-compatibility/2006"
  xmlns:d="http://schemas.microsoft.com/expression/interactivedesigner/2006"
  mc:Ignorable="d"
  x:Class="InputExamples.PointHitTest"
  x:Name="Page"
  WindowTitle="Page"
  FlowDirection="LeftToRight"
  Width="640"
  Height="480"
  WindowWidth="640"
  WindowHeight="480"
  >
  <Grid
    Background="#FFFFFFFF"
    x:Name="DocumentRoot"
    Width="640"
    Height="480"
    >
      <Rectangle Fill="sc#1, 0, 0.08110714, 1" Margin="202,123,238,157" Width="200"
        Height="200" x:Name="RectangleArea"/>
      <Label d:LayoutOverrides="Height" VerticalAlignment="Bottom"
        Margin="125.685,0,149.479999999981,99" Width="Auto" Height="28"
          x:Name="HitLabel" Content="Label"/>
  </Grid>

</Page>
```

4. Add the following `using` directives to the code-behind file:

```csharp
using System;
using System.Windows;
using System.Windows.Input;
using System.Windows.Media;
```

5. Add the following private member to the class definition:

```
private string hitStatus;
```

6. Add the following `OnInitialized` override:

```
protected override void OnInitialized(EventArgs e)
{
  base.OnInitialized(e);

  CompositionTarget.Rendering += this.CompositionTarget_Rendering;
}
```

7. In order to get real-time results to your hit test per frame, you will need to include a method to work in concert with the `CompositionTarget` class to perform the hit test and display the results. Copy the following method declaration into the code-behind file:

```
private void CompositionTarget_Rendering(object sender, EventArgs e)
{
  // Retrieve the coordinate of the Ellipse position.
  Point position = Mouse.GetPosition(RectangleArea);

  hitStatus = "no hit";

  // Set up a callback to receive the hit test result enumeration.
  VisualTreeHelper.HitTest(
    RectangleArea,
    null,
    new HitTestResultCallback(HitTestResultHandler),
    new PointHitTestParameters(position)
  );

  // Alert the status of the hit test
  this.HitLabel.Content = String.Format(
    "Result of the hit test: {0}",
    hitStatus
  );
}
```

8. You'll need your `HitTestResultCallback` method. Copy the following into the code-behind file. This will output the point that was hit to the screen as well as notify you that the hit test occurred.

```
public HitTestResultBehavior HitTestResultHandler(HitTestResult result)
{
  PointHitTestResult hitResult = (PointHitTestResult)result;

  hitStatus = String.Format(
    "{0} was hit at this point: {1}",
    ((FrameworkElement)hitResult.VisualHit).Name,
    hitResult.PointHit.ToString()
  );

  // Stop since no other testing required.
  return HitTestResultBehavior.Stop;
}
```

9. Build the project in Debug to view the hosted control in WPF. Figure 5-7 shows the compiled result.

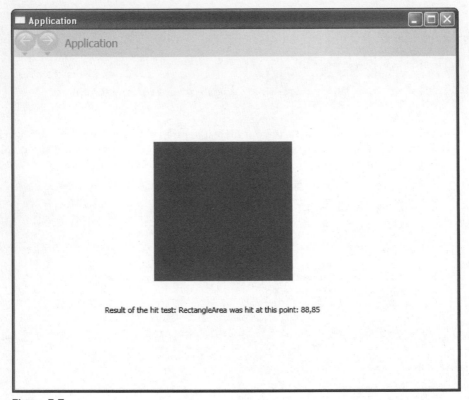

Figure 5-7

Detecting a Hit Test with Geometry

When performing a hit test between geometries, it is important to note that the HitTestResultCallback delegate returns a subclass of the HitTestResult as the method argument, GeometryHitTestResult. The GeometryHitTestResult class contains an additional property called VisualHit that is an enumeration type. VisualHit specifies the type of intersection that occurs when the two geometries collide. The values of the enumeration are as follows:

❑ Empty—The target and the hit test objects do not intersect.

❑ Intersects—The target and the hit test objects intersect.

❑ FullyContains—The hit test object completely contains the target object within its boundaries.

❑ FullyInside—The target object is completely inside the hit test object.

In the next example you will hit test two visual objects according to their geometry and display the type of intersection that occurs between them to the screen.

1. Using the same project created previously, add a new page to the project by selecting File ⇨ New Item from the main menu, and then choosing Page from the list of installed templates. Name the page **CircleHitTest.xaml** and click OK.

2. Double-click the new XAML page, and create a new Canvas, name it **SceneCanvas,** and alter its dimensions so that it occupies roughly the top two-thirds of the Scene. (You can locate the Canvas by right-clicking on the Grid in the Toolbox to reveal the other containers available to you.) You will be using a Canvas so that you can take advantage of its ability to position elements absolutely. Follow the same procedure used in the previous example to add a new Rectangle and Label to the page. Set the Ellipse Width and Height property to 94 and then set the name property to be DragEllipse. Set the Name property of the rectangle to RectangleArea. Once the Rectangle and Ellipse elements are created, add them as child controls to the Canvas container by selecting them all and dragging them onto the Canvas control while pressing the Alt key. Place the Label control at the bottom, below the Canvas container.

Or, copy the following markup into the file through the XAML view.

```
<Page
  xmlns="http://schemas.microsoft.com/winfx/2006/xaml/presentation"
  xmlns:x="http://schemas.microsoft.com/winfx/2006/xaml"
  xmlns:mc="http://schemas.openxmlformats.org/markup-compatibility/2006"
  xmlns:d="http://schemas.microsoft.com/expression/interactivedesigner/2006"
  mc:Ignorable="d"
  x:Class="InputExamples.CircleHitTest"
  x:Name="Page"
  WindowTitle="Page"
  FlowDirection="LeftToRight"
  Width="640"
  Height="480"
  WindowWidth="640"
  WindowHeight="480"
  >
  <Grid
    Background="#FFFFFFFF"
    x:Name="DocumentRoot"
    Width="640"
    Height="480"
    MinWidth="640"
    MaxHeight="480"
    MaxWidth="640"
    MinHeight="480"
    Canvas.Left="0"
    Canvas.Top="0"
    >
    <Label HorizontalAlignment="Stretch" VerticalAlignment="Bottom"
      Margin="4.6850000000003,0,25.7399999999999,71" Width="Auto" Height="28"
        x:Name="HitLabel" Content="Label"/>
    <Canvas
      Margin="5.99999999999204,6.0000000000001,3.00000000000591,129.210526315788"
        x:Name="SceneCanvas" VerticalAlignment="Stretch" Height="Auto">
      <Ellipse Stroke="{x:Null}" Fill="sc#1, 0.9257866, 0.5352878, 0"
        HorizontalAlignment="Left" VerticalAlignment="Top" Width="94" Height="94"
          x:Name="DragEllipse" MinWidth="94" MaxHeight="94" MaxWidth="94"
            MinHeight="94" d:LayoutOverrides="Height" Canvas.Left="500"
```

```
                Canvas.Top="81"/>
      <Rectangle Fill="sc#1, 0, 0.08110714, 1" HorizontalAlignment="Stretch"
        VerticalAlignment="Stretch" Width="200" Height="200" Canvas.Left="203"
          Canvas.Top="74" x:Name="RectangleArea"/>
    </Canvas>
  </Grid>
</Page>
```

3. Add the following `using` directives to the code-behind file:

```
using System;
using System.Windows;
using System.Windows.Controls;
using System.Windows.Input;
using System.Windows.Media;
using System.Windows.Shapes;
```

4. Add the following private members to the class definition.

```
private string hitStatus = "no hit";
private Path ellipseTrace;
```

5. Add the following `OnInitialized` override:

```
protected override void OnInitialized(EventArgs e)
{
  base.OnInitialized(e);

  CompositionTarget.Rendering += this.CompositionTarget_Rendering;
}
```

6. To get real-time results to your hit test per frame, you will need to include a method to work in concert with the `CompositionTarget` class to perform the hit test and display the results. Copy the following method declaration into the code-behind file:

```
private void CompositionTarget_Rendering(object sender, EventArgs e)
{
  // Retrieve the coordinate of the Ellipse position.
  Point position = Mouse.GetPosition(SceneCanvas);

  // Get the Geometry of the colliding object
  EllipseGeometry hitTestArea = new EllipseGeometry(
    position,
    DragEllipse.Width / 2,
    DragEllipse.Height / 2
  );

  hitStatus = "no hit";

  this.SceneCanvas.Children.Remove(ellipseTrace);

  ellipseTrace = new Path();
  ellipseTrace.Data = hitTestArea;
```

```
  ellipseTrace.Stroke = Brushes.Black;

  this.SceneCanvas.Children.Add(ellipseTrace);

  // Set up a callback to receive the hit test result enumeration.
  VisualTreeHelper.HitTest(
    this.SceneCanvas,
    MyHitTestFilter,
    new HitTestResultCallback(HitTestResultHandler),
    new GeometryHitTestParameters(hitTestArea)
  );

  // Alert the status of the hit test
  this.HitLabel.Content = String.Format(
    "Result of the hit test: {0}",
    hitStatus
  );

  Canvas.SetLeft(DragEllipse, position.X - (DragEllipse.Width / 2));
  Canvas.SetTop(DragEllipse, position.Y - (DragEllipse.Height / 2));
}
```

7. On each successful callback, you will examine the `GeometryHitTestResult` argument that is returned to determine what type of intersection occurred. You will add that to the output string of the hit status to our Label control. Copy the following code into the class definition.

```
public HitTestResultBehavior HitTestResultHandler(HitTestResult result)
{
  GeometryHitTestResult hitResult = (GeometryHitTestResult)result;

  // Retrieve the results of the hit test.
  IntersectionDetail intersectionDetail = hitResult.IntersectionDetail;

  switch (intersectionDetail)
  {
    case IntersectionDetail.FullyContains:
      hitStatus = "hit - FullyContains";
      break;
    case IntersectionDetail.Intersects:
      hitStatus = "hit - Intersects";
      break;
    case IntersectionDetail.FullyInside:
      hitStatus = "hit - FullyInside";
      break;
    case IntersectionDetail.Empty:
      default:
      hitStatus = "no hit";
      break;
  }

  // Set the behavior to return visuals at all z-order levels.
  return HitTestResultBehavior.Stop;
}
```

8. In your hit test, you are specifying a custom filter that will make sure that the Canvas and the Ellipse will be excluded from the hit test because all you care about is the effect on the Rectangle in your scene. Copy the following code into the scene class definition:

```
public HitTestFilterBehavior MyHitTestFilter(DependencyObject o)
{
  // Test for the object value you want to filter.
  if (o.GetType() == typeof(Canvas) || o.GetType() == typeof(Ellipse))
  {
    return HitTestFilterBehavior.ContinueSkipSelf;
  }
  else
  {
    return HitTestFilterBehavior.Continue;
  }
}
```

9. Build the project in Debug to view the hosted control in WPF. Figure 5-8 shows the compiled result.

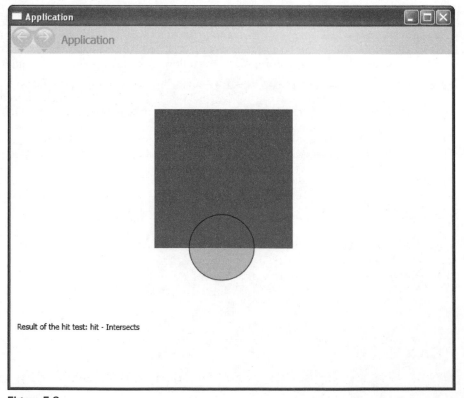

Figure 5-8

The WPF Animation API

Designing animations in Expression Blend is an easy and straightforward process. Expression Blend provides tools that allow you to easily create timelines and animation for visuals, eliminating the cumbersome task of writing code for each segment of an animation.

However, it may be the case that the desired animation falls out of any predefined animation patterns supplied by Expression Blend. In this case, you will need to program your animation procedurally. For example, you may wish to create a particle engine that simulates a firework effect where each individual particle is a sprite that contains a fade out animation segment. Animating each particle, as the explosion expands, could become tedious and it would be difficult to model the realistic physical effect of the explosion by hand.

Be cautious about re-inventing the wheel. It may be in a programmer's nature to define animation in code, but Expression Blend is a productivity tool designed to streamline workflow thereby decreasing production time. If a certain animation doesn't require a programmatic definition, use the timeline and animate it through the Artboard panel instead. You'll save loads of production time.

Animation Classes

The Animation API provides classes that encapsulate the timing calculations required to perform the work of redrawing the scene during each frame.

Each animation watches for property changes on an object. Each animation class allows you to specify "To" and "From" values for the property it watches that designate when the animation starts and ends. The animation class will interpolate the property changes over the specified duration of the animation. This process is easily visualized by the use of the Timeline sub-panel.

The following table shows a sample of the animation types available through the API and the properties to which they apply change.

Animation Type	Behavior
ColorAnimation	Performs an animation between two values on a color property of a UIElement.
DoubleAnimation	Performs an animation on any property that is of type Double, such as the Width, Height, and Opacity of a UIElement.
PointAnimation	Performs an animation between two values on a property of a UIElement that is of type Point.

Creating a Dynamic Animation Procedurally with Code

In this example, we cover the basic steps for creating an animation class on-the-fly procedurally and applying it to the opacity property of a shape.

1. In Expression Blend, select File ⇨ New Project. From the Project Types view, select the Standard Application (.exe) option and then name the project **AnimationExamples**.

2. Add a new Page to the project by selecting File ⇨ New Item and then choosing Page from the Add New Item dialog box. Name the page **AnimationInCode.xaml** and click OK.

3. Double-click the new XAML scene file and create a new Ellipse shape on the drawing area. Alter the fill and stroke properties to your liking. Next, add a Slider control to the scene and place it below the Ellipse shape. In the properties panel, modify the Minimum property to 0 and the Maximum to 100. This will create your value range.

   Or, copy the following markup into the file through the XAML view.

```xml
<Page
  xmlns="http://schemas.microsoft.com/winfx/2006/xaml/presentation"
  xmlns:x="http://schemas.microsoft.com/winfx/2006/xaml"
  xmlns:mc="http://schemas.openxmlformats.org/markup-compatibility/2006"
  xmlns:d="http://schemas.microsoft.com/expression/interactivedesigner/2006"
  mc:Ignorable="d"
  x:Class="AnimationExamples.AnimationInCode"
  x:Name="Page"
  WindowTitle="Page"
  FlowDirection="LeftToRight"
  Width="640"
  Height="480"
  WindowWidth="640"
  WindowHeight="480"
  >
  <Grid
    Background="#FFFFFFFF"
    x:Name="DocumentRoot"
    Width="640"
    Height="480"
    >
    <Grid.Resources>
      <Storyboard x:Key="OnLoaded"/>
    </Grid.Resources>

    <Grid.Triggers>
      <EventTrigger RoutedEvent="FrameworkElement.Loaded">
        <BeginStoryboard x:Name="OnLoaded_BeginStoryboard"
          Storyboard="{DynamicResource OnLoaded}"/>
      </EventTrigger>
    </Grid.Triggers>

    <Grid.ColumnDefinitions>
      <ColumnDefinition/>
    </Grid.ColumnDefinitions>
    <Grid.RowDefinitions>
      <RowDefinition/>
    </Grid.RowDefinitions>
    <Slider d:LayoutOverrides="Width, Height" HorizontalAlignment="Right"
      VerticalAlignment="Bottom" Margin="0,0,212,87" Width="105" Height="33"
        x:Name="WidthControl" Maximum="100" Minimum="0"/>
    <Label d:LayoutOverrides="Width, Height" HorizontalAlignment="Left"
```

```
        VerticalAlignment="Bottom" Margin="208,0,0,97.893333333333" Width="100"
          Height="23.2766666666667" x:Name="ContentLabel" Content="Circle Opacity:"
            RenderTransformOrigin="0.5,0.5" TabIndex="4"/>
      <Ellipse Stroke="{x:Null}" HorizontalAlignment="Stretch"
        VerticalAlignment="Stretch" Margin="228,163,233,138" Width="Auto"
          Height="Auto" x:Name="MyControl">
        <Ellipse.Fill>
          <RadialGradientBrush>
            <GradientStop Color="#FFFFFFFF" Offset="0"/>
              <GradientStop Color="#FF87001C" Offset="0.73735921399473"/>
              <GradientStop Color="#FF4C000F" Offset="1"/>
          </RadialGradientBrush>
        </Ellipse.Fill>
      </Ellipse>
    </Grid>

</Page>
```

4. Add the following using directives to the code-behind file:

```
using System;
using System.Windows;
using System.Windows.Controls.Primitives;
using System.Windows.Input;
using System.Windows.Media;
using System.Windows.Media.Animation;
using System.Windows.Shapes;
```

5. In the .cs code-behind file, you will customize (in code) the slider control so that you can add some visual ticks as well as tooltips to describe the selected value. Copy the following code within the default constructor. The code contains an OnInitialized event handler override to handle setting your slider control properties as well as attaching a MouseUp event handler for when the control is released.

```
protected override void OnInitialized(EventArgs e)
{
  base.OnInitialized(e);

  DoubleCollection tickMarks = new DoubleCollection();
  tickMarks.Add(0);
  tickMarks.Add(25);
  tickMarks.Add(50);
  tickMarks.Add(75);
  tickMarks.Add(100);

  this.WidthControl.Ticks = tickMarks;
  this.WidthControl.TickPlacement = TickPlacement.BottomRight;
  this.WidthControl.AutoToolTipPlacement = AutoToolTipPlacement.TopLeft;
  this.WidthControl.AutoToolTipPrecision = 0;
  this.WidthControl.Value = this.WidthControl.Maximum;
  this.WidthControl.PreviewMouseUp += new
    MouseButtonEventHandler(WidthControl_MouseUp);
}
```

6. Define the behavior of what happens after the slider value has been modified. The event handler will modify the opacity of the Ellipse shape you created earlier based on the selected value of the slider. Because the opacity value is a double from the range of 0.0 to 1.0, you take the ratio of the selected value over the maximum value to define your opacity value. The DoubleAnimation you create will animate the property change from the current opacity value of the shape to the new opacity value.

```
private void WidthControl_MouseUp(object sender, MouseButtonEventArgs e)
{
    DoubleAnimation moveAnimation = new DoubleAnimation();
    moveAnimation.From = this.MyControl.Opacity;
    moveAnimation.To = this.WidthControl.Value / this.WidthControl.Maximum;
    moveAnimation.Duration = new Duration(TimeSpan.FromSeconds(.5));
    moveAnimation.DecelerationRatio = .5;

    MyControl.BeginAnimation(Shape.OpacityProperty, moveAnimation);
}
```

7. Build the project in Debug to view the hosted control in WPF. Figure 5-9 shows the compiled result.

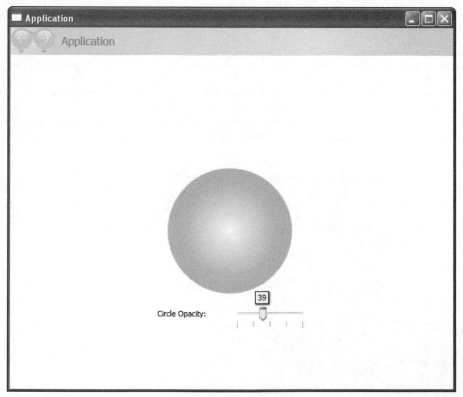

Figure 5-9

Programmatic Animation

When an animated effect cannot be interpolated in a linear fashion, it will require that you set custom values in order to achieve the desired effect. At this point you will need to time the animation yourself while updating the values of the property through the animation.

The CompositionTarget Class

To create animations where you need more control over the rendered output, you need to utilize the CompositionTarget class. The CompositionTarget class represents the display surface to which your application is drawn and rendered. Every time a scene is drawn to screen, the CompositionTarget class raises the Rendering event to notify any event handlers that a frame has been rendered.

To create custom animation, you need to create an event handler and subscribe to the CompositionTarget.Rendering event. The CompositionTarget class is static and can be easily accessed within your code-behind file. In your event handler, you can add any additional logic that is required to create custom drawing to the screen on a frame-by-frame basis.

There are a couple of important points to remember about CompositionTarget rendering. The first is that the frames-per-second (fps) rate may differ from machine to machine. Factors such as hardware and system workload will affect how many times per second the rendering event will be fired.

Second, the order in which the subscribed rendering event handlers are called is not pre-determined nor do they follow any order. Therefore, it is suggested that you coordinate the sequence in which things are drawn in one event handler; otherwise, your animation may be subject to random sequencing.

Animating Frame-by-Frame Using CompositionTarget

In this example, we cover how to control the frame-by-frame rendering of a scene. In this case, you will create a shape that rotates about a fixed point in the center of the screen and you will offer the control to dynamically change the radius length. You will also include code to trace the path of the object's rotation.

1. Using the same AnimationExamples project you created for the earlier example, create a new page by selecting File ➪ New from the main menu and then selecting Page from the Add New Item dialog box. Name the page **Rotation.xaml**.

2. In the design view, create a new shape (any will do) and name it **MyControl**. In the Library palette, drag a new Slider control into the scene.

   Or, copy the following markup into the file in XAML view:

```
<Page
  xmlns="http://schemas.microsoft.com/winfx/2006/xaml/presentation"
  xmlns:x="http://schemas.microsoft.com/winfx/2006/xaml"
  xmlns:mc="http://schemas.openxmlformats.org/markup-compatibility/2006"
  xmlns:d="http://schemas.microsoft.com/expression/interactivedesigner/2006"
  mc:Ignorable="d"
  x:Class="AnimationExamples.Rotation"
  x:Name="Page"
  WindowTitle="Page"
  FlowDirection="LeftToRight"
  Width="640"
  Height="480"
```

```
WindowWidth="640"
WindowHeight="480"
>
<Grid
  Background="#FFFFFFFF"
  x:Name="DocumentRoot"
  Width="640"
  Height="480"
  >

<Grid.ColumnDefinitions>
  <ColumnDefinition/>
</Grid.ColumnDefinitions>
<Grid.RowDefinitions>
  <RowDefinition/>
</Grid.RowDefinitions>

<Slider HorizontalAlignment="Right" VerticalAlignment="Top"
  Margin="0,55,48,0" Width="105" Height="33" x:Name="RadiusControl"/>

<Label d:LayoutOverrides="Width, Height"
  HorizontalAlignment="Right" VerticalAlignment="Top"
    Margin="0,23.83,58,0" Width="100" Height="23.2766666666667"
      x:Name="ContentLabel" RenderTransformOrigin="0.5,0.5" Content="Radius
        Length:" TabIndex="4"/>

<Rectangle Stroke="sc#1, 0.32030192, 0.293796659, 0.9098395"
  RadiusX="14.5" RadiusY="14.5" Width="Auto" Height="Auto"
    x:Name="MyControl" Margin="291,197,294,228" HorizontalAlignment="Stretch"
      VerticalAlignment="Stretch" MinHeight="0">
  <Rectangle.Fill>
    <LinearGradientBrush StartPoint="0,0.5" EndPoint="1,0.5">
      <LinearGradientBrush.RelativeTransform>
        <TransformGroup>
          <TranslateTransform X="-0.5" Y="-0.5"/>
          <ScaleTransform ScaleX="1" ScaleY="1"/>
          <SkewTransform AngleX="0" AngleY="0"/>
          <RotateTransform Angle="-90"/>
          <TranslateTransform X="0.5" Y="0.5"/>
          <TranslateTransform X="0" Y="0"/>
        </TransformGroup>
      </LinearGradientBrush.RelativeTransform>
      <LinearGradientBrush.GradientStops>
        <GradientStopCollection>
          <GradientStop Color="#FE1216A1" Offset="0"/>
          <GradientStop Color="sc#0.996078432, 1, 1, 1" Offset="1"/>
          <GradientStop Color="sc#0.996078432, 0, 0.00211989, 0.222403333"
            Offset="0.41529898672755938"/>
          <GradientStop Color="sc#0.996078432, 0.05701078, 0.05701078,
            0.05701078" Offset="0.82974168688454564"/>
          <GradientStop Color="sc#0.996078432, 0, 0.004114673, 0.639381647"
            Offset="0.12644498358784184"/>
          <GradientStop Color="#FE000893" Offset="0.30226915941201776"/>
          <GradientStop Color="#FE8E8EA0" Offset="0.89253603539317994"/>
        </GradientStopCollection>
      </LinearGradientBrush.GradientStops>
```

```
        </LinearGradientBrush.GradientStops>
      </LinearGradientBrush>
    </Rectangle.Fill>
    <Rectangle.RenderTransform>
      <TransformGroup>
        <TranslateTransform X="0" Y="0"/>
        <ScaleTransform ScaleX="1" ScaleY="1"/>
        <SkewTransform AngleX="0" AngleY="0"/>
        <RotateTransform Angle="0"/>
        <TranslateTransform X="0" Y="0"/>
        <TranslateTransform X="0" Y="0"/>
      </TransformGroup>
    </Rectangle.RenderTransform>
  </Rectangle>

  </Grid>

</Page>
```

3. Add the following using directives to the code-behind file:

```
using System;
using System.Windows;
using System.Windows.Media;
using System.Windows.Shapes;
```

4. Add the following private members to the code-behind for this page. These members will help support the calculations for your rotation.

```
private double radius = 20;
private double maxRadius;
private double currTheta = 0;
private Point center;
private TranslateTransform translation = new TranslateTransform();
private Path outline = new Path();
```

5. In the .cs code-behind file, you will again override the OnInitialized event handler. In the method, you set up the base values for rotation and you add an event handler to the CompositionTarget.Rendering event.

```
protected override void OnInitialized(EventArgs e)
{
  base.OnInitialized(e);

  // Set up the center of the coordinate plane
  center = new Point(DocumentRoot.Width / 2, DocumentRoot.Height / 2);

  // Set the maximum radius length
  maxRadius = this.Width / 3;

  // Default the radius
  RadiusControl.Value = 2;

  // hook up a handler to be called each time the scene is rendered.
```

```
CompositionTarget.Rendering += this.CompositionTarget_Rendering;

// Draw the rotation outline
EllipseGeometry rotationOutline = new EllipseGeometry(
  center, radius, radius
);

outline.Data = rotationOutline;
outline.Stroke = Brushes.Black;
outline.StrokeThickness = .25;
DocumentRoot.Children.Add(outline);

// assign the transform
MyControl.RenderTransform = this.translation;
}
```

6. You need to perform the calculations for rotating and translating your shape. The following event handler finds the current angle (the angle is incremented every scene redraw) as well as the correct X and Y position values and applies them to the transform object:

```
private void CompositionTarget_Rendering(object sender, EventArgs e)
{
    double angleInRadians = DegreeToRad(currTheta);
    double sliderRatio = this.RadiusControl.Value * .1;

    // Adjust the radius to the current slider position
    radius = sliderRatio * this.maxRadius;

    // Apply the coordinate transformation
    translation.X = this.radius * Math.Cos(angleInRadians);
    translation.Y = this.radius * Math.Sin(angleInRadians);

    // increment angle
    currTheta = currTheta + (1 * sliderRatio);

    // Adjust the path trace
    EllipseGeometry pathOutline = (EllipseGeometry)outline.Data;
    pathOutline.Center = this.center;
    pathOutline.RadiusX = this.radius;
    pathOutline.RadiusY = this.radius;
}
```

7. Copy the following support method into the code-behind file. This method just converts angles in degrees to its radian equivalent. The `Math.Cos()` and `Math.Sin()` methods accept angle arguments only in radian form.

```
private double DegreeToRad(double theta)
{
  return Math.PI / 180 * theta;
}
```

8. Build the project in Debug to view. Interact with the radius length by moving the slider back and forth. Figure 5-10 shows the compiled result.

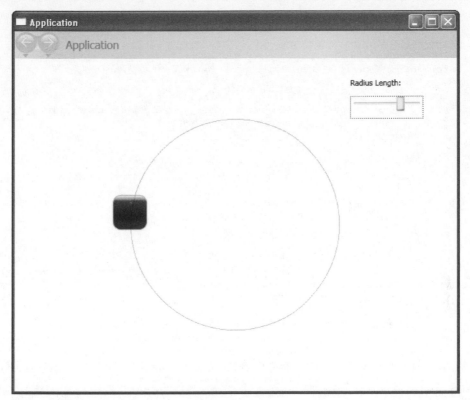

Figure 5-10

This effect could easily be accomplished using a `RotateTransform`; *however, to illustrate the creation of custom frame-by-frame animation, we're going to re-invent the wheel. Hey, it's only an example.*

Interacting with Storyboards

In Expression Blend, each scene can have multiple storyboards. Each storyboard is represented as a new timeline in the Timelines palette.

Storyboards can contain multiple animations, which are treated as a collection of timelines (animations are considered timelines, with interpolation information) with targeting information for each object for which they contain property animations. You can think of a storyboard as a mechanism for organizing and orchestrating all the animations of a particular scene or object.

Within the scene, each timeline you create is added as a resource of the containing control that represents your scene. The following example code illustrates the markup that results whenever a new timeline with animations is created using the Timeline palette of the designer.

```
....
<Grid.Resources>
  <Storyboard x:Key="OnLoaded"/>

  <Storyboard x:Key="BallMotion" d:StoryboardName="BallMotion">

    <DoubleAnimationUsingKeyFrames
Storyboard.TargetProperty="(UIElement.RenderTransform).(TransformGroup.Children)[5]
    .(TranslateTransform.X)" BeginTime="00:00:00"
      Storyboard.TargetName="Ellipse_Copy">

      <SplineDoubleKeyFrame d:KeyEase="Linear;Linear;0.5;0.5;0.5;0.5"
        KeySpline="0.5,0.5,0.5,0.5" Value="0" KeyTime="00:00:00"/>

      <SplineDoubleKeyFrame d:KeyEase="Linear;Linear;0.5;0.5;0.5;0.5"
        KeySpline="0.5,0.5,0.5,0.5" Value="360" KeyTime="00:00:04"/>
    </DoubleAnimationUsingKeyFrames>

    <DoubleAnimationUsingKeyFrames
Storyboard.TargetProperty="(UIElement.RenderTransform).(TransformGroup.Children)[5]
    .(TranslateTransform.Y)" BeginTime="00:00:00"
      Storyboard.TargetName="Ellipse_Copy">

      <SplineDoubleKeyFrame d:KeyEase="Linear;Linear;0.5;0.5;0.5;0.5"
        KeySpline="0.5,0.5,0.5,0.5" Value="0" KeyTime="00:00:00"/>

      <SplineDoubleKeyFrame d:KeyEase="Linear;Linear;0.5;0.5;0.5;0.5"
        KeySpline="0.5,0.5,0.5,0.5" Value="0" KeyTime="00:00:04"/>
    </DoubleAnimationUsingKeyFrames>

  </Storyboard>
</Grid.Resources>
....
```

You can manipulate the playback of the Storyboard timeline through the Timeline Properties palette. From there you can attach the storyboard playback behavior you want to trigger on a property event.

Accessing and manipulating the storyboard in code is a very easy thing to do. Each storyboard is accessible in code by accessing the Resources collection of the container control. To access the desired storyboard, you just index into the collection with the name of the storyboard object as the key. The following code snippet shows how to access a scene storyboard:

```
private void StartStoryboard()
{
  Storyboard myStoryboard = (Storyboard) this.Resources["BallMotion"];
  selectedStoryboard.Begin(this, true);
}
```

The following table lists the basic playback methods. Each method may have its own set of overloads.

Method	Behavior
Begin	Starts the storyboard
Pause	Pauses the storyboard
Resume	Resumes the storyboard from the pause point
Stop	Stops the storyboard playback

Through the use of the storyboard, you can dynamically change the timing behavior of each child animation. For instance, in the designer you may have animated a sequence of property changes on different objects where the timing is spaced at a pre-determined interval. Based on a specified event, you may want to delay or alter the timing of when one property animation ends and the next begins. You can approach this in two ways. You can either separate or manage each set of property changes on two separate storyboards (Timelines in the Designer view), or you can access the child animations of a storyboard and offset the `BeginTime` property of the animation by the desired amount.

```
...
Storyboard selectedStoryboard = (Storyboard) this.Resources["MyStoryboard"];

DoubleAnimationUsingKeyFrames first =
   (DoubleAnimationUsingKeyFrames)selectedStoryboard.Children[2];
DoubleAnimationUsingKeyFrames second =
   (DoubleAnimationUsingKeyFrames)selectedStoryboard.Children[3];

first.BeginTime = TimeSpan.FromSeconds(2);
second.BeginTime = TimeSpan.FromSeconds(2);

selectedStoryboard.Begin(this);
...
```

WPF Drawing API

Expression Blend provides the visual tools required to create and draw objects, eliminating the need for writing large amounts of tedious code. However, there may be times when your application will require dynamic drawing. For example, your application may provide support for drawing and writing, or you may be developing a game where images and objects must be generated at runtime.

Geometry

The Geometry classes are used to define geometrical regions for rendering two-dimensional graphics. They can either define the geometry to be rendered or the hit test and clipping areas.

Geometry objects contain no information regarding how they are to be rendered onscreen. Stroke, Fill, and Opacity cannot be applied to geometry. They contain only the necessary information about the regions within the drawing space they occupy. Each geometry object contains a set of coordinate relations that are used by a drawing or path object to actually render the geometry as a visual element.

An instance of a Geometry class can be used to define any two-dimensional shape. Complex geometries can also be created that define structures of line and curve segments. In fact, the `Path` class is represented by geometry objects

Shapes

Shape classes allow you to introduce 2D geometric shapes into your page or window. The shape classes are much more than just geometry objects in that they take part in creating the rendered display of geometry. Fill, Stroke, and Opacity can be applied to Shape objects as they are actual accessible objects within the WPF scene.

In GDI+ shapes and drawings were rasterized. It was difficult to manipulate a shape or line onscreen. Basically, the GDI+ API allowed you to generate shapes and drawings onscreen but didn't provide the capability to manipulate them once drawn. Finding the position of drawing or shape elements, and where they intercepted each other, was often a painstaking process that required math and elbow grease.

Shapes in WPF are objects that support events and have accessible properties that allow them to be candidates for controls or for the visual elements that make up controls.

Creating a Dynamic Clipping Region with Geometry and Shapes

In this example, we will cover how to use shapes in Expression Blend to create clipping regions and how to dynamically control the clipping region in code.

1. In Expression Blend, select File ⇨ New Project from the menu. From the Project Types view, select the Standard Application (.exe) option and then name the project **PaintDrawExamples**.

2. Add a new page to the project by selecting File ⇨ New from the main menu and then choosing Page from the list of installed templates in the Add New Item dialog box. Name the page **DynamicClipping.xaml** and click OK.

3. In the designer, select and create a new Canvas control from the Library palette. Place the canvas as close to the center of the scene as possible. In the properties panel, modify the height value to 100 and the width value to 436.

4. From the Tools palette, select the Rectangle tool and draw a new rectangle on the scene. In the Properties palette, change the Rectangle's Width and Height values to match that of the Canvas. Click and drag the newly created Rectangle onto the Canvas control. You will be prompted by the Designer to press the Alt key to add the Rectangle as a child control of the Canvas container. Press the Alt key to add it.

5. In the Properties palette, set the `Canvas.Left` and `Canvas.Top` properties of the Rectangle control to 0.

6. Select and create a new Label control from the Library palette. Change the Content property to "This is my clipped space." Add the Label control to the Canvas using the procedure described in the preceding steps. Once the Label has been added, place it relatively in the center of the Rectangle shape. The Canvas and its child elements will become the object that you will clip.

7. Select and create a new Ellipse from the Tools palette. In the Properties palette, modify its Width and Height property to 150. Place the Ellipse on top of the Canvas control roughly in the center.

8. Select the Ellipse shape first and then select the Canvas (the order which you select the elements is important). From the main menu select Tools ➪ Make Clipping Path.

All the work just created should result in the following XAML:

```
<Page
  xmlns="http://schemas.microsoft.com/winfx/2006/xaml/presentation"
  xmlns:x="http://schemas.microsoft.com/winfx/2006/xaml"
  xmlns:mc="http://schemas.openxmlformats.org/markup-compatibility/2006"
  xmlns:d="http://schemas.microsoft.com/expression/interactivedesigner/2006"
  mc:Ignorable="d"
  x:Class="PaintDrawExamples.DynamicClipping"
  x:Name="Page"
  WindowTitle="Page"
  FlowDirection="LeftToRight"
  Width="640"
  Height="480"
  WindowWidth="640"
  WindowHeight="480"
  >
  <Grid
    Background="#FFFFFFFF"
    x:Name="DocumentRoot"
    Width="640"
    Height="480"
    >
    <Grid.Resources>
      <Storyboard x:Key="OnLoaded"/>
    </Grid.Resources>

    <Grid.Triggers>
      <EventTrigger RoutedEvent="FrameworkElement.Loaded">
        <BeginStoryboard x:Name="OnLoaded_BeginStoryboard"
          Storyboard="{DynamicResource OnLoaded}"/>
      </EventTrigger>
    </Grid.Triggers>

    <Grid.ColumnDefinitions>
      <ColumnDefinition/>
    </Grid.ColumnDefinitions>
    <Grid.RowDefinitions>
      <RowDefinition/>
    </Grid.RowDefinitions>
    <Canvas VerticalAlignment="Stretch" Margin="119.5,175,120.5,195" Height="100"
      x:Name="Canvas" Width="436">
      <Canvas.Clip>
        <PathGeometry>
          <PathFigure StartPoint="299,52.5" IsClosed="True" IsFilled="True">
            <BezierSegment IsSmoothJoin="True" Point1="299,93.9213562373095"
              Point2="265.42135623731,127.5" Point3="224,127.5" IsStroked="True"/>
            <BezierSegment IsSmoothJoin="True" Point1="182.57864376269,127.5"
              Point2="149,93.9213562373095" Point3="149,52.5" IsStroked="True"/>
            <BezierSegment IsSmoothJoin="True" Point1="149,11.0786437626905"
              Point2="182.57864376269,-22.5" Point3="224,-22.5" IsStroked="True"/>
            <BezierSegment IsSmoothJoin="True" Point1="265.42135623731,-22.5"
```

```
                   Point2="299,11.0786437626905" Point3="299,52.5" IsStroked="True"/>
           </PathFigure>
         </PathGeometry>
       </Canvas.Clip>
       <Rectangle d:LayoutOverrides="Height" Stroke="{x:Null}" Fill="sc#1,
           0.8597243, 0.805513, 0.805513" VerticalAlignment="Bottom" Width="436"
             Height="100" x:Name="Rectangle" Canvas.Left="0" Canvas.Top="0"/>
       <Label FontSize="30" VerticalAlignment="Stretch" Height="Auto" x:Name="Label"
           Content="This is my clipped space." Canvas.Left="46" Canvas.Top="26"
             d:IsHidden="True"/>
     </Canvas>
   </Grid>
</Page>
```

9. In the .cs code-behind file, add the following using declarations:

```
using System;
using System.Windows;
using System.Windows.Input;
using System.Windows.Media;
```

10. Add the following code into the default constructor below the `InitializeComponent()` method call.

```
this.Canvas.VerticalAlignment = VerticalAlignment.Center;
this.Canvas.HorizontalAlignment = HorizontalAlignment.Center;

CompositionTarget.Rendering += CompositionTarget_Rendering;
```

11. Provide the `CompositionTarget.Rendering` event handler. The following event handler definition will perform the process of accessing the clipping region of the Canvas you create in the designer and will translate its X and Y position relative to the movement of the mouse.

```
private void CompositionTarget_Rendering(object sender, EventArgs e)
{
  Point mousePos = Mouse.GetPosition(this.Canvas);
  Geometry clippingRegion = this.Canvas.Clip;

  TranslateTransform newPos = new TranslateTransform();
  newPos.X = mousePos.X - (this.Canvas.Width / 2);
  newPos.Y = mousePos.Y - (this.Canvas.Height / 2);

  clippingRegion.Transform = newPos;
}
```

12. Build the project in Debug to view the final effect. Figure 5-11 shows the compiled result.

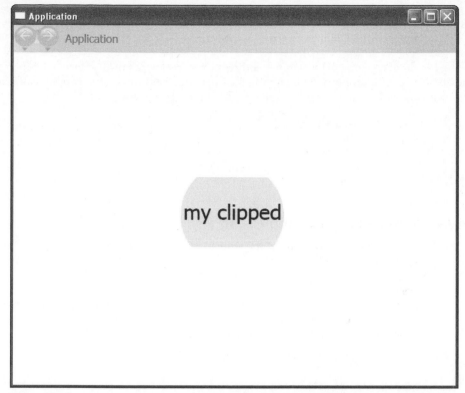

Figure 5-11

Brushes

The WPF brush classes are responsible for painting all elements to the screen. Brushes are quite versatile in that they can be used to create basic fills or complex fills, such as gradients, images, and patterns.

The following table describes the different kinds of brushes and their default behaviors.

Brush Class	Description
SolidColorBrush	Paints a region with solid color.
LinearGradientBrush	Paints a region with a linear gradient.
RadialGradientBrush	Paints a region with a radial gradient.
ImageBrush	Paints a region with an image.
DrawingBrush	Paints a region with a drawing that can include text, images, and shapes.
VisualBrush	Paints a region with a Visual. This could be any UIElement class or ContainerVisual class that is a collection of many Visual objects.

Within the Expression Blend design environment, the Appearance palette enables you to interact with and alter the fill appearance for an object. At design time, Expression Blend will dynamically construct the XAML to represent the fill appearance of an object.

Changing the fill of an element at runtime requires either creating a new instance of a brush and applying the brush to the fill property or modifying the brush that has already been applied as a fill. The following code segment illustrates changing the fill of a rectangle instance:

```
Rectangle rectangle = new Rectangle();
rectangle.Width = 100;
rectangle.Height = 50;

SolidColorBrush brush = new SolidColorBrush(Colors.Black);
rectangle.Fill = brush;
```

Creating a Custom Drawing and Brush Fill

In this example, you will incorporate all of the aforementioned drawing components into one application. The application will allow the user to click on four different points in the scene and, in code, you will generate a new `Path` object and animate it into view.

1. In the PaintDrawExamples project you created in the previous example, create a new page for the project by selecting File ⇨ New Item from the main menu and then selecting Page from the Add New Item dialog box. Name the page **DynamicFill.xaml** and click OK.

2. Open up the DynamicFill.xaml file and modify the markup as follows:

```
<Page
    xmlns="http://schemas.microsoft.com/winfx/2006/xaml/presentation"
    xmlns:x="http://schemas.microsoft.com/winfx/2006/xaml"
    x:Class="PaintDrawExamples.DynamicFill"
    x:Name="Page"
    WindowTitle="Page"
    FlowDirection="LeftToRight"
    Width="640" Height="480"
    WindowWidth="640" WindowHeight="480">

    <Canvas x:Name="LayoutRoot" Background="White"  Width="640" Height="480" />
</Page>
```

This XAML sets the properties of your page and also creates a canvas that you will use to add your dynamically generated elements to.

3. In the code-behind file, add the following `using` directives:

```
using System;
using System.Collections.Generic;
using System.Windows;
using System.Windows.Input;
using System.Windows.Media;
using System.Windows.Media.Animation;
using System.Windows.Shapes;
```

4. Add the following private members to the class definition. The max point count (which you can alter later after the example) will determine at what point you stop counting user clicks to define a path shape. The points generic list will keep track of each point that is clicked.

```
private int maxPointCount = 4;
private List<Point> points = new List<Point>();
```

5. Add the following line of code to the default constructor below the `InitializeComponent` method call. This will attach an event handler that you will define next to the `MouseDown` event.

```
this.LayoutRoot.MouseDown += new MouseButtonEventHandler(MouseDownHandler);
```

6. Before you define your event handling procedure for each mouse click, you need a couple of support methods. The first support method, `DrawPoint`, dynamically creates a new circular path that visually shows where the user has currently clicked in the cycle.

```
private void DrawPoint(Point point)
{
  EllipseGeometry visualPoint = new EllipseGeometry(
       new Point(point.X, point.Y), 3, 3
  );

  Path visualPointPath = new Path();
  visualPointPath.Data = visualPoint;
  visualPointPath.Stroke = Brushes.Gray;

  this.LayoutRoot.Children.Add(visualPointPath);
}
```

7. The `AnimateFill` method will take a `PathGeometry` that is created when the user clicks one of the four points, and create a `Path` object that will visually represent the geometry and animate it. Using the same technique for creating animation in code that you used earlier, you create a double animation to fade in your `Path` shape to a random opacity.

```
private void AnimateFill(PathGeometry pathLines)
{
    Path path = new Path();
    path.Data = pathLines;
    path.Fill = Brushes.Blue;
    path.Stroke = Brushes.DarkBlue;
    this.LayoutRoot.Children.Add(path);

    DoubleAnimation moveAnimation = new DoubleAnimation();
    moveAnimation.From = 0;
    moveAnimation.To = (new Random()).NextDouble();
    moveAnimation.Duration = new Duration(TimeSpan.FromSeconds(.5));
    moveAnimation.DecelerationRatio = .5;

    path.BeginAnimation(Shape.OpacityProperty, moveAnimation);
}
```

8. You need to define the actions that must be performed when a user clicks on a point in the scene. In the following event handler definition, you get the point that the user clicked relative to the scene and add it to your collection of points. If four points have been selected, you create a new `PathGeometry` class and create a `PathFigure` with a collection of segments that define the shape created by your four points. Once the figure is created, you add it to the `PathGeometry`, call the `AnimateFill()` method to create your shape, and then clear the points collection for the next series.

```
private void MouseDownHandler(object sender, MouseButtonEventArgs e)
{
  Point mousePos = Mouse.GetPosition(this);
  points.Add(new Point(mousePos.X, mousePos.Y));

  // Draw visual point to screen
  DrawPoint(mousePos);

  if (points.Count == maxPointCount)
  {
    PathGeometry pathLines = new PathGeometry();
    PathFigure figure = new PathFigure();
    figure.StartPoint = points[0];

    for (int i = 1; i <= points.Count; i++)
      figure.Segments.Add(
      new LineSegment(points[i % points.Count], true)
      );

    pathLines.Figures.Add(figure);

    // Animate in the shape
    AnimateFill(pathLines);

    // Clear out the points
    points.Clear();
  }
}
```

9. Build the project in Debug to view the hosted control in WPF. Figure 5-12 shows the compiled result.

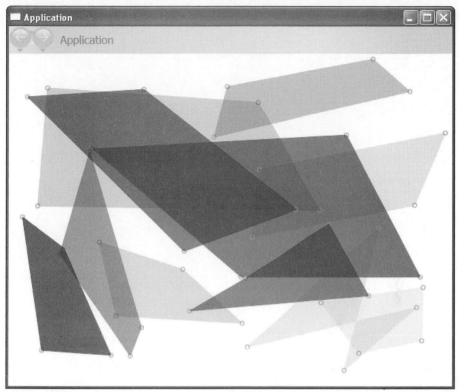

Figure 5-12

Summary

Expression Blend allows the designer/developer to quickly and easily create custom controls and graphical elements visually while offering the capability to add programmatic activity to a WPF application page or window. In this chapter, you worked with the WPF API in concert with the workflow provided by Expression Blend and Visual Studio 2005. The chapter covered the following:

❑   Handling user input and adding events and event handlers

❑   Creating and controlling animation programmatically by accessing the storyboard and using the Animation API

❑   Creating custom animation on a per-frame basis using the `CompositionTarget` class

❑   Creating real-time drawings with the 2D drawing API

Special Effects

6

WPF provides built-in functionality that you can use to create graphically rich applications. Bitmap effects, transformations, a wide variety of brushes, transparency, and animation provide a vast toolset for creating unique special effects. Furthermore, you can combine any or all of these to create advanced special effects to enhance the look and feel of your applications.

In WPF, a brush is more than just a means of applying color to pixels. WPF provides a set of brushes that allow you to paint with color, gradient, image, drawing, and even visual objects as output. Painting with gradients provides you with a way to present glass effects or the illusion of depth and a third dimension. Painting with an image provides a means to stretch, tile, or fill an area with a specified bitmap. Most interesting in WPF is the ability to paint an area with any visual object defined in the application. The `VisualBrush` allows you to fill an area with a visual from another part of the applications visual tree. You can use this to create grand illusions of reflection or magnification in your UI. WPF provides a set of bitmap effects and transformations that you can apply to your elements. Specifically, the bitmap effects offer you a means to apply filters to your elements. Using bitmap effects you can, for example, apply drop shadows and blurring to graphical elements. Transformations, on the other hand, provide the opportunity to adjust the coordinates of an element. Using transformations, you can scale, skew, move, and rotate elements.

Using brushes, bitmap effects, and transformations in conjunction with animation, you will find yourself truly equipped with a powerful arsenal for creating visually stunning applications. For instance, if desired you could rotate an element that has a drop shadow applied by first using a transform in response to an event trigger fired by a button and then by using animation to control the speed of the rotation. Furthermore, you could accomplish all of this directly in XAML, if desired. This is powerful stuff!

In this chapter, you explore each of the concepts mentioned thus far, and a few others as well. Specifically, you will learn about the following:

❑   Brushes
❑   Bitmap effects

❑ Transformations

❑ Opacity masks

❑ Combining effects

As you move through the chapter, your ability to create special effects will increase as you explore much of what is available to you in WPF. Finally, with all of the basics under your belt, you'll combine these features to create some advanced special effects in WPF.

Brushes

In WPF, brushes are responsible for painting each visual element. If an element is visible on a screen, it is because a brush painted it. Brushes are responsible for painting both the `Fill` and `Stroke` of a visual element. Control properties, such as `Background`, `Foreground`, and `Border`, all use a brush as a mechanism to paint. Brushes are capable of painting solid colors, gradients, images, drawings, and even other visual objects.

WPF provides a number of brush classes you can use to paint pixels, all of which ultimately derive from the `Brush` base class. The brush classes reside in the `System.Windows.Media` namespace. The WPF framework provides six types of brushes you can use: `SolidColorBrush`, `LinearGradientBrush`, `RadialGradientBrush`, `DrawingBrush`, `ImageBrush`, and `VisualBrush`. The table that follows illustrates these brushes and the functionality provided by each.

Brush	Description
SolidColorBrush	Paints a specific area of the screen with a solid color.
LinearGradientBrush	Paints a specific area of the screen with a linear gradient.
RadialGradientBrush	Paints a specific area of the screen with a radial gradient.
ImageBrush	Paints a specific area of the screen with an image.
DrawingBrush	Paints a specific area of the screen with a custom drawing.
VisualBrush	Paints a specific area of the screen with an object that derives from `Visual`.

As the preceding table illustrates, a brush can indeed provide output other than simply solid colors. Utilizing the various brushes available, you can create some interesting effects such as gradient and lighting effects, tiled backgrounds, thumbnail views, and visual reflection, among others. Brushes, along with other topics covered in this chapter, make up the primary toolset you can use to create a great UI.

SolidColorBrush

The most common brush, and the simplest to use, is the `SolidColorBrush`. A `SolidColorBrush` simply paints a specific area of the screen with a solid color. But don't confuse a brush with a color: In WPF they are not the same. A brush is an object that tells the system to paint specific pixels with a specified output defined by the brush. A `SolidColorBrush` paints a color to a specific area of the screen, such as Red, DarkRed, or even PapayaWhip. The output for a `SolidColorBrush` is a `Color` whereas the output for an `ImageBrush` is an `Image`.

A `SolidColorBrush` can be defined by simply providing a value for its `Color` property. In WPF, you can define color in a number of ways, such as declaring RGB or ARGB values, using hexadecimal notation, or by specifying a predefined color. In addition, you can supply an alpha value for the `Color` you define, providing transparency. (That explains the *A* in ARGB.) The `Brush` class also exposes an `Opacity` property you can use to define an alpha value for a brush.

Additionally, WPF also provides some handy classes for working with brushes and colors. The `Brushes` class, for example, exposes a set of predefined brushes based on solid colors. This provides a syntactical shortcut you can use for creating common solid color brushes. Similarly, the `Colors` class exposes a set of predefined colors.

Here's a quick example in which you can define a `SolidColorBrush` using the different methods just described:

```
using System.Windows;
using System.Windows.Documents;
using System.Windows.Controls;
using System.Windows.Media;
using System.Windows.Shapes;

namespace WPFBrushes
{

  public partial class SolidColorBrushInCode : System.Windows.Window
  {

    public SolidColorBrushInCode()
    {

      InitializeComponent();

      this.Width = 600;
      this.Title = "SolidColorBrush Definition";

      StackPanel sp = new StackPanel();
      sp.Margin = new Thickness(4.0);
      sp.HorizontalAlignment = HorizontalAlignment.Left;
      sp.Orientation = Orientation.Vertical;

      TextBlock tb1 = new TextBlock(new Run(@"Predefined Brush [ .Fill =
        Brushes.Red; ]"));
      Rectangle rect1 = new Rectangle();
      rect1.HorizontalAlignment = HorizontalAlignment.Left;
      rect1.Width = 60;
      rect1.Height = 20;
      rect1.Fill = Brushes.Red;

      TextBlock tb2 = new TextBlock(new Run(@"Brush from Predefined Color [ .Fill =
        new SolidColorBrush(Colors.Green); ]"));
```

```
Rectangle rect2 = new Rectangle();
rect2.HorizontalAlignment = HorizontalAlignment.Left;
rect2.Width = 60;
rect2.Height = 20;
rect2.Fill = new SolidColorBrush(Colors.Green);

TextBlock tb3 = new TextBlock(new Run(@"Brush from RGB Color [ .Fill = new
    SolidColorBrush(Color.FromRgb(0, 0, 255)); ]"));
Rectangle rect3 = new Rectangle();
rect3.HorizontalAlignment = HorizontalAlignment.Left;
rect3.Width = 60;
rect3.Height = 20;
rect3.Fill = new SolidColorBrush(Color.FromRgb(0, 0, 255));

TextBlock tb4 = new TextBlock(new Run(@"Brush from ARGB Color [ .Fill = new
    SolidColorBrush(Color.FromArgb(100, 0, 0, 255)); ]"));
Rectangle rect4 = new Rectangle();
rect4.HorizontalAlignment = HorizontalAlignment.Left;
rect4.Width = 60;
rect4.Height = 20;
rect4.Fill = new SolidColorBrush(Color.FromArgb(100, 0, 0, 255));

TextBlock tb5 = new TextBlock(new Run(@"Brush from Hex Color [ .Fill = new
    SolidColorBrush((Color)ColorConverter.ConvertFromString(""#FFFFEFD5""));
    ]"));
Rectangle rect5 = new Rectangle();
rect5.HorizontalAlignment = HorizontalAlignment.Left;
rect5.Width = 60;
rect5.Height = 20;
rect5.Fill = new
    SolidColorBrush((Color)ColorConverter.ConvertFromString("#FFFFEFD5"));

sp.Children.Add(tb1);
sp.Children.Add(rect1);
sp.Children.Add(tb2);
sp.Children.Add(rect2);
sp.Children.Add(tb3);
sp.Children.Add(rect3);
sp.Children.Add(tb4);
sp.Children.Add(rect4);
sp.Children.Add(tb5);
sp.Children.Add(rect5);

this.Content = sp;

    }

  }
}
```

In the preceding code, you create five rectangles and define a `SolidColorBrush` for each of them:

❑   In `rect1`, you use a predefined `SolidColorBrush` from the `Brushes` class to define a red brush.

❑   For `rect2`, you create a new instance of a `SolidColorBrush` and pass a predefined color from the `Colors` class in the constructor.

❑ For `rect3`, you use the method `ColorFromRgb` of the `Color` class to create a color from RGB values you've supplied, which you pass to the constructor of your `SolidColorBrush`.

❑ In `rect4`, you'll do the same thing, only in this case you'll supply an alpha channel value to set the color transparency to 100. The range for alpha is 0–255, with zero being fully transparent (no color value).

❑ For `rect5`, you create a `Color` from a hexadecimal string representation using a `TypeConverter` class provided by WPF, the `ColorConverter`.

You typically wouldn't use hexadecimal notation and a TypeConverter in procedural code as it requires unnecessary overhead. The TypeConverter is really provided for using hexadecimal notation in XAML.

Figure 6-1 illustrates the results of running the sample application.

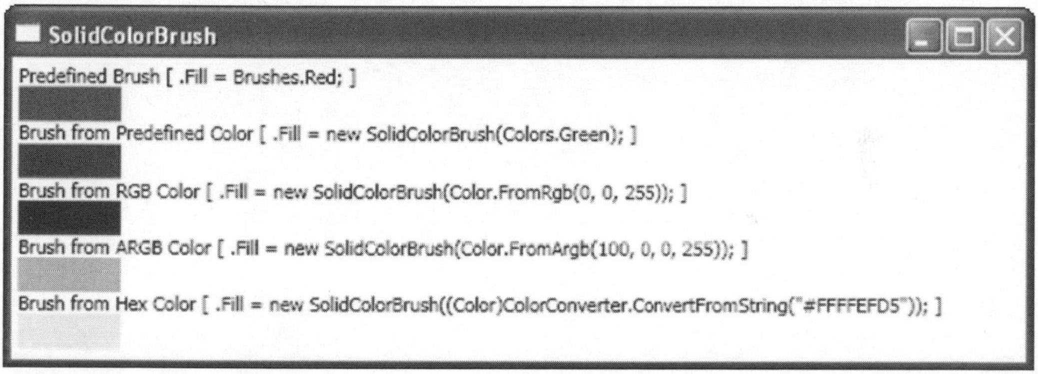

Figure 6-1

Of course, you can just as easily define and apply brushes using XAML. The following example is the XAML equivalent of the last example and will yield the same results illustrated in Figure 6-1.

```xaml
<Window x:Class="WPFBrushes.SolidColorBrushInXAML"
  xmlns="http://schemas.microsoft.com/winfx/2006/xaml/presentation"
  xmlns:x="http://schemas.microsoft.com/winfx/2006/xaml"
  Title="SolidColorBrush" Height="300" Width="600"
  >
<StackPanel Margin="4" Orientation="Vertical" HorizontalAlignment="Left">

  <TextBlock Text="Predefined Brush [ .Fill = Brushes.Red; ]"/>
  <Rectangle HorizontalAlignment="Left" Width="60" Height="20" Fill="Red"/>

  <TextBlock Text="Brush from Predefined Color [ .Fill = new
    SolidColorBrush(Colors.Green); ]"/>
  <Rectangle HorizontalAlignment="Left" Width="60" Height="20">
    <Rectangle.Fill>
      <SolidColorBrush Color="Green"/>
    </Rectangle.Fill>
  </Rectangle>

  <TextBlock Text="Brush from RGB Color [ .Fill = new
    SolidColorBrush(Color.FromRgb(0, 0, 255)); ]"/>
```

```
<Rectangle HorizontalAlignment="Left" Width="60" Height="20">
  <Rectangle.Fill>
    <SolidColorBrush>
      <SolidColorBrush.Color>
        <Color A="255" R="0" G="0" B="255" />
      </SolidColorBrush.Color>
    </SolidColorBrush>
  </Rectangle.Fill>
</Rectangle>

<TextBlock Text="Brush from ARGB Color [ .Fill = new
  SolidColorBrush(Color.FromArgb(100, 0, 0, 255)); ]"/>
<Rectangle HorizontalAlignment="Left" Width="60" Height="20">
  <Rectangle.Fill>
    <SolidColorBrush>
      <SolidColorBrush.Color>
        <Color A="100" R="0" G="0" B="255" />
      </SolidColorBrush.Color>
    </SolidColorBrush>
  </Rectangle.Fill>
</Rectangle>

<TextBlock Text="Brush from Hex Color [ .Fill = new
  SolidColorBrush((Color)ColorConverter.ConvertFromString('#FFFFEFD5')); ]"/>
<Rectangle HorizontalAlignment="Left" Width="60" Height="20" Fill="#FFFFEFD5"/>

</StackPanel>
</Window>
```

Before you move on, take a quick look at defining a color's alpha channel. The alpha channel specifies the level of transparency for a color. The values are 0–255, with zero being fully transparent. The following example creates a blue rectangle with white grid lines, and with three overlapping red rectangles. Each of the red rectangles sets a different value for transparency.

```
<Window x:Class="WPFBrushes.ColorAndAlpha"
  xmlns="http://schemas.microsoft.com/winfx/2006/xaml/presentation"
  xmlns:x="http://schemas.microsoft.com/winfx/2006/xaml"
  Title="Alpha Channel" Height="300" Width="300"
  >
<Grid VerticalAlignment="Center" HorizontalAlignment="Center">

<Rectangle Height="200" Width="200">
  <Rectangle.Fill>
    <DrawingBrush Viewport="0,0,10,10" ViewportUnits="Absolute" TileMode="Tile">
      <DrawingBrush.Drawing>
        <DrawingGroup>
          <GeometryDrawing Brush="Blue">
            <GeometryDrawing.Geometry>
              <RectangleGeometry Rect="0,0,10,10" />
            </GeometryDrawing.Geometry>
          </GeometryDrawing>
          <GeometryDrawing Brush="#CCCCFF" Geometry="M0,10 L 0,0 10,0
            10,1 1,1 1,10Z">
```

```
            </GeometryDrawing>
          </DrawingGroup>
        </DrawingBrush.Drawing>
      </DrawingBrush>
    </Rectangle.Fill>
  </Rectangle>

  <StackPanel Orientation="Horizontal" VerticalAlignment="Center"
    HorizontalAlignment="Center">

  <Rectangle Height="50" Width="50" Stroke="Black" StrokeThickness="4" Margin="4">
    <Rectangle.Fill>
      <SolidColorBrush>
        <SolidColorBrush.Color>
          <Color A="0" R="255" G="0" B="0"/>
        </SolidColorBrush.Color>
      </SolidColorBrush>
    </Rectangle.Fill>
  </Rectangle>

  <Rectangle Height="50" Width="50" Stroke="Black" StrokeThickness="4" Margin="4">
    <Rectangle.Fill>
      <SolidColorBrush>
        <SolidColorBrush.Color>
          <Color A="125" R="255" G="0" B="0"/>
        </SolidColorBrush.Color>
      </SolidColorBrush>
    </Rectangle.Fill>
  </Rectangle>

  <Rectangle Height="50" Width="50" Stroke="Black" StrokeThickness="4" Margin="4">
    <Rectangle.Fill>
      <SolidColorBrush>
        <SolidColorBrush.Color>
          <Color A="255" R="255" G="0" B="0"/>
        </SolidColorBrush.Color>
      </SolidColorBrush>
    </Rectangle.Fill>
  </Rectangle>

  </StackPanel>

  </Grid>

</Window>
```

The example code defines a large blue rectangle with a grid pattern you'll use as a background so you can see the opacity of each brush color. Next, place three smaller red rectangles over the grid pattern and change the alpha channel value for each color specified. Each of the red rectangles sets a different value for alpha as follows: 0, 125, and 255. Figure 6-2 illustrates the results.

When you run the example, you can see that the first rectangle shows none of the red color value. Its alpha value is zero, so it is fully transparent. The second rectangle has an alpha value of 125, and therefore is semi-transparent. The last rectangle has an alpha value of 255, so there is no transparency.

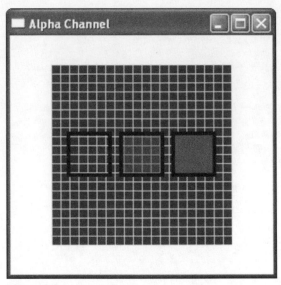

Figure 6-2

GradientBrush

Now that you understand the roles of a brush and colors in WPF, and the SolidColorBrush in particular, you can take a look at gradient brushes. Gradient brushes paint an area with multiple colors. The colors blend together at specific points you specify in your brush definition. The points line up along an axis, referred to as the gradient-axis, the direction of which you also define. You can use gradients to achieve visually appealing effects, such as metal, glass, water, and shadows, or even to present the illusion of depth or a third dimension. WPF provides two flavors of gradient brushes that not surprisingly derive from the GradientBrush base class: LinearGradientBrush and RadialGradientBrush.

As its name implies, the LinearGradientBrush follows a linear axis. You can define the direction of the axis to achieve vertical, horizontal, or diagonal gradients. The gradient-axis is defined by two points, a StartPoint and an EndPoint. These points map to a 1 × 1 matrix. So a StartPoint of (0,0) and an EndPoint of (1,1) will produce a diagonal gradient, while a StartPoint of (0,0.5) and an EndPoint of (1,0.5) will product a horizontal gradient. Along the axis you define a series of GradientStop objects, which are points on the axis where you want colors to blend and transition to other colors. You can define as many GradientStop objects as you like. A GradientStop has two properties of interest: Color and Offset. The Offset property defines a distance, ranging from 0 to 1, from the start point of the axis, from which the color specified in the Color property should begin.

The RadialGradientBrush is defined in a similar fashion; however, this brush blends colors in a radial pattern. A radial gradient is defined as a circle. The axis of the RadialGradientBrush starts from a point of origin you can define called the GradientOrigin and runs to the outer edge of the circle, the axis end point. You define GradientStop objects along the gradient-axis, just as you do for a LinearGradientBrush. You can define the circle of the gradient by specifying the Center, RadiusX, and RadiusY properties. The Center property specifies the center of the circle. The RadiusX and RadiusY properties specify the distance from center to the outer edge of the circle on the X and Y axis. This means you don't have to define a perfect circle: It could be an ellipse.

Now, create an example using the LinearGradientBrush and RadialGradientBrush.

```xml
<Window x:Class="WPFBrushes.GradientBrushInXAML"
  xmlns="http://schemas.microsoft.com/winfx/2006/xaml/presentation"
  xmlns:x="http://schemas.microsoft.com/winfx/2006/xaml"
  Title="Gradient Brushes" Height="300" Width="300"
  >
  <Grid>
    <Grid.RowDefinitions>
      <RowDefinition/>
      <RowDefinition/>
    </Grid.RowDefinitions>
    <Grid.ColumnDefinitions>
      <ColumnDefinition/>
      <ColumnDefinition/>
    </Grid.ColumnDefinitions>

    <Rectangle Grid.Row="0" Grid.Column="0" Width="100" Height="100"
      StrokeThickness="4" Margin="4">
      <Rectangle.Fill>
        <LinearGradientBrush>
          <GradientStop Color="Gray" Offset=".3"/>
          <GradientStop Color="Black" Offset=".4"/>
          <GradientStop Color="Gray" Offset=".8"/>
        </LinearGradientBrush>
      </Rectangle.Fill>
      <Rectangle.Stroke>
        <SolidColorBrush Color="Blue"/>
      </Rectangle.Stroke>
    </Rectangle>

    <Rectangle Grid.Row="0" Grid.Column="1"  Width="100" Height="100"
      StrokeThickness="8" Margin="4">
      <Rectangle.Fill>
        <LinearGradientBrush StartPoint="0.5,0" EndPoint="0.5,1">
          <GradientStop Color="Gray" Offset=".3"/>
          <GradientStop Color="Black" Offset=".4"/>
          <GradientStop Color="Gray" Offset=".8"/>
        </LinearGradientBrush>
      </Rectangle.Fill>
      <Rectangle.Stroke>
        <LinearGradientBrush StartPoint="0,0" EndPoint="0,1">
          <GradientStop Color="Red" Offset=".3"/>
          <GradientStop Color="Blue" Offset=".4"/>
        </LinearGradientBrush>
      </Rectangle.Stroke>
    </Rectangle>

    <Rectangle Grid.Row="1" Grid.Column="0"  Width="100" Height="100"
      StrokeThickness="4" Margin="4">
      <Rectangle.Fill>
        <RadialGradientBrush GradientOrigin="0.5,0.5" Center="0.5,0.5"
          RadiusX="0.5" RadiusY="0.5">
          <GradientStop Color="Black" Offset="0" />
```

```
              <GradientStop Color="Gray" Offset="0.45" />
              <GradientStop Color="Black" Offset="0.85" />
          </RadialGradientBrush>
        </Rectangle.Fill>
        <Rectangle.Stroke>
          <SolidColorBrush Color="Blue"/>
        </Rectangle.Stroke>
      </Rectangle>

      <Rectangle Grid.Row="1" Grid.Column="1"  Width="100" Height="100"
        StrokeThickness="8" Margin="4">
        <Rectangle.Fill>
          <RadialGradientBrush GradientOrigin="0.5,0.5" Center="0.5,0.5"
            RadiusX="0.5" RadiusY="0.5">
            <GradientStop Color="Red" Offset="0" />
            <GradientStop Color="Green" Offset="0.45" />
            <GradientStop Color="Yellow" Offset="0.85" />
          </RadialGradientBrush>
        </Rectangle.Fill>
        <Rectangle.Stroke>
          <RadialGradientBrush GradientOrigin="0.5,0.5" Center="0.5,0.5"
            RadiusX="0.5" RadiusY="0.5">
            <GradientStop Color="Black" Offset="0.95" />
            <GradientStop Color="Gray" Offset="0.95" />
          </RadialGradientBrush>
        </Rectangle.Stroke>
      </Rectangle>

    </Grid>
  </Window>
```

The first two rectangles are filled by LinearGradientBrush objects, the first along a diagonal gradient-axis, and the second along a horizontal gradient-axis. The second rectangle also uses a LinearGradientBrush to fill its Stroke property with red and blue. The last two rectangles are filled by a RadialGradientBrush. The second rectangle uses a RadialGradientBrush to fill its Stroke property, creating an interesting pattern. Figure 6-3 illustrates the results of this example.

The GradientBrush examples presented thus far are intended to illustrate how LinearGradientBrush and RadialGradientBrush objects can be defined. The best way to get to know gradient brushes and the various properties covered in the chapter so far is to dive in and start using them. In the case of a LinearGradientBrush, change the StartPoint and EndPoint properties to get a feel for the gradient axis. Add variable numbers of GradientStops and play with the Color and Offset properties of each to see the results and how the colors transition. For a RadialGradientBrush, change the size of the circle and point of origin to get a feel for the many options available to you.

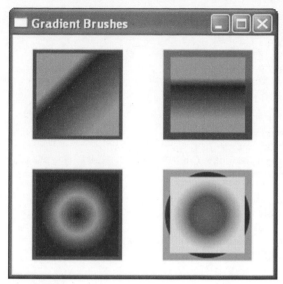

Figure 6-3

ImageBrush

The `ImageBrush` allows you to specify an image to be painted to an output area. Quite simply, the `ImageBrush` paints a specified area with its output, a bitmap. `ImageBrush` derives from `TileBrush`, so a pattern can be specified based on the image. Using the `ImageBrush`, you can specify an image to be used as the background of a button as follows:

```xml
<Window x:Class="WPFBrushes.ImageBrushInXAML"
  xmlns="http://schemas.microsoft.com/winfx/2006/xaml/presentation"
  xmlns:x="http://schemas.microsoft.com/winfx/2006/xaml"
  Title="ImageBrush" Height="425" Width="300"
  >

<StackPanel Margin="4">

  <StackPanel.Resources>
    <Style TargetType="Button">
      <Setter Property="Foreground" Value="White"/>
      <Setter Property="FontWeight" Value="DemiBold"/>
      <Setter Property="FontSize" Value="18"/>
      <Setter Property="Width" Value="250"/>
      <Setter Property="Height" Value="65"/>
      <Setter Property="Margin" Value="4"/>
    </Style>
  </StackPanel.Resources>

  <Button Content="FILL">
    <Button.Background>
      <ImageBrush ImageSource="Images/Flower.jpg" Stretch="Fill"/>
```

```
        </Button.Background>
      </Button>

      <Button Content="FILL + OPACITY">
        <Button.Background>
          <ImageBrush ImageSource="Images/Flower.jpg" Stretch="Fill" Opacity=".25"/>
        </Button.Background>
      </Button>

      <Button Content="UNIFORM">
        <Button.Background>
          <ImageBrush ImageSource="Images/Flower.jpg" Stretch="Uniform"/>
        </Button.Background>
      </Button>

      <Button Content="NONE">
        <Button.Background>
          <ImageBrush ImageSource="Images/Flower.jpg" Stretch="None"/>
        </Button.Background>
      </Button>

      <Button Content="UNIFORM TO FILL">
        <Button.Background>
          <ImageBrush ImageSource="Images/Flower.jpg" Stretch="UniformToFill"/>
        </Button.Background>
      </Button>

    </StackPanel>

  </Window>
```

The preceding code defined five buttons. For each button, an ImageBrush was defined in order to be used for setting the button's Background property. Also, the ImageSource property of each Brush was set to point at an image resource defined in your Visual Studio project. (Be sure to set the Build Action of the image to Resource.) Additionally, the Stretch property of each ImageBrush was set differently, in order to illustrate each of the values of the stretch enumeration. Figure 6-4 illustrates the results of running the application.

For the first button, setting the Stretch property of your ImageBrush to Fill will stretch the image to fill the button's background. By default, the ImageBrush will stretch an image to fill its output area. In the second button, add an Opacity value of .25 to your ImageBrush. (All brushes expose an Opacity property.) In the third button, set the Stretch property to Uniform. Uniform will maintain the image ratio, but make sure to resize the image to fit into the buttons content area. In the fourth button, set the Stretch property to None, which has the effect of preserving the original image size and centering it in the output content area. In the last button, set the Stretch property to UniformToFill, which resizes the image to best-fit while preserving the original image ratio. In this case, the best-fit is still larger than the content area of the button, so the image is essentially clipped.

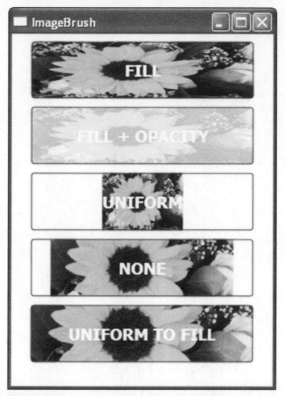

Figure 6-4

DrawingBrush

A DrawingBrush paints a specified area with a Drawing object. The Drawing class represents a two-dimensional drawing and is the base class for other drawing objects, including GeometryDrawing, GlyphRunDrawing, ImageDrawing, and VideoDrawing. The GeometryDrawing class allows you to define and render shapes with a specified Fill and Stroke, and the GlyphRunDrawing supports text operations. The latter two are self-explanatory. So, because the output of a DrawingBrush is a Drawing object, and because these various objects derive from Drawing, this means that a drawing brush can paint shapes, text, images, and video.

Additionally, one other class derives from Drawing, the DrawingGroup class. The DrawingGroup class allows you to group multiple Drawing objects together in order to create a composite Drawing object.

The following example applies a DrawingBrush to the background of a button. You will now create a Drawing using a GeometryDrawing object.

```
<Window x:Class="WPFBrushes.DrawingBrushInXAML"
  xmlns="http://schemas.microsoft.com/winfx/2006/xaml/presentation"
  xmlns:x="http://schemas.microsoft.com/winfx/2006/xaml"
  Title="DrawingBrush" Height="300" Width="300"
```

```
>

<Window.Resources>
  <DrawingBrush x:Key="MyCustomDrawing">
    <DrawingBrush.Drawing>
      <GeometryDrawing Brush="Red">
        <GeometryDrawing.Geometry>
          <GeometryGroup>
            <EllipseGeometry RadiusX="22" RadiusY="25" Center="25,50" />
            <EllipseGeometry RadiusX="22" RadiusY="55" Center="50,50" />
          </GeometryGroup>
        </GeometryDrawing.Geometry>
        <GeometryDrawing.Pen>
          <Pen Thickness="1.5" Brush="LightBlue" />
        </GeometryDrawing.Pen>
      </GeometryDrawing>
    </DrawingBrush.Drawing>
  </DrawingBrush>
</Window.Resources>

<Grid>
  <Button Name="MyVisual" Content="DrawingBrush" Height="125" Width="275"
    Background="{StaticResource MyCustomDrawing}"/>
</Grid>

</Window>
```

The previous example uses a `DrawingBrush` to define the background of a button. In this example, you created your drawing as a resource, but you don't have to — this is just for convenience should you want to reuse this drawing elsewhere. Here, simply use a couple of `EllipseGeometry` classes to define a couple of shapes in a `GeometryDrawing`. The `GeometryDrawing` object is the `Drawing` that will be used by the `DrawingBrush` you define.

Figure 6-5 illustrates the results of running the example.

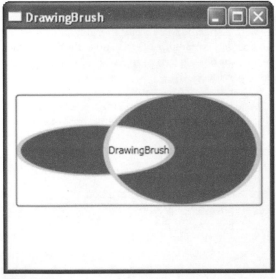

Figure 6-5

The DrawingBrush is quite flexible and very powerful. It allows you to paint with many low-level objects from the WPF framework. These objects are not derivatives of UIElement, so they do not participate in the layout system, which is why they are so lightweight.

VisualBrush

The VisualBrush paints an area with any object that derives from Visual. Any visual element you specify, along with the children of that element, will be output by the VisualBrush. You can apply transformations to the VisualBrush in order to add additional effects if you choose. Note that the VisualBrush is "copying" the visual tree of an element, not the transformations, animations, events, and so on, which are associated with that element.

```xml
<Window x:Class="WPFBrushes.VisualBrushInXAML"
  xmlns="http://schemas.microsoft.com/winfx/2006/xaml/presentation"
  xmlns:x="http://schemas.microsoft.com/winfx/2006/xaml"
  Title="VisualBrush" Height="500" Width="300"
  >

<Window.Resources>
  <DrawingBrush x:Key="MyCustomDrawing">
    <DrawingBrush.Drawing>
      <GeometryDrawing Brush="Red">
        <GeometryDrawing.Geometry>
          <GeometryGroup>
            <EllipseGeometry RadiusX="22" RadiusY="25" Center="25,50" />
            <EllipseGeometry RadiusX="22" RadiusY="55" Center="50,50" />
          </GeometryGroup>
        </GeometryDrawing.Geometry>
        <GeometryDrawing.Pen>
          <Pen Thickness="1.5" Brush="LightBlue" />
        </GeometryDrawing.Pen>
      </GeometryDrawing>
    </DrawingBrush.Drawing>
  </DrawingBrush>
</Window.Resources>

<Grid>
  <StackPanel Margin="4,4,4,4">

    <TextBlock Margin="4,4,4,4">Source Visual:</TextBlock>
    <Button Content="DrawingBrush" Height="125" Width="275" Name="MyVisual"
      Background="{StaticResource MyCustomDrawing}"/>

    <TextBlock Margin="4,4,4,4">VisualBrush:</TextBlock>
    <Button Foreground="Blue" Height="125" Width="275">
      <Button.Background>
        <VisualBrush Visual="{Binding ElementName=MyVisual}"/>
      </Button.Background>
    </Button>

    <TextBlock Margin="4,4,4,4">Tiled VisualBrush:</TextBlock>
    <Button Foreground="Blue" Height="125" Width="275">
      <Button.Background>
        <VisualBrush Visual="{Binding ElementName=MyVisual}"
```

```
                TileMode="Tile">
                <VisualBrush.Transform>
                  <ScaleTransform ScaleX=".25" ScaleY=".25" CenterX=".5" CenterY=".5"/>
                </VisualBrush.Transform>
              </VisualBrush>
            </Button.Background>
          </Button>

      </StackPanel>
    </Grid>
  </Window>
```

The previous example extends the DrawingBrush example you created previously. What you are doing here is adding two more buttons below the original button. Each of these new buttons uses a VisualBrush to paint its background. In this example, the second button simply uses the VisualBrush to essentially "copy" the first button and use it as its background. The third button does the same, only this time scales the "copy" to 25 percent and then tiles its background. The scaling is achieved using a ScaleTransform, which you'll get to know later in this chapter. Figure 6-6 illustrates the results of running the example.

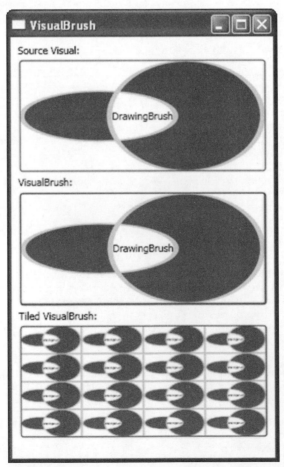

Figure 6-6

The background for the bottom two buttons is created using a `VisualBrush`. By default, when you mouse over a button, the button is highlighted yellow. Notice that if you mouse over the first button, the background of the other buttons becomes highlighted as well. In fact, in the third button, each of the tiles of the `VisualBrush` are highlighted. This is because the `VisualBrush` "copies" the entire visual tree of its source object. Part of the button's visual tree is the border and the event trigger associated with it.

The `VisualBrush` is extremely powerful and opens the door for creating lots of special effects. For example, there are already a lot of examples on the Internet of using a `VisualBrush` to achieve a reflection effect. You will see how to use a `VisualBrush` later in this chapter in the Bouncing Ball example.

Bitmap Effects

WPF bitmap effects allow you to add artistic filters to your visual elements such as blurring, drop shadows, and glows. If you're a designer, you can think of these as blending options. These effects can be applied to any `Visual` or `UIElement` in the WPF Framework. `UIElement` exposes a `BitmapEffect` property, whereas `Visual` exposes a `VisualBitmapEffect` property. Both of these properties accept a `BitmapEffect` object as a value.

Bitmap effects are classes in the WPF framework that derive from `BitmapEffect` base class. These are found in the `System.Windows.Media.Effects` namespace. Currently, the WPF Framework provides six flavors of bitmap effects, as illustrated in the table that follows.

Bitmap Effect	Description
BevelBitmapEffect	Creates a raised surface effect on an element.
BlurBitmapEffect	Creates a blurring effect on an element.
DropShadowBitmapEffect	Creates a shadow behind an element.
EmbossedBitmapEffect	Creates an illusion of depth on an element.
OuterGlowBitmapEffect	Creates a glowing effect around the perimeter of an element.
BitmapEffectGroup	Allows multiple effects to be applied to a `BitmapEffect` property.

A bitmap effect accepts a visual element as input, applies the effect, and produces a graphical result. Bitmap effects are software rendered and, therefore, can be expensive for large visual objects. Some effects work better on vector content and others work better with images, but they can all be applied to either. What works best in a given situation is completely up to you. Also, you can create custom bitmap effects, but an explanation of that is beyond the scope of this chapter.

The best way to get familiar with these effects is to get your hands dirty and write some code. Rather than create a separate code example for each of the bitmap effects, this chapter presents a single example to demonstrate all of them. In this code example, you will create a number of elements, bitmap effects, sliders, and text boxes, which will illustrate the various bitmap effects provided by WPF.

```
<Window x:Class="BitmapEffects.Window4"
  xmlns="http://schemas.microsoft.com/winfx/2006/xaml/presentation"
  xmlns:x="http://schemas.microsoft.com/winfx/2006/xaml"
```

```
    Title="Bitmap Effects" Height="538" Width="600"
>
<Window.Resources>
  <Style TargetType="TextBox">
    <Setter Property="FontFamily" Value="Verdana"/>
    <Setter Property="Margin" Value="4"/>
    <Setter Property="FontWeight" Value="DemiBold"/>
    <Setter Property="Width" Value="40"/>
    <Setter Property="HorizontalAlignment" Value="Center"/>
    <Setter Property="VerticalAlignment" Value="Center"/>
  </Style>
  <Style TargetType="TextBlock">
    <Setter Property="FontFamily" Value="Verdana"/>
    <Setter Property="Margin" Value="4"/>
    <Setter Property="FontWeight" Value="DemiBold"/>
    <Setter Property="HorizontalAlignment" Value="Center"/>
    <Setter Property="VerticalAlignment" Value="Center"/>
  </Style>
  <Style TargetType="Slider">
    <Setter Property="Margin" Value="4"/>
    <Setter Property="Width" Value="100"/>
    <Setter Property="TickFrequency" Value="1"/>
    <Setter Property="IsSnapToTickEnabled" Value="True"/>
  </Style>
</Window.Resources>
<Grid Margin="4">
  <Grid.RowDefinitions>
    <RowDefinition Height="110"/>
      <RowDefinition Height="35"/>
      <RowDefinition Height="110"/>
      <RowDefinition Height="35"/>
      <RowDefinition Height="165"/>
      <RowDefinition Height="35"/>
  </Grid.RowDefinitions>
  <Grid.ColumnDefinitions>
    <ColumnDefinition/>
    <ColumnDefinition/>
  </Grid.ColumnDefinitions>

  <Grid Grid.Column="0" Grid.Row="0" HorizontalAlignment="Center">
    <Rectangle Height="50" Width="200" Fill="Red" Stroke="Black">
      <Rectangle.BitmapEffect>
        <BevelBitmapEffect
          BevelWidth="{Binding ElementName=sliderBevel, Path=Value}"
          />
      </Rectangle.BitmapEffect>
    </Rectangle>
    <TextBlock>Bevel</TextBlock>
  </Grid>
  <StackPanel Grid.Column="0" Grid.Row="1"
    Orientation="Horizontal" HorizontalAlignment="Center">
    <Slider Minimum="0" Maximum="20" Name="sliderBevel" Value="14"/>
    <TextBox Text="{Binding ElementName=sliderBevel, Path=Value}"/>
  </StackPanel>

  <Grid Grid.Column="0" Grid.Row="2" HorizontalAlignment="Center">
```

```xml
      <Ellipse Height="100" Width="100" Fill="Blue" Stroke="Black">
        <Ellipse.BitmapEffect>
          <BlurBitmapEffect
            Radius="{Binding Path=Value, ElementName=sliderBlur}"
            />
        </Ellipse.BitmapEffect>
      </Ellipse>
      <TextBlock>Blur</TextBlock>
    </Grid>
    <StackPanel Grid.Column="0" Grid.Row="3"
      Orientation="Horizontal" HorizontalAlignment="Center">
      <Slider Minimum="0" Maximum="10" Name="sliderBlur" Value="14"/>
      <TextBox Text="{Binding ElementName=sliderBlur, Path=Value}"/>
    </StackPanel>

    <Grid Grid.Column="1" Grid.Row="0"
      Height="50" Width="200" HorizontalAlignment="Center">
      <Rectangle Height="50" Width="200" Fill="White" Stroke="Black">
        <Rectangle.BitmapEffect>
          <DropShadowBitmapEffect
            ShadowDepth="{Binding Path=Value, ElementName=sliderDrop}"
            />
        </Rectangle.BitmapEffect>
      </Rectangle>
      <TextBlock>Drop Shadow</TextBlock>
    </Grid>
    <StackPanel Grid.Column="1" Grid.Row="1"
      Orientation="Horizontal" HorizontalAlignment="Center">
      <Slider Minimum="0" Maximum="10" Name="sliderDrop" Value="14"/>
      <TextBox Text="{Binding ElementName=sliderDrop, Path=Value}"/>
    </StackPanel>

    <Grid Grid.Column="1" Grid.Row="2" HorizontalAlignment="Center">
      <Canvas>
        <Ellipse Height="100" Width="100" Fill="Blue" Stroke="Black"/>
        <Canvas.BitmapEffect>
          <OuterGlowBitmapEffect
            GlowSize="{Binding Path=Value, ElementName=sliderGlow}"
            />
        </Canvas.BitmapEffect>
      </Canvas>
      <TextBlock>Outer Glow</TextBlock>
      <Button Grid.Column="1" Grid.Row="2" Height="50" Width="200">
        Outer Glow
        <Button.BitmapEffect>
          <OuterGlowBitmapEffect
            GlowSize="{Binding Path=Value, ElementName=sliderGlow}"
            />
        </Button.BitmapEffect>
      </Button>
    </Grid>
    <StackPanel Grid.Column="1" Grid.Row="3"
      Orientation="Horizontal" HorizontalAlignment="Center">
      <Slider Minimum="0" Maximum="20" Name="sliderGlow" Value="14"/>
      <TextBox Text="{Binding ElementName=sliderGlow, Path=Value}"/>
```

```
          </StackPanel>

          <Border Grid.Column="0" Grid.Row="4" Grid.ColumnSpan="2"
            Width="300" Height="150">
            <Border.Background>
              <ImageBrush ImageSource="Images/Rain.jpg" Stretch="Uniform"/>
            </Border.Background>
            <Border.BitmapEffect>
              <EmbossBitmapEffect
                Relief="{Binding Path=Value, ElementName=sliderEmboss}"
                />
            </Border.BitmapEffect>
            <TextBlock Foreground="White" FontSize="18">EMBOSS</TextBlock>
          </Border>
          <StackPanel Grid.Column="0" Grid.Row="5" Grid.ColumnSpan="2"
            Orientation="Horizontal" HorizontalAlignment="Center">
            <Slider Minimum="0" Maximum="1" Name="sliderEmboss" Value=".5"
              TickFrequency=".1"/>
            <TextBox Text="{Binding ElementName=sliderEmboss, Path=Value}"/>
          </StackPanel>

      </Grid>
  </Window>
```

In order to illustrate the various bitmap effects, you need some elements to apply them to. Create a couple of rectangles, a couple of ellipses, a button, and an image reference. Then, place all of these elements in a `Grid` for presentation alignment purposes. For each element, create a `BitmapEffect` object and then supply the specific effect to be used. For each of these effects, create a `Slider` object and bind the appropriate effect property to the slider's `Value` property. For example, you can bind your drop shadows `ShadowDepth` property to your drop shadow slider. Finally, create a `TextBox` next to each slider and bind the `TextBox.Text` property to the slider's `Value` property to display the value of the slider.

For the Emboss effect, you can use any image you like. Simply add the image to your Visual Studio project, right-click, select Properties, and then change the Build property to Resource.

Figure 6-7 illustrates the results of running the example.

Figure 6-7 illustrates the use of each bitmap effect provided by WPF. The example application suggests that these effects can be applied to any element, and that is, in fact, true. What this example does not show is that you can indeed combine bitmap effects and apply them as one to any visual element. To do this, you can add your effects to a `BitmapEffectGroup` class as follows:

```
<Rectangle.BitmapEffect>
  <BitmapEffectGroup>
    <BevelBitmapEffect
      BevelWidth="{Binding ElementName=sliderBevel, Path=Value}" />
    <OuterGlowBitmapEffect GlowColor="Aqua" GlowSize="3"/>
  </BitmapEffectGroup>
</Rectangle.BitmapEffect>
```

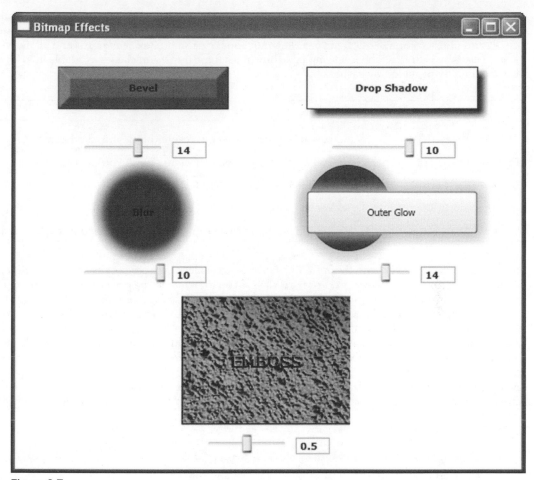

Figure 6-7

In the previous code, you simply created a `BitmapEffectGroup` object and then added two bitmap effects to it: one `BevelBitmapEffect` and one `OuterGlowBitmapEffect`. The ability to combine bitmap effects in WPF is very effective in creating an interesting UI.

Transformations

WPF transformations can be used to apply effects such as rotation, scaling, and skewing to visual elements. For example, using transformations you can rotate a button, scale text, or skew a rectangle to give the impression of depth. Taking this one step further, you can add animation to transformation to achieve even more effects. For example, you can magnify visual elements, move controls around in your UI (referred to as translation), and do just about anything else you can think of.

Transformation classes live in the `System.Windows.Media` namespace. WPF provides several transform classes for convenience that let you easily scale, translate, rotate, and skew objects. These classes are: `ScaleTransform`, `TranslateTransform`, `RotateTransform`, and `SkewTransform` and all derive from the base class `Transform`. The following table illustrates these transform classes available in WPF and the functionality provided by each.

Transform	Description
RotateTransform	Rotates an element based on a center point you can define.
ScaleTransform	Resizes an element based on a center point you can define.
SkewTransform	Shears an element in a non-uniform manner.
TranslateTransform	Moves an element along an X and Y axis.
MatrixTransform	Provides a 3×3 matrix you can use to define a custom transformation.

I refer to the first four classes in the preceding table as convenience classes because transformations can be created directly using a `MatrixTransform` class if you understand the principles of mapping points from one coordinate space to another. The `MatrixTransform` class exposes six properties: `m11`, `m12`, `m21`, `m22`, `offsetX`, and `offsetY`, which let you define the values of a transform matrix, a 3×3 matrix of values that define a transformation. All transforms have a matrix. While creating transformations such as scale and translate is very easy using a `MatrixTransform`, rotate and skew are far more complex. This is why WPF offers the convenient transform classes that it does.

The following code creates a scale transform using a `MatrixTransform` object:

```
<Grid>
  <Rectangle Width="50" Height="50" Fill="Blue"/>
  <Rectangle Width="50" Height="50" Fill="#AAFF0000">
    <Rectangle.RenderTransform>
      <MatrixTransform>
        <MatrixTransform.Matrix>
          <Matrix M11=".75" M12="0" M21="0" M22=".75" OffsetX="-20" OffsetY="-20"/>
        </MatrixTransform.Matrix>
      </MatrixTransform>
    </Rectangle.RenderTransform>
  </Rectangle>
</Grid>
```

The following code creates the same scale transform using a `ScaleTransform` object:

```
<Grid>
  <Rectangle Width="50" Height="50" Fill="Blue"/>
  <Rectangle Width="50" Height="50" Fill="#AAFF0000">
    <Rectangle.RenderTransform>
      <ScaleTransform ScaleX=".75" ScaleY=".75" CenterX="-20" CenterY="-20"/>
    </Rectangle.RenderTransform>
  </Rectangle>
</Grid>
```

There are two types of transforms you can apply to elements in WPF: `RenderTransform`, defined by `UIElement`, and `LayoutTransform`, defined by `FrameworkElement`. A `RenderTransform` is applied to an element as the element is rendered. What this means is that the transform is applied after layout. Because of this, you may transform an element and find it overlaps other elements, or moves outside of the bounding box of its parent element. This is not necessarily a bad thing; in fact, it might be desirable in a specific situation. Alternatively, a `LayoutTransform` applies the transform to an element prior to layout. The WPF layout engine will take into account the transform during the `Measure` and `Arrange` phase of layout and will size and arrange the elements appropriately.

The following example creates three rectangles placed side by side. You can then place a `RotateTransform` on the rectangle in the center to rotate it 45 degrees. The rectangle will rotate 45 degrees as expected, but it overlaps the left-most rectangle. Again, this may be the desired effect.

```
<StackPanel Orientation="Horizontal">
  <Rectangle Width="50" Height="50" Fill="Blue"/>
  <Rectangle Width="50" Height="50" Fill="Red">
    <Rectangle.RenderTransform>
      <RotateTransform Angle="45"/>
    </Rectangle.RenderTransform>
  </Rectangle>
  <Rectangle Width="50" Height="50" Fill="Green"/>
</StackPanel>
```

In the following example, simply swap out the `RenderTransform` with a `LayoutTransform`. The result is that the layout engine takes into account the space required for the rotated rectangle, and sizes the controls respectfully. This results in no overlapping of elements.

```
<StackPanel Orientation="Horizontal">
  <Rectangle Width="50" Height="50" Fill="Blue"/>
  <Rectangle Width="50" Height="50" Fill="Red">
    <Rectangle.LayoutTransform>
      <RotateTransform Angle="45"/>
    </Rectangle.LayoutTransform>
  </Rectangle>
  <Rectangle Width="50" Height="50" Fill="Green"/>
</StackPanel>
```

Additionally, you can apply any number of transformations that you wish to a single element using a `TransformGroup` class. If you want to scale an item to twice its size and then rotate it 45 degrees, you can do this by adding both transforms to a `TransformGroup` object. You would then assign the `TransformGroup` object to the `RenderTransform` or `LayoutTransform` property of the element, and both would be applied.

```
<Rectangle Width="200" Height="50" Fill="Red">
  <Rectangle.RenderTransform>
    <TransformGroup>
      <ScaleTransform ScaleX="2" ScaleY="2"/>
      <RotateTransform Angle="45"/>
    </TransformGroup>
  </Rectangle.RenderTransform>
</Rectangle>
```

The rest of this section provides a thorough overview of the first four transform classes provided by WPF.

TranslateTransform

The `TranslateTransform` is one of the simplest transformations you can perform. Similar in simplicity is the `ScaleTransform`, which will be covered next. The `TranslateTransform` simply moves (translates) an element along a two-dimensional X and Y axis. A positive X value moves the element to the right; a negative value moves it to the left. Similarly, a positive Y value moves the element down, and a negative value moves it up. This is really an offset from the element's original position. `TranslateTransform` is really just a convenience wrapper for setting the `OffsetX` and `OffsetY` properties of the transform `Matrix` structure.

Most containers in WPF provide layout mechanisms that control the position of an element, such as `Margin`, `HorizontalAlignment`, and `VerticalAlignment`. Sometimes, however, you still cannot set a child element's position as you would like. One solution is to apply a `TranslateTransform` to the element and then position the element to your liking. This is but one example of the use of a `TranslateTransform`. In an example later in this chapter, you'll use a `TranslateTransform` with animation in order to make an element bounce up and down . . . so stay tuned.

In the following example, you create a `ListBox` and two sliders that you can use to move the `ListBox` from its original position.

```
<Window x:Class="WPFTransformations.Translate"
  xmlns="http://schemas.microsoft.com/winfx/2006/xaml/presentation"
  xmlns:x="http://schemas.microsoft.com/winfx/2006/xaml"
  Title="Translate Transform" Height="300" Width="300"
  >
<Window.Resources>
  <Style TargetType="TextBox">
    <Setter Property="FontFamily" Value="Verdana"/>
    <Setter Property="Margin" Value="4"/>
    <Setter Property="FontWeight" Value="DemiBold"/>
    <Setter Property="Width" Value="40"/>
  </Style>
  <Style TargetType="TextBlock">
    <Setter Property="FontFamily" Value="Verdana"/>
    <Setter Property="Margin" Value="4"/>
    <Setter Property="FontWeight" Value="DemiBold"/>
  </Style>
  <Style TargetType="Slider">
    <Setter Property="Margin" Value="4"/>
    <Setter Property="Width" Value="100"/>
    <Setter Property="Maximum" Value="100"/>
    <Setter Property="Minimum" Value="-100"/>
    <Setter Property="Value" Value="0"/>
    <Setter Property="TickFrequency" Value="2"/>
    <Setter Property="IsSnapToTickEnabled" Value="True"/>
  </Style>
</Window.Resources>
<Grid>
  <StackPanel Margin="8">

    <ListBox Height="100" Width="200" BorderBrush="Blue" BorderThickness="2">
      <ListBoxItem Content="Item 1" Background="Beige" Height="22"/>
```

```
                 <ListBoxItem Content="Item 2" Background="LightGray" Height="22"/>
                 <ListBoxItem Content="Item 3" Background="Beige" Height="22"/>
                 <ListBoxItem Content="Item 4" Background="LightGray" Height="22"/>
                 <ListBox.RenderTransform>
                   <TranslateTransform
                     X="{Binding Path=Value, ElementName=sliderX}"
                     Y="{Binding Path=Value, ElementName=sliderY}"/>
                 </ListBox.RenderTransform>
               </ListBox>

               <TextBlock Height="65" Width="100"/>
               <Grid HorizontalAlignment="Center" Margin="2">
                 <Grid.RowDefinitions>
                   <RowDefinition/>
                   <RowDefinition/>
                 </Grid.RowDefinitions>
                 <Grid.ColumnDefinitions>
                   <ColumnDefinition/>
                   <ColumnDefinition Width="110"/>
                   <ColumnDefinition/>
                 </Grid.ColumnDefinitions>

                 <TextBlock Grid.Row="0" Grid.Column="0" Text="X:"/>
                 <Slider Grid.Row="0" Grid.Column="1" Name="sliderX"/>
                 <TextBox Grid.Row="0" Grid.Column="2" Text="{Binding Path=Value,
                   ElementName=sliderX}"/>

                 <TextBlock Grid.Row="1" Grid.Column="0" Text="Y:"/>
                 <Slider Grid.Row="1" Grid.Column="1" Name="sliderY"/>
                 <TextBox Grid.Row="1" Grid.Column="2" Text="{Binding Path=Value,
                   ElementName=sliderY}"/>

               </Grid>
             </StackPanel>
             <StackPanel Margin="8">
               <Border BorderBrush="Red" BorderThickness="1" Width="200" Height="100">
                 <Rectangle Height="100" Width="200" Stroke="Red" Fill="Red" Opacity=".05"/>
               </Border>
             </StackPanel>
           </Grid>
         </Window>
```

In the preceding code, you also created a `Rectangle` the same size as the `ListBox`. The rectangle will serve as a point of reference for you while you move the `ListBox` along the X and Y axis. You'll also add a `RenderTransfrom` to the `ListBox` and specify a `TranslateTransform` transformation. The `TranslateTransform` exposes two properties you're concerned with, X and Y. Both of these accept a double, and can be either positive or negative in value. In this example, you bind the X and Y properties of your transform to the `Value` property of the X and Y sliders. Figure 6-8 illustrates the results of running your example.

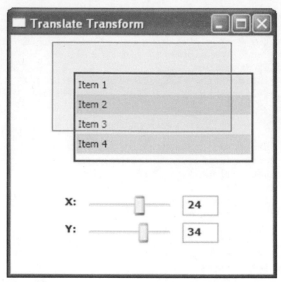

Figure 6-8

Moving the X and Y sliders moves the ListBox control accordingly. Because this transformation is applied after rendering, you'll find that you can effectively move an element right out of its container. For example, change the Background of the topmost StackPanel to gray and rerun the application. You'll see that you can move outside of the StackPanel bounds. This behavior exists because you are applying a RenderTransform.

Now, if you change the RenderTransform to a LayoutTransform, you'll see a completely different behavior. When you move the sliders, nothing happens. This is by design because a LayoutTransform will ignore a TranslateTransform.

ScaleTransform

When you want to resize an element, you can use a ScaleTransform. Applying a scale transformation is also very simple. You can scale an object using a ScaleTransform by specifying the value for the ScaleX and ScaleY properties. As their names suggest, these properties represent factors for scaling along the X and Y axis. If you were to specify 2 for ScaleX and 2 for ScaleY, you would be scaling your element by 200 percent. Similarly, if you were to specify .5 for both properties, you would be resizing your element by 50 percent.

In addition to defining a scale factor for your element, you may also specify a point from which to scale. You can specify these values by setting the CenterX and CenterY properties of the ScaleTransform object. By default, these both have a value of zero. This means your element will scale from the top-left corner of the object (for example, the top-left corner will remain intact). If you wanted to scale from the center of the element, you would specify CenterX = Width/2 and CenterY=Height/2, where Width and Height are values of your element.

Similar to the prior example, you'll now create a ListBox and some Slider objects you can use to scale the ListBox and define the center point from which you will scale, using the following code:

```xml
<Window x:Class="WPFTransformations.Scale"
  xmlns="http://schemas.microsoft.com/winfx/2006/xaml/presentation"
  xmlns:x="http://schemas.microsoft.com/winfx/2006/xaml"
  Title="Scale Transform" Height="381" Width="300"
  >
  <Window.Resources>
    <Style TargetType="TextBox">
      <Setter Property="FontFamily" Value="Verdana"/>
      <Setter Property="Margin" Value="4"/>
      <Setter Property="FontWeight" Value="DemiBold"/>
      <Setter Property="Width" Value="40"/>
    </Style>
    <Style TargetType="TextBlock">
      <Setter Property="FontFamily" Value="Verdana"/>
      <Setter Property="Margin" Value="4"/>
      <Setter Property="FontWeight" Value="DemiBold"/>
    </Style>
    <Style TargetType="Slider">
      <Setter Property="Margin" Value="4"/>
      <Setter Property="Width" Value="100"/>
      <Setter Property="Maximum" Value="100"/>
      <Setter Property="Minimum" Value="-100"/>
      <Setter Property="Value" Value="0"/>
      <Setter Property="TickFrequency" Value="2"/>
      <Setter Property="IsSnapToTickEnabled" Value="True"/>
    </Style>
  </Window.Resources>
  <Grid>
    <StackPanel Margin="8">
      <TextBlock Height="25" Width="100"/>

      <ListBox Height="100" Width="200" BorderBrush="Blue" BorderThickness="2">
        <ListBoxItem Content="Item 1" Background="Beige" Height="22"/>
        <ListBoxItem Content="Item 2" Background="LightGray" Height="22"/>
        <ListBoxItem Content="Item 3" Background="Beige" Height="22"/>
        <ListBoxItem Content="Item 4" Background="LightGray" Height="22"/>
        <ListBox.RenderTransform>
          <ScaleTransform
            ScaleX="{Binding Path=Value, ElementName=sliderScaleX}"
            ScaleY="{Binding Path=Value, ElementName=sliderScaleY}"
            CenterX="{Binding Path=Value, ElementName=sliderScaleCX}"
            CenterY="{Binding Path=Value, ElementName=sliderScaleCY}"
            />
        </ListBox.RenderTransform>
      </ListBox>

      <TextBlock Height="65" Width="100"/>
      <Grid HorizontalAlignment="Center" Margin="2">
        <Grid.RowDefinitions>
          <RowDefinition/>
          <RowDefinition/>
          <RowDefinition/>
          <RowDefinition/>
        </Grid.RowDefinitions>
        <Grid.ColumnDefinitions>
```

```
                  <ColumnDefinition/>
                  <ColumnDefinition Width="110"/>
                  <ColumnDefinition/>
               </Grid.ColumnDefinitions>

               <TextBlock Grid.Row="0" Grid.Column="0" Text="Scale X:"/>
               <Slider Grid.Row="0" Grid.Column="1" Name="sliderScaleX"
                  Maximum="2.5" Minimum="0" Value="1" TickFrequency=".1"/>
               <TextBox Grid.Row="0" Grid.Column="2"
                  Text="{Binding Path=Value, ElementName=sliderScaleX}"/>

               <TextBlock Grid.Row="1" Grid.Column="0" Text="Scale Y:"/>
               <Slider Grid.Row="1" Grid.Column="1" Name="sliderScaleY"
                  Maximum="2.5" Minimum="0" Value="1" TickFrequency=".1"/>
               <TextBox Grid.Row="1" Grid.Column="2"
                  Text="{Binding Path=Value, ElementName=sliderScaleY}"/>

               <TextBlock Grid.Row="2" Grid.Column="0" Text="Center X:"/>
               <Slider Grid.Row="2" Grid.Column="1" Name="sliderScaleCX"/>
               <TextBox Grid.Row="2" Grid.Column="2"
                  Text="{Binding Path=Value, ElementName=sliderScaleCX}"/>

               <TextBlock Grid.Row="3" Grid.Column="0" Text="Center Y:"/>
               <Slider Grid.Row="3" Grid.Column="1" Name="sliderScaleCY"/>
               <TextBox Grid.Row="3" Grid.Column="2"
                  Text="{Binding Path=Value, ElementName=sliderScaleCY}"/>

         </Grid>
      </StackPanel>
      <StackPanel Margin="8">
         <TextBlock Height="25" Width="100"/>
         <Border BorderBrush="Red" BorderThickness="1" Width="200" Height="100">
            <Rectangle Height="100" Width="200" Stroke="Red" Fill="Red" Opacity=".05"/>
         </Border>
      </StackPanel>
   </Grid>
</Window>
```

This code is very similar to the last example. The primary difference is that this time you are using a ScaleTransform rather than a TranslateTransform. In addition you are adding a couple more sliders. This time the sliders represent the ScaleX, ScaleY, CenterX, and CenterY properties of the ScaleTransform. Figure 6-9 illustrates the results of running your example.

Running your program, you can see that by changing the ScaleX slider, the ListBox gets larger and smaller along the X axis. Similarly, changing the ScaleY slider stretches the ListBox along the Y axis. Your top-left corner, however, will not change, unless you move the CenterX and CenterY sliders away from zero. Once you change these, you'll see you lose the default top-left corner position. Figure 6-9 illustrates this point. The original ListBox position is represented by the red rectangle in the center.

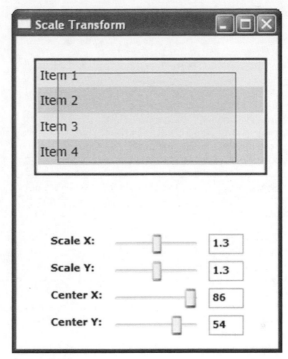

Figure 6-9

SkewTransform

The term *skew* literally means to turn or place something at an angle or on its side. In a 2D world, this would be hard to do, but you can create an effect that will give the appearance of a skewed object. The SkewTransform will skew (a.k.a. shear) an element's coordinates in a non-uniform manner. Skewing an element can create the illusion of depth or a third dimension. You can control the skewing of an element by defining four property values of the SkewTransform class: AngleX, AngleY, CenterX, and CenterY. AngleX and AngleY define the skew angle, while CenterX and CenterY the center point from which to skew. By default, all these properties are set to zero.

Next, modify your prior example to perform a skew transformation and change the sliders to manipulate the SkewTransform properties.

```
<Window x:Class="WPFTransformations.Transforms"
  xmlns="http://schemas.microsoft.com/winfx/2006/xaml/presentation"
  xmlns:x="http://schemas.microsoft.com/winfx/2006/xaml"
  Title="Skew Transform" Height="350" Width="300"
  >
  <Window.Resources>
    <Style TargetType="TextBox">
      <Setter Property="FontFamily" Value="Verdana"/>
      <Setter Property="Margin" Value="4"/>
      <Setter Property="FontWeight" Value="DemiBold"/>
      <Setter Property="Width" Value="40"/>
```

```
        </Style>
        <Style TargetType="TextBlock">
          <Setter Property="FontFamily" Value="Verdana"/>
          <Setter Property="Margin" Value="4"/>
          <Setter Property="FontWeight" Value="DemiBold"/>
        </Style>
        <Style TargetType="Slider">
          <Setter Property="Margin" Value="4"/>
          <Setter Property="Width" Value="100"/>
          <Setter Property="Maximum" Value="100"/>
          <Setter Property="Minimum" Value="-100"/>
          <Setter Property="Value" Value="0"/>
          <Setter Property="TickFrequency" Value="2"/>
          <Setter Property="IsSnapToTickEnabled" Value="True"/>
        </Style>
  </Window.Resources>
  <Grid>
    <StackPanel Margin="8">

      <ListBox Height="100" Width="200" BorderBrush="Blue" BorderThickness="2">
        <ListBoxItem Content="Item 1" Background="Beige" Height="22"/>
        <ListBoxItem Content="Item 2" Background="LightGray" Height="22"/>
        <ListBoxItem Content="Item 3" Background="Beige" Height="22"/>
        <ListBoxItem Content="Item 4" Background="LightGray" Height="22"/>
        <ListBox.RenderTransform>
          <SkewTransform
            CenterX="{Binding Path=Value, ElementName=sliderSkewCX}"
            CenterY="{Binding Path=Value, ElementName=sliderSkewCY}"
            AngleX="{Binding Path=Value, ElementName=sliderSkewX}"
            AngleY="{Binding Path=Value, ElementName=sliderSkewY}"
            />
        </ListBox.RenderTransform>
      </ListBox>

      <TextBlock Height="65" Width="100"/>
      <Grid HorizontalAlignment="Center" Margin="2">
        <Grid.RowDefinitions>
          <RowDefinition/>
          <RowDefinition/>
          <RowDefinition/>
          <RowDefinition/>
        </Grid.RowDefinitions>
        <Grid.ColumnDefinitions>
          <ColumnDefinition/>
          <ColumnDefinition Width="110"/>
          <ColumnDefinition/>
        </Grid.ColumnDefinitions>

        <TextBlock Grid.Row="0" Grid.Column="0" Text="Angle X:"/>
        <Slider Grid.Row="0" Grid.Column="1" Name="sliderSkewX"/>
        <TextBox Grid.Row="0" Grid.Column="2"
          Text="{Binding Path=Value, ElementName=sliderSkewX}"/>

        <TextBlock Grid.Row="1" Grid.Column="0" Text="Angle Y:"/>
```

```
            <Slider Grid.Row="1" Grid.Column="1" Name="sliderSkewY"/>
            <TextBox Grid.Row="1" Grid.Column="2"
              Text="{Binding Path=Value, ElementName=sliderSkewY}"/>

            <TextBlock Grid.Row="2" Grid.Column="0" Text="Center X:"/>
            <Slider Grid.Row="2" Grid.Column="1" Name="sliderSkewCX"/>
            <TextBox Grid.Row="2" Grid.Column="2"
              Text="{Binding Path=Value, ElementName=sliderSkewCX}"/>

            <TextBlock Grid.Row="3" Grid.Column="0" Text="Center Y:"/>
            <Slider Grid.Row="3" Grid.Column="1" Name="sliderSkewCY"/>
            <TextBox Grid.Row="3" Grid.Column="2"
              Text="{Binding Path=Value, ElementName=sliderSkewCY}"/>

          </Grid>
        </StackPanel>
        <StackPanel Margin="8">
          <Border BorderBrush="Red" BorderThickness="1" Width="200" Height="100">
            <Rectangle Height="100" Width="200" Stroke="Red" Fill="Red" Opacity=".05"/>
          </Border>
        </StackPanel>
      </Grid>
</Window>
```

Again, this code is very similar to the other transform samples you've created. This time, however, you're applying a skew transformation. Also, the previous code creates a slider for each value that affects the skew effect you place on the `ListBox`. Figure 6-10 illustrates the results of running the example.

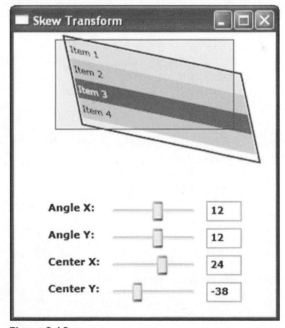

Figure 6-10

Running this sample and applying the various values, you can really get a sense of what "skewing" is. You can make an element appear to be on its side, tilted backward or forward giving the illusion of depth, or stretched in very odd ways. One of my favorite aspects of this example is the fact that the `ListBox` still works! You can select items, wire up routed events, and do any other thing you can think of with a `ListBox` control. That is the power of WPF.

RotateTransform

WPF also provides the `RotateTransform` class. As you've probably guessed already, the `RotateTransform` class allows you to rotate an element. There are three properties of interest: `Angle`, `CenterX`, and `CenterY`. The `Angle` property specifies the distance to rotate, for example, 45, 90, 180 degrees, and so on. Together, the `CenterX` and `CenterY` properties specify the center point around which the element will rotate. The default for all three properties is zero. To rotate an element on center, you would set `CenterX = Width/2` and `CenterY=Height/2`, where `Width` and `Height` are values of the element. This assumes you are using a `RenderTransform`. If you rotate an element in a `LayoutTransform`, it will rotate on center because you cannot translate the element in this mode.

You don't always know the height and width of your elements because the WPF layout engine may resize them during the `Measure` and `Arrange` phase of layout, which is performed at runtime. For this scenario, you can use a property called `RenderTransformOrigin` which is part of the `UIElement` class. `RenderTransformOrigin` is defined as a `Point` object. You're not specifying a location when you set this value; rather, you are specifying a factor, between 0 and 1 for both `X` and `Y`, which you will use as the base for the transformation. `RenderTransformOrigin` can be applied to any transformation. So, to rotate on center, you simply supply the value of 0.5 for both `X` and `Y` of the `Point` structure.

```
<Window x:Class="WPFTransformations.Rotate"
  xmlns="http://schemas.microsoft.com/winfx/2006/xaml/presentation"
  xmlns:x="http://schemas.microsoft.com/winfx/2006/xaml"
  Title="Rotate Transform" Height="350" Width="300"
  >
  <Window.Resources>
    <Style TargetType="TextBox">
      <Setter Property="FontFamily" Value="Verdana"/>
      <Setter Property="Margin" Value="4"/>
      <Setter Property="FontWeight" Value="DemiBold"/>
      <Setter Property="Width" Value="40"/>
    </Style>
    <Style TargetType="TextBlock">
      <Setter Property="FontFamily" Value="Verdana"/>
      <Setter Property="Margin" Value="4"/>
      <Setter Property="FontWeight" Value="DemiBold"/>
    </Style>
    <Style TargetType="Slider">
      <Setter Property="Margin" Value="4"/>
      <Setter Property="Width" Value="100"/>
      <Setter Property="Maximum" Value="100"/>
      <Setter Property="Minimum" Value="-100"/>
      <Setter Property="Value" Value="0"/>
      <Setter Property="TickFrequency" Value="2"/>
      <Setter Property="IsSnapToTickEnabled" Value="True"/>
    </Style>
```

```xml
    </Window.Resources>
<Grid>
  <StackPanel Margin="8">
    <TextBlock Height="25" Width="100"/>

    <ListBox Height="100" Width="200" BorderBrush="Blue" BorderThickness="2">
      <ListBoxItem Content="Item 1" Background="Beige" Height="22"/>
      <ListBoxItem Content="Item 2" Background="LightGray" Height="22"/>
      <ListBoxItem Content="Item 3" Background="Beige" Height="22"/>
      <ListBoxItem Content="Item 4" Background="LightGray" Height="22"/>
      <ListBox.RenderTransform>
        <RotateTransform
          Angle="{Binding ElementName=sliderAngle, Path=Value}"
          CenterX="{Binding ElementName=sliderCenterX, Path=Value}"
          CenterY="{Binding ElementName=sliderCenterY, Path=Value}"
          />
      </ListBox.RenderTransform>
    </ListBox>

    <TextBlock Height="65" Width="100"/>
    <Grid HorizontalAlignment="Center" Margin="2">
      <Grid.RowDefinitions>
        <RowDefinition/>
        <RowDefinition/>
        <RowDefinition/>
        <RowDefinition/>
      </Grid.RowDefinitions>
      <Grid.ColumnDefinitions>
        <ColumnDefinition/>
        <ColumnDefinition Width="110"/>
        <ColumnDefinition/>
      </Grid.ColumnDefinitions>

      <TextBlock Grid.Row="0" Grid.Column="0" Text="Angle:"/>
      <Slider Grid.Row="0" Grid.Column="1" Name="sliderAngle" Maximum="360"
        Minimum="-360"/>
      <TextBox Grid.Row="0" Grid.Column="2" Text="{Binding
        ElementName=sliderAngle, Path=Value}"/>

      <TextBlock Grid.Row="1" Grid.Column="0" Text="Center X:"/>
      <Slider Grid.Row="1" Grid.Column="1" Name="sliderCenterX"/>
      <TextBox Grid.Row="1" Grid.Column="2" Text="{Binding
        ElementName=sliderCenterX, Path=Value}"/>

      <TextBlock Grid.Row="2" Grid.Column="0" Text="Center Y:"/>
      <Slider Grid.Row="2" Grid.Column="1" Name="sliderCenterY"/>
      <TextBox Grid.Row="2" Grid.Column="2" Text="{Binding
        ElementName=sliderCenterY, Path=Value}"/>

    </Grid>
  </StackPanel>
  <StackPanel Margin="8">
    <TextBlock Height="25" Width="100"/>
    <Border BorderBrush="Red" BorderThickness="1" Width="200" Height="100">
```

```
                <Rectangle Height="100" Width="200" Stroke="Red" Fill="Red" Opacity=".05"/>
            </Border>
        </StackPanel>
    </Grid>
</Window>
```

This time you're using a `RotateTransform`, and the sliders represent the `Angle`, `CenterX`, and `CenterY`. Moving the Angle slider will rotate the `ListBox`. Changing the `CenterX` and `CenterY` sliders will move the center point of the rotation. By this, the fourth example in this style, the rest of the code should look pretty familiar.

Figure 6-11 illustrates the results of running the example.

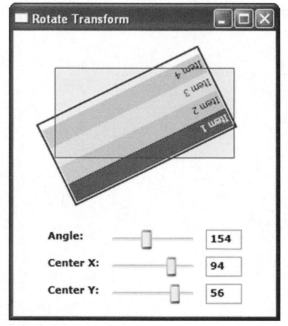

Figure 6-11

In Figure 6-11, you see that you've rotated the `ListBox` 154 degrees clockwise. In order to keep your element on the screen while rotating, you must change the `CenterX` and `CenterY` properties. If you didn't, you wouldn't see much of your `ListBox` at 154 degrees because, by default, you'd be rotating at the coordinates (0,0).

Opacity Masks

Opacity masks provide another way to create interesting effects in WPF. You can create the appearance of an element or image fading into the background. You can also create glass-like surface effects in order to make an element look glossy or semi-transparent. You can apply an opacity mask to any element via the `OpacityMask` property.

Typically, you create an opacity mask using a gradient, but you can use any type of `Brush` object as an opacity mask. The way an opacity mask works is based on the alpha value of each pixel defined in the brush. The actual color of the pixel is ignored; rather, the opacity mask simply determines the alpha value (opacity level) of each pixel. The value of the alpha is then applied to the element to which you are applying the opacity mask. If an area of the opacity mask's brush is fully transparent, then the corresponding area of the element is made transparent.

The following example illustrates the use of an opacity mask. You'll use a drawing brush to create a grid pattern to use as the background of a rectangle. You'll then define an opacity mask for the rectangle, which will create a fading effect.

```xml
<Window x:Class="OpacityMasks.Window1"
  xmlns="http://schemas.microsoft.com/winfx/2006/xaml/presentation"
  xmlns:x="http://schemas.microsoft.com/winfx/2006/xaml"
  Title="Opacity Masks" Height="300" Width="300"
  >
<Window.Resources>
  <DrawingBrush x:Key="Grid" Viewport="0,0,.1,.1" TileMode="Tile">
    <DrawingBrush.Drawing>
      <GeometryDrawing>
        <GeometryDrawing.Geometry>
          <GeometryGroup>
            <RectangleGeometry Rect="0, 0, 10, 10"/>
            <RectangleGeometry Rect="5, 5, 10, 10"/>
            <RectangleGeometry Rect="0, 5, 10, 10"/>
            <RectangleGeometry Rect="5, 0, 10, 10"/>
          </GeometryGroup>
        </GeometryDrawing.Geometry>
        <GeometryDrawing.Pen>
          <Pen Thickness=".5" Brush="Blue"/>
        </GeometryDrawing.Pen>
      </GeometryDrawing>
    </DrawingBrush.Drawing>
  </DrawingBrush>
</Window.Resources>
<Grid>
  <Rectangle VerticalAlignment="Center" HorizontalAlignment="Center" Width="200"
    Height="200" StrokeThickness="0" Fill="{StaticResource Grid}">
    <Rectangle.OpacityMask>
      <LinearGradientBrush StartPoint="0.5,0" EndPoint="0.5,1">
        <GradientStop Color="Transparent" Offset="0"/>
        <GradientStop Color="Black" Offset=".1"/>
        <GradientStop Color="Transparent" Offset=".5"/>
        <GradientStop Color="Black" Offset=".9"/>
        <GradientStop Color="Transparent" Offset="1"/>
      </LinearGradientBrush>
    </Rectangle.OpacityMask>
  </Rectangle>
  <Rectangle VerticalAlignment="Center" HorizontalAlignment="Center" Width="205"
    Height="205" StrokeThickness="0">
    <Rectangle.Fill>
      <LinearGradientBrush StartPoint="0,0.5" EndPoint="1,0.5">
        <GradientStop Color="White" Offset="0"/>
        <GradientStop Color="Transparent" Offset=".5"/>
```

```
            <GradientStop Color="White" Offset="1"/>
         </LinearGradientBrush>
      </Rectangle.Fill>
   </Rectangle>
   <TextBlock VerticalAlignment="Center" HorizontalAlignment="Center"
      FontWeight="DemiBold" FontFamily="Verdana" Foreground="Blue"
      FontSize="24">Opacity Mask</TextBlock>
  </Grid>
 </Window>
```

In the preceding example code, you create a `DrawingBrush` resource that defines your grid pattern. You then create a rectangle and assign your grid pattern to the `Fill` property as a `StaticResource`. You now have a visual element to play with. Next, you assign an opacity mask to the rectangle, defined as a `LinearGradientBrush`. You set the `StartPoint` and `EndPoint` properties of the brush to (0.5,0) and (0.5,1) so that you get a nice horizontal gradient. Next you define your gradient stops, and here's where the opacity mask gets interesting. Notice that the colors you are using for your stops are `Black` and `Transparent`. The predefined color `Black` is defined by WPF as fully opaque, meaning it has no transparency. The predefined `Transparent` value, of course, exhibits full transparency. The result of this is that the `GradientStops`, which define `Black` as a color will expose the element underneath, while the `GradientStops`, which define `Transparent` as a color will expose whatever is behind the element (for example, make the portion of the element transparent as well).

To add a bit more style to your example, you create a second rectangle, whose fill is a `LinearGradientBrush`, in order to feather the left and right edges of your element. You set the `StartPoint` and `EndPoint` values to (0, 0.5) and (1, 0.5) to create a vertical gradient. Because this is not an opacity mask, you will use background color `White`, and the color `Transparent` to get a similar effect to that of the opacity mask. Because this rectangle will overlay your previous rectangle, you can simply define the edges of the gradient as white, and the center as transparent. Remember that this is not an opacity mask, so you're not dealing with alpha values now; you're dealing with color again.

Figure 6-12 illustrates the end result, which is a grid that appears to be burned into the background of your window.

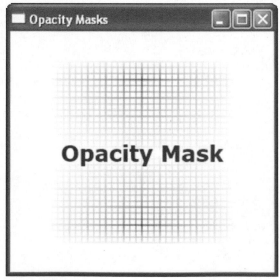

Figure 6-12

Putting It All Together — Combining Effects

Now that you've explored many of the effects available to you in WPF, it's time to build some examples that combine these effects. In this section, you create two projects that utilize many of the concepts that have been covered throughout this chapter. In the first example, you create a bouncing ball project. Your bouncing ball will bounce up and down on a glass table, casting a dynamic reflection. In the second example, you create an image viewer application. The image viewer displays a set of thumbnail images horizontally along the bottom of the window. When the mouse passes over one of the thumbnail images, the image will "fly in" to the image preview area, and the last image viewed will "fly out" of view.

Bouncing Ball with Reflection Example

We are all familiar with the Hello World scenario used to introduce a new language or platform in the programming world. I think the bouncing ball animation may be just as predominant in the graphics world. If not, maybe I can get the trend started as it is one of my favorite examples. The following example will combine animation, render transformations, opacity mask, and gradient brushes to create a bouncing ball. This bouncing ball will bounce up and down continuously on a plate of black glass, and its reflection will grow and shrink as the ball bounces. In addition, just to spice things up a bit, you'll make your bouncing ball "draggable" horizontally.

Start by creating your XAML page. Open Visual Studio and create a new project using the .NET Framework 3.0 Windows Application template. Name the project **BouncingBall** and modify the default Window1.xaml as follows.

```xml
<Window x:Class="BouncingBall.Window1"
  xmlns="http://schemas.microsoft.com/winfx/2006/xaml/presentation"
  xmlns:x="http://schemas.microsoft.com/winfx/2006/xaml"
  xmlns:local="clr-namespace:BouncingBall"
  Title="Red Ball Bouncing on Glass"
  Height="400"
  Width="400"
  VerticalAlignment="Center"
  HorizontalAlignment="Center"
  Background="Black"
  MouseMove="BouncingBall_MouseMove"
  MouseDown="BouncingBall_MouseDown"
  MouseUp="BouncingBall_MouseUp"
  >

  <Window.Resources>
    <local:FlipConverter x:Key="FlipConverter" />
  </Window.Resources>

  <Grid VerticalAlignment="Stretch" HorizontalAlignment="Stretch">
    <Grid.ColumnDefinitions>
      <ColumnDefinition Width="*"/>
    </Grid.ColumnDefinitions>
    <Grid.RowDefinitions>
      <RowDefinition Height="*"/>
      <RowDefinition Height="*"/>
    </Grid.RowDefinitions>
```

First, modify the Window element as illustrated in the previous code. You are adding an XMLNamespace so you'll be able to reference a TypeConverter that you'll be creating shortly. Also, you're adding events definitions for the MouseMove, MouseDown, and MouseUp events. These will wire-up your event handlers, which will provide the code to handle dragging your bouncing ball horizontally. Change the other Window attributes to match the previous code. You are also defining a single window resource, which contains your TypeConverter declaration. (You'll create the TypeConverter shortly.) Last, you've added some row and column definitions to your Grid container.

```xml
<!-- Bouncing Ball Background -->
<Border Grid.Row="0" Grid.Column="0"
  x:Name="BouncingBallContainer"
  VerticalAlignment="Stretch"
  BorderBrush="White"
  BorderThickness="0"
  >
  <Border.Background>
    <LinearGradientBrush StartPoint="0.5,0" EndPoint="0.5,1">
      <GradientStop Color="Gray" Offset="0.8"/>
      <GradientStop Color="Black" Offset="0.99"/>
    </LinearGradientBrush>
  </Border.Background>
</Border.Background>
```

Here, you're simply creating a Border object, which will surround your bouncing ball and give you a chance to add a gradient background behind it. For the background, you define a simple LinearGradientBrush with a gradient flowing horizontally, made up of two colors, black and gray.

```xml
<!-- Bouncing Ball -->
<Canvas
  x:Name="BouncingBall"
  Background="Transparent"
  VerticalAlignment="Stretch"
  >

  <Ellipse Width="100" Height="100"
    Fill="Red" Opacity=".8" />
  <Ellipse Width="100" Height="100"
    Fill="Red" Opacity="1">
    <Ellipse.OpacityMask>
      <LinearGradientBrush StartPoint="0,1" EndPoint="0,0">
        <GradientStop Color="White" Offset="0.04"/>
        <GradientStop Color="#00000000" Offset="0.5"/>
      </LinearGradientBrush>
    </Ellipse.OpacityMask>
  </Ellipse>
  <Ellipse Width="60" Height="60"
    Fill="White" Opacity="0.3"
    Margin="20,0,0,0" >
    <Ellipse.OpacityMask>
      <LinearGradientBrush StartPoint="0,0" EndPoint="0,1">
        <GradientStop Color="White" Offset="0"/>
        <GradientStop Color="#00000000" Offset="0.8"/>
      </LinearGradientBrush>
    </Ellipse.OpacityMask>
```

```
        </Ellipse>

        <Canvas.RenderTransform>
          <TranslateTransform Y="0" X="0" x:Name="bounce"/>
        </Canvas.RenderTransform>

        <Canvas.Triggers>
          <EventTrigger RoutedEvent="Canvas.Loaded">
            <BeginStoryboard>
              <Storyboard>
                <DoubleAnimation
                  Storyboard.TargetName="bounce"
                  Storyboard.TargetProperty="Y"
                  From="1.0" To="55.0"
                  Duration="0:0:.25"
                  AutoReverse="True"
                  RepeatBehavior="Forever"
                  />
              </Storyboard>
            </BeginStoryboard>
          </EventTrigger>
        </Canvas.Triggers>

      </Canvas>
      <!-- End Bouncing Ball -->

    </Border>
    <!-- End Bouncing Ball Background -->
```

Next, you are to define your bouncing ball. The bouncing ball is made up of three `Ellipses` and two opacity masks placed on a `Canvas`. Together, these elements make up the glassy, 3D visual effect of your ball. Opacity masks were covered earlier in the chapter, so you should be familiar with what's happening thus far. This last example defines your ball, but now you'll want to get it bouncing.

To get the ball bouncing, you've added a `TranslateTransform` to the outermost container for your bouncing ball, which is the `Canvas`. You aren't actually moving anything in your transform definition; you're letting the animation take care of this instead. This brings you to the next piece of functionality you need to add to your ball: the bounce. Before you can do that, however, you need to figure out when to start bouncing.

You want your animation to kick-off as soon as your `Canvas` completes loading. In your `Canvas.Triggers` object, you define a single `EventTrigger`, the target of which is the `Canvas.Loaded` event. When the `Canvas.Loaded` event fires, your `EventTrigger` will kick-off your `Storyboard` animation.

Finally, you need to create your animation. The animation will target the `TranslateTransform` you created earlier, specifically the `Y` property. You'll move the ball along a `Y` axis from 1 to 55. This gets the ball bouncing up, but to get it back down you'll need to do something else. To do this, you set the `AutoReverse` property to true. This will reverse the animation when it completes, sending the ball back down to its starting point. Finally, you want to keep this animation going, so you set the `RepeatBehavior` to a repeat value of `Forever`.

Next you need to create the reflection.

```xml
<!-- Glass -->
<Border Grid.Column="0" Grid.Row="1" Height="300" Background="Black"
  Opacity=".8">

  <!-- Reflection -->
  <Border>

    <Border.Background>
      <VisualBrush
        Visual="{Binding ElementName=BouncingBall}"
        Opacity=".35"
        Stretch="None"
        AlignmentX="Left">
        <VisualBrush.Transform>
          <TransformGroup>
            <ScaleTransform
              ScaleX="1"
              ScaleY="-1"
              CenterX="150"
              CenterY="104"
              />
            <TranslateTransform
              Y="{Binding ElementName=bounce, Converter={StaticResource
                FlipConverter}, Path=Y}"
              X="{Binding ElementName=bounce, Path=X}"/>
          </TransformGroup>
        </VisualBrush.Transform>
      </VisualBrush>
    </Border.Background>

    <Border.OpacityMask>
      <LinearGradientBrush StartPoint="0,0" EndPoint="0,1">
        <GradientStop Offset="0" Color="Black"/>
        <GradientStop Offset=".9" Color="Transparent"/>
      </LinearGradientBrush>
    </Border.OpacityMask>

  </Border>
  <!-- End Reflection -->

</Border>
<!-- End Glass -->

  </Grid>
</Window>
```

Here you are creating a `Border` object for the background glass effect. Within your black border, you are going to create the actual reflection of the bouncing ball. You use another `Border` object to define the reflection. You will use a `VisualBrush` to create the background of this border and, you guessed it, the visual you will target is your bouncing ball.

A `VisualBrush` is itself an object, so although it copies your bouncing ball, it does not copy the transform or animation. So you simply create a `TranslateTransform` for the reflection object. You don't have to create another animation, however. If you were to create another animation, it might be hard to sync up the bounce with the reflection. In order to keep things in sync, you'll take advantage of WPF data binding. You bind the X and Y properties of the `TranslateTransform` to the X and Y values defined in the bouncing ball `TranslateTransform`. That seems pretty great, but you want the reflection to translate in the opposite direction of your bouncing ball. When the bouncing ball goes up, the reflection should go down. In order to accomplish this, you need the inverse value of the Y property. For this, you'll use a `TypeConverter`, which you'll create shortly. You bind the X property as well so that when you drag the bouncing ball, your reflection will drag as well. In addition, you add a `ScaleTransform` to shrink up the reflection a bit, which will enhance your illusion of reflection on glass.

Finally, you also add an opacity mask to the reflection. This gives the impression of depth to the reflection.

Next you need to modify the `Window1.xaml.cs` code-behind file to add your dragging logic. You'll simply define event handlers for `MouseDown`, `MouseMove`, and `MouseUp` events. In addition, you'll create a `TypeConverter`, which simply returns the inverse value of an integer. This is part of how you get your reflected ball to move in the opposite direction of the main bouncing ball.

```
using System;
using System.Windows;
using System.Windows.Data;
using System.Windows.Input;
using System.Windows.Media;

namespace BouncingBall
{

  public partial class Window1 : System.Windows.Window
  {

    private bool _dragging = false;

    public Window1()
    {
      InitializeComponent();
    }

    private void BouncingBall_MouseDown(object sender, MouseEventArgs e)
    {
      _dragging = true;
    }

    private void BouncingBall_MouseUp(object sender, MouseEventArgs e)
    {
      _dragging = false;
    }

    private void BouncingBall_MouseMove(object sender, MouseEventArgs e)
    {
      if (!_dragging)
```

```
        return;

    double x = Mouse.GetPosition(this.BouncingBallContainer).X;

    Vector vector = VisualTreeHelper.GetOffset(this.BouncingBall);
    double pX = vector.X;

    TranslateTransform t = (TranslateTransform)this.bounce;
    t.X = x - pX;
    }

}

public class FlipConverter : IValueConverter
{
  public object Convert(object value, Type targetType, object parameter,
    System.Globalization.CultureInfo culture)
  {
    return (((double)value) * -1);
  }
  public object ConvertBack(object value, Type targetType, object parameter,
    System.Globalization.CultureInfo culture)
  {
    return (((double)value) * -1);
  }
}

}
```

The logic for dragging the ball is quite simple. You grab the x position of the mouse, the x position of your bouncing ball, and then perform a translate transform on the ball, using the formula (Mouse X Position – BouncingBall X Position).

You also finally get around to defining a TypeConverter, which will return the inverse of any integer passed to it. This is what you will use to get the opposite value of your bouncing ball TranslateTransform y-coordinate to your reflection. When the ball moves up 10 degrees, the reflection will move down 10 degrees (–10).

Figure 6-13 illustrates the results of running your example.

Of course Figure 6-13 can't demonstrate the animation, but you get the idea. When you run the application, you can click any area of the window and drag the bouncing ball horizontally. The bouncing ball will follow the mouse. As the mouse moves horizontally, it continues to bounce up and down, and the reflection will follow.

Figure 6-13

Animated Image Viewer Example

In this example, you create an animated image viewer application. The structure of your application is going to be simple. You're going to focus on bells and whistles rather than functionality. Your image viewer application will display a number of thumbnails across the bottom of the screen. When the mouse passes over a thumbnail, you'll display the image at a larger size in a preview area, similar to the Windows Picture and Fax Viewer. When an image is selected, it will rotate into your preview area. While it rotates, the selected image will scale from its thumbnail size to full size. Similarly, when another image is selected, the current image will rotate and scale smaller until out of view. This gives the effect of an image "flying" into and out of the preview area. You'll be using transformations and animation to make all of this happen. You'll also use a VisualBrush to display the selected image in the preview area. Additionally, you'll use a couple of bitmap effects to give your application some polish, and a Slider object to control the animation speed.

Now that you know what you are going to build, it's time to jump into the code. Open Visual Studio and create a new project using the .NET Framework 3.0 Windows Application template. Name the project **ImageViewer**. You will need to add an Images directory to your project, and add some images to it. Make sure all images have their Build Action property set to Resource. Open the Window1.xaml file and modify it as follows:

```xml
<Window x:Class="ImageViewer.Window1"
  xmlns="http://schemas.microsoft.com/winfx/2006/xaml/presentation"
  xmlns:x="http://schemas.microsoft.com/winfx/2006/xaml"
  Title="Image Viewer"
  Height="413"
  Width="643"
  Margin="10"
  Name="ThisWindow"
  >

  <Window.Resources>
    <Style TargetType="Image">
      <Setter Property="Margin" Value="5"/>
    </Style>
  </Window.Resources>

<DockPanel LastChildFill="True" Margin="5">

  <StackPanel DockPanel.Dock="Top" Margin="4" VerticalAlignment="Center"
    HorizontalAlignment="Center">
    <StackPanel Orientation="Horizontal">
      <TextBlock FontWeight="Bold">Animation Duration:</TextBlock>
      <Slider
        Minimum="1"
        Maximum="1500"
        TickFrequency="1"
        IsSnapToTickEnabled="True"
        Width="100"
        Value="{Binding ElementName=ThisWindow, Path=AnimationDuration}"
        />
    </StackPanel>
  </StackPanel>
```

Up to this point, you've simply defined your Window element, a Style for your Image objects, and a Slider object to control the animation speed. The Slider control binds to a dependency property in your Window1 code-behind, which you'll create shortly. Next you create your image thumbnails.

```xml
<StackPanel Orientation="Horizontal" DockPanel.Dock="Bottom"
  VerticalAlignment="Center" HorizontalAlignment="Center">
  <Image Source="Images/Beach.jpg" Width="50" MouseEnter="Image_MouseEnter"/>
  <Image Source="Images/Blossoms.jpg" Width="50" MouseEnter="Image_MouseEnter"/>
  <Image Source="Images/Flower.jpg" Width="50" MouseEnter="Image_MouseEnter"/>
  <Image Source="Images/Hills.jpg" Width="50" MouseEnter="Image_MouseEnter"/>
  <Image Source="Images/Water.jpg" Width="50" MouseEnter="Image_MouseEnter"/>
</StackPanel>
```

You are simply placing five images into a horizontal StackPanel and setting the Width property of each Image to 50. This is what we meant by not focusing on functionality. If you wanted to extend this example later, you could create a custom thumbnail Panel, read in files from disk, or load the images dynamically using an XMLDataProvider. You're focusing on effects in this chapter so we'll leave these details up to you. For now, this suits your purpose.

```
<TextBlock Name="txtImageName" FontFamily="Verdana" FontWeight="DemiBold"
  DockPanel.Dock="Bottom" VerticalAlignment="Center"
  HorizontalAlignment="Center"
  Margin="5"/>
```

Here you simply add a TextBlock to display the image name when an image is loaded into the preview area. You're placing all of your elements in a DockPanel. You set the DockPanel.Dock property for your TextBlock to Bottom. You also set the DockPanel.Dock property to Bottom for the StackPanel. When two or more objects define the same value for the Dock property of a DockPanel, each will get docked in the order in which it is defined. So your StackPanel is docked to the bottom-most edge of your DockPanel because it is defined in your XAML file first, and your TextBlock is docked to the top edge of your StackPanel because it is defined second.

```
<Border BorderBrush="White">
  <Border Margin="50" ClipToBounds="True">
    <Border.Background>
      <LinearGradientBrush StartPoint="0.5,0" EndPoint="0.5,1">
        <GradientStop Color="LightBlue" Offset=".2"/>
        <GradientStop Color="Blue" Offset=".5"/>
        <GradientStop Color="LightBlue" Offset=".8"/>
      </LinearGradientBrush>
    </Border.Background>
    <Border.BitmapEffect>
      <BitmapEffectGroup>
        <DropShadowBitmapEffect ShadowDepth="2"/>
        <BevelBitmapEffect BevelWidth="1.5"/>
      </BitmapEffectGroup>
    </Border.BitmapEffect>
      <Canvas Name="imageCanvas"/>
    </Border>
  </Border>

</DockPanel>

</Window>
```

Finally, you define your image preview area as a Canvas, named imageCanvas. You'll use the canvas to display your image previews by painting the canvas's Background property with a VisualBrush that points to the selected thumbnail. Your canvas in this example is surrounded by two Border objects. The first Border you define will provide a white border area around your preview area. For the nested Border, you create a LinearGradientBrush to fill the background of your preview area. You also add a couple of bitmap effects, a drop shadow, and a slight bevel to give your preview area some depth and polish.

Now that you've defined your UI in XAML, let's jump to the code behind, where you'll add your transformation logic and animation to get the images "flying." Open up the Window1.xaml.cs file and modify it as follows.

```
using System;
using System.Windows;
using System.Windows.Controls;
using System.Windows.Input;
```

```
using System.Windows.Media;
using System.Windows.Media.Animation;

namespace ImageViewer
{

  public partial class Window1 : System.Windows.Window
  {

    object _sender;

    public Window1()
    {
      InitializeComponent();

      TransformGroup group = new TransformGroup();
      ScaleTransform scale = new ScaleTransform();
      group.Children.Add(scale);
      RotateTransform rot = new RotateTransform();
      group.Children.Add(rot);
      this.imageCanvas.RenderTransform = group;
    }

    public static DependencyProperty AnimationDurationProperty =
      DependencyProperty.Register("AnimationDuration", typeof(double),
        typeof(Window1), new PropertyMetadata(500.0, null));

    public double AnimationDuration
    {
      get { return (double)GetValue(AnimationDurationProperty); }
      set { SetValue(AnimationDurationProperty, value); }
    }


    private void Image_MouseEnter(object sender, MouseEventArgs e)
    {
      _sender = sender;
      if (this.imageCanvas.Background != null)
        FlyOutCurrentImage();
      else
        FlyInNewImage(sender);
    }
```

Up to this point, you've simply defined some basic class constructs. In the Window1 constructor, you've added a TransformGroup to your imageCanvas. You've placed two transforms in the group — a ScaleTransform and RotateTransform. You've added a single dependency property named AnimationDurationProperty to your class. This will be used by the animation code you'll write shortly. This is also the property that the Slider you created earlier binds to. Additionally, you create an event handler named Image_MouseEnter. This event will fire off the animation and transformation code whenever the mouse moves over a thumbnail.

Next, you define three methods: FlyInNewImage, FlyOutCurrentImage, and Animation_Completed. These methods control the animations and transformations you will apply to your preview area canvas.

```csharp
private void FlyInNewImage(object sender)
{

  if (this.imageCanvas.RenderTransform == null)
    return;

  string imageName = ((Image)sender).Source.ToString();
  imageName = imageName.Substring(imageName.LastIndexOf("/") + 1);
  this.txtImageName.Text = imageName;

  VisualBrush vb = new VisualBrush((Visual)sender);
  this.imageCanvas.Background = vb;

  TransformGroup group = (TransformGroup)this.imageCanvas.RenderTransform;
  ScaleTransform scale = (ScaleTransform)group.Children[0];
  RotateTransform rot = (RotateTransform)group.Children[1];

  this.imageCanvas.RenderTransformOrigin = new Point(0, 0);

  scale.ScaleX = .5;
  scale.ScaleY = .5;
  rot.Angle = 45;

  DoubleAnimation rotAnimation = new DoubleAnimation(0,
    TimeSpan.FromMilliseconds(AnimationDuration));
  rot.BeginAnimation(RotateTransform.AngleProperty, rotAnimation);
  DoubleAnimation scaleAnimation = new DoubleAnimation(1,
    TimeSpan.FromMilliseconds(AnimationDuration));
  scale.BeginAnimation(ScaleTransform.ScaleXProperty, scaleAnimation);
  scale.BeginAnimation(ScaleTransform.ScaleYProperty, scaleAnimation);
}
```

The FlyInNewImage method accepts a parameter of type object, which will be the image that the mouse is over, and is passed in from your MouseEnter event handler. The FlyInNewImage method essentially does four things:

❑ Sets the Text property TextBlock to display the currently selected image name

❑ Adds the image the mouse is currently over to the Background property of the imageCanvas by setting the Visual property of the VisualBrush

❑ Sets up the scale and rotate transformation values for the imageCanvas

❑ Kicks off the animations.

```csharp
private void FlyOutCurrentImage()
{

  if (this.imageCanvas.RenderTransform == null)
    return;

  TransformGroup group = (TransformGroup)this.imageCanvas.RenderTransform;
  ScaleTransform scale = (ScaleTransform)group.Children[0];
```

```
    RotateTransform rot = (RotateTransform)group.Children[1];

    this.imageCanvas.RenderTransformOrigin = new Point(1, 0);

    DoubleAnimation rotAnimation = new DoubleAnimation(45,
      TimeSpan.FromMilliseconds(AnimationDuration));
    rotAnimation.Completed += Animation_Completed;
    rotAnimation.AccelerationRatio = 0.2;
    rotAnimation.DecelerationRatio = 0.7;
    rot.BeginAnimation(RotateTransform.AngleProperty, rotAnimation);

    DoubleAnimation scaleAnimation = new DoubleAnimation(.5,
      TimeSpan.FromMilliseconds(AnimationDuration));
    scale.BeginAnimation(ScaleTransform.ScaleXProperty, scaleAnimation);
    scale.BeginAnimation(ScaleTransform.ScaleYProperty, scaleAnimation);
  }

  void Animation_Completed(object sender, EventArgs e)
  {
    FlyInNewImage(_sender);
  }
}
}
```

The FlyOutCurrentImage is very similar to the FlyInNewImage method. There are two key differences, however. First, the values you set for your transformations are different, and the RenderTransformOrigin is set to the upper-right corner of the preview area. Second, the rotAnimation object defines a callback method that will be called when the animation completes. This callback ensures the "fly out" will finish before the "fly in" begins. Finally, the Animation_Completed method simply calls the FlyInNewImage method.

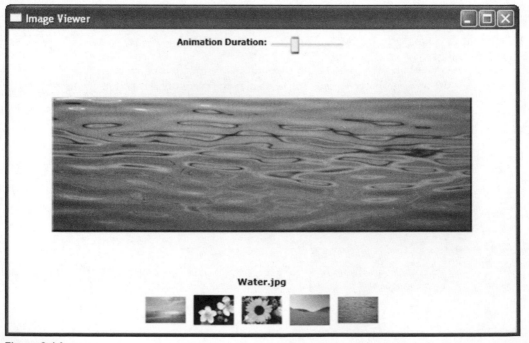

Figure 6-14

As with the last example, Figure 6-14 doesn't really do the application justice. When you run the application, and mouse over the image thumbnails, you'll see the animation and transformations in action. Moving the Animation Duration slider to the right slows the animation speed and, of course, moving it left speeds the animation up. You can see the drop shadow and bevel of the preview area provide a nice framing effect for the image you are previewing.

Summary

WPF offers a lot of effects you can use to achieve some pretty cool UI. Using the foundations provided, the possibilities are truly endless. In this chapter you have explored all of the brushes, bitmap effects, and transformations provided by WPF. You've seen how they work, how you can apply them to elements in your UI, and how you can combine them to achieve a unique and visually appealing UI. You also explored triggering animations off of events and using animations to perform transformations. Finally, you created a couple of sample applications by combining the concepts that you have learned about in this chapter.

After reading this chapter you can now:

❑ Describe the various brushes available to you in WPF, including the `SolidColorBrush`, `LinearGradientBrush`, `RadialGradientBrush`, `ImageBrush`, `DrawingBrush`, and `VisualBrush`.

❑ Understand the functionality and capabilities of each `Brush` class.

❑ Describe the various bitmap effects provided by WPF including the `BevelBitmapEffect`, `BlurBitmapEffect`, `DropShadowBitmapEffect`, `EmbossedBitmapEffect`, and `OuterGlowBitmapEffect`.

❑ Understand the functionality and capabilities of each `BitmapEffect` class.

❑ Describe the various transformations provided by WPF, including `TranslateTransform`, `ScaleTransform`, `SkewTransform`, and `RotateTransform`.

❑ Understand the functionality and capabilities of each `Transform` class.

❑ Understand the difference between a `LayoutTransform` and a `RenderTransform`, and when to use each.

❑ Describe and use an opacity mask.

7

Custom Controls

Windows Presentation Foundation controls are based on the concept of composition. Controls can contain other controls. For instance, a button may contain another button as its content, or it may contain an image, video, animation, or even a text box. The power of composition in WPF is that it provides a tremendous amount of flexibility right out of the box for customizing controls. In addition, WPF introduces styling, control templates, and triggers, which further enhance the extensibility of controls. Still there may be times when you need to create a custom control and, of course, WPF supports that as well.

The purpose for any application user interface is to present users with a set of visual components that coordinate user input and organize workflow. Controls are the individual visual elements that are logically grouped to accept, organize, and validate user input. In both Windows and web applications today, you commonly see these elements as text boxes, drop-down lists, radio buttons, and checkboxes.

WPF controls are referred to as *lookless controls*, which refers to the separation of visual appearance from behavior. WPF allows you to modify or extend the visual appearance of any control without affecting the control's behavior. Developers can modify the visual appearance of any pre-existing control, enhancing its visual impact while allowing the user to retain familiarity with the expected behavior. For example, with the media and animation capabilities provided in WPF, a button can exhibit animation features when the user interacts with it, but the button's behavior does not change. The button may "spin" or "glow" in reaction to a user clicking on it but the button still fires the expected click event.

Within WPF, the developer also has the ability to author custom controls tailored to the specific data input and validation needs of their application. The base classes provided by WPF for extending and creating controls provide the developer with great flexibility in the design of their control's visual appearance. Such flexibility in visual appearance is made available through the styling and control template features of WPF.

The following concepts are covered in this chapter:

❏   Choosing a control base class

❏   Custom control authoring via the `UserControl` base class

❏   Data binding to controls using both declarative XAML and procedural code

❏   Customizing a control's look and feel with styles and templates

Overview

WPF offers the developer an extensive feature set for constructing dynamic controls that push the boundaries of what users expect from conventional Windows application development. For instance, WPF controls can now be animated quickly and easily and 3D graphics and video can be incorporated to give controls a new level of interactivity and dynamism.

In spite of the advances that WPF provides, the problem-solving process for controls remains unchanged. Controls are still intended to serve a purpose and should define behavior accordingly. When developing a control, the developer must ask himself basic design questions, such as the following:

❏   What are the requirements of my new control?

❏   What behavior or functionality should my control provide?

❏   Does a control already exist that I can customize using styling or control templates in order to get the behavior I desire?

❏   How flexible does the control need to be for stylizing and extension by the control consumer?

❏   What type of user will be interacting with the control?

❏   Does the functionality meet the specified business requirements?

The answers to these questions will define not only the path you take — customizing an existing control or creating a new control — but also will define your control's behavior, referred to as its *API*. Designing a streamlined, flexible, and well–thought out API is the goal of the custom control author.

In WPF, the choice of base class for your control is also dependent on the answers to these questions. The amount of customization required for your control will indicate the starting point for extending a new control.

Before heading down the path of creating a new control, it is important to note that many of the default controls within the WPF Framework allow for custom styling, triggers, and templating. If, for example, the need of your control is only to introduce an animation behavior, then creating a subclassed control would be overkill.

Control Base Classes

Once you have determined that creating a new control is the way to go, it's time to select a base class. In WPF, you can create custom controls based on a number of base classes, including `Control`, `UserControl`, and `FrameworkElement`. Selecting which base class to inherit from when creating a new control is contingent on the level of flexibility and customization you desire for your control. For example, the questions that you should ask yourself about the purpose of your control include the following:

❑   Will your control be composed of existing WPF elements?

❑   How flexible does your control need to be?

❑   Will you be doing custom low-level rendering in your control?

❑   What is the application context of the control? Will it be used by one application or many?

❑   How much visual customization will be required by consumers of your control? Should users be able to override the visual appearance of your control?

If you are simply composing existing elements in your control and consumers will not need to override its visual appearance, then most likely subclassing `UserControl` is the way to go. If separation of visual appearance from your control behavior is important in order that it may be visually changed by a consumer, then subclassing `Control` is the way to go. If you can't get the visuals you want out-of-the-box with WPF and you'll be doing custom rendering, then subclassing `FrameworkElement` is your best choice. There may be other factors that affect your choice of base class as well. Becoming familiar with these classes will go a long way in helping you make the right choice.

The UserControl Class

Subclassing the `UserControl` class is the simplest way to create a new control and is the method you will explore in this chapter. A user control is composed of standard controls that together perform a particular interface function. Because a user control typically is meant to be used within a certain application context, its ability to be customized doesn't warrant as much attention as perhaps its reusability.

Within your user control you can apply styles to individual elements as well as handle specific events and raise custom events specific to the functionality of your control.

Creating a User Control

In this example, you will create a new user control that inherits from the `System.Windows.Controls.UserControl` base class. The control will be one that I'm sure many developers have come across before: a pie graph chart. This control will be a good example of using the dynamic drawing features of WPF and container controls.

Before you get started in the code, let's expand on the process of defining the behavior (API) of this control, the logic necessary to generate the graph, and the WPF objects that you will use to draw the graph.

With WPF, a piece of constructed geometry that is drawn to screen is a visual element. Therefore, it is a targetable object that can be accessed directly in code rather than having to be redrawn as pixels to a screen as would have been the case prior to WPF. This means that it becomes much easier for you to detect collisions (hit-testing) as well as apply transformations and animation to the geometry object.

In order to draw to specific coordinate locations you will use a Canvas as the container for your pie drawing. A Path object will represent each pie slice. In WPF, a Path object can be made up of multiple geometry objects. Therefore, each pie section of your pie graph will be a Path object, which contains a PathGeometry object.

In WPF, the PathGeometry object represents a complex shape that is made up of any combination of arcs, curves, ellipses, lines, or rectangles. In WPF geometry, these arcs, curves, lines, and rectangles are represented by PathFigure and PathSegment objects. This will provide you with the flexibility to operate on each segment of the graph individually. For example, you can apply individual animations (if you so desire) to each piece rather than to the graph as a whole. You can also capture events on a piece-by-piece basis making it easier to respond to an input event as it pertains to each segment of the graph. Similarly, you can utilize the WPF routed event model to allow events fired by any pie piece to bubble up to the pie graph's parent container.

In order to create the PathGeometry object, you must first create a PathFigure object for each side of the pie graph piece. The PathFigure class represents a subsection of the PathGeometry object you will create. The PathFigure is itself made up of one or more PathSegment objects, which are specific types of geometric segments, such as the LineSegment and ArcSegment. You will use two LineSegment classes to create the initial and terminal sides of the piece. An instance of the ArcSegment class will construct the circular arc that attaches the two line segments together. Figure 7-1 illustrates how each pie piece will be constructed using the Segment classes.

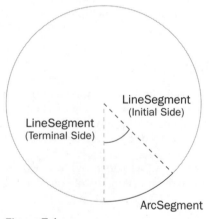

Figure 7-1

The ArcSegment Class

The ArcSegment constructs an elliptical arc based on the initial starting point of the PathFigure object and a terminal point. Alternatively, you can construct the elliptical arc from the sibling, preceding it within the collection of PathSegment objects in its Segments property. The following table outlines the argument list used to construct an ArcSegment.

Argument	Specification
Point	The terminal point for the arc segment.
Size	Specifies the x and y radius of the arc. The more circular the arc desired, the closer the x and y radius will be.
RotationAngle	The x-axis rotation angle.
IsLargeArc	Flags if the arc to be drawn is greater than 180 degrees.
SweepDirection	Enumeration value that specifies whether the arc sweeps clockwise or counter-clockwise.

The following XAML defines an `ArcSegment` that will start from the initial point based on the `PathFigure` to which it belongs.

```xml
<Path Stroke="Black" Fill="Gray" StrokeThickness="2" Width="Auto">
  <Path.Data>
    <PathGeometry>
      <PathGeometry.Figures>
        <PathFigureCollection>
          <PathFigure StartPoint="200,200">
            <PathFigure.Segments>
              <PathSegmentCollection>
                <ArcSegment
                    Point="300,200"
                    Size="200,50"
                    RotationAngle="90"
                    IsLargeArc="False"
                    SweepDirection="Clockwise"
                    />
              </PathSegmentCollection>
            </PathFigure.Segments>
          </PathFigure>
        </PathFigureCollection>
      </PathGeometry.Figures>
    </PathGeometry>
  </Path.Data>
</Path>
```

The following procedural code generates the equivalent to the declarative XAML:

```csharp
PathGeometry pathGeometry = new PathGeometry();

PathFigure figure = new PathFigure();
figure.StartPoint = new Point(200,200);

figure.Segments.Add(
new ArcSegment(
  new Point(300,200),
```

```
    new Size(200,50),
    90,
    false,
    SweepDirection.Clockwise,
    true
    )
);

pathGeometry.Figures.Add(figure);

Path path = new Path();
path.Data = pathGeometry;
path.Fill = Brushes.Gray;
path.Stroke = Brushes.Black;

myContainer.Children.Add(path);
```

Figure 7-2 illustrates the ArcSegment created in the preceding code examples.

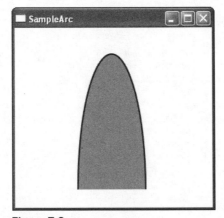

Figure 7-2

Each subsequent arc segment that is drawn for each piece in the pie graph will have to start at the last terminal point of the former segment. To calculate this you'll need to use some trigonometry to determine each pie piece's initial and terminal points relative to the angle of each pie piece. The pie piece angle will be determined by the percentage it represents of the underlying data. Figure 7-3 illustrates the incremental process.

To keep track of the next starting point you'll create a private local variable that you'll increment by the angle of the current pie piece.

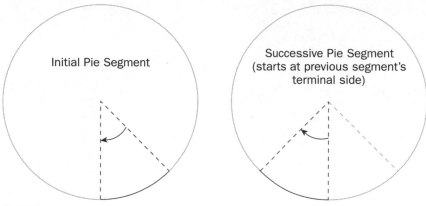

Figure 7-3

Now that you have established a basis for your control, you can build it in Visual Studio. The steps are as follows:

1. In Visual Studio, select File ➪ New Project from the menu. From the Project Types tree view, select Visual C# ➪ Windows (.NET Framework 3.0) Node, and then click on the Windows Application (WPF) icon from the list. Name your project **WPFWindowsApplication**, and click OK. This new project should create a `Window1.xaml` file, and a supporting partial class code-behind file.

2. Right-click on the project node and select Add ➪ New Item. Select User Control (WPF) and rename the file to **PieGraphControl**.

3. Open the PieGraphControl.xaml.cs file and add the following `using` directives, if they don't exist:

```
using System;
using System.Collections.Generic;
using System.Net;
using System.Windows;
using System.Windows.Controls;
using System.Windows.Data;
using System.Windows.Input;
using System.Windows.Media;
using System.Windows.Media.Animation;
using System.Windows.Navigation;
using System.Windows.Shapes;
```

4. Within the pie graph control, you will create a private class named `PiePieceData` that will hold the data required to generate each section of the pie graph. Specifically, it will contain properties pertinent to the construction of each `ArcSegment` for a `PathFigure`.

   In the PieGraphControl.xaml.cs file, add the following private class declaration:

```
private class PiePieceData
{
  private double percentage;
```

```
private string label;
private bool isGreaterThan180;
private Point initialSide;
private Point terminalSide;
private Brush color;

public Brush Color
{
  get { return color; }
  set { color = value; }
}

public double Percentage
{
  get { return percentage; }
  set { percentage = value; }
}

public string Label
{
  get { return label; }
  set { label = value; }
}

public bool IsGreaterThan180
{
  get { return isGreaterThan180; }
  set { isGreaterThan180 = value; }
}

public Point InitialSide
{
  get { return initialSide; }
  set { initialSide = value; }
}

public Point TerminalSide
{
  get { return terminalSide; }
  set { terminalSide = value; }
}

public PiePieceData()
{

}

public PiePieceData(double percentage, string label)
{
  this.percentage = percentage;
  this.label = label;
}
}
```

5. Shifting focus back to our `PieGraphControl` class, you will need to perform a little math to determine where each segment will be placed within the area of the pie graph.

❑ The `ConvertToRadians` method will take an angle measured in degrees and convert it to its radian measure equivalent so that you can use the `Math.Cos()` and `Math.Sin()` methods to find the point positions.

❑ The `CalcAngleFromPercentage` will take the percentage value that the pie segment represents and calculate the angle that represents the given percentage.

❑ The `CreatePointFromAngle` will take the radian angle and produce a point that intersects the pie graph circle for the given angle. This will help you determine the initial and terminal sides.

Add the following private methods to your `PieGraphControl` class definition:

```
private Point CreatePointFromAngle(double angleInRadians)
{
  Point point = new Point();

  point.X = radius * Math.Cos(angleInRadians) + origin.X;
  point.Y = radius * Math.Sin(angleInRadians) + origin.Y;

  return point;
}


private double CalcAngleFromPercentage(double percentage)
{
  return 360 * percentage;
}


private double ConvertToRadians(double theta)
{
  return (Math.PI / 180) * theta;
}
```

6. You now need to include some private members that will aid in calculations and hold the collection of data from which you'll want to generate the graph. You'll also include a list of colors for each piece. For the sake of this example, you'll create a finite number of colors that will be used with the pie pieces. For a more flexible control, you would probably include a more dynamic color creation mechanism.

Include the following code in the `PieGraphControl` class definition:

```
private Point origin = new Point(100, 100);
private int radius = 100;
private double percentageTotal = 0;
private double initialAngle = 0;
private List<PiePieceData> piePieces = new List<PiePieceData>();

private Brush[] brushArray = new Brush[]
{
  Brushes.Aquamarine,
  Brushes.Azure,
  Brushes.Blue,
  Brushes.Chocolate,
```

```
   Brushes.Crimson,
   Brushes.DarkGreen,
   Brushes.DarkGray,
   Brushes.DarkSlateBlue,
   Brushes.Maroon,
   Brushes.Teal,
   Brushes.Violet
};
```

7.   The following code constructs a `PathFigure` based on the `PiePieceData`, which is passed into the method.

Include the following code in the `PieGraphControl` class definition:

```
private PathFigure CreatePiePiece(PiePieceData pieceData)
{
    PathFigure piePiece = new PathFigure();
    piePiece.StartPoint = origin;

    // Create initial side
    piePiece.Segments.Add(new LineSegment(pieceData.InitialSide, true));

    // Add arc
    Size size = new Size(radius,radius);

    piePiece.Segments.Add(
        new ArcSegment(
            pieceData.TerminalSide,
            size,
            0,
            pieceData.IsGreaterThan180,
            SweepDirection.Clockwise,
            true
            )
    );

    // Complete the terminal side line
    piePiece.Segments.Add(new LineSegment(new Point(origin.X,origin.Y), true));

    return piePiece;
}
```

8.   The next method definition will be a public method to allow developers to add a new pie percentage value. This method also checks to make sure that the total percentage doesn't exceed the value of 100 so that there is no overlap in the pie segments.

Add the following to the `PieGraphControl` class definition:

```
public void AddPiePiece(double percentage, string label)
{
    if (percentageTotal + percentage > 1.00)
        throw new Exception("Cannot add percentage. Will make total greater than
            100%.");

    PiePieceData pieceData = new PiePieceData();
```

```
    pieceData.Percentage = percentage;
    pieceData.Label = label;

    // Calculate initial and terminal sides
    double angle = CalcAngleFromPercentage(percentage);
    double endAngle = initialAngle + angle;
    double thetaInit = ConvertToRadians(initialAngle);
    double thetaEnd = ConvertToRadians(endAngle);

    pieceData.InitialSide = CreatePointFromAngle(thetaInit);
    pieceData.TerminalSide = CreatePointFromAngle(thetaEnd);
    pieceData.IsGreaterThan180 = (angle > 180);

    // Update the start angle
    initialAngle = endAngle;

    piePieces.Add(pieceData);
}
```

9. Once the values have been added to the control, it is now ready to proceed in rendering the data. The following method creates a new `PathGeometry` object for each pie piece figure so that it can be drawn to screen. Add the following `RenderGraph` method to your `PieGraphControl` class definition:

```
public void RenderGraph()
{
    int i = 0;

    foreach (PiePieceData piePiece in piePieces)
    {
        PathGeometry pieGeometry = new PathGeometry();
        pieGeometry.Figures.Add(CreatePiePiece(piePiece));

        Path path = new Path();
        path.Data = pieGeometry;
        path.Fill = brushArray[i++ % brushArray.Length];
        piePiece.Color = (Brush)brushArray[i++ % brushArray.Length];
        canvas1.Children.Add(path);
    }
}
```

10. In the default Window1.cs code-behind file that was generated when the project was created, include the following code in the constructor of the `PieGraphControl` class:

```
public partial class Window1 : Window
{
    public Window1()
    {
        InitializeComponent();

        PieGraphControl ctrl = new PieGraphControl();

        ctrl.AddPiePiece(.20, "Latino");
        ctrl.AddPiePiece(.20, "Asian");
        ctrl.AddPiePiece(.30, "African-American");
```

```
      ctrl.AddPiePiece(.30, "Caucasian");

      ctrl.RenderGraph();
      this.myGrid.Children.Add(ctrl);
   }
}
```

11. The following XAML code contains the drawing canvas to which the drawing output will be directed.

Copy the following XAML code into the PieGraphControl.xaml file:

```xml
<UserControl x:Class="WPFWindowsApplication.PieGraphControl"
  xmlns="http://schemas.microsoft.com/winfx/2006/xaml/presentation"
  xmlns:x="http://schemas.microsoft.com/winfx/2006/xaml" Width="300" Height="400">
  <Grid>
    <Canvas Margin="50,38,51,162" MinHeight="50" MinWidth="50" Name="canvas1" />
  </Grid>
</UserControl>
```

12. Modify the Window1.xaml code generated by the New Project Wizard so that it looks like this:

```xml
<Window x:Class="WPFWindowsApplication.Window1"
  xmlns="http://schemas.microsoft.com/winfx/2006/xaml/presentation"
  xmlns:x="http://schemas.microsoft.com/winfx/2006/xaml"
  Title="WPFWindowsApplication" Height="300" Width="300"
  >
  <Grid Name="myGrid"/>
</Window>
```

13. Build the project in Debug to view the custom user control in WPF. Figure 7-4 shows the compiled result.

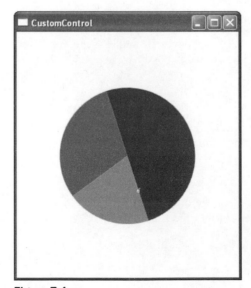

Figure 7-4

Data Binding in WPF

In WPF, data binding is an integral part of the platform. Data binding creates a connection between the properties of two objects. When the property of one object (the source) changes, the property of the other object (the target) is updated. In the most common scenario, you will use data binding to connect application interface controls to the underlying source data that populates them. A great example of data binding is using a Slider control to change a property of another control. The Value property of the Slider is bound to a specified property of some control such as the width of a button. When the slider is moved, its Value property changes and through data binding the Width property of the button is updated. The change is reflected at runtime, so as you might imagine, data binding is a key concept in animation. WPF introduces new methods for implementing data binding, but the concept remains the same: a source object property is bound to a target object property.

Prior to WPF, developers created data bindings by setting the DataSource property of a binding target object and calling its DataBind method. In the case of binding to a collection of objects, sometimes event handling methods would perform additional logic on an item-by-item basis to produce the output result. In WPF, the process for creating a binding between object and data source can be done procedurally through code or declaratively using XAML markup syntax.

Binding Markup Extensions

WPF introduces a new XAML markup extension syntax used to create binding associations in XAML. A markup extension signals that the value of a property is a reference to something else. This could be a resource declared in XAML or a dynamic resource determined at runtime. Markup extensions are placed within a XAML element attribute value between a pair of curly braces. You can also set properties within markup extensions. The following code example illustrates a markup extension for a binding:

```
<TextBlock
  Text="{Binding Source={StaticResource resourceKey},Path= Property}"
  Margin="2,2,2,2"
  FontSize="12"
  />
```

In the preceding XAML code, you designate that the Text property of the TextBox control is data bound by using a Binding extension. Within the Binding markup extension you specify two properties: the source object to bind from and the property of the source object to bind to. The source object is defined using another extension that denotes the source is a static resource defined within the XAML document. As you can see from this example, markup extensions can be nested within other markup extensions as well.

Binding Modes

Binding modes allow you to specify the binding relationship between the target and source objects. In WPF, a binding can have one of four modes, as the following table illustrates.

Mode	Description
OneWay	The target object is updated to reflect changes to the source object.
TwoWay	The target and source objects are updated to reflect changes on either end.
OneWayToSource	The converse of OneWay binding where target object changes are propagated back to the source object.
OneTime	The target object is populated to the source data once and changes between the target and source aren't reflected upon one another.

To operate within a OneWay or TwoWay binding mode, the source data object needs to be able to notify the target object of source data changes. The source object must implement the INotifyPropertyChanged interface to allow the target object to subscribe to the PropertyChanged event to refresh the target binding.

Data Binding to a List<T>

To pull all of these concepts together, you will modify the pie graph control you created previously to include some data bound elements. In this example, you will add a ListBox control to your user control that will display the percentage and description for each segment of the pie chart. You will bind the ListBox items to the pie pieces.

Because the source data object is a private list within the custom user control, you will need to set the context of the binding to the private list. To do this you will add a line of code to the constructor of the PieGraphControl that initializes the DataContext property of the user control to the list of pie pieces. The DataContext property allows child elements to bind to the same source as its parent element.

```
public PieGraphControl()
{
  InitializeComponent();
  this.DataContext = piePieces;
}
```

Next, in the XAML code for the PieGraphControl, you'll replace the current Grid with the following markup to introduce a ListBox control into the element tree. You will need to add a Binding markup extension to the ItemSource property of the ListBox to designate that it is data bound. Because you set the DataContext of the control to the list of pie pieces, you don't need to specify the source in the binding extension. You only need to include the binding extension itself within the curly braces. The following code segment illustrates the XAML markup required for this.

```
<Grid>
  <Canvas
    Margin="50,38,51,162"
    MinHeight="50"
    MinWidth="50"
    Name="canvas1"
    />
  <ListBox
    Height="138"
    Margin="49,0,49,13"
```

```
        Name="listBox1"
        VerticalAlignment="Bottom"
        ItemsSource="{Binding}">
    </ListBox>
  </Grid>
```

At this point, the process creates the binding but gives you no visualization of the data elements with which you would like to populate the ListBox. If you were to compile this project and view the resulting list box, you would see that all of the list items would just be ToString() representations of each PiePieceData object. To customize the result of each ListBox item and to display the data you want you'll need to use a data template.

Data Templates

Data templates provide you with a great deal of flexibility in controlling the visual appearance of data in a binding scenario. A data template can include its own unique set of controls, elements, and styles, resulting in a customized look and feel.

To customize the visual appearance of each data bound item that appears in the ListBox you will define a DataTemplate as a resource of the PieGraphControl. Defining our data template as a PieGraphControl resource will allow child elements within the custom control to use the same template if so desired. The following code segment defines a data template that you will apply to each list item in our PieGraphControl.

```
<UserControl.Resources>
  <DataTemplate x:Key="ListTemplate">
    <Grid>
      <Border
        BorderBrush="{Binding Path=Color}"
        BorderThickness="1"
        CornerRadius="3"
        Width="150">
        <StackPanel Orientation="Horizontal">
          <TextBlock
            Text="{Binding Path=Percentage}"
            Margin="2,2,2,2"
            FontSize="12"
            />
          <TextBlock
            Text="{Binding Path=Label}"
            Margin="2,2,2,2"
            FontSize="12"
            />
        </StackPanel>
      </Border>
    </Grid>
  </DataTemplate>
</UserControl.Resources>
```

Within the data template, you will notice that Binding Extensions have been added to those elements that will display the source data. The template includes a Border whose border brush will be specified by the color of the pie piece that is bound to it. Within the BorderBrush attribute of the Border element, you include a binding extension to specify that it binds to the Color property of the pie piece.

Now that the template has been created, you need to add an attribute to the `ListBox` element to specify that it should use the new template. Within the `ItemTemplate` attribute of the `ListBox` element, you add a binding extension to define the template as a `StaticResource` that you've defined in XAML. The resource key serves as the name of the template — in this case the name is `ListTemplate`.

```
<Grid>
  <Canvas
    Margin="50,38,51,162"
    MinHeight="50"
    MinWidth="50"
    Name="canvas1"
    />
  <ListBox
    Height="138"
    Margin="49,0,49,13"
    Name="listBox1"
    VerticalAlignment="Bottom"
    ItemsSource="{Binding}"
    ItemTemplate="{StaticResource ListTemplate}">
  </ListBox>
</Grid>
```

Figure 7-5 shows the newly formatted data bound ListBox as is defined in the template.

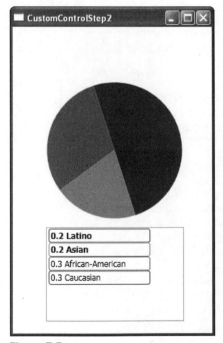

Figure 7-5

Data Conversions

Within a binding, you can also specify if any type conversions need to take place before data is bound to the target control. In order to support a custom conversion, you need to create a class that implements the IValueConverter interface. IValueConverter contains two methods that need to be implemented: Convert and ConvertBack.

In the pie chart, recall that each pie piece on the graph represents a fraction of the total pie. This fraction is stored within each PiePieceData object as a double. While it is common knowledge that decimals can be thought of in terms of percentages, it would be nice to display to the user the double value as a percentage to make the data easier to read.

In your PieGraphControl, you will now define a new class that converts the decimal value to a string value for its percentage representation. Copy the following code sample, which contains the class definition for the converter into the PieGraphControl.xaml.cs file:

```
[ValueConversion(typeof(double), typeof(string))]
public class DecimalToPercentageConverter : IValueConverter
{
  public object Convert(object value, Type targetType, object parameter,
    System.Globalization.CultureInfo culture)
  {
    double decimalValue = (double)value;
    return String.Format("{0:0%}", decimalValue);
  }

  public object ConvertBack(object value, Type targetType, object parameter,
    System.Globalization.CultureInfo culture)
  {
    throw new InvalidOperationException("Not expected");
  }

  public DecimalToPercentageConverter()
  {
  }
}
```

In order to use the type converter within XAML, you will need to create a new XML namespace that maps to the CLR namespace. To do so, add the following xmlns attribute to the UserControl element of the PieGraphControl.xaml file.

```
xmlns:local="clr-namespace:WPFWindowsApplication"
```

Next you must add an additional property to the Binding markup extension to denote that you would like to use a type converter during the binding. In the following code example, you add the Converter property to the binding and set it to the DecimalToPercentageConverter resource you've defined in the control resources and assign it the given key:

```
<UserControl.Resources>
  <local:DecimalToPercentageConverter x:Key="decimalConverter" />
  <DataTemplate x:Key="ListTemplate">

    ...
```

```
        <StackPanel Orientation="Horizontal">
        <TextBlock
          Text="{Binding Path=Percentage, Converter={StaticResource decimalConverter}}"
          Margin="2,2,2,2"
          FontSize="12"
          />
        <TextBlock
        ...
      </DataTemplate>
    </UserControl.Resources>
```

Figure 7-6 shows the results of the modified PieGraphControl that now includes the data conversion for each percentage within the ListBox item list.

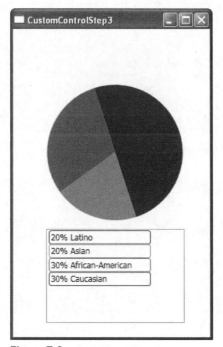

Figure 7-6

Creating and Editing Styles

WPF styles allow you to uniformly apply a specific group of property settings to controls in order to define a desired look and feel. WPF has a styling mechanism similar to CSS and its application to HTML elements. Styles provide a centralized location where you define the visual appearance for your controls. In addition, styles propagate those attributes to any element that inherits the style. Styles also allow the definition of custom triggers that can change the visual behavior of a control.

Before you begin applying styles to controls, you will cover the basics of styles and how to apply them to standard controls.

Styles are declared in the `Resources` property of a window, container, or application. Where you place your style definition depends on the scope of your style. For styles that have a global context within your application, you can add your style to the `Resources` property of the `App.xaml` file. The following code segment illustrates a global application-level style defined in the `<Application>` element of an App.xaml file:

```
<Application x:Class="WinFxBrowserApplication1.App"
  xmlns="http://schemas.microsoft.com/winfx/2006/xaml/presentation"
  xmlns:x="http://schemas.microsoft.com/winfx/2006/xaml"
  StartupUri="Window1.xaml"
  >
  <Application.Resources>
    <Style x:Key="GlobalTextStyle">
      <Setter Property="TextElement.FontSize" Value="14"></Setter>
    </Style>
  </Application.Resources>
</Application>
```

To apply this style to an element, you simply set the `Style` attribute of the control to the name of the defined style:

```
<Label Style="{StaticResource GlobalTextStyle}" Name="label1" >My Label
  Text</Label>
```

Figure 7-7 illustrates your label with an application-level style applied.

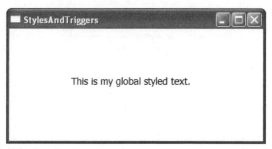

Figure 7-7

Specifying a Style's Target Type

The previous example illustrated a generic style definition that could be applied to any WPF element in your application, provided that it had a `FontSize` attribute to set. The style is generic because it does not specify a `TargetType` attribute. You use the `TargetType` attribute to indicate a specific control type to which the style will apply. If no `x:Key` attribute is specified along with the `TargetType` attribute, then the style will be applied to all elements of the specified target type.

The following code segment illustrates the use of the `TargetType` attribute. This style will be applied to elements of type `Label`. Additionally, the code defines an `x:Key` attribute so that only `Label` elements that specify the style property `LabelStyle` will inherit the style.

```
<Grid.Resources>
  <Style x:Key="LabelStyle" TargetType="{x:Type Label}">
    <Setter Property="Background" Value="BlueViolet" />
    <Setter Property="Foreground" Value="White" />
    <Setter Property="FontSize" Value="20" />
    <Setter Property="Width" Value="50" />
    <Setter Property="Height" Value="30" />
  </Style>...
</Grid.Resources>
```

As mentioned, specifying a target type for a style can also create a default style that is to be added to any element of the specified type by default. By removing the x:Key attribute, the style will be applied by default to elements of the specified target type — in this case, labels.

```
<Application.Resources>
  <Style TargetType="{x:Type Label}">
    <Setter Property="Background" Value="LightGray" />
    <Setter Property="Foreground" Value="White" />
    <Setter Property="FontSize" Value="14" />
    <Setter Property="Width" Value="100" />
    <Setter Property="Height" Value="50" />
  </Style>...
</Application.Resources>
```

The preceding code snippet declares a style that will be applied to all elements of type Label. Figure 7-8 illustrates the results of a simple label without a Style property defined. The style is picked up simply because the label is of type Label.

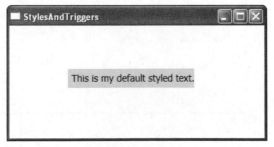

Figure 7-8

Inheriting and Overriding Styles

A style is a class just like any other in WPF, so it can be inherited from and extended easily. Inheriting from a style class comes in handy if you want to define a global style to apply to all of your elements. For instance, maybe you want all of your text elements to conform to one font face. Of course, you may also want a small subset of text elements to use other text styles. In this case you adjust the weight and decoration by overriding the global style, either with an additional style, or by setting the element attributes directly.

To inherit from a style in XAML, you simply specify the BasedOn attribute of the Style element and create a markup extension that points to the base style. The following code segment defines a base style that is applied to a button, as well as a derived style that inherits from the base style.

```xml
<Window.Resources>
  <Style x:Key="BaseStyle">
    <Setter Property="TextElement.FontSize" Value="12"></Setter>
  </Style>
  <Style x:Key="BoldStyle" BasedOn="{StaticResource BaseStyle}">
    <Setter Property="TextElement.FontWeight" Value="Bold"></Setter>
  </Style>
  <Style x:Key="ItalicStyle" BasedOn="{StaticResource BoldStyle}">
    <Setter Property="TextElement.FontStyle" Value="Italic"></Setter>
  </Style>
</Window.Resources>
<Grid Name="myGrid">
  <Label Style="{StaticResource BaseStyle}" Height="29" VerticalAlignment="Top"
    Margin="91,31,100,0">This is my base styled text.</Label>
  <Label Style="{StaticResource BoldStyle}" Margin="55,79,49,92"  >This is my base
    derived bold styled text.</Label>
  <Label Style="{StaticResource ItalicStyle}" Margin="57,0,47,41" Height="26"
    VerticalAlignment="Bottom">This is my bold derived italic styled text.</Label>
</Grid>
```

Figure 7-9 illustrates the results.

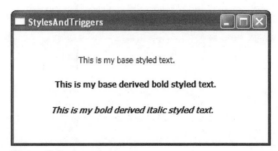

Figure 7-9

Style properties are overridden by in-line styles in WPF. In the following code segment, you adjust the italicized styled label in the previous code block but override the FontSize inline.

```xml
<Label Style="{StaticResource ItalicStyle}" FontSize="16" Margin="17,61,22,58">This
  is my bold derived italic styled text at 16pt.</Label>
```

The results are illustrated in Figure 7-10.

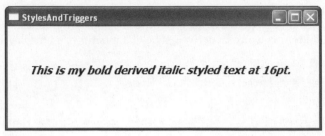

Figure 7-10

Style Triggers

Triggers enable you to develop interaction logic based on conditions or events. They allow you to alter the behavior of controls depending on which conditions of the control are true. Triggers can apply a new set of style changes or can initiate more complex actions, such as animating properties of the control. Triggers fall into three categories: properties, events, and data.

Property triggers watch specific properties and fire when their values change. In the following example, you define a style for a button that contains a property trigger that fires when the IsMouseOver property change occurs. The trigger alters the background and foreground properties of the button.

```
<Style x:Key="ButtonStyle" TargetType="{x:Type Button}">
  <Setter Property="Background" Value="LightBlue" />
  <Setter Property="Foreground" Value="Blue" />
  <Setter Property="FontSize" Value="14" />
  <Setter Property="Width" Value="100" />
  <Setter Property="Height" Value="50" />
  <Setter Property="TextElement.FontSize" Value="12"></Setter>
  <Style.Triggers>
    <Trigger Property="IsMouseOver" Value="True">
      <Setter Property="Background" Value="Orange" />
      <Setter Property="Foreground" Value="Black"></Setter>
    </Trigger>
  </Style.Triggers>
</Style>
```

The important thing to note about triggers is that they are designed to handle the return to original state automatically. Therefore, there is no need to apply an additional trigger to return the button back to its original state once the property condition isn't true.

Triggers can also have multiple conditions, which must hold true before new property changes are applied. Triggers with multiple conditions are modeled with a MultiTrigger element. The MultiTrigger element contains a collection of Condition child elements for each logical condition that must be applied before the trigger is fired. The following code segment illustrates a sample MultiTrigger for a button where the IsMouseOver and IsEnabled properties must be true before applying new property changes:

```
<Style.Triggers>
  <MultiTrigger>
    <MultiTrigger.Conditions>
```

```
            <Condition Property="IsMouseOver" Value="True"/>
            <Condition Property="IsEnabled" Value="True" />
        </MultiTrigger.Conditions>
        <Setter Property="Background" Value="Orange" />
        <Setter Property="Foreground" Value="Black"></Setter>
    </MultiTrigger>
</Style.Triggers>
```

Unlike property triggers, event triggers listen for specific events rather than watching for property changes.

A data trigger can be used when an element participates in data binding. A data trigger will fire when a value that is bound to an element is equal to the value specified in the data trigger's `Value` attribute. Using data triggers allows you to define styles or behaviors based on runtime data. For example, you may have a list box containing items that represent tasks in a queue that are color-coded based on a priority level.

To illustrate the application of a data trigger, add the following code representing a new style to the resources collection of the PieGraphControl. The data trigger specifies the binding path that maps to the `PiePieceData` object's `Percentage` property. It also specifies a target value of .2 which, if matched during the binding, will apply a bold font weight to the text element of the list box item. Figure 7-11 illustrates the compiled result.

```
<Style TargetType="ListBoxItem">
  <Style.Triggers>
    <DataTrigger Binding="{Binding Path=Percentage}" Value=".2">
      <Setter Property="TextElement.FontWeight" Value="Bold" />
    </DataTrigger>
  </Style.Triggers>
</Style>
```

20% Latino
20% Asian
30% African-American
30% Caucasian

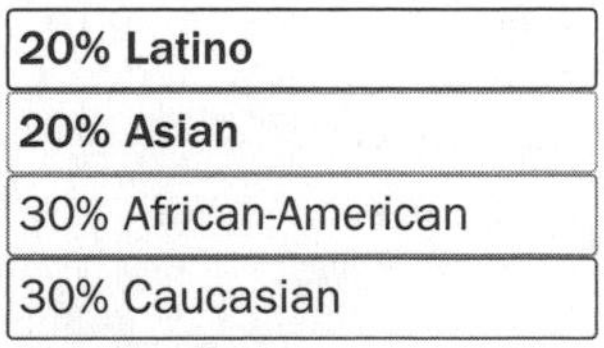

Figure 7-11

An important thing to remember about all of the trigger types is that they can coexist with one another within a style definition. Each type of trigger can also have multiple declarations for multiple properties or multiple events. If your control requires the use of event, property, and data triggers, they can simply be placed as sibling elements within the `Style.Triggers` XAML declaration.

```
<Style TargetType="ListBoxItem">
  <Style.Triggers>
    <EventTrigger ...="">
    </EventTrigger>
    <DataTrigger ...>
    </DataTrigger>
    <Trigger ...>
    </Trigger>
  </Style.Triggers>
</Style>
```

Customizing Existing Controls with Templates

The composition design model of WPF offers such an unprecedented level of control customization that creating and implementing a custom control is often unnecessary. Using templates, the entire look and behavior of a control can be customized easily within XAML.

To customize a control in WPF, you can define and apply a control template. A control template allows you to change the composition of a control to any degree you like. As mentioned earlier, in WPF this is possible because controls are *lookless*, meaning their visual appearance is separate from the behavior. Control templates differ from styles. Styles allow you to customize a control's visual appearance based on setting properties that exist on the elements that make up the control (the default control template). A control template, however, can extend and even completely replace the elements that make up the control.

The one thing to remember when customizing an existing control with templates is that to offer a complete implementation of a new template, it is good practice to make sure you include overrides for all of the common triggers for events and property changes. For example, when creating a template for a button, it would be a good idea to create property and event triggers for mouse property changes and events.

The following example walks you through the basics of creating a custom control template for a button and then applying that template to a button.

1. In Visual Studio, add a new WPF window to the application you created for the custom user control. Leave the default name intact, as it is of no importance to this example.

2. Create a set of brushes as static resources, which you will use to define the mouse over, mouse out, and mouse pressed look and feel of the button. Place the following code within the `Window.Resources` element of the window XAML file.

```
<RadialGradientBrush x:Key="ButtonOffStateColor">
  <GradientStop Color="sc#1, 0, 0.05307113, 0.8078084" Offset="1"/>
  <GradientStop Color="#FFFFFFFF" Offset="0"/>
  <GradientStop Color="#FF5D87F0" Offset="0.64595660749506867"/>
</RadialGradientBrush>

<RadialGradientBrush x:Key="ButtonOnStateColor">
  <GradientStop Color="sc#1, 0.0145082464, 0.0145082464, 0.0145082464" Offset="1"/>
  <GradientStop Color="sc#1, 0, 0.07862101, 0.451001883"
    Offset="0.64595660749506867"/>
  <GradientStop Color="#FF7DA5D8" Offset="0"/>
</RadialGradientBrush>

<RadialGradientBrush x:Key="ButtonPressedStateColor">
  <GradientStop Color="sc#1, 0, 0.07862101, 0.451001883"
    Offset="0.63872452333990792"/>
  <GradientStop Color="#FF7DA5D8" Offset="0.85568704799474"/>
  <GradientStop Color="#FF074492" Offset="1"/>
  <GradientStop Color="#FF12345F" Offset="0"/>
  <GradientStop Color="#FF0A3F83" Offset="0"/>
</RadialGradientBrush>
```

3. You now need to define the style and control template for the button. The following XAML code defines a new control template for a button and includes property triggers for the IsMouseOver and IsPressed properties. It applies the appropriate brush you previously defined to each trigger respectively. Include the following code in the Windows.Resources declaration:

```xaml
<Style x:Key="RadialButton" TargetType="Button">
  <Setter Property="SnapsToDevicePixels" Value="true"/>
  <Setter Property="OverridesDefaultStyle" Value="true"/>
  <Setter Property="MinHeight" Value="60"/>
  <Setter Property="MinWidth" Value="60"/>
  <Setter Property="Template">
    <Setter.Value>
      <ControlTemplate TargetType="Button">
        <Ellipse
          Stroke="{x:Null}"
          Fill="{StaticResource ButtonOffStateColor}"
          HorizontalAlignment="Center"
          VerticalAlignment="Center"
          Width="60"
          Height="60"
          x:Name="Ellipse">
        </Ellipse>
        <ControlTemplate.Triggers>
          <Trigger Property="IsMouseOver" Value="true">
            <Setter TargetName="Ellipse" Property="Fill" Value="{StaticResource
              ButtonOnStateColor}" />
          </Trigger>
          <Trigger Property="IsPressed" Value="true">
            <Setter TargetName="Ellipse" Property="Fill" Value="{StaticResource
              ButtonPressedStateColor}" />
            <Setter TargetName="Ellipse" Property="Stroke" Value="Black" />
          </Trigger>
        </ControlTemplate.Triggers>
      </ControlTemplate>
    </Setter.Value>
  </Setter>
</Style>
```

4. Add a Button declaration to the default window Grid and apply the RadialButton style as follows:

```xaml
<Grid HorizontalAlignment="Center" VerticalAlignment="Center">
  <Button Style="{StaticResource RadialButton}" />
</Grid>
```

5. Compile the application and run the new Window file. The compile result is illustrated in Figures 9-12 through 9-14.

Figure 7-12 illustrates the default state of your button.

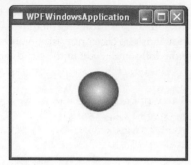

Figure 7-12

Figure 7-13 illustrates the `IsMouseOver` state of your button.

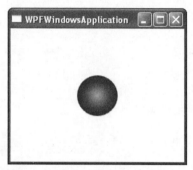

Figure 7-13

Figure 7-14 illustrates the `IsPressed` state of your button.

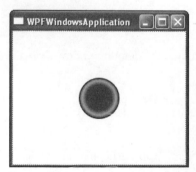

Figure 7-14

Summary

Custom user control authoring now enables the control designer to easily add the graphics capabilities of WPF while leveraging common controls. This offers a new level of design capability to create user controls that are more engaging and interactive than older counterparts.

In WPF, control customization is accomplished with relative ease without the need to implement a custom control. WPF allows the developer and application UI designer to easily customize the look and feel of the default controls through styles and templates, altering the visual appearance and behavior of the control without having to reinvent the wheel.

In this chapter you have looked at the following:

❑ A custom control is no longer the necessary first choice when you need to encapsulate behaviors and visual appearance. The WPF composition model is a robust and flexible model that provides a means for customizing most aspects of almost any control.

❑ After asking the right questions and determining that customizing an existing control won't meet your requirements, sometimes creating a custom control is the right choice. You've seen one way to do so through the implementation of a WPF User Control.

❑ WPF data binding is a powerful tool at your disposal. You've seen how data binding creates a connection between the properties of two objects complete with runtime change notification. You've also explored the various modes of data binding and have seen how to use data binding in your code.

❑ Data templates allow you to stylize the visual output of a bound data source.

❑ Data type conversions are easily handled by creating a class that implements the `IValueConverter` interface and then adding that class as a resource in XAML.

❑ WPF styles provide a convenient way to create reusable property settings that customize visual appearance of a control or set of controls.

❑ Styles can contain triggers that watch for and take action based on changes in properties, events, or data.

❑ Control templates provide a way to partially customize or completely replace the visual appearance of an existing control.

Using WPF in the Enterprise

8

Previous chapters have focused on the building blocks of WPF, such as creating application UI, framework classes and methods, and the various subsystems available to developers. Enterprise application development, however, is more than simply building UI, coding behavior, and animating elements. Enterprise application developers must also consider the ecosystem their application will live in and the needs of system users. These considerations will influence the decisions you make regarding the type of application to build and how best to deploy it. Knowing the right questions to ask and taking a systematic approach to application design is a requirement of professional application development.

WPF provides a number of different application models you can choose from to meet your needs. Traditional standalone windows applications are supported but now provide two distinct navigation models: menu-based and navigation-based. Browser-based applications are also supported. Standalone XAML files can be published to a web server or launched directly from the file system. Additionally, a new type of browser-based application is offered called the XAML Browser Application (XBAP), which is a compiled application that can be deployed in a browser environment similar to a .NET Smart-Client application. Regardless of the application model you choose, the WPF development platform does not change. You use the same CLR code base and XAML to create you application. Only your deployment model will differ depending on your target environment.

In WPF, as with any other platform, state management is important. The WPF `Application` object provides a global-scope collection that you can use to store state data during the life of your application. For a scenario in which longer term persistence is desired, a new construct called *isolated storage* is available. Isolated storage allows browser-based applications to write and read files to and from the local disk. No direct file system access is provided. Rather, WPF manages this access for you so that security is kept intact. You will explore these new state management techniques later in the chapter.

WPF applications are typically made up of a collection of pages. Users navigate between these pages to retrieve content and access functionality provided by the application. Navigation has traditionally been menu-driven in standalone Windows applications and link-driven in web applications. These methods are considered unstructured navigation models because pages are unaware of actions performed in other pages. This has, in part, been a result of the stateless environment of the web. WPF offers a new navigation model you can use to build your application. Navigation in WPF is called structured navigation. Structured navigation provides a mechanism in which pages can interact intelligently. A calling page can call a target page, be notified when the target page completes an action and, optionally, get a value in return. You will explore this mechanism and build some examples that use structured navigation in this chapter.

World-ready applications require localization in order to support the cultural constructs of your target locales. Support for multilingual text and cultural differences within elements, such as calendar dates and currencies, are provided in WPF. Planning your UI to support this can be challenging, but WPF provides content controls and best practices that will enable you to localize your applications in a snap. In this chapter, you will explore Microsoft's guidelines for developing world-ready applications.

Deploying your WPF applications comes in three flavors: XCopy, Windows Installer, and ClickOnce. You will look at the features supported by each of these deployment models and which are best to use in relation to your application model. As mentioned earlier, the development code base does not change based on application model. Only your deployment method will change. Based on the target hosting environment, security considerations, and application management requirements, you will be able to pick the best deployment model for your scenario.

In this chapter, you explore best practices and important guidelines for creating WPF applications that meet the demands of today's enterprise. The points that will be covered include:

❑ Contrasting application models and selecting the best fit for your organization's needs

❑ Implementing WPF state management features in your applications

❑ Exploring the new WPF navigation features

❑ Making applications world-ready with globalization and localization techniques

❑ Deployment options in WPF

WPF Application Models

Choosing the right application model is one of the most important decisions you make when starting a new project. There are usually many factors to consider when making your decision. However, in WPF the choice of application model really boils down to the hosting environment, and so your choices are either browser-based or Windows-based applications. In this section, you learn about the application models WPF provides and explore the points you'll want to consider when choosing between these models.

One of the greatest benefits provided by the WPF platform is a unified development environment for creating both browser and Windows-based applications. Both utilize the same code base. They are not separate technologies. Regardless of the WPF application model you choose, a WPF application consists of a collection of XAML pages and a navigation model. The way in which these application models differ lies primarily in how you intend to deliver your solution to users. Therefore, in WPF, the decision about whether to develop browser- or Windows-based applications is really a question of which hosting environment you intend to target. Additionally, you must consider the security context of the target environment—in particular, the browser-based environment, as it may be restrictive to the functionality you seek to provide.

As previously mentioned, there are really two ways to deliver your WPF application: through the browser as pages, or as a standalone windows application, which, of course, makes use of the familiar windows and dialog boxes to deliver content and forms. In WPF, a browser-based application is called a XAML Browser Application (XBAP). An XBAP is a compiled application that runs in a browser rather than as a standalone windows application. The primary benefit of the XBAP model is that it can deliver all the same rich visual content provided by WPF that a standalone windows application model can, only it can deliver this content through the browser. Additionally, an XBAP is centrally deployed just like a standard web application.

Another way you can deliver content through a browser in WPF is by publishing standalone XAML files. This is referred to as *loose XAML* and, unlike with an XBAP, you cannot have any code-behind files with your loose XAML application.

> *It is important to stress that an XBAP is a compiled application that simply runs in a browser. To clarify, this is not a web application as you might think. The client is required to have the .NET Framework 3.0 installed on his computer, and the application will run within the security context of the browser (just think smart-client here). Therefore, ASP.NET still holds an important place in the .NET development landscape as a platform for developing thin-client applications with a wide reach.*

A standalone windows application model is, of course, familiar to anyone who has ever run an application on a computer. This model delivers its content through familiar windows and dialog boxes. In WPF, however, two flavors of navigation are available to you for standalone windows application development: the common menu-based model, or the new navigation-based model that uses hyperlinks and has an HTML-like navigation feel. You'll look at these shortly.

> *Both XBAP and windows applications require the client to have the .NET Framework 3.0 installed.*

Standalone Applications

WPF standalone windows applications are designed to be full featured, highly responsive, rich-client applications. These applications have full access to system resources, as they run within the full-trust security model. Standalone applications also utilize the full processing power of the computer on which they run. Historically, windows applications have been chosen because of their ability to harness this processing power and for their rich UI capabilities. WPF levels the playing field to some extent with the introduction of the XBAP, but because of security restrictions of running in the Internet zone security sandbox, the standalone application model still has value because it behaves as a full trust client.

You should consider implementing a windows application if:

❑ Your application requires full access to system resources such as the file system or registry.

❑ You need to use WPF elements that are not allowed for XBAPs.

❑ You want the application to run in a standalone window.

❑ You want the user to be able to use the application offline.

The following table illustrates common features of standalone windows applications.

Issue	Specification
Hosting	Hosted within a standalone window and cannot be run in a browser.
Deployment	Windows applications can be deployed over the web via ClickOnce or MSI.
Security	Windows applications have full access to system resources.
User permission	Users must specifically grant permission to install because of the full-trust access to system resources.
Installation	Installed on the machine (and provides shell presence) until a user explicitly uninstalls the application.
Offline use	Capability to work offline.
Persistence	Windows applications have access to the file system to write out data that will persist between application instances.
Updating	If the application is installed using ClickOnce, it contains support for automatic updating. A custom updating solution is required if deploying via MSI.

There are two flavors of windows applications you can develop in WPF. The standalone windows application behaves just like WinForms applications today. This style utilizes common menu-based navigation between windows and dialog boxes. The new windows navigation application utilizes hyperlinks that provide an HTML-like navigation feel. This style of windows application runs inside a host window that provides browser-like navigation complete with forward, back, and history navigation.

Standalone Windows Application

Standalone windows applications are the familiar window, dialog box, and menu-driven applications you've been using forever. Content is hosted in a standard window defined as XAML and includes an associated code-behind file. The application runs on the desktop and typically appears in your Start menu, and you usually install/uninstall them from the Control Panel. These are compiled applications that typically require full access to local resources.

Figure 8-1 illustrates a typical standalone windows application that uses standard menu-based navigation.

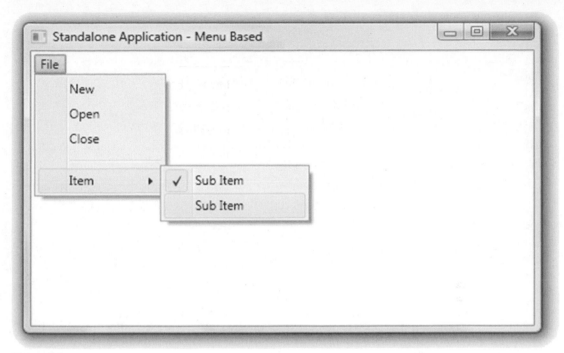

Figure 8-1

Standalone Windows Navigation Application

Windows navigation applications are hosted inside a navigation window and provide the UI look and feel of a browser-based application. Like standalone windows applications, navigation applications run on the desktop. Unlike standalone windows applications, content is created using pages rather than windows, although pages, like windows, are defined as XAML with an associated code-behind. Also, unlike standalone windows applications, content in a windows navigation application is typically hosted inside of a NavigationWindow object, rather than inside of a Window because a Page is a content control and not a Window. The Page class requires a host of type Window, NavigationWindow, or Frame in order to display content. The nature of the Page class makes it ideal for navigation.

When a Page is hosted inside a NavigationWindow object, the UI feels like a browser. This is because the NavigationWindow provides the basic navigation features found in a Web browser, such as forward and back buttons and a history menu. A Page can also be hosted inside a Window as the content of that Window. Furthermore, a Page can also be hosted within a Frame object, which itself can be placed within the content of any other control. A Frame can also contain HTML, allowing you to embed web content directly in your WPF application.

Figure 8-2 illustrates the new standalone windows navigation application hosted in a NavigationWindow.

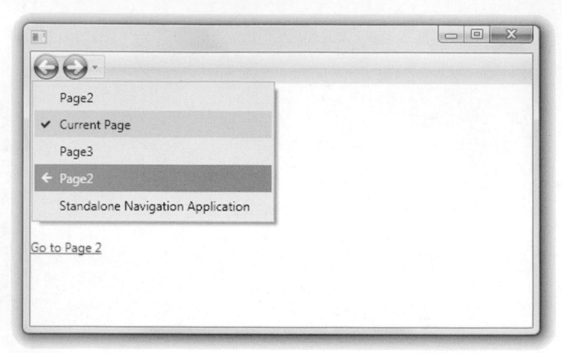

Figure 8-2

In this case, each application `Page` is hosted inside a `NavigationWindow`, which itself derives from `Window`. The `NavigationWindow` provides the forward and back buttons as well as the history menu referred to as a `Journal`. The `Hyperlink` displayed simply links to another `Page` in the application. Implementing navigation will be explained in more detail later in this chapter.

Browser-Based Applications

In WPF, browser-based applications are compiled applications that run in a browser. These applications are hosted by a WPF application called PresentationHost.exe. PresentationHost.exe is responsible for loading the CLR runtime, managing security permissions, and for registering HTML handlers that will host WPF content. PresentationHost.exe resides at the top level of the browser hierarchy or within an HTML IFrame.

Unlike standalone windows applications that execute in a full trust security environment, browser-based applications run in a partial trust security sandbox. The term "security sandbox" or "sandbox" refers to any environment with a restricted set of privileges in which an application executes. In relation to browser-based applications, security is restricted to the default Internet zone permission set. These restrictions exist to safeguard applications downloaded from the Internet because the source of the executable is typically unknown. As with any security model, this imposes restrictions on what you can and cannot do with XBAPs. Later in this chapter, you explore these security considerations in more detail.

Standalone or "Loose" XAML

Standalone or "loose XAML" is delivered through a browser. Loose XAML is merely markup and is not compiled; therefore, you can simply navigate to or open from your local disk any XAML file to view it in a browser. Of course, you can also embed loose XAML into an HTML web page. This would enable you to create a bit of rich content that can make your web page even more visually appealing. Similarly, you could use loose XAML to provide a richer layout than say, HTML, but this would require that the client viewing your content have the .NET Framework 3.0 installed locally.

> *Loose XAML uses the* Page *element as its root element rather than the* Window *element.*

A collection of loose XAML files does not constitute an application because they are not compiled. Loose XAML files are simply independent files that can be published on a web server such as any content file, including HTML. Hence, they are not really an application model, but worth mentioning briefly in this section as they relate to browser-based applications. An XBAP, for instance, could navigate to and from a loose XAML file (or any other type of content file, for that matter) and the transition would be seamless.

Standalone XAML is hosted within the browser by the PresentationHost.exe. PresentationHost.exe performs a number of functions, including managing the communication between XAML and the browser. For instance, when the browser's Back button is clicked, PresentationHost.exe communicates this to your XAML application. Within PresentationHost.exe, another WPF application, XAMLViewer, runs the loose XAML.

XAML Browser Applications

XBAPs are compiled applications made up of a collection of XAML pages. Notice that we say XAML pages rather than files. XAML pages have code-behind and therefore are far more functional that loose XAML files. XBAPs are also click-once applications. When a user navigates to the URL of the XBAP, the whole application will be downloaded and cached locally on the client computer.

XBAPs are intended to combine the best of web-based and Windows-based application models, utilizing the rich visuals and powerful processing capabilities of a thick-client application, as well as taking advantage of the simplistic deployment of a web-based application. Developers who have attempted to create dynamic, visually engaging, and user-friendly web-based applications in the past can relate to the frustration of trying to build cross-browser–compatible HTML and JavaScript. Similarly, developers who have managed the deployment and update process of a Windows-based application have endured their own set of frustrations.

Instead of being bound to the confines of HTML and client-side scripting to try and emulate a fraction of the capability of rich-clients, XBAPs have access to all of the rich media and graphic capabilities provided by WPF. If you want to build an application with a rich UI but would also like to deliver the content via the browser, then XBAP is for you. However, it is worth reiterating that XBAP is not a replacement for websites built with ASP.NET or straight HTML. XBAPs are for delivering compiled applications to users via the browser. XBAPs not only simplify deployment but also deliver the application and its navigation model in an environment with which users are now deeply familiar: the browser. ASP.NET and HTML, on the other hand, are for delivering websites (collections of content pages) to a wide range of users on a wide range of browser platforms.

The following table illustrates common features of XBAPs.

Issue	Specification
Hosting	XBAPs are always hosted in the browser. The client, however, must have the .NET Framework 3.0 installed.
Deployment	XBAPs are deployed to an IIS version 5 or higher server. The application is invoked by navigating to the .xbap deployment manifest file, and the execution of the application is handled by ClickOnce.
Security	XBAPs run within a sandbox with Internet zone permissions. They do not have access to important system resources such as the Windows registry or the local file system.
User permission	Because of the XBAP security context, no explicit user permission to execute the application is required.
Installation	XBAPs aren't installed on the user machine and therefore have no shell presence (meaning there are no shortcuts, file associations, or application folders). To execute the application, the user must navigate to the .xbap file.
Offline use	XBAPs are available online only. XBAPs have access to isolated storage used to store data that will be used when the next instance of the application is started.
Caching	Applications are cached locally on the user's system for some duration of time. They are scavenged and removed from the cache if latent for longer than the cache expiration date.

Both XBAPs and windows applications share the same code base for development. Each application consists of a set of XAML pages that declare elements for each screen and a code-behind file to drive the logic of the page.

Integrating XBAPs with Existing Web Content

As much as you might wish for change to come rapidly, you can assume that it may take some time for WPF to reach mainstream acceptance in the enterprise. Even though the general benefits of XBAPs may be overwhelming, certain constraints or user requirements may prevent converting some existing applications to XBAPs.

In spite of these constraints, there are steps you can take to start integrating XBAPs with your existing web-based applications.

One option you have is to create composite sites that consist of HTML forms and XBAP pages. For example, you could create a corporate website product demonstration leveraging the multimedia capabilities of WPF and the .NET Framework 3.0 runtime. The demonstration could be launched in a separate browser window from a standard HTML form via a simple hyperlink. This way, sections of your Web application that are XBAP-driven can coexist with standard HTML forms.

Another technique is to create a composite site by placing the sections of a web page that are XBAP-driven within IFrames. This would require additional code to coordinate the event handling of form submissions, data entry, or mouse clicks, but it may well be worth the effort.

Yet another technique for mixing XBAP and web application environments is to enable HTML to WPF communication. You have several options to enable communication between XBAP hosted in HTML or vice versa:

❑ Use the server to bridge the gap for communication via HTTP web requests.

❑ Use first-party Internet Explorer cookies.

❑ Leverage URI parameters on the hosted HTML or XBAP URI.

For example, the `System.Windows.Navigation.NavigationService` class provides a method to look up the current URI of the page a user is on.

```
Uri currUri = NavigationService.CurrentSource;

string[] paramList = currUri.Query.Split('&');

foreach (string param in paramList)
{
  // Process each param in the query...
}
```

By accessing the URI, you can collect any query parameters stored in the URI's `Query` property.

XBAPs and Data Access

Data access is an important part of most applications. As described earlier, XBAPs run in a security sandbox. The security sandbox does not support direct database connectivity. However, you can gain access to data through the use of web services. By utilizing a service-oriented model, you enable a mechanism for transporting data to and from your XBAP.

The following example demonstrates how to access data through an XBAP using services. Working under the assumption that this sample application will execute with Internet zone permissions, you will access data using an `.asmx` web service. The web service authenticates users logging in to the application. The service will return data that you will assume is required in the context of your application: the user's first name, the user's last name, and the last product the user viewed in the system. Because the primary purpose of this example is to illustrate the use of a web service in an XBAP, the authentication mechanism is very basic.

To create and run this example, you need to have IIS installed on your machine.

1. Create the web service. In Visual Studio, select File ➪ New Web Site. From the templates view, choose the ASP.NET Web Service template. Set the location for the web service to HTTP from the location drop-down list. Set the path to http://localhost/AuthenticationService. Click OK to create the new website. The location of your new website will be C:\Inetpub\wwwroot\AuthenticationService.

   If you are running IIS 7, you will need to ensure Visual Studio 2005 can access your web server in order to run/debug locally. If access is denied, you may receive an error indicating Front Page Extensions are not installed on the web server. To avoid this issue, enable IIS 6 Management Capabilities from within the Windows Features dialog box (Control Panel ➪ Programs and Features ➪ Turn Windows Features On or Off).

2. Create a class that will store the details of the authenticated user. For this example, it will contain the first and last name of the user and the ID of the last product viewed by the user. Right-click on the App_Code directory of your web service project and choose Add ➪ New Item, select Class from the Add New Item dialog box, name the class **UserState**, and click Add. Modify the UserState.cs file as follows:

```csharp
using System;

[Serializable]
public class UserState
{
  private int lastViewProductID;
  private string firstName = "";
  private string lastName = "";

  public UserState()
  {
  }

  public int LastViewProductID
  {
    get { return lastViewProductID; }
    set { lastViewProductID = value; }
  }

  public string FirstName
  {
    get { return firstName; }
    set { firstName = value; }
  }

  public string LastName
  {
    get { return lastName; }
    set { lastName = value; }
  }
}
```

3. Now you are ready to create the service method that will be used to authenticate users. Open the Service.cs file in the App_Code directory and modify as follows:

```csharp
using System;
using System.Web;
using System.Web.Services;
using System.Web.Services.Protocols;

[WebService(Namespace = "http://tempuri.org/")]
[WebServiceBinding(ConformsTo = WsiProfiles.BasicProfile1_1)]
public class Service : System.Web.Services.WebService
{
  public Service ()
  {
  }

  [WebMethod]
```

```
public UserState AuthenticateUser(string userName, string password)
{
  UserState state = null;

  // Very basic, unsecure authentication procedure
  if (!String.IsNullOrEmpty(userName) && !String.IsNullOrEmpty(password))
    state = RetrieveUserState();

  // Assuming the user exists, return
  // the user state
  return state;
}

public UserState RetrieveUserState()
{
  UserState state = new UserState();
  state.FirstName = "Christopher";
  state.LastName = "Andrade";

  // Return a dummy id
  state.LastViewProductID = 1;

  return state;
}
}
```

Your web service is now ready for consumption. You can test the service if you like by navigating to `http://localhost/AuthenticationService/Service.asmx`.

4. Create the XBAP that will consume the service. In Visual Studio, right-click on your solution and select Add ➪ New Project from the context menu. From the Project Types tree view, choose the Visual C# ➪ .NET Framework 3.0 Node, and then select the XAML Browser Application (WPF) icon from the list. Name your project **XbapApplication** (case sensitive), and then click OK. This new project should create a `Page1.xaml` file and a supporting partial class code-behind file.

5. To consume the service, you will need to add a reference to it in your XbapApplication project. Right-click the XbapApplication project in the Solution Explorer and select Add Web Reference from the context menu. In the URL text box, type **http://localhost/AuthenticationService/Service.asmx** and press Go.

    Once the service is found, accept the default Web reference name of "localhost" and then click the Add Reference button to add it to the project.

6. You need to get a UI put together. The UI will consist of two pages. The first page will contain the controls necessary to log in. The second page will be the landing page after a successful login. Open the Page1.xaml file and modify as follows:

```
<Page x:Class="XbapApplication.Page1"
  xmlns="http://schemas.microsoft.com/winfx/2006/xaml/presentation"
  xmlns:x="http://schemas.microsoft.com/winfx/2006/xaml"
  Title="Page1"
  >
  <Grid>

    <Button VerticalAlignment="Bottom" HorizontalAlignment="Left"
```

```
            Grid.Column="0" Grid.ColumnSpan="1" Grid.Row="0" Grid.RowSpan="1"
          Margin="21,0,0,21" Width="75" Height="23"
            Name="login">Login</Button>

      <TextBox VerticalAlignment="Top" HorizontalAlignment="Stretch"
        Grid.Column="0" Grid.ColumnSpan="1" Grid.Row="0" Grid.RowSpan="1"
          Margin="21,110.276666666667,99,0" Width="Auto" Height="20"
            Name="password"></TextBox>

      <TextBox VerticalAlignment="Top" HorizontalAlignment="Stretch"
        Grid.Column="0" Grid.ColumnSpan="1" Grid.Row="0" Grid.RowSpan="1"
          Margin="21,60,99,0" Width="Auto" Height="20"
            Name="userName"></TextBox>

      <Label VerticalAlignment="Top" HorizontalAlignment="Left"
        Grid.Column="0" Grid.ColumnSpan="1" Grid.Row="0" Grid.RowSpan="1"
          Margin="21,37.276666666667,0,0" Width="100" Height="23.276666666666685"
            Name="label1">User Name:</Label>

      <Label VerticalAlignment="Top" HorizontalAlignment="Left"
        Grid.Column="0" Grid.ColumnSpan="1" Grid.Row="0" Grid.RowSpan="1"
          Margin="21,87,0,0" Width="100" Height="23.276666666666642"
            Name="label2">Password:</Label>

    </Grid>
  </Page>
```

7. Now, modify the Page1.xaml.cs code-behind file as follows:

```
using System;
using System.Windows;
using System.Windows.Navigation;

// Include reference to our web service
using XbapApplication.localhost;

namespace XbapApplication
{
  public partial class Page1 : System.Windows.Controls.Page
  {

    public Page1()
    {
      InitializeComponent();
      this.login.Click += new RoutedEventHandler(login_Click);
    }

    void login_Click(object sender, RoutedEventArgs e)
    {
      try
      {
        Service service = new Service();
        service.AuthenticateUserCompleted += new
          AuthenticateUserCompletedEventHandler(service_AuthenticateUserCompleted);
```

```
          service.AuthenticateUserAsync(userName.Text, password.Text);
        }
        catch (Exception ex)
        {
          // Perform exception handling....
        }
      }

    static void service_AuthenticateUserCompleted(object sender,
      AuthenticateUserCompletedEventArgs e)
    {
      UserState prevState = e.Result;

      if (prevState != null)
      {
        // Store the data from the service result within
        // the application properties so that the next
        // page can access it.
        Application.Current.Properties["FirstName"] = prevState.FirstName;
        Application.Current.Properties["LastName"] = prevState.LastName;
        Application.Current.Properties["CurrentProductID"] =
          prevState.LastViewProductID;

        // Create the landing page and navigate to it
        Page2 page2 = new Page2();
        page2.InitializeComponent();

        NavigationWindow navWindow =
          (NavigationWindow)Application.Current.MainWindow;

        navWindow.Navigate(page2);
      }
    }
  }
}
```

The code-behind hooks up a click event handling procedure for the login button that will create the service call to authenticate the user. The code also uses the asynchronous method of attaching an event handler to listen for when the service call completes. Once completed, the code stores the data in the application properties collection to pass on to the landing page.

8. You need to create the landing Page in order to show the login was successful. Add a new Page to your XbapApplication project and accept the default Page2 name. Modify the Page2.xaml file as follows:

```
<Page x:Class="XbapApplication.Page2"
  xmlns="http://schemas.microsoft.com/winfx/2006/xaml/presentation"
  xmlns:x="http://schemas.microsoft.com/winfx/2006/xaml"
  Title="Page2"
  >
  <Grid>
    <Label VerticalAlignment="Top" Margin="21,37.276666666667,22,0"
      Height="23.276666666666685" Name="label1"></Label>
  </Grid>
</Page>
```

9. Modify the Page2.xaml.cs code-behind file as follows:

```
using System;
using System.Windows;

namespace XbapApplication
{
  public partial class Page2 : System.Windows.Controls.Page
  {
    public Page2()
    {
      InitializeComponent();
    }

    protected override void OnInitialized(EventArgs e)
    {
      this.Loaded += new RoutedEventHandler(Page2_Loaded);
      base.OnInitialized(e);
    }

    void Page2_Loaded(object sender, RoutedEventArgs e)
    {
      string firstName = (string)Application.Current.Properties["FirstName"];
      string lastName = (string)Application.Current.Properties["LastName"];

      label1.Content = firstName + " " + lastName + " is Authenticated.";
    }
  }
}
```

The code loads up the user's first and last name retrieved from the service and displays it in a message label.

10. That's it for coding the example, but before you can run the application you need to deploy it to the Web server. Right-click on the XbapApplication project and select Properties from the context menu. Select Publish from the left menu to view the Publish settings pane. In the Publish pane's Location combo box, type **http://localhost/AuthenticationService/** in order to publish the XBAP files one directory level below the AuthenticationService directory (be sure to include the "/" at the end of the path). Save the settings and click the Publish Now button on the bottom right.

11. Once the publish cycle has successfully completed. Navigate through Internet Explorer to `http://localhost/AuthenticationService/XbapApplication.xbap`. To test the UI, type in anything into the user name and password text boxes (because the authentication mechanism requires only that the text isn't null) and press the Login button.

It is important to note that when using Web services with your XBAP the default security settings for the Internet zone allow web requests only to the application's site of origin. This conforms to the web cross-domain security model, which allows web pages to access the DOM of pages from the same domain.

Outside of these security constraints, images and video elements can display content from domains other than the site of origin. This is considered by the framework to be a safe operation.

Security Considerations

WPF security is based on the .NET Framework Code Access Security (CAS) model. This model restricts code access to protected system resources such as the local disk or system registry based on the origin of the executing code. Covering CAS in its entirety is beyond the scope of this book, but a quick overview will help you understand the implications of WPF security that must be considered when choosing an application model. WPF applications execute based on the permissions and restrictions of a particular CAS permission set. A CAS permission set is a collection of permissions, each of which is assigned to a particular system resource. CAS includes some predefined permission sets such as Full Trust, Local Intranet, and Internet as well as allowing for the creation of custom permission sets. Unless explicitly defined to do otherwise, WPF applications execute based on the permissions of the zone within which they run. A zone refers to the area from which an application is deployed, such as My_Computer_Zone, LocalIntranet_Zone, or Internet_Zone. Zones are grouped into Code Groups, which are sets of conditions an application must meet to participate in the security model. Based on the code group or groups that an application belongs to, a particular permission set is applied. When an application executes based on the permission set that imposes security restraints, it is said to be running in a security *sandbox*.

> You can access the CAS administration console by selecting Start ⇨ Programs ⇨ Administrative Tools ⇨ Microsoft .NET Framework 2.0 Configuration. Within the administration console, expand .NET Framework Configuration ⇨ My Computer ⇨ Runtime Security Policy.

Standalone applications execute from the local file system and, as such, run in the CAS Full Trust zone. Because full trust implies no restrictions, standalone applications do not run in a sandbox. On the other hand, loose XAML and XBAPs run in the browser and therefore must adhere to the security restraints imposed by the Internet zone permission set. Browser-based applications therefore are "sandboxed." Applications running in a local intranet can run with fewer restrictions than those running on the Internet.

You must take security sandboxing into consideration when choosing an application model. If you require access to registry and I/O operations against the local file system, then a standalone Windows-based application is most appropriate. If your needs are more limited, then a browser-based application model may be appropriate. Additionally, it is possible to request additional permissions for your browser-based application using Visual Studio through the Project Properties dialog box on the Security tab. For more information on this, see the MSDN.

For a full list of security restrictions for each zone, see the WPF security topic on the MSDN. For more details on the CAS security model, see the Security in the .NET Framework topic located in the .NET Framework Technologies section of the MSDN.

You'll now create a simple example that illustrates running the same code in a standalone and XBAP application. This simple example will write to the EventLog when a button is clicked. The standalone application will execute as expected because it runs with full permissions. However, the same code executing in an XBAP will throw a System.Security.SecurityException because the Event permission is not granted to the Internet zone in which the XBAP runs.

1. Create a new WPF windows application, delete the default Window1.xaml file, and create a new Page accepting the default name Page1.xaml.

2. Add the following Button declaration to the Page1.xaml file:

```
<Button Name="button1" Click="button1_Click">Write to Event Log</Button>
```

3. Add the following button event-handler method to the Page1.xaml.cs code-behind file:

```
private void button1_Click(object sender, RoutedEventArgs e)
{
    if (!System.Diagnostics.EventLog.SourceExists("TestSource"))
    {
        System.Diagnostics.EventLog.CreateEventSource("TestSource", "TestLog");
    }
    System.Diagnostics.EventLog.WriteEntry("TestSource", "Log message text...");
}
```

4. Run the application and click the button.

5. View the log entry in the Event Viewer. To access the Event Viewer, select Start ⇨ Programs ⇨ Administrative Tools ⇨ Event Viewer. In the Event Viewer dialog box, expand the Applications and Services Logs node, and then highlight TestLog. You will find your log entry in the center pane.

6. Create a new XBAP and repeat Steps 2 through 4. This time when you click the button, a SecurityException will be thrown, illustrating that there is indeed a different set of permissions applied to XBAPs.

State Management

In WPF, as with any other platform, state management is an important function. WPF introduces several new methods that you can use to manage state data throughout the life of the application, or in a more persistent manner beyond application lifecycle. In this section, you will explore these state management techniques and build some examples to get you up and running quickly.

Application Object

WPF applications consist of one or more pages, and you will often want to share data across these pages. For example, in a traditional e-commerce application, items are selected for purchase from one or many pages and will be stored in a shopping cart. Items in the cart will need to be accessed by a review and order page when the user checks out. This example illustrates a common need in most applications. Application data often needs to be accessed globally within your application and stored independently of a single page.

In WPF, each Application object contains a collection property called Properties. The Properties collection is a key-value collection that can be indexed very much like a Hashtable or Dictionary object. This object is available globally to all windows or pages of your application, so it can be used as a storage location for state data.

The following sample code illustrates accessing the `Properties` collection and assigning a list of objects to it:

```
// Store a list of products to be purchased
List<Product> products = new List<Product>();
products.Add(new Product("shirt"));
products.Add(new Product("shorts"));
products.Add(new Product("socks"));

MyApplication.Properties["productList"] = products;
```

In staying with our traditional e-commerce application scenario, the preceding sample code creates a list of various products purchased by a customer. The list will need to be accessed throughout the application's lifetime by one or many pages. The `products` list is placed in the `Properties` collection of the application object `MyApplication`.

The following code sample illustrates how the `products` list can be retrieved from the `Properties` collection:

```
// Retrieve the list to be processed
List<Product> products = (List<Product>) MyApplication.Properties["productList"];
```

Notice that the object retrieved must be cast to the appropriate list type. Items stored in the `Properties` collection are stored as type `Object` and, therefore, must be type-cast on retrieval.

Now that you have a mechanism for storing state data, the challenge lies in organizing the retrieval of that data among the different pages that need access to it. As illustrated in the preceding example code, the `Properties` collection stores values as objects and therefore you must use caution to cast the return value to the appropriate type.

To avoid the potential pitfalls just mentioned, you may find it beneficial to create a class that can manage the retrieval and type-casting of values stored in the application object's `Properties` collection.

Still keeping with the e-commerce application scenario, the following example creates a class named `AppState` that can organize state information about a current shopper and the list of products they have in their cart:

```
// Wrapper class that organizes state information as properties
using System.Collections.Generic;
using System.Windows;

class AppState
{
    private string firstNameKey = "firstName";
    private string lastNameKey = "lastName";
    private string productListKey = "productList";

    public static string ShopperFirstName
    {
        get
        {
            return (string)Application.Current.Properties[firstNameKey];
```

```
        }
        set
        {
          Application.Current.Properties[firstNameKey] = value;
        }
      }

      public static string ShopperLastName
      {
        get
        {
          return (string)Application.Current.Properties[lastNameKey];
        }
        set
        {
          Application.Current.Properties[lastNameKey] = value;
        }
      }

      public static List<Product> ProductList
      {
        get
        {
          return (List<Product>)Application.Current.Properties[productListKey];
        }
        set
        {
          Application.Current.Properties[productListKey] = value;
        }
      }
    }
```

This code example illustrates the encapsulation of the `Application` object's `Properties` property. Utilizing a class such as `AppState` enables an application to retrieve session values in a type-safe manner because each member of `AppState` is a typed value. Remember that `Application.Properties` is a collection of Object types and so any value stored within the collection must be cast when retrieved.

Isolated Storage

Depending on the application model you choose, state data could be stored in a variety of locations. For instance, because standalone windows applications run within a Full-Trust environment, data can be stored locally as a file on the client machine. However, because of the security restrictions imposed on applications running in a browser, an XBAP will have to store data in an out-of-process database or in a new WPF mechanism called *isolated storage*.

Isolated storage is a new data storage mechanism that allows partial-trust applications running in a security sandbox to store data in a way that is controlled by the computer's security policy. Because file I/O operations violate Internet zone security settings, isolated storage offers XBAPs a viable option to store pieces of data on the client which can be retrieved the next time the application is started. By default, code running on the local computer, local network, or the Internet is granted the right to use isolated storage.

The `Application` object has two specific events where the capture and re-creation of state should occur. The `Application.Startup` and `Exit` events occur when the application is starting up and shutting down. You can override the event handlers for the startup and exit events in order to inject your own logic that can either retrieve or capture and store the current state of the application.

The following code segment illustrates overriding the `Application.OnExit` event handler to save state data in isolated storage:

```
// Wrapper class that organizes state information as properties
protected override void OnExit(ExitEventArgs e)
{
  try
  {
    IsolatedStorageFile persistedState =
      IsolatedStorageFile.GetStore(IsolatedStorageScope.User |
        IsolatedStorageScope.Domain |
          IsolatedStorageScope.Assembly, null, null);

    StreamWriter stateWriter = new StreamWriter(new
      IsolatedStorageFileStream("state.txt", FileMode.Create, persistedState));

    stateWriter.WriteLine(...);
  // Write out the state data
  }
  catch (System.Security.SecurityException ex)
  {
    // If we do not have access to Isolated storage, perhaps
    // provide a secondary means of saving state information...
  }
}
```

The preceding code obtains a reference to the isolated storage data store. The store is specific to the executing assembly. Once a store is obtained, you can create and write files, placing them in the store for retrieval at a later time. The key takeaway is that WPF provides a managed subsystem that actually stores the files and provides security.

The following code segment illustrates retrieving state information from isolated storage when your application starts:

```
// Wrapper class that organizes state information as properties
private void OnStartup(object sender, StartupEventArgs e)
{
  try
  {
    IsolatedStorageFile isoLastState =
      IsolatedStorageFile.GetStore(IsolatedStorageScope.User |
        IsolatedStorageScope.Domain |
          IsolatedStorageScope.Assembly, null, null);

    StreamReader stateReader = new StreamReader(new
      IsolatedStorageFileStream("state.txt", FileMode.OpenOrCreate, isoLastState));

    //Open the isolated storage from the previous instance and read the data
    if (stateReader == null)
```

```
    {
      // Add code to react to no state information
      ....
    }
    else
    {
      // Add code to read the state information back
      ....
    }

    stateReader.Close();
  }
  catch (Exception ex)
  {

  }
}
```

Similar to the previous code example, the first step is to get a reference to the store. With the reference obtained, retrieving values is a simple matter of reading the text file.

State Management Example

It's time to put the state management concepts we've covered thus far into the context of a real-world scenario and build an example. The sample application you build next demonstrates the concepts discussed so far. In this example you create a portion of an ecommerce application that will allow a user to add products to a list. The sample application makes use of the `Product` class, which represents a product for purchase. The `Product` class is very simple and is intended only as a means of illustrating state management concepts.

The steps are as follows:

1. In Visual Studio, select File ⇨ New Project from the menu. From the Project Types tree view, select the Visual C# ⇨ .NET Framework 3.0 Node, and then click the XAML Browser Application (WPF) icon from the list. Name your project **XBAPStatePersistence**, and click OK. This new project should create a Page1.xaml file, and a supporting partial class code-behind file.

2. Add the following Product class definition to your Page1.xaml.cs file:

```
[Serializable]
public class Product
{
  private string name = "";
  private string color = "";
  private string type = "";
  private string brand = "";

  public Product()
  {
  }

  public string Name
  {
```

```
        get { return name; }
        set { name = value; }
    }

    public string Color
    {
      get { return color; }
      set { color = value; }
    }

    public string Type
    {
      get { return type; }
      set { type = value; }
    }

    public string Brand
    {
      get { return brand; }
      set { brand = value; }
    }
}
```

3. Employing the concept of the managed state object, the next class definition encapsulates your state information in typed property procedures that any page in the workflow can access to retrieve state information. Add the following AppState class to your Page1.xaml.cs file.

```
public class AppState
{
  private static string productListKey = "productList";

  public static List<Product> ProductList
  {
    get
    {
      List<Product> products =
        (List<Product>)Application.Current.Properties[productListKey];
      if (products == null)
      {
        products = new List<Product>();
        Application.Current.Properties[productListKey] = products;
      }
        return products;
    }
    set
    {
      Application.Current.Properties[productListKey] = value;
    }
  }
}
```

4. The next code listing provides a class definition for the Application object. It contains the event handling methods for the Application.Startup and Application.Exit events to write out the current user name and product list to a persistent `IsolatedStorageFile` and retrieve it on the next application start. Modify the `Application` class found in your App.xaml.cs file as follows:

```csharp
using System;
using System.Windows;
using System.Windows.Navigation;
using System.Data;
using System.Xml;
using System.Configuration;

using System.IO;
using System.IO.IsolatedStorage;

namespace XBAPStatePersistence
{
  public partial class App : System.Windows.Application
  {
    protected override void OnStartup(StartupEventArgs e)
    {
      IsolatedStorageFile isoLastState = IsolatedStorageFile.GetStore(
        IsolatedStorageScope.User |
        IsolatedStorageScope.Domain |
        IsolatedStorageScope.Assembly,
        null,
        null
      );

      StreamReader stateReader = new StreamReader(
        new IsolatedStorageFileStream(
          "MyLastState.txt",
          FileMode.OpenOrCreate,
          isoLastState
        )
      );

      // Open the isolated storage from the previous instance
      // and read each line of product data
      if (stateReader != null)
      {
        while (!stateReader.EndOfStream)
        {
          string productLine = stateReader.ReadLine();

          if (!String.IsNullOrEmpty(productLine))
          {
            string[] tokens = productLine.Split('|');

            if (tokens != null)
            {
              if (tokens.Length != 4)
              {
                throw new ApplicationException(
                  "Malformed product string."
```

```
                    );
                }
                else
                {
                  Product product = new Product();
                  product.Name = tokens[0];
                  product.Type = tokens[1];
                  product.Brand = tokens[2];
                  product.Color = tokens[3];

                  AppState.ProductList.Add(product);
                }
              }
            }
          }
        }
      stateReader.Close();
    }

    protected override void OnExit(ExitEventArgs e)
    {
      IsolatedStorageFile isoLastState = IsolatedStorageFile.GetStore(
        IsolatedStorageScope.User |
        IsolatedStorageScope.Domain |
        IsolatedStorageScope.Assembly,
        null,
        null
      );

      StreamWriter stateWriter = new StreamWriter(
        new IsolatedStorageFileStream(
          "MyLastState.txt",
          FileMode.Create,
          isoLastState
        )
      );

      // Write out a line for each product entered.
      foreach (Product product in AppState.ProductList)
        stateWriter.WriteLine(
          String.Format(
            "{0}|{1}|{2}|{3}\n",
            product.Name,
            product.Type,
            product.Brand,
            product.Color
          )
        );

      stateWriter.Close();
    }

  }
}
```

5. The following XAML markup defines your product selection page. It contains the controls to display what you currently have in your cart and provides the capability to add more products to your list. Modify your Page1.xaml file as follows:

```
<Page x:Class="XBAPStatePersistence.Page1"
  xmlns="http://schemas.microsoft.com/winfx/2006/xaml/presentation"
  xmlns:x="http://schemas.microsoft.com/winfx/2006/xaml"
  Title="Page1"
  >
  <Grid>

    <Grid.Resources>
      <DataTemplate x:Key="ListTemplate">
        <TextBlock Text="{Binding Path=Name}" FontSize="11" Margin="1" />
      </DataTemplate>
    </Grid.Resources>

    <Grid.ColumnDefinitions>
      <ColumnDefinition Width="100" />
      <ColumnDefinition Width="100" />
      <ColumnDefinition Width="30" />
      <ColumnDefinition Width="200" />
    </Grid.ColumnDefinitions>

    <Grid.RowDefinitions>
      <RowDefinition Height="50"/>
      <RowDefinition Height="50"/>
      <RowDefinition Height="50"/>
      <RowDefinition Height="50"/>
      <RowDefinition Height="50"/>
    </Grid.RowDefinitions>

    <Label Grid.Column="0" Grid.Row="0" Height="23">Product Name:</Label>

    <Label Grid.Column="0" Grid.Row="1" Height="23">Product Color: </Label>

    <Label Grid.Column="0" Grid.Row="2" Height="23">Product Type:</Label>

    <Label Grid.Column="0" Grid.Row="3" Height="23">Brand:</Label>

    <TextBox Grid.Column="1" Grid.Row="0" Height="20"
      Name="productName" TabIndex="1"></TextBox>

    <TextBox Grid.Column="1" Grid.Row="1" Height="20"
      Name="productColor" TabIndex="2"></TextBox>

    <TextBox Grid.Column="1" Grid.Row="2" Height="20"
      Name="productType" TabIndex="4"></TextBox>

    <TextBox Grid.Column="1" Grid.Row="3" Height="20"
      Name="productBrand" TabIndex="3"></TextBox>

    <Button Grid.Column="1" Grid.Row="4" Height="23"
```

```
          Name="save" Width="80">Save</Button>

      <Label Height="23" Grid.Column="3"
        Grid.Row="0">Products Entered Last Time:</Label>

      <ListBox ItemTemplate="{StaticResource ListTemplate}"
        Name="productList" Grid.Column="3" Grid.Row="1" Grid.RowSpan="4" />

    </Grid>

  </Page>
```

6. To finish, we'll modify the code-behind for the page to wire up the event handling procedures necessary to interact with the state wrapper class to access data and store it. Modify the Page1 class in the Page1.xaml.cs file as follows:

```csharp
public partial class Page1 : System.Windows.Controls.Page
{
  public Page1()
  {
    InitializeComponent();
    this.save.Click += new RoutedEventHandler(save_Click);
    this.Loaded += new RoutedEventHandler(Page1_Loaded);
  }

  void Page1_Loaded(object sender, RoutedEventArgs e)
  {
    // Bind the previously entered products
    this.productList.ItemsSource = AppState.ProductList;
  }

  void save_Click(object sender, RoutedEventArgs e)
  {
    Product product = new Product();
    product.Name = this.productName.Text;
    product.Type = this.productType.Text;
    product.Brand = this.productBrand.Text;
    product.Color = this.productColor.Text;

    AppState.ProductList.Add(product);
  }
}
```

7. You're finished! Press F5 to run the application.

When you run the application, you are presented with a form for entering product information. Enter the product information and choose Save. You can continue entering product information and saving until your heart is content. When finished, close the application. Now, run the application again. The product information you entered will now be displayed in the list box on the right side of the form, pulled from isolated storage.

Navigation

During the Internet "boom," websites and web applications became responsible for introducing a new means of navigation to users known as the *hyperlink*. Most people spend a fair amount of time on the Internet and have become comfortable with and accustomed to navigating the pages of a site or application via hyperlinks. This is fine for websites strictly geared to displaying content. However, for the developer creating web applications based on the familiar hyperlink style of navigation, a new set of challenges arose.

Web applications consist of one or more pages that represent functional units of a system as a whole. Each page or functional unit of a web application typically needs to interact either directly with another page or with data that another page modifies. This is where the challenge begins. For instance, a calling page has no knowledge of the actions subsequently taken by the user on the target page or if the target page action completed successfully. Additionally, the calling page cannot get a result back from the target page. This type of navigation is referred to as *unstructured navigation* and can be implemented in WPF applications just as it can in web applications. However, WPF introduces a new model for navigation — referred to as structured navigation — that solves many of the problems encountered in a stateless environment using unstructured navigation.

Elements of Navigation

This section focuses on the new navigation capabilities of WPF. However, before diving into the new navigation model in detail you should become familiar with the components of navigation.

To begin, any element can be navigated to in WPF. Typically, however, the target of navigation will be either a `Page` or a `PageFunction`. The `PageFunction` class derives from `Page` and is a new concept in WPF that allows for structured navigation in your application. More about page functions in the next section.

A `Page`, or any other element that you navigate to, will require a host. The host will be different depending on your application model. For standalone navigation applications, the host will be a `NavigationWindow`. The `NavigationWindow` class derives from and extends `Window` by providing support for content navigation. You can explicitly define a `NavigationWindow` for your application or you can let WPF do it for you by setting the `StartupURI` of your application to a `Page`. In the case of an XBAP or loose XAML, the host will be PresentationHost.exe, which is loaded for you by the browser.

Given some content and a host, you will need a mechanism to perform navigation. The mechanism you choose for navigation can be a simple `Hyperlink` or it can be implemented procedurally using the new WPF class called the `NavigationService`. The `NavigationService` class is the core of the navigation subsystem in WPF for navigable applications. In fact, the WPF `Hyperlink` control uses the `NavigationService` class under the covers to locate and load a page specified in its `NavigateURI` property.

Within navigable applications, you will notice that a history-like drop-down is added to the host. This is called the journal. Standalone navigation applications do not run in a browser; therefore a mechanism is needed to manage navigation history. XBAPs also require this feature because they are loaded by the browser as a single file. Loose XAML, on the other hand, is managed by the browser because each file is served individually and therefore a journal is not present. You manage the journal using the `NavigationService`.

Structured Navigation

WPF structured navigation is a framework you can use in your applications to organize pages and page navigation. Structured navigation is WPF's answer to the issues presented when using unstructured navigation in your applications. Structured navigation introduces the concept of navigation topologies. A navigation topology is defined by the organization of pages and the navigation between them. (Actually, unstructured navigation is itself a navigation topology as well.) Using structured navigation, you can create topologies that would be difficult or impossible to create with unstructured navigation. The structure of these topologies can be determined at compile time or at runtime. You'll see examples of these shortly.

The primary benefit of using structured navigation is the ability to have multiple pages working together in your application that perform a specific function or task. These pages can pass data to each other and also return data to one another. This allows a browser-based application to function more like a standalone application would using dialog boxes. The term "structure" in structured navigation therefore refers to the fact that you are adding logical structure to an otherwise unstructured foundation.

The cornerstone of structured navigation is a new generic class called a `PageFunction`, which inherits indirectly from the `Page` class. A `PageFunction` is a construct that allows a calling page to call a target page similar to how one method calls another in code. In doing so, the calling page can pass to and accept data from the target page.

Any target page that participates in structured navigation must inherit from the `PageFunction`. Rather than creating and navigating to pages, content can be created and navigated to as page functions. The key benefit of this is that a `PageFunction` returns a value to the calling page. The value that it returns is specified at the page function's class definition, both in XAML by specifying the `x:TypeArguments` attribute and in the code-behind by specifying the type of the generic `PageFunction` class.

> After the calling page has been returned to by the target page, the target page is still in the browser's history. You can remove the target URI by calling the `RemoveFromJournal` property of the page function. This way an application user will not navigate back to a target page by using the browser history.

The following code illustrates the class definition of a page function:

```
public partial class MyPageFunction : PageFunction<int>
{
  public MyPageFunction() { }
  ...
}
```

In order to navigate to a `PageFunction`, a calling page would create a new instance of a `PageFunction` and navigate to it directly. The following code illustrates the code used to accomplish this:

```
public partial class MyCallingPage : Page
{
  NavigationWindow myWindow;

  // Button event handler to navigate to the
```

```
// desired page function
private void NavigateToMyPageFunction(object sender, RoutedEventArgs e)
{
  MyPageFunction nextPage = new MyPageFunction();
  nextPage.InitializeComponent();
  nextPage.Return += new ReturnEventHandler<int>(nextPage_Return);
  myWindow = (NavigationWindow)MyApplication.MainWindow;
  myWindow.Navigate(nextPage);
}

// Event handling method that listens
// for the OnReturn method call from the
// page function class
void nextPage_Return(object sender, ReturnEventArgs<int> args)
{
  switch (args.Result)
  {
    // Perform some logic based on the return value...
    // of the page function
    case 1:
      ...
  }
}
}
```

The benefit of page functions lies in the fact that they aren't tied directly to the application of which they are a part. Therefore, page functions can be reused in other applications or parts of the same application. Page functions have only the responsibility of returning a value to the calling page. Some key points to remember when implementing structured navigation with page functions are:

❑ **You implement page function objects and define the behavior of each subclass** — All page function objects inherit from the `System.Windows.Navigation.PageFunction` base class.

❑ **Data can be passed from the calling page to the target page by passing constructor parameters** — As with any other class, one or more constructors can be defined.

❑ **The navigation function that is called by the calling page to the target page is managed and kept track of in a navigation journal** — To return to the previous or calling page, you simply call the `OnReturn` method of the target page function. The system returns you to the previous page. This allows for a decoupling between page functions. No two page functions need to know about each other. They can operate independently of their implementation.

❑ **Once the `OnReturn` method of the target page function has been invoked, the calling page is notified of the event and the return data is made available to the calling page** — The calling page can access the return data through the `OnReturn` event handler `ReturnEventArgs` argument.

❑ **When the `OnReturn` method is called to return to the calling page, the target page can be "pruned" so that it is no longer kept alive in the navigation journal** — This can ensure that users navigate only to pages determined by the navigation hub or controller. The `System.Windows.Navigation.JournalEntry` class has a `SetKeepAlive` method that can be used to determine whether the journal should keep items active or inactive. Or, the `RemoveFromJournal` property for a `Page` class can be set to `true`.

> It is important to note that while page functions can be associated with a UI, it isn't a requirement. They can be "UI-less." This feature is explored in more detail as you dive into adaptive navigation topologies where UI-less page functions can be used as a controller or navigation hub to dynamically decide at runtime, based on the state of the application, where to navigate next.

To better understand the concept of structured navigation using page functions, you will now create a simple page flow that includes obtaining a user's address information. A calling page will launch the data collection task by calling a PageFunction. The PageFunction will present the user with a simple form that will collect address, city, state, and ZIP code data. That captured data will then be returned to and displayed on the calling page.

To do this, you'll create a PageFunction named Address.xaml to capture address data from a user. You will also create a second "UI-less" PageFunction that will act as a controller (Controller.cs), the value of which will not be immediately apparent, but will make sense as you build on this example in the sections that follow. The page flow will be initiated from a simple Page named CallingPage.xaml.

Figure 8-3 illustrates the components of the page flow example.

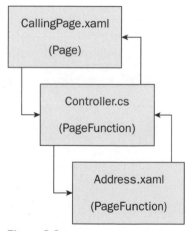

Figure 8-3

As you can see in Figure 8-3, CallingPage.xaml is the start of your page flow. CallingPage.xaml will initiate your address data collection task by making a call to the task controller. The controller calls Address.xaml, which collects the data from the user and passes the results back to the controller. The controller then passes the results back to CallingPage.xaml, where the results are displayed.

1. In Visual Studio, select File ➪ New Project from the menu. From the Project Types tree view, select the Visual C# ➪ .NET Framework 3.0 Node, and then click the XAML Browser Application (WPF) icon from the list. Name your project **StructuredNavigation**, and click OK.

2. Delete the default `Page1.xaml` file and its supporting code-behind file. Add a new Page to the project and name it **CallingPage**. Modify the App.xaml file by setting the `StartupUri` property to CallingPage.xaml.

```
StartupUri="CallingPage.xaml"
```

3. You are going to need a data structure to store the address data you collect in the Address `PageFunction`. Add a new class to your project and name it **AddressData**. Modify the AddressData.cs file as follows:

```
/*
 *  AddressData
 */

using System;
using System.Collections.Generic;
using System.Text;

namespace StructuredNavigation
{
  public class AddressData
  {

    private string _address1;
    public string Address1
    {
      get { return _address1; }
      set { _address1 = value; }
    }

    private string _address2;
    public string Address2
    {
      get { return _address2; }
      set { _address2 = value; }
    }

    private string _city;
    public string City
    {
      get { return _city; }
      set { _city = value; }
    }

    private string _state;
    public string State
    {
      get { return _state; }
      set { _state = value; }
    }

    private string _zip;
    public string Zip
    {
```

```
        get { return _zip; }
        set { _zip = value; }
    }


  }
}
```

AddressData is a very simple class that stores the various data fields you will be collecting, such as address, city, state, and ZIP code. The benefit of creating the class is that you can pass your data between the calling page, controller, and Address `PageFunction` easily.

4. In the examples that follow this one, you will be collecting additional data. To accommodate upcoming examples and in order to make it easy to build upon this example, you will define another class named `UserData`. In this example, `UserData` will store a reference to the `AddressData` class. In upcoming examples, it will also support additional data you will be adding. The `UserData` class will be the actual type you pass between the calling page, controller, and address page function. Add a new class to your project and name it **UserData**. Modify the `UserData` class as follows:

```
/*
 *   UserData
 */

using System;
using System.Collections.Generic;
using System.Text;

namespace StructuredNavigation
{
  public class UserData
  {

    private AddressData addressInfo;
    public AddressData AddressInfo
    {
      get
      {
        return addressInfo;
      }
      set
      {
        addressInfo = value;
      }
    }

  }
}
```

5. Add the Address `PageFunction` that will capture address data from the user and return the data to the calling page via the controller. Right-click on your StructuredNavigation project and select Add ⇨ New Item and choose PageFunction (WPF) from the Add New Item Templates dialog box. Name the `PageFunction` **Address** and click Add. Modify the Address.xaml file as follows:

```
<PageFunction
  xmlns="http://schemas.microsoft.com/winfx/2006/xaml/presentation"
  xmlns:x="http://schemas.microsoft.com/winfx/2006/xaml"
  xmlns:local="clr-namespace:StructuredNavigation"
  x:Class="StructuredNavigation.Address"
  x:TypeArguments="local:UserData"
  Title="Address"
  >

  <Grid ShowGridLines="False">

    <Grid.ColumnDefinitions>
      <ColumnDefinition Width="75"/>
      <ColumnDefinition Width="150"/>
    </Grid.ColumnDefinitions>

    <Grid.RowDefinitions>
      <RowDefinition Height="40"/>
      <RowDefinition Height="40"/>
      <RowDefinition Height="40"/>
      <RowDefinition Height="40"/>
      <RowDefinition Height="40"/>
      <RowDefinition Height="40"/>
      <RowDefinition Height="40"/>
    </Grid.RowDefinitions>

    <TextBox Name="address1" Grid.Column="1" Grid.Row="0"
        Width="150" Height="20"></TextBox>

    <TextBox Name="address2" Grid.Column="1" Grid.Row="1"
        Width="150" Height="20"></TextBox>

    <TextBox Name="city" Grid.Column="1" Grid.Row="2"
        Width="150" Height="20"></TextBox>

    <TextBox Name="state" Grid.Column="1" Grid.Row="3"
        Width="150" Height="20"></TextBox>

    <TextBox Name="zip" Grid.Column="1" Grid.Row="4"
        Width="150" Height="20"></TextBox>

    <Label Grid.Column="0" Grid.Row="0">Address:</Label>

    <Label Grid.Column="0" Grid.Row="1">Address 2:</Label>

    <Label Grid.Column="0" Grid.Row="2">City:</Label>

    <Label Grid.Column="0" Grid.Row="3">State:</Label>

    <Label Grid.Column="0" Grid.Row="4">Zip:</Label>

    <Button Name="submit" Grid.Column="1" Grid.Row="5"
        HorizontalAlignment="Right" Width="100" Height="20"
```

```
                    Click="submit_Click">Submit</Button>

  </Grid>

</PageFunction>
```

In the Address XAML, you are simply creating the fields for collecting address data. Using a Grid as a container, a Label and TextBox is added for each field: address1, address2, city, state and zip. A submit Button is also added for completing the task. The XAML should look pretty familiar by this point in the book. What is different, however, is the x:TypeArguments attribute of the PageFunction element. Because PageFunction is a generic class, this attribute is used to specify the type of value that will be returned.

6. You need to add some logic to the Address page function code-behind. The code-behind file for the Address page function wires an event to the submit button that collects the user input data, populates an instance of an AddressData class, and then calls the OnReturn method to bubble the data up to the calling page via the controller. Modify the Address.xaml.cs file as follows:

```csharp
using System;
using System.Windows;
using System.Windows.Controls;
using System.Windows.Navigation;

namespace StructuredNavigation
{
  public partial class Address : PageFunction<UserData>
  {
    public Address()
    {
    }

    void submit_Click(object sender, RoutedEventArgs e)
    {
      if (IsInputComplete())
      {
        // Collect the data and add it to the class
        UserData data = new UserData();
        data.AddressInfo = new AddressData();
        data.AddressInfo.Address1 = this.address1.Text;
        data.AddressInfo.Address2 = this.address2.Text;
        data.AddressInfo.City = this.city.Text;
        data.AddressInfo.State = this.state.Text;
        data.AddressInfo.Zip = this.zip.Text;

        // Bubble the data up to the calling function
        OnReturn(new ReturnEventArgs<UserData>(data));
      }
      else
      {
        MessageBox.Show("Please complete all fields.");
        this.address1.Focus();
        return;
      }
```

```
      }

      private bool IsInputComplete()
      {
        return !(this.address1.Text == "" ||
          this.address2.Text == "" ||
            this.city.Text == "" ||
              this.state.Text == "" ||
                this.zip.Text == "");
      }
    }
  }
}
```

In the submit button click event handler, you are simply populating the fields of your
`AddressInfo` object with the data collected in the form. The `AddressInfo` object is then added
to a `UserData` object that will serve as the return type of the `PageFunction`. Notice that the
definition of the `PageFunction` class includes a data type, UserData, which specifies the type
that will be returned to the caller. This corresponds to the `x:TypeAttribute` defined in the
associated XAML for this `PageFunction` class.

7. Rather than simply call the `Address` page function directly from the CallingPage.xaml page, we
will use a `PageFunction` as a controller so that we can expand on this example in upcoming
sections. This code sample represents your task controller, which will initiate the task of collecting the address information. This is the "UI-less" page function referred to earlier in this chapter. Add a new class (not a `PageFunction`) to your project. Name the class **Controller** and
modify the class as follows:

```
/*
 *  Controller
 */

using System;
using System.Windows;
using System.Windows.Controls;
using System.Windows.Navigation;

namespace StructuredNavigation
{
  // Return type indicates the task is done.
  public class Controller : PageFunction<UserData>
  {
    private UserData userData = new UserData();

    protected override void Start()
    {

      // Create and initialize the page function
      Address address = new Address();
      address.InitializeComponent();
      address.Return += new ReturnEventHandler<UserData>(address_Return);

      Navigate(address);
    }

    void address_Return(object sender, ReturnEventArgs<UserData> e)
```

```
      {
         // Remove task from journal to avoid re-navigating
         this.RemoveFromJournal = true;

         // Perform any further validation or ancillary logic before
         // ...

         // Return control to the calling page.
         OnReturn(new ReturnEventArgs<UserData>(e.Result));
      }

      void Navigate(Page page)
      {
         NavigationWindow navWindow =
            (NavigationWindow)Application.Current.MainWindow;

         navWindow.Navigate(page);
      }


   }
}
```

There are some important things to note from the previous class definition. First, the
AddressTaskController class is not a partial class because it represents a UI-less page function and serves only as the navigation hub. Therefore, there is no need for the compiler to merge
a partial class with a XAML file because there is no UI.

The second thing to note in this class is the Start method. Start is a member of the
PageFunction class and serves as the initialization method for the class the first time it is navigated to. In this case, you are overriding the Start method in order to add the logic required to
launch the Address PageFunction task. This is also where you specify the event handler to be
called when the Address PageFunction returns.

The third thing to note is setting the RemoveFromJournal property. By doing this, you disable
the user from any further navigation to this task. Future navigation can be determined by the
application instead.

8.   You will now modify the default CallingPage.xaml page so that the user can launch the address
     task and kick off the page flow. You'll add a button to launch the task. Modify the
     CallingPage.xaml file as follows:

```
<Page
  x:Class="StructuredNavigation.CallingPage"
  xmlns="http://schemas.microsoft.com/winfx/2006/xaml/presentation"
  xmlns:x="http://schemas.microsoft.com/winfx/2006/xaml"
  Title="CallingPage"
  >
<StackPanel Margin="10">

   <Button Name="button1" Click="button1_click" Width="200"
     HorizontalAlignment="Left">Begin Navigation</Button>

   <Label Name="output"/>

  </StackPanel>
</Page>
```

9. Now modify the Page1.xaml.cs code-behind file to launch the page function as follows:

```csharp
using System;
using System.Windows;
using System.Windows.Navigation;

namespace StructuredNavigation
{

  public partial class CallingPage : System.Windows.Controls.Page
  {

    public CallingPage()
    {
      InitializeComponent();
    }

    public void OnAddressReturned(object sender, ReturnEventArgs<UserData> e)
    {
      UserData userData = (UserData)e.Result;

      string result = "";

      result += "Address data captured: " + Environment.NewLine;

      result += "Address1: " + userData.AddressInfo.Address1 + Environment.NewLine;
      result += "Address2: " + userData.AddressInfo.Address2 + Environment.NewLine;
      result += "City: " + userData.AddressInfo.City + Environment.NewLine;
      result += "State: " + userData.AddressInfo.State + Environment.NewLine;
      result += "Zip: " + userData.AddressInfo.Zip + Environment.NewLine;

      this.output.Content = result;
    }

    private void button1_click(object sender, RoutedEventArgs e)
    {
      // --- using the controller
      Controller pageFunction = new Controller();
      pageFunction.Return += new ReturnEventHandler<UserData>(OnAddressReturned);
      this.NavigationService.Navigate(pageFunction);
    }
  }
}
```

In the code-behind for CallingPage, you are adding an event handler for the button that will launch the task. In the button, you create a new Controller PageFunction, specify the return event handler for when the controller returns, and then navigate to the controller. When the controller returns from the address task, it passes back a UserData object. In the return event handler, you simply display the results back to the user.

10. You're finished! Press F5 to run the application.

The example illustrates how to use structured navigation in your WPF applications. The use of page functions provides a powerful tool you can use for developing task-oriented applications. We hope this simple example has demonstrated just how useful structured navigation can be in your applications.

Navigation Topologies

Structured navigation provides a framework that defines the `Page-to-Page`, or `PageFunction`-to-`PageFunction`, navigation of a task or workflow. This model is defined by its topological structure.

Structured navigation has two distinct topological structures:

❑ **Fixed** — In a fixed topology, a navigation path is predefined at *compile time* and fixed regardless of user input or state information. A fixed topology is best exemplified by wizards where users navigate through each individual task in sequence from beginning to end.

❑ **Adaptive** — In an adaptive topology, a navigation path is flexible to the point where the next step in a task can be determined at *runtime* based on user input or state information. Adaptive topologies are more reactive to interaction where steps can be added or eliminated from a task.

While developing a UI for your application, you will find that it is useful to implement some tasks with a fixed topology and others with an adaptive topology. The requirements of each task will dictate the topological structure you should use.

You may also find that your tasks that are implemented as fixed or adaptive topologies can have hierarchies of other topologies. When using UI-less page functions, you can have multiple navigation hubs that are linked in a hierarchical fashion. To a user, it may seem as though they are engaging in one large task when in actuality it is a composite structure of both adaptive and fixed topologies.

For example, you could have an application that represents a user checking out through an e-commerce site. The checkout process follows a sequence of steps to gather the user information required to total their shopping cart items and collect their method of payment. Within this process, the user may have to create an account in order to check out. The process of creating an account could be represented as another fixed task that is called through another UI-less page function.

Fixed Linear Topology

As mentioned, this topology is best described as a fixed sequence of steps that a user is required to proceed through from beginning to end. Typically, the application UI will guide users through from page to page with an option to cancel at any of the individual steps. Figure 8-4 illustrates the page-by-page flow of a typical fixed linear topology.

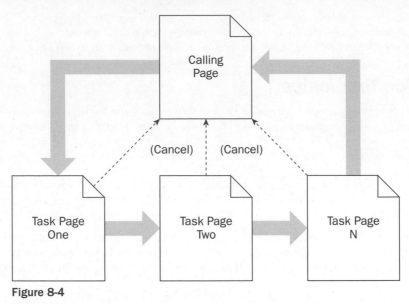

Figure 8-4

There are two methods you can use to initiate program flow:

❑ **Set the startup URI to that of the initial page in the task** — Each `Application` object has a `StartupUri` property. If there's no need to return to the calling page, then this approach will work.

❑ **Create a page function object explicitly in code and then navigate to it** — This allows you to easily pass any initial data to the page function through a constructor. This also eliminates the need for any hard-coded URIs in the application. The `OnReturn` method can be called from the start page of the task and automatically return to the calling page. This allows you to maintain the loose coupling between pages or sets of pages where they can be called from multiple parts of a larger application.

In order to illustrate the fixed topology in code, you will now expand on the previous example by adding an additional task as well as the logic required to drive the navigation within the controller so that the tasks are accessed in sequence.

In this example, you will add an additional task that will collect contact data from the user. This task will also be implemented as a `PageFunction`. In this example, the benefit of using a controller will become clear. The controller will call each task in succession, adding both address data and contact data to your `UserData` class, and returning all of this data to the calling page. The controller will also handle the case when a user cancels out of either task. The benefit of the controller is that it provides a centralized module where your navigation can live.

Figure 8-5 illustrates the addition of an additional task to our previous example:

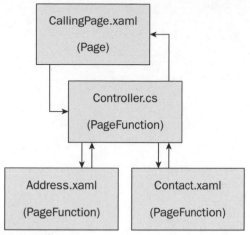

Figure 8-5

Looking at Figure 8-5 you will see the addition of the contact task, represented by the Contact.xaml `PageFunction`. The controller will call the address task first, and upon completion will then call the contact task before returning the collected data to the calling page. There won't be a lot of code descriptions in this example as the concepts should be quite familiar by now.

1. Add a new class file to your project and name it **ContactData**. The ContactData class will store the user's contact data, which will be the return type passed back to the controller. Add a new class to your project and name it **ContactData**. Modify the ContactData.cs file as follows:

```
/*
 *  ContactData
 */

using System;
using System.Collections.Generic;
using System.Text;

namespace StructuredNavigation
{
  public class ContactData
  {
    private string homePhoneNumber;
    public string HomePhoneNumber
    {
      get { return homePhoneNumber; }
      set { homePhoneNumber = value; }
    }

    private string cellPhoneNumber;
    public string CellPhoneNumber
    {
      get { return cellPhoneNumber; }
      set { cellPhoneNumber = value; }
```

```
      }

      private string faxNumber;
      public string FaxNumber
      {
        get { return faxNumber; }
        set { faxNumber = value; }
      }

      private string emailAddress;
      public string EmailAddress
      {
        get { return emailAddress; }
        set { emailAddress = value; }
      }
    }
  }
}
```

There's nothing special in this code. Here you are simply defining a data structure that will store the fields collected by the Contact PageFunction.

2. Now that you are collecting two sets of data (address and contact) you need to modify the UserData class to hold a reference to both AddressData and ContactData. Modify the UserData class as follows:

```
using System;
using System.Collections.Generic;
using System.Text;

namespace StructuredNavigation
{
  public class UserData
  {
    private AddressData addressInfo;
    public AddressData AddressInfo
    {
      get
      {
        return addressInfo;
      }
      set
      {
        addressInfo = value;
      }
    }

    private ContactData contactInfo;
    public ContactData ContactInfo
    {
      get
      {
        return contactInfo;
      }
      set
      {
```

```
        contactInfo = value;
      }
    }
  }
}
```

3. Add a new `PageFunction` named Contact that collects contact information from the user. Modify the Contact.xaml file as follows:

```xml
<PageFunction
  xmlns="http://schemas.microsoft.com/winfx/2006/xaml/presentation"
  xmlns:x="http://schemas.microsoft.com/winfx/2006/xaml"
  xmlns:local="clr-namespace:StructuredNavigation"
  x:Class="StructuredNavigation.Contact"
  x:TypeArguments="local:UserData"
  Title="Contact">
  <Grid>

    <Grid.ColumnDefinitions>
      <ColumnDefinition Width="75"/>
      <ColumnDefinition Width="150"/>
    </Grid.ColumnDefinitions>

    <Grid.RowDefinitions>
      <RowDefinition Height="40"/>
      <RowDefinition Height="40"/>
      <RowDefinition Height="40"/>
      <RowDefinition Height="40"/>
      <RowDefinition Height="40"/>
      <RowDefinition Height="40"/>
    </Grid.RowDefinitions>

    <TextBox Name="homeNumber" Grid.Column="1" Grid.Row="0"
        Width="150" Height="20"></TextBox>

    <TextBox Name="cellNumber" Grid.Column="1" Grid.Row="1"
        Width="150" Height="20"></TextBox>

    <TextBox Name="faxNumber" Grid.Column="1" Grid.Row="2"
        Width="150" Height="20"></TextBox>

    <TextBox Name="emailAddress" Grid.Column="1" Grid.Row="3"
        Width="150" Height="20"></TextBox>

    <Label Grid.Column="0" Grid.Row="0">Home #:</Label>

    <Label Grid.Column="0" Grid.Row="1">Cell #:</Label>

    <Label Grid.Column="0" Grid.Row="2">Fax:</Label>

    <Label Grid.Column="0" Grid.Row="3">Email:</Label>

    <Button Name="submit" Grid.Column="1" Grid.Row="4"
  HorizontalAlignment="Right" Width="100" Height="20"
```

```
      Click="submit_Click">Submit</Button>

      <Button Name="cancel" Grid.Column="1" Grid.Row="5"
        HorizontalAlignment="Right" Width="100" Height="20"
          Click="cancel_Click">Cancel</Button>

    </Grid>

</PageFunction>
```

The Contact XAML basically mirrors the Address XAML created earlier, only with different fields and a Cancel button.

4. The code-behind for your new contact `PageFunction` will perform the task of populating your data object and returning it to the controller. To indicate that the user has cancelled the action, you simply return a null reference. The task controller determines the next course of action based on the returned value. Modify the Contact.xaml.cs file as follows:

```
using System;
using System.Windows;
using System.Windows.Controls;
using System.Windows.Data;
using System.Windows.Documents;
using System.Windows.Media;
using System.Windows.Media.Imaging;
using System.Windows.Navigation;
using System.Windows.Shapes;

namespace StructuredNavigation
{

  public partial class Contact : PageFunction<UserData>
  {

    public Contact()
    {
    }

    void cancel_Click(object sender, RoutedEventArgs e)
    {
      // Return null to indicate the user cancelled.
      OnReturn(new ReturnEventArgs<UserData>(null));
    }

    void submit_Click(object sender, RoutedEventArgs e)
    {
      if (IsInputComplete())
      {
        // Collect the data and add it to the class
        UserData data = new UserData();
        data.ContactInfo = new ContactData();
        data.ContactInfo.HomePhoneNumber = this.homeNumber.Text;
        data.ContactInfo.CellPhoneNumber = this.cellNumber.Text;
        data.ContactInfo.FaxNumber = this.faxNumber.Text;
```

```
            data.ContactInfo.EmailAddress = this.emailAddress.Text;

            // Bubble the data up to the calling function.
            OnReturn(new ReturnEventArgs<UserData>(data));
        }
        else
        {
            MessageBox.Show("Please complete all fields.");
            this.homeNumber.Focus();
            return;
        }
    }

    private bool IsInputComplete()
    {
        return !(this.homeNumber.Text == "" ||
                 this.cellNumber.Text == "" ||
                 this.faxNumber.Text == "" ||
                 this.emailAddress.Text == "");
    }
  }
}
```

As with the UI definition, the code-behind looks very similar to the Address `PageFunction` created earlier. However, new logic has been added to allow the user to cancel the task. Additionally, validation code has been added so that the user may not complete the task without filling in all required fields. The `IsInputComplete` method provides the validation logic for the `PageFunction`.

5. Now you need to update your previous address input screen. You will need to add a button to allow the user to cancel the task. Simply add the following XAML to the Address.xaml page function and place it just beneath the Submit button.

```
<Button Name="cancel" Grid.Column="1" Grid.Row="6"
  HorizontalAlignment="Right" Width="100" Height="20"
    Click="cancel_Click">Cancel</Button>
```

6. You'll also need to add an event handler to handle the click event for the Cancel button as well as the validation for the task form. The cancel event handler follows the same pattern as the address page and returns a null reference if the user decides to cancel the current action. Add the following `cancel_Click` event handler to the Address.xaml.cs file:

```
void cancel_Click(object sender, RoutedEventArgs e)
{
  // Return null to indicate the user cancelled.
  OnReturn(new ReturnEventArgs<UserData>(null));
}

private bool IsInputComplete()
{
  return !(this.Address1.Text == "" ||
    this.Address2.Text == "" ||
    this.City.Text == "" ||
    this.State.Text == "" ||
    this.Zip.Text == "");
}
```

7. You have to make some significant changes to the controller. The controller initiates a task by creating an instance of the Address `PageFunction` and navigating to it. When the page function returns, the contact task will be initiated. The controller now has to handle the possibility that the user can choose to cancel any step in the overall task workflow. Modify Controller.cs as follows:

```csharp
/*
 *  Controller
 */

using System;
using System.Windows;
using System.Windows.Controls;
using System.Windows.Navigation;

namespace StructuredNavigation
{

  public class Controller : PageFunction<UserData>
  {
    private UserData userData = new UserData();

    protected override void Start()
    {

      this.KeepAlive = true;

      // Create and initialize the page function
      Address address = new Address();
      address.InitializeComponent();
      address.Return += new ReturnEventHandler<UserData>(address_Return);

      //this.NavigationService.Navigate(address);
      Navigate(address);
    }

    void address_Return(object sender, ReturnEventArgs<UserData> e)
    {

      if (e != null)
      {
        // Remove task from journal to avoid re-navigating
        this.RemoveFromJournal = true;

        // Perform any further validation or ancillary logic before
        // ...

        userData.AddressInfo = ((UserData)e.Result).AddressInfo;

        // Navigate to the next page in the task
        Contact contact = new Contact();
        contact.InitializeComponent();
        contact.Return += new ReturnEventHandler<UserData>(contact_Return);

        //this.NavigationService.Navigate(contact);
```

```
        Navigate(contact);
      }
      else
      {
        // Return null if the user cancelled
        OnReturn(new ReturnEventArgs<UserData>(null));
      }
    }

    void contact_Return(object sender, ReturnEventArgs<UserData> e)
    {
      // Remove task from journal to avoid re-navigating
      this.RemoveFromJournal = true;

      // Add contact data if user didn't cancel
      if (e != null)
      {
        // Add data
        userData.ContactInfo = ((UserData)e.Result).ContactInfo;
      }

      // Return control to calling page
      OnReturn(new ReturnEventArgs<UserData>(userData));
    }

    void Navigate(Page page)
    {
      NavigationWindow navWindow =
        (NavigationWindow)Application.Current.MainWindow;

      navWindow.Navigate(page);
    }

  }
}
```

The event handling methods for both the Address and Contact OnReturn events check to see if null is returned, which, as you defined earlier, would be the mechanism for determining if the user cancelled the task. If the user proceeds through each step, the controller adds each of the return values to the UserData object.

The other thing to note is that the Address OnReturn event handler navigates to the next step in the task and the Contact OnReturn event handler signals the end of the task by calling the TaskController's OnReturn method.

8. You'll also need to modify the OnAddressReturned method in your calling page to display the additional contact data captured. Modify the CallingPage.xaml.cs file as follows:

```
public void OnAddressReturned(object sender, ReturnEventArgs<UserData> e)
{
  UserData userData = (UserData)e.Result;

  string result = "";

  result += "Address data captured: " + Environment.NewLine;
```

```
result += "Address1: " + userData.AddressInfo.Address1 + Environment.NewLine;
result += "Address2: " + userData.AddressInfo.Address2 + Environment.NewLine;
result += "City: " + userData.AddressInfo.City + Environment.NewLine;
result += "State: " + userData.AddressInfo.State + Environment.NewLine;
result += "Zip: " + userData.AddressInfo.Zip + Environment.NewLine;


result += Environment.NewLine;
result += "Contact data captured: " + Environment.NewLine;
result += "Home: " + userData.ContactInfo.HomePhoneNumber +
  Environment.NewLine;
result += "Cell: " + userData.ContactInfo.CellPhoneNumber +
  Environment.NewLine;
result += "Fax: " + userData.ContactInfo.FaxNumber + Environment.NewLine;
result += "Email: " + userData.ContactInfo.EmailAddress +
  Environment.NewLine;

    this.output.Content = result;
  }
```

9. Press F5 to run the fixed topology example.

This example illustrated the fixed topology navigation model. The application executes a predefined series of tasks in a specified order. The controller became a centralized hub for managing the tasks and centralizing the navigation logic. A fixed topology is a great model to use when your steps must execute in a specific order, but sometimes you might need tasks to be ordered based on events at runtime. The solution for this scenario is to use an adaptive topology, and you look at this next.

Adaptive Topology

Adaptive topologies are intended for applications that require flexibility in determining page navigation. This may also involve varying the order in which they are presented. For example, let's say you have an application that helps students study varying levels of high school mathematics. One part of the application may include sample tests to help students gauge their readiness for an actual exam. The first screen displays the difficulty level of the math class in which the student is currently enrolled in. Based on that selection, the system determines the test questions to present to the student. As the student proceeds through the test, each subsequent question is based on the student's response to the previous question.

In the hypothetical example just outlined, you can see that a fixed topology will not fit because the selection of pages to show must be determined at runtime. Figure 8-6 illustrates the way page flow control is always routed through the navigation hub.

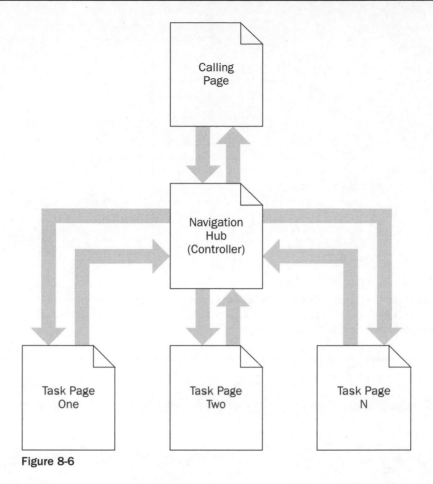

Figure 8-6

You will now expand, once again, on the previous example by adding some functionality within the controller to evaluate if additional data is needed based on user input. The controller will again manage the navigation and will contain the logic required to implement an adaptive topology.

In this example, you add an additional task to the application. This task collects credit card data from the user and is implemented as a PageFunction just like the other tasks you have defined thus far. The order in which tasks execute is completely random in order to simulate a scenario in which logic might dictate the ordering of tasks.

Figure 8-7 illustrates the addition of an additional task to your previous example. Notice that tasks are executed in no particular order

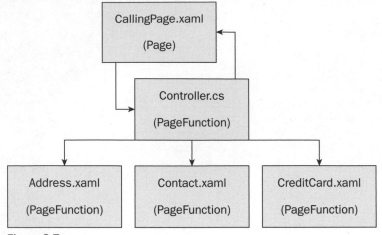

Figure 8-7

Looking at Figure 8-7, you will see the addition of the credit card task, represented by the CreditCarad.xaml `PageFunction`. The controller randomly calls each task and, upon completion, returns the collected data to the calling page.

1. Add a new class to your project, name it **CreditCardData**, and modify it as follows:

```
/*
 *  CreditCardData
 */

using System;
using System.Collections.Generic;
using System.Text;

namespace StructuredNavigation
{
    public class CreditCardData
    {
        private string type;
        public string Type
        {
            get { return type; }
            set { type = value; }
        }

        private string number;
        public string Number
        {
            get { return number; }
            set { number = value; }
        }

        private string code;
        public string Code
```

```
        {
            get { return code; }
            set { code = value; }
        }
    }
}
```

2. You now need to add a reference to that `CreditCardData` class you just created within the `UserData` class so that you can collect and store the information gathered on the screen. Open the `UserData` class file and modify it as follows:

```
/*
 *  UserData
 */

using System;
using System.Collections.Generic;
using System.Text;

namespace StructuredNavigation
{
  public class UserData
  {

    private AddressData addressInfo;
    public AddressData AddressInfo
    {
      get
      {
        return addressInfo;
      }
      set
      {
        addressInfo = value;
      }
    }

    private ContactData contactInfo;
    public ContactData ContactInfo
    {
      get
      {
        return contactInfo;
      }
      set
      {
        contactInfo = value;
      }
    }

    private CreditCardData creditCardInfo;
    public CreditCardData CreditCardInfo
    {
      get
```

```
      {
        return creditCardInfo;
      }
      set
      {
        creditCardInfo = value;
      }
    }


  }
}
```

3. Now, you need a to create a task that will collect the credit card data from the user. Create a new
    `PageFunction`, name it **CreditCard**, and modify it as follows:

```
<PageFunction
  xmlns="http://schemas.microsoft.com/winfx/2006/xaml/presentation"
  xmlns:x="http://schemas.microsoft.com/winfx/2006/xaml"
  xmlns:local="clr-namespace:StructuredNavigation"
  x:Class="StructuredNavigation.CreditCard"
  x:TypeArguments="local:UserData"
  Title="CreditCard"
  >
<Grid>

  <Grid.ColumnDefinitions>
    <ColumnDefinition Width="75"/>
    <ColumnDefinition Width="150"/>
  </Grid.ColumnDefinitions>

  <Grid.RowDefinitions>
    <RowDefinition Height="40"/>
    <RowDefinition Height="40"/>
    <RowDefinition Height="40"/>
    <RowDefinition Height="40"/>
    <RowDefinition Height="40"/>
    <RowDefinition Height="40"/>
  </Grid.RowDefinitions>

  <TextBox Name="cardType" Grid.Column="1" Grid.Row="0"
       Width="150" Height="20"></TextBox>

  <TextBox Name="cardNumber" Grid.Column="1" Grid.Row="1"
      Width="150" Height="20"></TextBox>

  <TextBox Name="cardCode" Grid.Column="1" Grid.Row="2"
      Width="150" Height="20"></TextBox>

  <Label Grid.Column="0" Grid.Row="0">Type:</Label>

  <Label Grid.Column="0" Grid.Row="1">Number:</Label>

  <Label Grid.Column="0" Grid.Row="2">Code:</Label>

  <Button Name="submit" Grid.Column="1" Grid.Row="3"
```

```
                HorizontalAlignment="Right" Width="100" Height="20"
                  Click="submit_Click">Submit</Button>

            <Button Name="cancel" Grid.Column="1" Grid.Row="6"
              HorizontalAlignment="Right" Width="100" Height="20"
                Click="cancel_Click">Cancel</Button>

        </Grid>
    </PageFunction>
```

4. Modify the CreditCard code-behind as follows:

```csharp
using System;
using System.Windows;
using System.Windows.Controls;
using System.Windows.Data;
using System.Windows.Documents;
using System.Windows.Media;
using System.Windows.Media.Imaging;
using System.Windows.Navigation;
using System.Windows.Shapes;

namespace StructuredNavigation
{
    public partial class CreditCard : PageFunction<UserData>
    {
        public CreditCard()
        {
        }

        void submit_Click(object sender, RoutedEventArgs e)
        {
            if (IsInputComplete())
            {
                // Collect the data and add it to the class
                UserData data = new UserData();
                data.CreditCardInfo = new CreditCardData();
                data.CreditCardInfo.Type = this.cardType.Text;
                data.CreditCardInfo.Number = this.cardNumber.Text;
                data.CreditCardInfo.Code = this.cardCode.Text;

                // Bubble the data up to the calling function.
                OnReturn(new ReturnEventArgs<UserData>(data));
            }
            else
            {
                MessageBox.Show("Please complete all fields.");
                this.cardType.Focus();
                return;
            }
        }

    void cancel_Click(object sender, RoutedEventArgs e)
    {
        // Return null to indicate the user cancelled.
```

```
            OnReturn(new ReturnEventArgs<UserData>(null));
        }

            private bool IsInputComplete()
            {
                return !(this.cardType.Text == "" ||
                        this.cardNumber.Text == "" ||
                        this.cardCode.Text == "");
            }
        }
    }
}
```

5. The task controller has gone through several changes and now must undergo one more. Modify the Controller.xaml.cs file as follows:

```
/*
 *   Controller
 */

using System;
using System.Windows;
using System.Windows.Controls;
using System.Windows.Navigation;

namespace StructuredNavigation
{

  public class Controller : PageFunction<UserData>
  {

    private UserData userData = new UserData();

    private Address address = new Address();
    private Contact contact = new Contact();
    private CreditCard creditCard = new CreditCard();

    protected override void Start()
    {
      this.KeepAlive = true;

      address.InitializeComponent();
      contact.InitializeComponent();
      creditCard.InitializeComponent();

      address.Return += new
        ReturnEventHandler<UserData>(ReturnEvaluator);
      contact.Return += new
        ReturnEventHandler<UserData>(ReturnEvaluator);
      creditCard.Return += new
        ReturnEventHandler<UserData>(ReturnEvaluator);

      // Pick a random screen to start since
      // navigation is non-linear
      Navigate(PickRandomStart());
```

```
      }

      void ReturnEvaluator(object sender, ReturnEventArgs<UserData> e)
      {
        //Populate our data based on the returned data
        switch (sender.GetType().ToString())
        {
          case "StructuredNavigation.Address":
            userData.AddressInfo = new AddressData();
            userData.AddressInfo = e.Result.AddressInfo;
            break;
          case "StructuredNavigation.Contact":
            userData.ContactInfo = new ContactData();
            userData.ContactInfo = e.Result.ContactInfo;
            break;
          case "StructuredNavigation.CreditCard":
            userData.CreditCardInfo = new CreditCardData();
            userData.CreditCardInfo = e.Result.CreditCardInfo;
            break;
        }

        // Check to see what page to navigate to next
        // based on the state of the UserData
        if (userData.AddressInfo == null)
          Navigate(address);
        else if (userData.ContactInfo == null)
          Navigate(contact);
        else if (userData.CreditCardInfo == null)
          Navigate(creditCard);

        // Return control to the calling page
        if (userData.AddressInfo != null && userData.ContactInfo != null
          && userData.CreditCardInfo != null)
          OnReturn(new ReturnEventArgs<UserData>(userData));
      }

    void Navigate(Page page)
    {
      NavigationWindow navWindow =
        (NavigationWindow)Application.Current.MainWindow;

      navWindow.Navigate(page);
    }

    Page PickRandomStart()
    {
      Page[] pages = new Page[] {
              address, contact, creditCard
          };

      return pages[(new Random()).Next(0, pages.Length - 1)];
    }

  }
}
```

The task controller (for the sake of this example) now initializes all pages within the task it controls and picks a random screen to start the task. There is now one `OnReturn` event handler that handles each of the task pages `Return` events and evaluates which page to go to based on the state of the data that has been collected.

6. You'll also need to modify the `OnAddressReturned` method in your calling page to display the additional contact data captured. Modify the CallingPage.xaml.cs file as follows:

```
public void OnAddressReturned(object sender, ReturnEventArgs<UserData> e)
{
  UserData userData = (UserData)e.Result;

  string result = "";

  result += "Address data captured: " + Environment.NewLine;

  result += "Address1: " + userData.AddressInfo.Address1 + Environment.NewLine;
  result += "Address2: " + userData.AddressInfo.Address2 + Environment.NewLine;
  result += "City: " + userData.AddressInfo.City + Environment.NewLine;
  result += "State: " + userData.AddressInfo.State + Environment.NewLine;
  result += "Zip: " + userData.AddressInfo.Zip + Environment.NewLine;

  result += Environment.NewLine;
  result += "Contact data captured: " + Environment.NewLine;
  result += "Home: " + userData.ContactInfo.HomePhoneNumber +
    Environment.NewLine;
  result += "Cell: " + userData.ContactInfo.CellPhoneNumber +
    Environment.NewLine;
  result += "Fax: " + userData.ContactInfo.FaxNumber + Environment.NewLine;
  result += "Email: " + userData.ContactInfo.EmailAddress + Environment.NewLine;

  result += Environment.NewLine;
  result += "Credit Card data captured: " + Environment.NewLine;
  result += "Type: " + userData.CreditCardInfo.Type + Environment.NewLine;
  result += "Number: " + userData.CreditCardInfo.Number + Environment.NewLine;
  result += "Code: " + userData.CreditCardInfo.Code + Environment.NewLine;

  this.output.Content = result;
}
```

7. Press F5 to run the application.

This example illustrates the use of an adaptive topology. The controller randomly calls each task, collects the data, and returns it to the calling page. An adaptive topology is a useful solution for creating applications that need to determine task order at runtime.

Application Localization

When writing world-ready applications, developers must consider the localization requirements of the specific geographical regions they intend to support. Localization involves adapting the application UI to different cultures. For instance, localization provides a means by which UI elements — such as text, dates and times, numbers, and currencies — can be adapted to the cultural norm of a target location.

Implementing a flexible layout for localized applications has been both time intensive and tedious in the past. WPF provides new features you can use to better manage the localized UI. By following localization guidelines when developing WPF applications, localized development is now easier, and you can reduce the impact of applying cultural resources to the UI.

Automatic Layout Guidelines

Building a localized application in the past was a time intensive and tedious process in which elements had to be resized on an individual basis relative to the cultural context of the application. In an effort to minimize the time it takes to develop localized applications, Microsoft recommends an approach to creating user interfaces called *automatic layout*.

Automatic layout isn't a feature but rather a set of guidelines and coding standards that developers should adhere to when creating application UIs that require localization.

By using the guidelines of automatic layout, UI localizers can focus on the language and resource specifics of the application rather than the pixel-by-pixel UI element adjustments previously required to accommodate different languages.

The benefits of using the standards of automatic layout in your UI design are:

❑   Your UI will display correctly regardless of the language.

❑   The need to adjust both the position and size of controls for the targeted culture will be reduced.

❑   The window and the layout of the page will render properly regardless of locale.

❑   Localization efforts will be reduced when translating strings.

The following sections represent the major guidelines to follow when developing an application user interface using automatic layout.

Do Not Use Absolute Positioning

The use of absolute positioning when placing elements in a panel control, such as Canvas, is too rigid in its approach. Each element will affect other elements adjacent to it on the UI display. To remedy this, use a `DockPanel`, `StackPanel`, or `Grid` as a container for positioning controls. These containers will perform the task of recalculating the position of each child element relative to the size of the window or parent container.

Do Not Set a Fixed Size for a Window

The `Window` class has two attributes that affect the size of a window and its content: `ResizeMode` and `SizeToContent`.

The `ResizeMode` property specifies the resize behavior of the window. The following values are acceptable for setting the `ResizeMode` property:

❑   `NoResize` — The user cannot resize the window. Minimize and maximize controls are not shown.

❑   `CanMinimize` — The user can only minimize the window and restore it from the task bar. Minimize and maximize controls are visible, but only the minimize control is enabled.

❑   `CanResize`—The user has the full ability to resize the window. Minimize and maximize controls are both visible and enabled.

❑   `CanResizeWithGrip`—This option exhibits the same functionality as `CanResize`, but adds a "resize grip" to the lower-right corner of the window.

The `SizeToContent` property determines how a window should be sized relative to its content. The following values are acceptable for setting the `SizeToContent` property:

❑   `Height`—Specifies that the window automatically sizes to the content's height, but not its width.

❑   `Manual`—Specifies that the window does not automatically size to fit the content.

❑   `Width`—Specifies that the window automatically sizes to the content's width, but not its height.

❑   `WidthAndHeight`—Specifies that the window automatically sizes to the content's height and width.

The following XAML code example sets the sizing properties of a window:

```
<Window
  xmlns="http://schemas.microsoft.com/winfx/2006/xaml/presentation"
  xmlns:x="http://schemas.microsoft.com/winfx/2006/xaml"
  SizeToContent="WidthAndHeight"
  ResizeMode="CanResize"
  >
....
</Window>
```

The preceding XAML code snippet sets the `Window` class's `SizeToContent` attribute to `WidthAndHeight`, indicating that the window should size itself to the space required by its content. The `Window` class's `ResizeMode` attribute is set to `CanResize`, indicating that the user will be unrestricted in sizing, minimizing, and maximizing the window.

Add a FlowDirection to the Root Element of Your Application

In WPF, each class that derives from `FrameworkElement` has a convenient way of supporting vertical, horizontal, and bidirectional layouts. The `FlowDirection` property of the `FrameworkElement` class is used to specify the layout direction.

❑   `LeftToRightThenTopToBottom (LrTb)`—Horizontal layout for Latin, East Asian, and so forth.

❑   `RightToLeftThenTopToBottom (RlTb)`—Bidirectional for Arabic, Hebrew, and so forth.

❑   `TopToBottomThenRightToLeft (TbRl)`— Vertical layout for Japanese, Chinese, and so forth.

❑   `TopToBottomThenLeftToRight (TbLr)`— Mongolian text flow.

Currently, only `LeftToRightThenTopToBottom` and `RightToLeftThenTopToBottom` are supported.

The following XAML code example sets the `FlowDirection` property of a window:

```
<Page
  xmlns="http://schemas.microsoft.com/winfx/2006/xaml/presentation"
  xmlns:x="http://schemas.microsoft.com/winfx/2006/xaml"
  FlowDirection="LeftToRightThenTopToBottom"
  >
....
</ Page>
```

The preceding XAML code snippet sets the `FlowDirection` attribute of the Window to `LeftToRightThenTopToBottom`, indicating that a horizontal layout should be applied.

Using Grids for Flexibility

The `Grid` control offers the most flexibility of the panel controls in regards to defining layout. The Grid is capable of dynamically sizing and arranging its child elements within the space available. Child elements of the `Grid` control are arranged as columns and rows. Individual elements can span multiple rows and columns. Grids can also contain other grids as child elements.

The real value of the `Grid` control is that it takes an active role in managing complex layouts of controls and elements. This makes the `Grid` control extremely valuable for localizing applications in which controls will require flexibility to adjust and fit to localized content.

Grids take advantage of the "Star" sizing unit type to distribute the remaining space between elements. With Star sizing, a column or row receives a weighted proportion of the available space remaining. If * is the Star sizing value, the row or column receives one times the available space. If 2* is the selected value, then the row or column receives two times the available space, and so on and so forth. This is not the same as Auto, which distributes the remaining space evenly based on the size of the content within a particular column or row.

Even though `Grid` panels are useful for dynamically repositioning and adjusting controls to fit content, there may be times when you want all the child elements within a row or column to share the same uniform size regardless of the content. For example, you may have buttons or labels that you want to align in a standard fashion. The Grid's `IsSharedSizeScope` property can be used to indicate where you would like the same sizing to be shared among multiple grid elements.

The following XAML demonstrates how to specify the `IsSharedSizeScope` property for a grid element:

```
<Window x:Class="Grids.Window1"
  xmlns="http://schemas.microsoft.com/winfx/2006/xaml/presentation"
  xmlns:x="http://schemas.microsoft.com/winfx/2006/xaml"
  Title="Grids" Height="300" Width="300"
  >
  <Grid
    MinHeight="50"
    MinWidth="50"
    VerticalAlignment="Stretch"
    HorizontalAlignment="Stretch"
    Margin="20"
    Name="grid1"
```

```
        Grid.IsSharedSizeScope="True"
        >

        <Grid.ColumnDefinitions>
          <ColumnDefinition Width="0*" />
          <ColumnDefinition Width="0.7*" />
          <ColumnDefinition Width="0.3*" />
        </Grid.ColumnDefinitions>

        <Grid.RowDefinitions>
          <RowDefinition Height="0.3*" />
          <RowDefinition Height="0.2*" />
          <RowDefinition Height="0.4*" />
        </Grid.RowDefinitions>

      </Grid>

    </Window>
```

Localization Attributes and Comments

Developers use localization attributes and free-form comments to indicate resources that are to be localized. Attributes and comments provide hints and information about localization:

❑ Attributes are used by the WPF Localization API to indicate which resources are to be localized.

❑ Free-form comments consist of any additional information that developers would like to include.

The `Localization.Attributes` property consists of a space-delimited list of values specifying what the localizer is able to do and not able to do. Each item in the list specifies the target property name and value. Specifying the actual content within the resource is done by using the `$Content()` token.

The following table provides a list of attributes that can be used for localization.

Attribute	Meaning
Modifiable	Specifies if the value can be modified.
Readable	Specifies that the content is visible to the localizer.
Category	Predefined category to aid the localizer in translating text. Text, Label, and Title are examples.
None	Indicates no predefined category.
Inherit	Target value inherits the category of its parent.
Ignore	The target value is ignored but any child elements aren't ignored.
NeverLocalize	The property is not to be localized.

The following code example shows how to add localization comments to a XAML file:

```
<Window x:Class="Grids.Window1"
  xmlns="http://schemas.microsoft.com/winfx/2006/xaml/presentation"
  xmlns:x="http://schemas.microsoft.com/winfx/2006/xaml"
  Title="Grids" Height="300" Width="300"
  >
  <Grid>
    <Button
      Localization.Attributes="$Content(Modifiable) $FontSize(Unmodifiable)"
      Localization.Comments="$Content(Submit Button)"
      VerticalAlignment="Stretch"
      HorizontalAlignment="Stretch"
      Margin="100"
      Width="NaN"
      Height="Auto"
      Name="submit"
      >
      Submit
    </Button>
  </Grid>

</Window>
```

The `Localization.Attributes` property in this example specifies that the content of the button is modifiable but that the font size of the button is unmodifiable. The `Localization.Comments` attribute lets the localizer know that this is the submit button.

> **If duplicate attributes appear within the** `Localization.Attributes` **declaration, the latter attribute will override the former. For example,** `Localization.Attributes="FontSize(Modifiable Unmodifiable)"` **will tell the localizer that the category is "Unmodifiable."**

WPF Deployment Models

WPF applications can be deployed in a number of ways, including XCopy, Windows Installer (MSI), and ClickOnce. The deployment options available depend on the application type being deployed. For instance, standalone windows applications may be deployed using MSI or ClickOnce, but not XCopy (unless the application is completely self-contained).

XCopy deployment is a command-line program that simply copies files from one location to another. XCopy is fairly limited in its functionality and probably most suitable only for browser-based applications, in particular loose XAML files, but this is not a hard and fast rule. XCopy will not integrate your application into the Windows shell, meaning startup icons will not be placed on the desktop or in the start menu, and the program will not be added to the Add and Remove Programs dialog box within the Control Panel. Furthermore, XCopy does not support versioning, uninstall, or rollback procedures.

Windows Installer (MSI) deployment is a common means for installing applications. Typically, when you download an application from the Internet, you get a self-contained executable file that, when run, will install the application files and resources for you automatically. MSI deployment will update the windows shell, if required, and is a great method for distribution. However, MSI does not support updating applications.

ClickOnce enables compiled applications to be installed and run inside of a browser. From an application management standpoint, ClickOnce is excellent in that you need only publish your application to a server. Clients will "browse" the applications from the browser. Because the application is installed on a web server, each time a client accesses the application, the server is checked for updates. If updates exist, they will be automatically downloaded to the client's machine. This provides easy management when publishing updates to your application.

In terms of application model, the differentiating factors between browser and Windows-based applications lie primarily in where they are hosted, security, and how they will be deployed. The following factors affect the deployment of the application include:

❑   How the application is hosted (in the browser or standalone window)

❑   The security context of the application (full-trust or partial-trust)

The following table provides a brief overview of how each of these factors differs by application model.

Issue	Browser-Based	Windows-Based
Hosting Environment	Hosted within the browser.	Hosted locally.
Security	Default Internet zone permissions. (Partial-trust)	Full access to the system resources (Full-trust). User permission is required before deployment.
Deployment	Deployed using XCopy or ClickOnce.	Deployed with ClickOnce or MSI package.

The following sections discuss the deployment models in relation to the type of application being installed.

Building Applications

Before you can deploy your application, you will need to build it. Visual Studio 2005 provides a very simple and automated solution to building projects. For each project type, you can simply define the build configuration settings for a project by right-clicking on the project in the Solution Explorer and accessing the Properties menu item.

Figure 8-8 displays the Publish pane of the property pages panel in Visual Studio 2005.

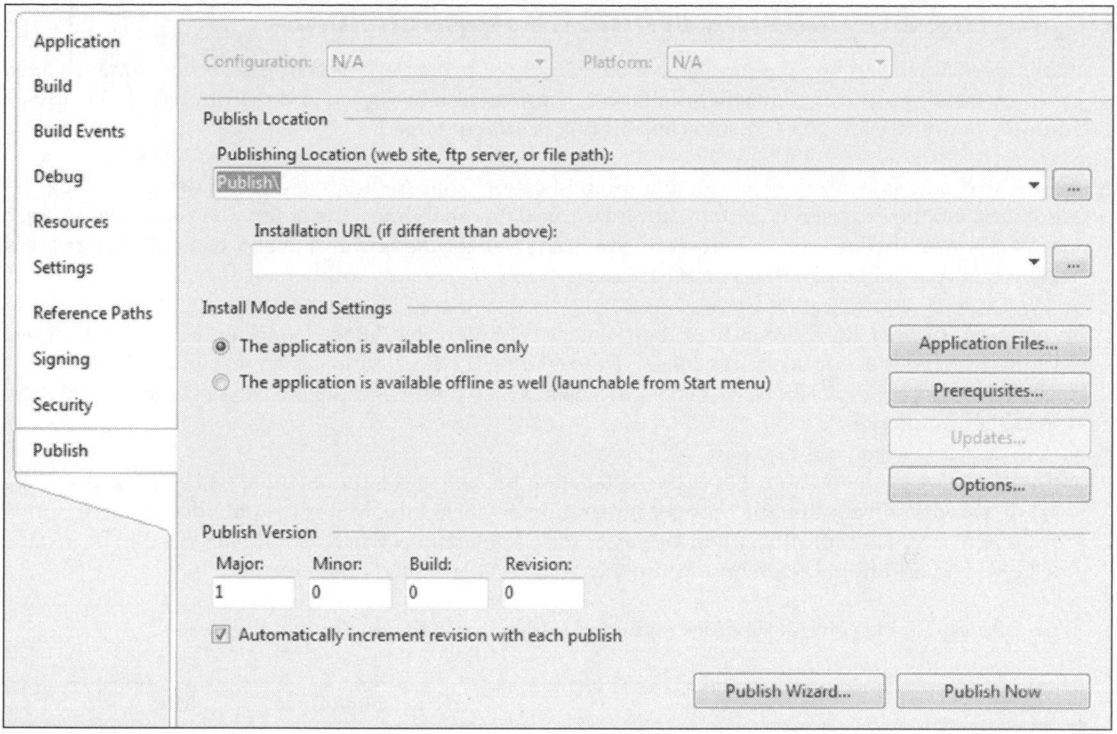

Figure 8-8

You can also build projects via the command line using Microsoft's MSBuild utility. MSBuild is the new build platform that ships with the Visual Studio 2005 and the Windows SDK. MSBuild uses an XML-based project file to define the build requirements of your application. In fact, Visual Studio uses MSBuild in the background to build a project for you. Once the MSBuild process completes, you will find the following files have been generated:

❑   An .exe file that contains the application's executable code.

❑   Referenced DLLs from dependent projects.

❑   An .exe.manifest file that contains metadata about the application including its trust information and dependencies.

❑   A .config file for the application configuration.

❑   A deployment manifest file. For WBAs the deployment manifest is suffixed with an .xbap extension. For installed applications, the suffix is .application.

Not all of these files are necessarily created; rather, the files created are based on the application model you are using.

> A complete overview of MSBuild is beyond the scope of this book. You can read more about it on the MSDN at http://msdn2.microsoft.com/en-us/library/wea2sca5.aspx. You can also learn more about how to build WPF applications using the MSBuild utility in the Windows SDK.

Deploying Standalone Windows Applications

Standalone windows applications have the flexibility of being deployed from a server using ClickOnce or from the desktop using an MSI installation. They can also be copied and distributed via XCopy from a storage medium, such as a CD, if the application is self-contained.

ClickOnce is by far the simplest solution for applications that are lightweight and designed to be deployed via the browser. It contains automatic update capabilities, the ability to rollback versions, clean uninstalls, and shell presence. In essence, you trade fine-grained control over the installation process for a much more reliable installation mechanism.

When you choose ClickOnce as your deployment type for a standalone Windows-based application, MSBuild includes a .application manifest. By executing the deployment manifest (either by URL or locally), a trust prompt will be displayed to a user. When a user accepts the trust prompt, ClickOnce performs the installation.

MSI offers fine-grained control over the installation process and requires more work on the developer's part. It also doesn't contain the browser integration of ClickOnce. MSI is the only deployment option for components. MSI is typically suited for larger scale applications where assemblies need to be installed in the GAC and additional referenced components must be installed on the system.

The following table provides a quick review of tradeoffs of each deployment type.

Feature	ClickOnce	MSI
Per machine	No	Yes
Per user	Yes	Yes
Specifies prerequisites: GAC dependencies	Yes	Yes
Specifies prerequisites: OS dependencies	Yes	Yes
Specifies prerequisites: other dependencies	No	Yes
Installs in GAC	No	Yes
Installs other components	No	Yes
Browser integration	Yes	No
URL activated	Yes	No
Appears in Start menu	Yes	Yes
Appears in Favorites	Yes	No
Customizes setup UI	No	Yes
On-demand installation	Yes	Yes
Supported by compiler	Yes	No
Supports localization	Yes	Yes
Displays trust dialog box	Yes	No

Feature	ClickOnce	MSI
Rolls back to earlier version	Yes	No
Always runs latest version	Yes	No
Guarantees clean uninstall	Yes	No
Added to Add or Remove Programs in the Control Panel	Yes	Yes
Scavenging	Yes	No
Automatic updates	Yes	No
Creates file associations	No	Yes
State management	Yes	Yes
Accepts URL arguments	Yes	No
Accepts command-line arguments	No	Yes
Supports browser-hosting	Yes	No

Deploying XAML Browser Applications

Three important files are generated when you build your XBAP. These files encompass the XBAP and are required for deployment to a web server. The name of each file depends on the project, but they have the following extensions:

❑ **.xbap** — This is the deployment manifest and is used by ClickOnce to deploy the application.

❑ **.exe.manifest** — This is the application manifest and contains metadata about the application.

❑ **.exe** — The application's executable code.

The deployment pattern for XBAPs is similar to that of ASP.NET applications. The XBAP is deployed to a server with Internet Information Services (IIS) version 5 or later. You simply copy the compiled output files (.xbap, .exe, and .exe.manifest) to the desired directory on the web server. You can also use the Publish pane of the property pages panel in Visual Studio 2005 by simply specifying the directory in which you would like your application installed.

The server does not require that the .NET Framework 3.0 runtime or SDK be installed in order to serve your application. However, you must configure the necessary MIME types and file extensions required for WPF applications. The following table lists the required MIME types that you will need to ensure are present.

Extension	MIME Type
.manifest	application/manifest
.xaml	application/xaml+xml
.application	application/x-ms-application
.xbap	application/x-ms-xbap
.deploy	application/octet-stream
.xps	application/vnd.ms-xpsdocument

To run your XBAP, create a link from a web page that navigates to the application's .xbap file. Once executed, ClickOnce will automatically handle the process of downloading and launching the application.

Although not mentioned specifically, loose XAML can simply be deployed by copying the file to the web server manually or by using XCopy.

Deploying the .NET Framework 3.0 Runtime

For standalone Windows-based applications, the .NET Framework 3.0 runtime can be included with the project, or a network administrator can implement a Group Policy to install the runtime on user machines.

For XBAPs, you need to detect the users' installed version of the runtime and notify them accordingly. The following is a JavaScript code snippet that detects what version of the runtime the user has installed on his or her machine. If the version is incorrect, the JavaScript alerts the user that he or she does not have the required version of the framework installed.

```
<script language="JavaScript">
<!--
  var RuntimeVersion = "3.0.50727";

  function window::onload()
  {
    var resultText="";
    if (HasRuntimeVersion(RuntimeVersion))
    {
      resultText += "This machine has the correct version of";
      resultText += ".NET Framework 3.0 Runtime: ";
      resultText += RuntimeVersion;
      resultText += ".\n\nThis machine's userAgent string is: ";
      resultText += navigator.userAgent;
      resultText += ".";
    }
    else
    {
      resultText += "This machine does not have correct version ";
      resultText += "of .NET Framework 3.0 Runtime.";
    }
    result.innerText = resultText;
```

```
    }

    //
    // Retrieve the version from the user agent string and compare
    // with specified version.
    //
    function HasRuntimeVersion(version)
    {
      var userAgentString = navigator.userAgent.match(/RunTime [0-9.]+/g);

      if (userAgentString != null)
      {
        var i;

        for (i = 0; i < userAgentString.length; ++i)
        {
          if (Compare(GetVersion(version), GetVersion(userAgentString[i])) <= 0)
            return true;
        }
      }

      return false;
    }

    //
    // Extract the numeric part of the version string.
    //
    function GetVersion(versionString)
    {
      var numericString = versionString.match(/([0-9]+)\.([0-9]+)\.([0-9]+)/i);
      return numericString.slice(1);
    }

    //
    // Compare the 2 version strings by converting them to numeric format.
    //
    function Compare(version1, version2)
    {
      for (i = 0; i < version1.length; ++i)
      {
        var number1 = new Number(version1[i]);
        var number2 = new Number(version2[i]);

        if (number1 < number2)
          return -1;

        if (number1 > number2)
          return 1;
      }

      return 0;
    }

  -->
</script>
```

Using the preceding code snippet, you can determine if the .NET Framework 3.0 is installed on the client's computer. If it is not, you may prompt the user to download the required redistributable and exit cleanly.

> **To determine which version of the .NET Framework 3.0 is installed on a machine, simply open the Registry Editor and browse to the** `HKEY_LOCAL_MACHINE\` `SOFTWARE\Microsoft\NET Framework Setup\NDP\v3.0\Setup\Windows` `Presentation Foundation` **key and check the** `Version` **value.**

Summary

In this chapter, you have learned both where and how WPF fits within the enterprise. You learned about the different application models you can choose when developing and deploying your solutions. You have been introduced to ways you can manage state in your WPF applications. You have learned about how applications can take advantage of the new structured navigation model in order to create a well-structured and flexible UI. You have seen how you can approach localization in WPF. Finally you've seen how you can build and deploy your applications using these tools.

Specifically, in this chapter you looked at the following:

❑ The differences between the browser-based and standalone Windows-based application types

❑ How to create a WPF data-driven XAML Browser Application (XBAP)

❑ State management and a structured approach to handling, persisting, and retrieving it

❑ Navigation topologies and how to use structured navigation to implement them

❑ Developing application UIs that are flexible and can be localized

❑ The UI Automation framework and how to use it to access UIs programmatically

9

Security

This chapter covers the essential security concerns involved with implementing solutions with the Visual Studio .NET IDE and WPF platform. Most of the security built into the WPF surrounds the concepts of critical versus non-critical code, as it stands in the .NET 2.0 Framework today. We cover how security plays out within web applications as opposed to desktop installed applications. We also take a look at the settings controlled within Internet Explorer 7, as several new security settings have been added to control WPF-specific features. These are of interest particularly for web deployments, and they add tremendous value for developers in their deployments and planning.

This chapter covers the following:

- ❑ Core OS security
- ❑ Common Language Runtime security
- ❑ Code Access Security
- ❑ Microsoft Internet Explorer security
- ❑ The security sandbox

WPF Security Model

The Windows Vista platform provides an additional layer of control on top of the core Vista operating system and .NET 3.0 Common Language Runtime. Figure 9-1 displays the layered view of the security model implemented in the WPF.

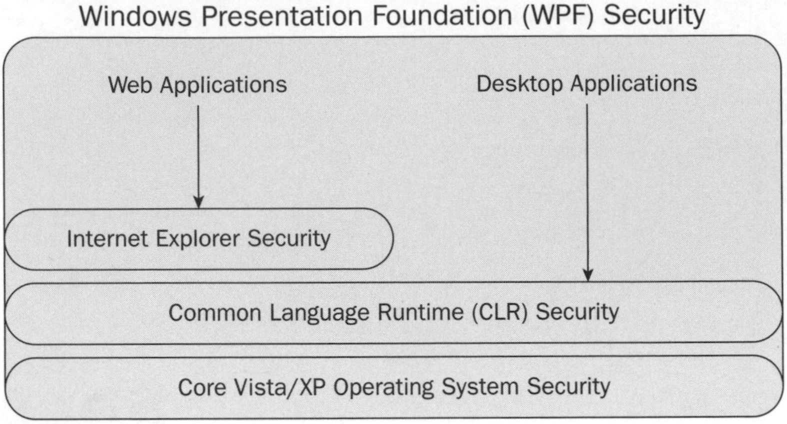

Windows Presentation Foundation (WPF) Security

Figure 9-1

One of the first layers is the CLR security model, which has existed since the .NET Framework was introduced, with some changes since then. At the time of this writing, it consisted of the Code Access Security model and several different .NET security control mechanisms.

The final and ground-level layer of security with WPF applications is the core OS layer, which is embedded into any Vista or XP (SP2)–based operating system. This OS layer consists of the base security for elements of an application, and what implications may exist.

Trusted Versus Express Applications

The two types of applications that are deployable within the WPF are:

❑ **Trusted applications** — Trusted applications are locally installed applications with full rights to the necessary operating system resources and application tools of the user's system. These launch within a window and establish their trust policy for their secure environment at the time of installation. The user who installs the application is prompted to accept the prompt for trust, giving consent to the installation.

❑ **Express applications** — Express applications are XAML Browser Applications (XBAPs), and run within the Internet Explorer limited sandbox (partial trust) environment. These do not require any sort of trust prompt for security confirmation.

Core OS Security

The core operating system security model covers WPF applications for both Windows XP SP2 and Windows Vista, and mandates certain ground-level framework security elements for application runtimes to utilize, whether they are aware or not. These new Windows Vista components include the following:

- ❑ Least-Privilege User Access (LUA)
- ❑ Virtualization
- ❑ Sandboxing
- ❑ Cryptography Next Generation
- ❑ Managed Cryptography API
- ❑ Certificate Enrollment API
- ❑ Managed Certificate API
- ❑ Rights Management Services

LUA

The Vista security model includes a Least-Privilege User Access (LUA) standard in its design sessions and development pieces. This provides a more leveraged use of the Windows *Standard Accounts*, designed to keep the use of the *Administrator* account to an all-time low. A vast majority of custom applications have been written with unnecessary use of the Windows Administrator user account.

Virtualization

Virtualization is the means by which Windows provides a safeguard against problems with sharing and reserving user-specific folder paths and file access issues. In a pre-WPF environment, an application would write files to user-specific locations and access files and folders of the operating system that were under strict security rules, reserved for Administrators only. As the applications were deployed out to the business users, the Administrator level user account was nowhere in sight, and the normal user accounts were not able to access the same areas of the operating system, causing countless errors in initial rollouts. This has been an all-too-common problem for the past decade of software development, and is addressed proactively within the Windows Vista security model. Only applications that specify their needs for administrator access within the application manifest file(s) or within a policy file will be permitted to assume the most-holy role of Administrator. This change also means that you don't have to worry about the exact file path of the location where you need to write files to a user's restricted file system paths (such as C:\Windows\ or C:\Program Files\), as the operating system interprets this location to be the specific file-folder location of the local Windows User Account running in context to the application. Virtualization thus provides the interpretation of what file or path the application needs, rather than just giving it what it asks for.

Sandboxing

Because WPF applications are deployable to both the user's desktop and to the web, they introduce a potential threat to the operating system. That is, there are some functionalities that can be safely executed within the security privileges of a typical desktop application without raising any eyebrows. However, if you try to run some of those same functionalities from a website application, there are some potential limitations to what you can do. Specifically, a web page accessed from a local machine should never be allowed to initiate a virus or damage critical Windows files. Architectures for Internet Explorer–contained applications are somewhat locked-down in previous versions of Windows development environments, and for very good reasons. The WPF required a means by which to wrap the runtime of a web-based application, eliminating security prompts, but protecting access to critical resources. After little debate, trust- and security-related prompts are by default removed from XBAPs in order to streamline the web development experience and prevent you from creating code that violates the security standards in place.

If you have developed within the VB6 web community (oh so long ago), you recall the design compromise to a speedy website known as the ActiveX control. These projects allowed IE to deliver deeper and system-intensive user interfaces and features. .NET applications, however, have deprecated and almost completely replaced any reason to continue using ActiveX controls to be downloaded to the browser. The roadmap for .NET development on the web continues to press toward abandoning the ActiveX control, with its heavy download potential and irritating security acceptance prompt to a user. If an application should require more system-intensive or driver-level access, a trust prompt can be conceded to, but only as needed. Sandboxing is the wrapping effect that the WPF framework takes advantage of in its hosted environment runtime at the operating system level.

Cryptography Next Generation

The Cryptography API: Next Generation (CNG) is the latest version of the Cryptography API. CNG provides generic and extensible regardless of the cryptography technology. The following table describes the Cryptography API components.

Name	Description
Managed Cryptography API	`System.Security.Cryptography` namespaces provide cryptographic tasks within managed code.
Certificate Enrollment API	The Certificate Enrollment API (CertEnroll) is an updated certificate enrollment programmatic interface new in Windows Vista.
Managed Certificate API	The `System.Security.Cryptography.X509Certificates` namespace provides managed code to access certificates and certificate stores.
Rights Management Services	Now included as a standard component of Windows Vista, Microsoft Windows Rights Management Services (RMS) SDK enforces rules for usage of encrypted digital assets, with the different available formats or contents.

CLR Security

The CLR layer of security is based on several important enhancements to the .NET Framework version 2.0. These include the following:

❑ Code Access Security

❑ Updated security methodology

❑ Verification

Code Access Security

The security model of the WPF sandbox used in Internet Explorer instances of WPF applications (XBAPs) is built on the baseline architecture of Code Access Security (CAS). The model for locking down the user experience requires numerous permission sets and zones in order to determine an application's needed security privileges. In order to configure web-based applications to run executable code locally on a server that requires elevated security permissions, your XBAP would need to be configured within the Code Access Security environment of that server. Leveraging the existing mode in the .NET Framework runtime, this CLR fundamental security model is able to provide a managed execution environment for an application. As a refresher to the CAS model, the goal of CAS is to protect resources and operations *from code*. Code Access Security allows code to be trusted at varying degrees depending on the code's origination, its trust levels, and its execution contents.

You must understand several key phrases and concepts before diving into the security model that the WPF adheres to:

- ❑ Permission
- ❑ Permission Set
- ❑ Zone
- ❑ Evidence
- ❑ Policy
- ❑ Policy system
- ❑ Code group
- ❑ AppDomain
- ❑ Membership rules

These will be covered in the following section.

The Verification Process

All of these terms have existed within the .NET code access security model long before the WPF drew its first breath, and are worthy of definition in order to fully understand Code Access Security. As a very high-level approach, let's walk through the basic.net runtime code security model and use the aforementioned terms as we go. Whenever an assembly loads within the .NET Runtime, it loads in the context of an AppDomain. At this time, the policy system accepts information known as evidence in the form of an evidence collection. This evidence is provided to the policy system in order to compare it to the membership rules of the code groups that existed in the policy. If the evidence does not compare appropriately to the membership rules, the assembly is prevented from running within the context of the code group. This provides a flexible model for configuring security and access privileges. Figure 9-2 depicts this security check between the code group's membership rules and the evidence of the assembly it is verifying.

As you can see in Figure 9-2, the evidence is the basis for verification in Code Access Security. It is the essential information that will allow the .NET Runtime Policy Evaluation process to verify the authenticity and legitimacy of a calling application.

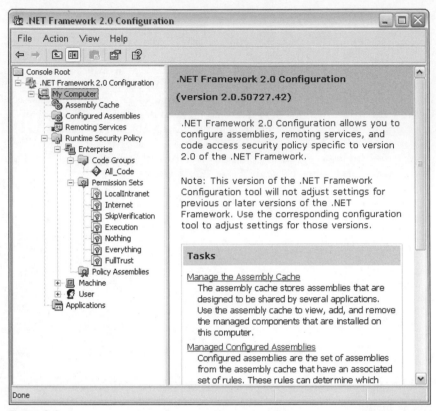

Figure 9-2

Permissions

Permissions are the basic element of the configurable security lockdown that is possible in CAS. Each granular area of usage can be assigned a specific permission. These permissions can be pointed to from a security perspective in order to configure access to them for user accounts. Some of the many permissions in use include:

- ❑ Printing
- ❑ File IO
- ❑ Reflection
- ❑ SQL Client Access
- ❑ Accessing the Registry
- ❑ File dialog boxes

Permissions are rolled up into permission sets for applying to code groups, as noted later in this section.

Zones

Zones are used in the Internet security settings as URL address groupings, which are used in order to identify where a URL address lives. An Internet domain address or local name address can be classified into a zone, which can be assigned security rights and constraints according to local or enterprise policies when applicable. All .NET managed code that requires Internet connectivity and address resolution accesses the intrinsic security infrastructure running within the Windows environment. This intrinsic Internet-centric security is a component of code access security as it pertains to trusted and untested zones.

A total of five built-in zones are provided within Code Access Security for trust level decisions:

❑   MyComputer

❑   LocalIntranet

❑   Internet

❑   TrustedSites

❑   UntrustedSites

Evidence

Numerous different types of evidence exist within the evidence collection. Each of these types is held within the `System.Security.Policy` namespace. The `Evidence` object exists as a collection, but is actually passed around within the runtime as two separate collections. These collections include the following:

❑   Host Evidence Collection

❑   Assembly Evidence Collection

The reason for this separation is basically to provide a clear separation between what the assembly *claims* as evidence in how and when the assembly loads into memory and what the operating system *has found* as evidence as to where and how the assembly came into contact with the machine. In this fashion, the host of the evidence collection acts as a sort of objective jury within a courtroom whose sole task is to capture and decipher the facts about the assembly in the context of what it is attempting to do. Following the same analogy, the assembly evidence collection could be compared to the defendant in a court case who is simply stating what he was trying to accomplish in an attempt to convince a jury of the innocence of his cause.

Evidence can be stored within either collection as objects of any data type. There are absolutely no restrictions on what sort of evidence can be used in this extensible policy system. Even so, there are usually three types of evidence that commonly follow an assembly in order to establish trust and pass the security checks of the .NET policy system in many cases. These three evidence types are:

❑   **Publisher signature** — The publisher signature indicates the author of the assembly and its authenticity as an embedded, compiled set of metadata. The publisher signature also contains a digital certificate that introduces a verification performed by a third party, which would further validate the authenticity of the assembly's publisher.

❑   **Strong name** — The strong name is contained within the `System.Security.Policy` `.StrongName` class, and is basically a set of evidence in the form of the name, version number, hash, and public key.

❑ **Hash** — The hash is contained within the `System.Security.Policy.Hash` class, and is essentially a unique identification number that is assigned to an assembly. This hash is a very useful tool, as it serves as a numeric value that correlates to an assembly as a direct correlation to the filename.

Policy Levels

There are four policy levels used within the 2.0 version of the .NET Framework. They are used to determine the applicable permission that can be assigned to a particular assembly. The four levels of policies are as follows:

❑ Enterprise

❑ Machine

❑ User

❑ AppDomain

Each policy contains one or more code groups, one or more policy assemblies, and one or more permission sets. The .NET Framework 2.0 Configuration tool is used to configure the policies at all levels and their contents.

The first policy on the list, Enterprise, reflects the interconnected machines with an AD (Active Directory) installation. The enterprise-level policy is at the top of the hierarchy, and supersedes the established policy settings at the sublevels of "machine" and "user."

The actual policy file for defining the policies on a server is located at `C:\WINDOWS\Microsoft.NET\Framework\v2.0.50727\config\enterprisesec.config`.

The machine policy configuration is specific to any user that exists on a specific machine. The user policy level applies only to a specific user on a specific machine. And finally, the AppDomain policy level must be explicitly called out programmatically, but refers to an application itself that can run in context to a system process on a machine or server.

Each policy level contains information on how it relates to code groups, defined in the next section.

Code Groups

Code groups provide security provisions for .NET assemblies based on fully configurable access controls. Microsoft defines code groups as *a set of permissions that requires a specific membership condition*. If the membership condition is not met, the assembly is not allowed to be granted access through this code group. Configuring a code group can be performed within the .NET Configuration tool, and provides numerous options for locking down code based on its origin, method of access, or type of application. The following membership conditions exist when creating the configuring code group for your WPF assembly:

❑ All Code

❑ Application Directory

❑ GAC

❑ Hash

❑ Publisher

❑ Site

❑ Strong Name

❑ URL

❑ Zone

❑ Custom

Each code group that has been configured contains a policy statement that explains what permissions set is configured to it. Permissions can be created within the code group creation wizard, which can be launched within the .NET configuration tool.

You can manage the trust level of an application by using any of the three tools provided in the .NET Framework as of version 1.1, including the following:

❑ Code Access Security Policy Tool (caspol.exe)

❑ .NET Configuration Tool (mscorcfg.msc)

❑ ClickOnce, which ships with the 2.0 version of the Framework and provides the ability to modify an applications trust level by way of approving the installation dialog box in a deployment request

The configuration tool for .NET assemblies in deployments has traditionally been the .NET Configuration Tool (mscorecfg.msc). To access this tool, simply navigate to a .NET command prompt and type **Mscorcfg.msc**. Alternatively, from any command prompt you can type the following elongated version: **%Systemroot%\Microsoft.NET\Framework\versionNumber\Mscorcfg.msc**. Figure 9-3 displays the tool.

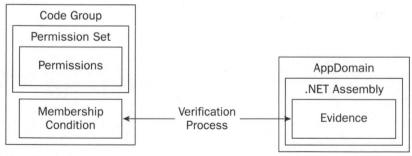

Figure 9-3

As displayed in Figure 9-3, the .NET Framework Configuration Tool (updated for .NET 2.0), allows you to configure assemblies, remoting services, and code access security policies specific to version 2.0 of the .NET Framework. It follows nearly the same security model as the 1.1 version of the .NET Framework but is used only for 2.0 version assemblies and applications. It supports the WPF security configurations. From the tree view, you can see that runtime security policies can be enforced at the enterprise, machine, and user levels. The security policies can be applied to WPF assemblies and groups of assemblies, as they normally would in the .NET 2.0 environment.

Creating a Code Group for Your WPF Application

A great way of determining the exact privileges that your WPF application will require you to create your own code group with the appropriate permission set and membership rules defined:

1. Create your application, compiling it in release mode.

2. Place the new DLL assembly in an accessible location on your machine.

3. Load the .NET Framework 2.0 Configuration Tool, expanding the tree view to the machine's Permission Sets section, as displayed in Figure 9-4.

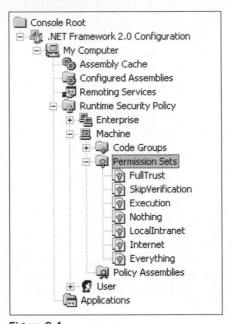

Figure 9-4

4. If you do not see the permission set you need within the list of standard permission sets, right-click the Permission Sets folder and select the New option from the contextual menu. Follow the prompts in order to fully create your custom permission set.

    If the permission set you want to use is in fact listed here, proceed to configure your Code Group by right-clicking the Code Groups folder and selecting the New option from the contextual menu (see Figure 9-5).

    From this new menu, several prompts appear, instructing you to enter specific information for your new code group to be created.

    Figure 9-6 displays the first window.

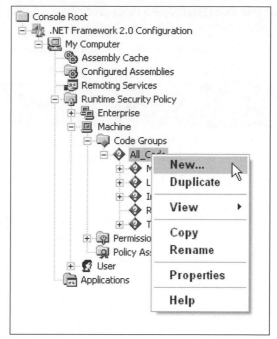

Figure 9-5

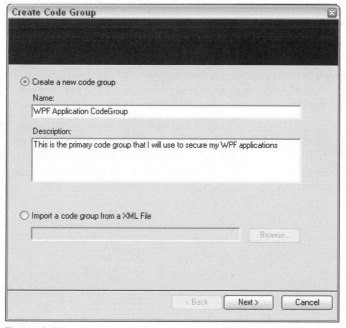

Figure 9-6

5.   Enter the name of the code group and a description that administrators will see when managing this within the .NET Framework 2.0 Configuration Tool.

Press Next to proceed to the next window, displayed in Figure 9-7.

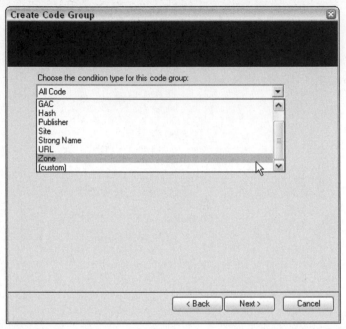

Figure 9-7

6.   Within each code group is the ability to store security conditions known as *membership rules*. There are numerous types of membership rules, as displayed in Figure 9-7. After selecting the appropriate membership rule and configuring its values, the next screen allows you to define the permission set this code group will utilize.

7.   Figure 9-8 shows the default local permission sets in use, which allow for varying levels of authority within the operating system for an assembly to operate within. Each Permission Set maintains a collection of permissions, which allow for a fine-grained level of access control over all areas of the system. Select a permission set to complete the process, or create your own permission set from the optional menu. Click Next to finish.

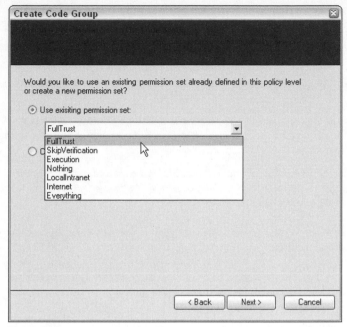

Figure 9-8

The Critical Code Methodology

The new security methodology in place for the Windows Presentation Foundation provides privilege-management in that it allows you to become aware of code that is requesting elevated privileges at the CLR level. If an assembly attempts to increase the security rights of one of its members, or of itself for that matter, the CLR will expect the assignment of a [SecurityCritical] attribute to the calling assembly method. System alerts and default processes can then be applied to such assembly logic as needed to provide a holistic approach to absorbing and validating such security requests. Once requests have been marked as security-critical using the attribute described, they can be funneled into the security-context-sensitive processing arm of the CLR for auditable decisions to be made on the security-related request and its implications. Our custom.net assemblies that sit on top of this area can provide further processing logic and special handling as desired.

As mentioned, there are two types of security-aware attributes that you can consider using while developing assemblies for the WPF in .NET 2.0 Framework:

❑   System.Security.SecurityTransparentAttribute

❑   System.Security.SecurityCriticalAttribute

The first one, System.Security.SecurityTransparentAttribute, carries with it the following very important considerations:

❑   The Assembly marked with this attribute will not contain any critical code, and won't attempt to elevate the privileges of the application's execution within a call stack.

❑   Code marked as such can't assert the necessary permissions in order to stop a "stack-walk" of execution from completing.

❑   Code marked as such can't satisfy what is known as a *link demand*. Full demands are used instead.

❑   Code marked as such can't use unverifiable code by default, whether or not it has the SkipVerification permission assigned to it. A *full demand* for specific unmanaged code would take place instead.

❑   Code marked as such can't make immediate or automatic calls to methods marked as P/Invoke, even if it has the SuppressUnmanagedCodeAttribute. A full demand for specific unmanagedCode would take place instead.

The next attribute, System.Security.SecurityCriticalAttribute, carries with it the following very important considerations:

❑   Code marked as SecurityCriticalAttribute is generally accessible from partially trusted application logic and provides limited access to local resources and/or system features.

❑   Development pieces marked as SecurityCriticalAttribute should be treated with greater caution and with more formal and thorough testing processes.

❑   By including the SecurityCriticalAttribute within your assembly (at the class declaration level), you're specifying that this assembly has the capacity to contain critical code.

The following is an example excerpt of these attributes:

```
[SecurityCritical]
public class A
{
    [SecurityCritical]
    public void TestThisDangerousStuff()
    {
        // Critical code would be placed here...
    }
    [SecurityTransparent]
    public void TestThisEasyStuff()
    {
        // Non-Critical code would be placed here...
    }
}
```

Notice in the previous logic the use of the attributes at both the class level and the method levels. The class-level decoration simply notes the possibility of the assembly containing any sort of security-critical logic. The actual members of the class must also explicitly state their attribute in order to make any real difference in the way it is handled within WPF.

Verification

For years, applications have been plagued by buffer overruns and memory leaks. Just-In-Time Compilation of the MSIL code includes a process of verification. This verification phase provides a safety net for such vulnerabilities, by way of the following security functions:

❑ Enforces type safety

❑ Prevents buffer overruns

❑ Isolates sub-processes

As the application runs in a managed state, the verification-related logic within the 2.0 of the .NET Framework is in overdrive. It protects the ability of the application to lose sight of memory management and closely watches its virtual memory allocations and requested subprocesses, among other indicators.

Microsoft Internet Explorer Security

Internet Explorer employs a strict security environment for provisioning and restricting applications for managed access to resources.

Zone Restrictions

The deployment manifest for the ClickOnce application will determine the full address of the application as it is launched in the .NET runtime. The launch addresses and their correlated zones listed in the table that follows provide insight into the way in which ClickOnce handles security.

Launch Address	Launch Zone
http://some.dotted.servername/Apps/CustomClickOnceApp.application	Internet
\\127.0.0.1\source\CustomClickOnceApp.application	Internet
http://yourservername/CustomClickOnceApp/CustomClickOnceApp.application	LocalIntranet
\\yourservername\CustomClickOnceApp\CustomClickOnceApp.application	LocalIntranet
C:\inetpub\wwwroot\CustomClickOnceApp\CustomClickOnceApp.application	MyComputer

Based on these potential addresses and zones being used, one would imagine you would need to apply it to your application by assigning the necessary zones and permissions.

The following table represents the default permission sets available within the Internet Zone.

Permission Set	Description
FileDialogPermission.Open	Allows you to open the File dialog box within the browser
IsolatedStorageFilePermission	Allows writing up to 512K to disk
UIPermission.SafeTopLevelWindows	Allows a single browser window
PrintingPermission.Safeprinting	Allows safe printing from the browser
WebPermission	Allows network access to the location of the website within the web server
WebBrowserPermission	Allows WPF frames to navigate to web content safely
MediaPermissionhim	Allows APF images, audio, and video to be hosted within the browser

The following table represents the permission sets that are not available within the Internet Zone.

Permission Set	Description
FileIOPermission	Reads and writes files to disk on the machine of the end user (from the browser)
RegistryPermission	Controls the ability to read/write to the registry on the machine of the end user (from the browser)
SecurityPermission.UnmanagedCode	Calls native Win32 functions (from the browser)

XBAP Sandbox Workarounds

The WPF sandbox environment is limiting in its allowable and disallowable features. As mentioned previously, it is built on top of the Code Access Security (CAS) model, which allows for configurable access to specific managed code within an application domain, as any .NET application would. When it comes to accessing resources or managed code within a web server that needs to do more than what the sandbox allows, there must be a workaround. There must be a means by which applications can call managed code from a web server in order to provide more robust, yet potentially vulnerable features to the application. In short, you need a way in which to call critical features from non-critical code. Applications may need to save files on the server that are more involved than a simple office document or image file. Applications may need to access network resources in order to provide more advanced business process flow or enterprise level application functionality. The solution provides an extension to the Internet Explorer sandbox environment by creating and deploying on a server your own assembly, which is marked with a special attribute. This attribute is named the `AllowPartiallyTrustedCallersAttribute` (APTCA), and marks the assembly as having a locally needed feature that is not accessible directly from your XBAP assembly. Your managed code is seen as trusted and deploys to the web server's Global Assembly Cache. Any highly secure operations that need to be performed should be located here, and callable from your local website deployments. As a chronological set of operations, the following would occur as an application is executed:

1. An assembly is requested as an XBAP request by the web server.

2. A WPF process creates a new restricted CLR application domain in order to provide a location for the application to exist under the WPF runtime.

3. The application is loaded into memory, limited to the Internet Zone permission set security profile.

4. The Internet Zone permissions limit access to the assembly throughout its lifespan.

5. Any requests — whether based on XAML declarative markup, code-behind assembly logic, or even system-level base class objects and methods — are validated against the application domain before they are handled within the website.

6. Permission-based resources runs through a stack-walk process, where the application domain is called into context and the methods listed in the stack are validated within the application domain before method processing continues.

XAML Browser Application Security

An XBAP differs from a traditional ASP.NET application in several areas. XBAPs carry with them a limited security level for accessing local system resources within the browser they are activated in. XAML markup moves from the server to its runtime on the client browser. From within the client browser, the application processes the XAML markup, accessing the resources available via the sandbox security available to it. Figure 9-9 displays the greeting screen upon creation of an XBAP.

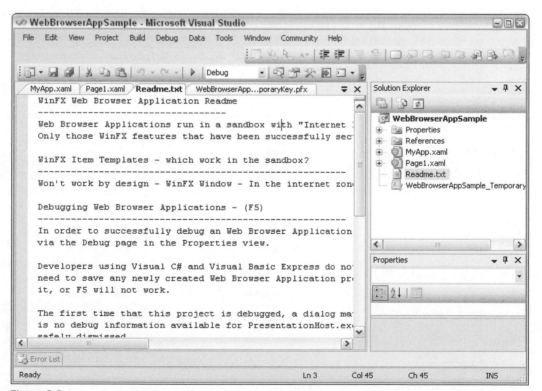

Figure 9-9

The readme.txt that is automatically generated with each new XBAP contains the following content:

```
.NET Framework 3.0 XAML Browser Application Readme
----------------------------------
XAML Browser Applications run in a sandbox with "Internet Permissions".
Only those .NET Framework 3.0 features that have been successfully security
reviewed and validated as safe by the .NET Framework 3.0 team will run inside the
sandbox.

.NET Framework 3.0 Item Templates - which work in the sandbox?
----------------------------------------------------------
Won't work by design - .NET Framework 3.0 Window - In the internet zone, you don't
have the permission to "popup" new windows.

Debugging XAML Browser Applications - (F5)
--------------------------------------------------
In order to successfully debug an XAML Browser Application in Visual Studio, you
must enable unmanaged code debugging
via the Debug page in the Properties view. Developers using Visual C# and Visual
Basic Express do not need to do this.

The first time that this project is debugged, a dialog may appear stating that
there
is no debug information available for PresentationHost.exe.  This dialog can be
safely dismissed.
```

The previous README file introduces a significant limitation to the user because it details their level of operation within the browser.

The coined phrase "partial trust" is used to describe the security for an application environment using Code Access Security (CAS). All XBAPs and any XAML files running as XBAPs are running in a partial trust mode.

The features shown in the following table are enabled while running in this partial trust mode.

Feature Category	Feature
General	Browser window
General	Site of origin access
General	Isolated Storage File IO
General	File Open dialog box
General	UIAutomation providers
General	Cicero IMEs
General	Commanding
General	Tablet stylus/ink
Web Integration	IE Download dialog box
Web Integration	Top Level User Initiated Navigation

Feature Category	Feature
Web Integration	HTML hosted in Frame or NavigationWindow
Web Integration	mailto: links
Web Integration	URI (cmd line) arguments
Web Integration	ASMX web services
Web Integration	XBAPs hosted in HTML IFrame
XPS Documents	XPS document viewer
Visuals	2D
Visuals	3D
Visuals	Animations
Media	Image
Media	Audio
Media	Video
Flow Documents	Pagination
Flow Documents	Text flow
Flow Documents	Optimal paragraph
Flow Documents	Hyphenation
Text	Embedded and system fonts
Text	Adobe CFF
Text	Glyphs
Editing	Text Box
Editing	Rich Text Box
Editing	Plaintext and Ink clipboard
Controls	Buttons
Controls	Sliders
Controls	Scroll viewers
Controls	Pop-up controls (bound to window limits)
Controls	Pop-up–based controls (for example, Menu)
Controls	Basic controls

The security settings for your XBAP are configurable within the project properties screen, in the Security tab, as displayed in Figure 9-9.

Figure 9-10 shows several permission settings necessary for ClickOnce Security for your assembly within the Internet Zone. The Zones that your application can be installed from are listed in a drop-down control, with the Zone's permissions listed below it.

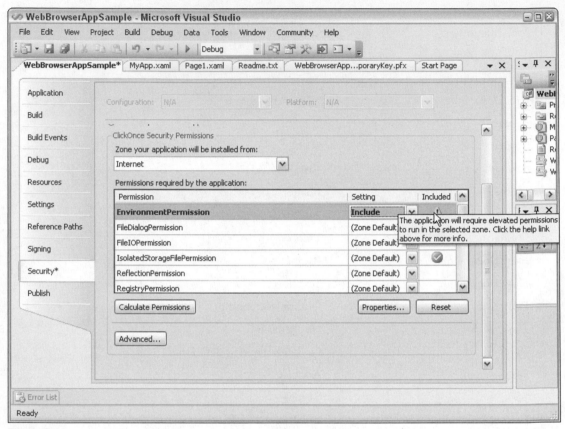

Figure 9-10

Figure 9-11 shows the preset permission settings for the "Intranet Zone." The Included column shows the actual status of the permission as it pertains to the currently selected zone from the list.

The Setting column has several possible values for each of the permissions listed:

❏   Zone Default

❏   Included

❏   Excluded

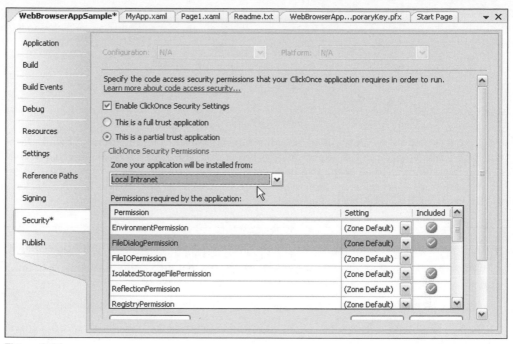

Figure 9-11

The default permissions provided by Internet Explorer are set as "Included," but more permissions can be added. By selecting the permission you would like to change and clicking on the Settings column drop-down, you can change the use of the permission for your application. Figure 9-11 shows the message that is displayed when a permission from the list that is normally set to "Zone Default" is set to "Included." The message displayed states that the application will require elevated permissions to run in the selected zone. This would infer that the user would be prompted with a security alert requesting explicit approval to run the application. Although it protects the user from unauthorized security breaches to unmonitored functions of windows accessible by the browser, this is still an undesirable prompt to the user. It prompts users to accept or deny the application logic, which may scare them away from the site. The protection of the Internet Explorer sandbox is explained earlier in this chapter. An alternative to these prompts is to provide a workaround using a locally installed assembly with all of the full-trust permissions in use, providing a local execution that the website can call upon.

The Calculate Permissions button provides a shortcut path to the Minimum Grant Set Determination Tool (Permcalc.exe). This utility ships with the .NET 2.0 Framework and is used to calculate the permissions that users must be granted in order to execute any part of the assembly. The result of a sample use of this tool is that the application is determined to require a full trust set of permissions, as displayed in Figure 9-12.

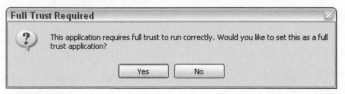

Figure 9-12

From the entry point of the application, the Minimum Grant Set Determination Tool walks through each of the code paths of the application and all of its referenced assemblies. It creates a generated call stack that contains references to all of the assemblies involved in the entire code path trace. Within each step of the code path trace, it searches for link demands, declarative demands, and declarative stack wall modifiers. These are defined in the table that follows.

Area	Description
Link Demands	Provide only the permissions that direct callers must have to link to your code
Declarative Demands	Place information into your code's metadata using attributes
Stack Wall Modifiers	Methods that allow you to override the outcome of security checks

Another button to consider within the project properties Security tab is the Advanced button. Clicking Advanced will load the additional properties window, as displayed in Figure 9-13.

Figure 9-13

This Advanced Security Settings dialog box provides a means by which the developer can simulate that he or she is downloading the application from a specific URL. This provides a great advantage to the developer in debug mode, where many troubleshooting complexities could exist.

> It is highly recommended that you develop and debug your application in the context of the zone that would be used in its final destination environment.

When you engage in debugging sessions with more restrictive permissions in use, your application will raise exceptions for code demands that haven't been allowed on the Security tab of the Project Properties screen in Visual Studio. This is accomplished by the Debug This Application with the Selected Permission Set checkbox in the Advanced tab, as shown in Figure 9-13. When you develop your application, IntelliSense provides a grayed-out reference to any members that are not accessible using the security permissions that you have configured.

As a sample execution of this security check, consider the following sample code, which attempts creating a text file on the server:

```
using System;
using System.Windows;
using System.Windows.Controls;
using System.Windows.Documents;
using System.IO;

namespace SecurityExceptionSample
{
    public partial class Page1 : Page
    {
        public Page1()
        {
            InitializeComponent();

            StreamWriter SW;
            SW = File.CreateText("c:\\shawnlivermore.blogspot.com.txt");
            SW.WriteLine("Elexzandreia is so smart!");
            SW.WriteLine("Shantell is a beauty queen");
            SW.Close();

        }

    }
}
```

The preceding logic would not be a concern in a full-trust application, such as a typical desktop application. However, XBAPs are constrained to their limited security sandbox as partial trust applications. If the previous logic were executed with the default .NET project security settings, an error would occur, as displayed in Figure 9-14.

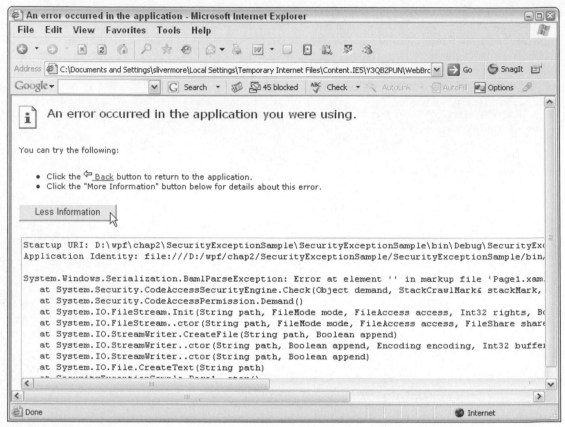

Figure 9-14

The error message is returned from running the stated code in the default security settings, which is a partial trust application mode. The actual error message is quite a bit longer, but includes the following statement:

```
System.Windows.Serialization.BamlParseException: Error at element '' in
markup file 'Page1.xaml' : Exception has been thrown by the target of an
invocation.. ---> System.Reflection.TargetInvocationException: Exception
has been thrown by the target of an invocation. --->
System.Security.SecurityException: Request for the permission of type
'System.Security.Permissions.FileIOPermission, mscorlib, Version=2.0.0.0,
Culture=neutral, PublicKeyToken=b77a5c561934e089' failed.
    at System.Security.CodeAccessSecurityEngine.Check(Object demand,
StackCrawlMark& stackMark, Boolean isPermSet)
```

The error is resolved and the file is written to the local file system if the project security settings are changed from a partial trust application to be a full-trust application or a custom zone.

ClickOnce Security

Several components of merit are introduced within the ClickOnce deployments of WPF applications that involve security. These are as follows:

❑   Trusted Publishers

❑   Personal Certificate File

❑   ClickOnce Security Invocations

Trusted Publishers

When an application is deployed using ClickOnce and loaded into memory in the .NET runtime, it will take a series of steps to ensure it is secure and authentic. That is, Trusted Publishers are created within a local machine in support of an installed application. They are created as a result of a three-step process in order to ensure the application has been provided safely from its originator(s). These three steps are essentially the following:

1.   Sign the deployment with a Certificate.

2.   Configure the local Certificate Store.

3.   Configure the local Trusted Root Certificate Authority.

Once this process is completed, the application is registered with a trusted publisher, and can continue issuing subsequent ClickOnce secure deployments. The process is somewhat involved, so the following steps will provide a bit more descriptive information on the details.

1.   Applications are deployed with a signed publisher certificate, among other deployment-specific files. A verification process is performed on these application manifest files in order to ensure they have not been tampered with.

2.   If they are clean, the application needs to reference the Trusted Root Certification Authority Store and validate that the same actual certificate used for the publisher is installed in that store. The application will perform a check of the publisher information for the certificate, verifying it exists within our Trusted Publishers store.

3.   If this signed publisher certificate is validated and the trusted Root certification Authority store is the same one used for the publisher, then the user will not be prompted for any sort of trust agreement when launching the application. The application is provided with the appropriate permissions and is allowed to continue processing.

4.   You can add what is known as an *application trust* to the user's .NET framework security policy file.

The application is now set up with a trusted publisher and accepts future ClickOnce deployments.

Personal Certificate File

After the initial creation of a Visual Studio 2005 .NET 3.0 application and its publishing to ClickOnce, a certificate is generated automatically for your application or order to be signed at the time it is published. At this moment, a personal certificate file (.pfx extension) is created and added to your project in Visual Studio.net. The file consists of the project name concatenated with _TemporaryKey.pfx. A certificate is also added to your personal certificate store on your local machine and enables the project to sign ClickOnce application manifests. This process is an automated function of the Visual Studio.net development environment and is considered a secure development baseline process for preemptively creating ClickOnce-enabled applications.

To secure your application within the ClickOnce secure deployment model, you must sign it with a certificate. Certificates can now be created from within Visual Studio 2005, and are used to sign the ClickOnce manifest for the applications installation process using the ClickOnce deployment model. The steps to secure your application for deployment for ClickOnce are as follows:

1. Within a Visual Studio 2005 XBAP, right-click the project file and select Properties from the menu. The project properties configuration screen is loaded. From within the project properties window, click the Signing tab, as shown in Figure 9-15.

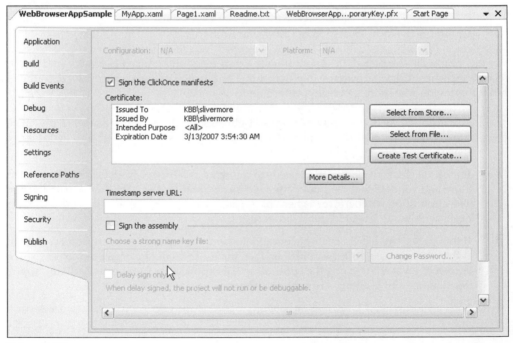

Figure 9-15

This user interface is new for developers within the Visual Studio 2005 environment, and provides a management tool for creating and signing certificates for assemblies to use in their deployments.

2. NET 2.0 applications (including the .NET 3.0 applications with the WPF) that will be securely deployed within ClickOnce can use test certificates. The use of these test certificates provides a means by which developers can expedite the development and deployment process prior to deploying to a production environment. In order to create a test certificate to develop with, click the Create Test Certificate button from the screen. The screen in Figure 9-16 appears, requesting a password for the certificate's signature.

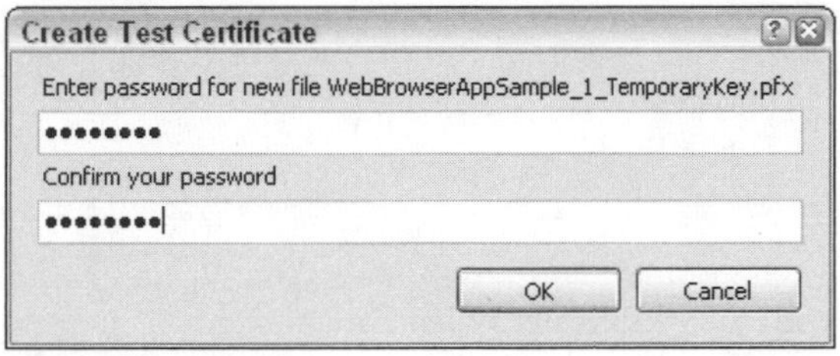

Figure 9-16

A new pfx file with a default name is created and added to your project. The file is provided by default with a XBAP, as was displayed in Figure 9-9. The name of the file by default is WebBrowserAppSample_TemporaryKey.pfx. This file can now be used in any development project on your local machine, and opened within the project properties of other Visual Studio 2005 projects.

> **Using a shared test certificate file for all of your local development saves you from creating numerous test certificates in your local development machine (specifically your _Local Certificate Test Store_), which makes things more difficult for you in the long run.**

3. Once a test certificate is created using the Create Test Certificate button on your local machine, you must designate it as the certificate to be used within your application. To configure the certificate as the _designated_ certificate, you must press the Select From File button in the Signing tab. After clicking, you are provided with an Open File dialog box, where you can select the certificate file from your local machine, as displayed in Figure 9-17.

Figure 9-17

Once you select the test certificate file you wish to use, a password prompt is displayed, allowing you to enter the certificate's password in order to consume this certificate and sign your assembly manifest file with it. Figure 9-18 displays this password prompt.

Figure 9-18

At this point you can publish your application from Visual Studio and the project's manifests will be signed with that certificate. When you are ready to publish a production version of your assemblies, you can purchase a certificate from third parties such as a VeriSign.

By clicking properties in the certificate selection, you can view the status of the certificate in your Trusted Root Certificate Authorities Store. If the certificate is not installed in your local machines trusted store, you can click the Install Certificate button. Figure 9-19 displays this information window.

Figure 9-19

When you configure the publisher certificate on the machine where the XBAP will be launched with ClickOnce, you avoid a user prompt referring to a trusted publisher deployment. This machine is very often a development machine.

.NET 3.0 Security Utilities

The security-related command-line utilities in the table that follows are available in the .NET Framework 3.0.

Utility Filename	Title	Description
Makecert.exe	Certificate Creation Tool	Generates X.509 certificates for development or testing only.
Certmgr.exe	Certificate Manager Tool	Manages certificates, certificate trust lists (CTLs), and certificate revocation lists (CRLs).
Caspol.exe	Code Access Security Policy Tool	Enables you to view and configure security policy. You can see the permissions that are granted to a specified assembly and the code groups that the assembly belongs to.
Storeadm.exe	Isolated Storage Tool	Manages isolated storage, providing options to list the user's stores and delete them.
Permview.exe	Permissions View Tool	Allows you to view an assembly's requested permissions.
Peverify.exe	PEVerify Tool	Determines whether the JIT compilation process can verify the type safety of the assembly.
Migpole.exe	Policy Migration Tool	Migrates security policy between two compatible versions of the .NET Framework.
Secutil.exe	Secutil Tool	Extracts strong name public key information or Authenticode publisher certificates from an assembly, in a format that can be incorporated into code.
SignTool.exe	Sign Tool	Digitally signs files, verifies signatures in files, and time stamps files.
Cert2spc.exe	Software Publisher Certificate Test Tool	Creates a Software Publisher's Certificate (SPC) from one or more X.509 certificates. This tool is for testing purposes only.
Sn.exe	Strong Name Tool	Helps create assemblies with strong names. Sn.exe provides options for key management, signature generation, and signature verification.

Most of these utilities are applicable in traditional .NET 2.0 and have not changed since the advent of this new presentation model.

Summary

In this chapter you learned about the various security-related components included in .NET 3.0 application deployments, including those with WPF components and features. You learned about the Windows presentation foundation layered security approach, extending from the browser down to the low-level operating system–related security components. You learned about verification and sandbox and how defense mechanisms exist as backup layers to an already robust checking mechanism. You learned about the following security-related development tasks:

❑ Determining which zones and permissions are needed for your application based on its various levels of security-related execution calls.

❑ Configuring your application to run with the correct permission sets in the user's local browser window.

❑ Creating a Code Group with the appropriate membership rules and permission set to run your application.

❑ Why and how would utilities that ship with the 2.0 version of the .NET Framework and .NET SDK allow you to view and modify the permissions for your application.

❑ Creating a certificate and installing the certificate to sign the assembly's manifest files to comply with ClickOnce deployment security protocols.

❑ Configuring a project to restrict or provide extended permissions to an application.

10

WPF and Win32 Interop

When it comes to adopting WPF for new application development, some developers may have the luxury of starting with a fresh code base to develop new controls and layouts for application UIs. But some organizations may have an existing code base of applications built on Win32 in the form of Windows Forms, ActiveX, MFC, or ATL applications. If significant investments are attached to these applications, this will probably mean that there will be some interop necessary to bridge the development gap between new and old. Either new development of WPF-based UIs and controls will need to be imported into existing applications or vice versa.

WPF provides an interop framework in the `System.Windows.Interop` and `System.Windows.Forms.Integration` namespaces with a set of base classes that make migrating HWND-based Win32 code to WPF windows and pages possible. The opposite is also possible, where WPF controls and UIs can be placed inside HWNDs to provide nested levels of WPF and/or Win32 elements.

This chapter covers the rules and guidelines to remember when migrating and interoperating WPF with existing HWND-based application UIs and provides an example of how this is achieved through code. The key topics to note are:

- ❑ How WPF and HWNDs differ in how they are rendered and managed by Windows
- ❑ How to cover the interop gaps of mixing managed with unmanaged code and WPF-based elements with HWND-based elements
- ❑ How to introduce HWNDs into WPF windows
- ❑ How to introduce WPF elements in HWND-based applications

Win32 User Interface Overview

The functionality provided by the Win32 API provides developers with a set of interfaces to interact with the Windows operating system to create applications. Within the Win32 API is a set of user interface functions to support development of the application UI such as creating windows and controls and managing user input.

When creating application UIs, code interacts with the Windows API through the `CreateWindow` function to request an HWND for each UI element (such as windows and controls). HWNDs are handles that serve as references to window objects that the OS manages but that you can use in your applications. HWNDs are used in a variety of Microsoft technologies, including MFC, ATL, DirectX, and ActiveX.

Managed Windows Forms from the .NET Framework are HWND-based as well. The Windows Forms API is designed to wrap the functionality of creating and accessing HWNDs in an abstracted way from the managed environment provided by the CLR.

How WPF and HWNDs Interoperate

HWND-based applications rely on the GDI subsystem to render most of their content. WPF differs in the way that it is rendered and managed in that it doesn't rely on GDI to render itself to the screen. WPF is an application development abstraction composed of managed and unmanaged components that sit on top of Microsoft DirectX. This is what provides WPF all the neat features of hardware acceleration and rendering. Figure 10-1 illustrates the WPF application stack.

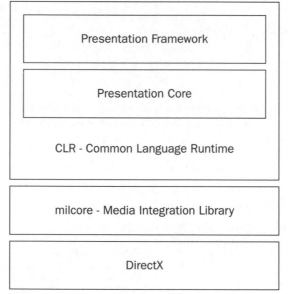

Figure 10-1

Although WPF applications ultimately rely on DirectX for display, they must cooperate with the Windows OS and exist within the context of an HWND. Under the covers, when you create a WPF window, an HWND is created that resides on the top-most level. In order to host your WPF content within the HWND, WPF creates an instance of the HwndSource class that is designed specifically to interoperate with Win32. The HwndSource class implements a Win32 window, and the parent WPF window of your application is assigned to the RootVisual property of the HwndSource. All the content within your application shares that one HWND.

An important thing to note is that when WPF interacts with HWNDs, WPF is constrained to Win32's rules for rendering and positioning. WPF rendering cannot be mixed with GDI rendering. WPF can do anything it wants in terms of rendering inside of its HWND — such as animating, transforming, and manipulating element transparency — but when WPF windows interact with other HWNDs, they are expected to act within HWND boundaries.

Interoperation between HWNDs and WPF can be described as falling into one of two categories (or both). Moving HWND-based controls and UIs into WPF windows or integrating unmanaged HWND applications with managed WPF.

Using Win32 HWNDs Inside of WPF

From the WPF architecture we know that elements on a page are rendered in a tree structure where elements are composed of parents and children. In order to introduce an HWND into your control tree, you need it to behave as a FrameworkElement object so that it fits in nicely with your WPF element tree.

The HwndHost class enables you to introduce HWNDs into WPF control hierarchies. The HwndHost class behaves more or less like any other FrameworkElement class, except that it is limited and bound to what HWNDs can actually do in terms of how they can be drawn and represented onscreen.

For example, HWNDs elements:

❏   Can't be rotated, scaled, skewed, or otherwise affected by a Transform.

❏   Can't have their opacity level manipulated. Any elements inside the HWND can have alpha transparencies but the HWND itself, as a whole, cannot have an opacity of less than 100 percent.

❏   Can't be clipped independent of the clipping region of their parent.

❏   Won't have all of the input behavior as other WPF elements. For example, when the HwndHost is moused-over, WPF won't receive any mouse events.

❏   Will appear on top of any other WPF elements in the same top-level window.

The HwndHost class is an abstract class that provides the necessary methods and events that are required for HWNDs and WPF to interoperate. The HwndHost class is meant to be derived from so that you can implement the specific details required for starting up your Win32 window.

Incorporating Win32 controls into your WPF application can be a tedious task but with enough tenacity and a heavy dose of P/Invoke it can be accomplished.

To host a Win32 window, implement a class that inherits from HwndHost. Depending on how complex your Win32 controls are, the steps in the process may require a heftier implementation.

The general process is summarized in the following general steps:

1. Create a host for the controls by implementing a subclass of the `HwndHost`.

2. Override the `BuildWindowCore` and `DestroyWindowCore` methods to build up and destroy the hosted window.

3. Handle messages sent to the hosted window. This can either be handled by WPF (by assigning a `MessageHook` for the host) or by the host (by overriding the `HwndHost WndProc` method).

4. Create a WPF element to host the window such as a Border.

If you have many Win32 controls to be hosted in WPF, it is generally easier to create a static host that contains the additional controls as children of that element and return the handle of that host from the `BuildWindowCore` method. This consolidates the messaging between one host rather than to multiple hosts.

Hosting a Win32 Button in WPF

In this example, you complete the basic steps of adding a Win32 Button control into a WPF window. The steps are as follows:

1. In Visual Studio, select File ⇨ New Project from the menu. From the Project Types tree view, select the Visual C# ⇨ Windows (WinFX) Node, and then click on the WinFX Windows Application icon from the list. Name your project **WPFwithWin32** and click OK. This new project should create a Window1.xaml file, and a supporting partial class code-behind file.

2. Add the following `using` directives:

```
using System.Windows.Interop;
using System.Runtime.InteropServices;
```

3. In the Window1.xaml.cs file, add the following code after the WPF window class definition:

```
public class Win32ButtonHost : HwndHost
{
    IntPtr hwndHost = IntPtr.Zero;
    IntPtr hwndButton = IntPtr.Zero;

    public int ButtonWidth = 0;
    public int ButtonHeight = 0;

    // Winuser.h constants for CreateWindowEx
    private const int WS_CHILD = 0x40000000;
    private const int WS_VISIBLE = 0x10000000;
    private const int WS_BORDER = 0x00800000;

    public Win32ButtonHost(int width, int height)
    {
        ButtonWidth = width;
        ButtonHeight = height;
    }
}
```

4. Provide your P/Invoke declarations and your `BuildWindowCore` method override in order to create the HWNDs using the user32.dll. Within the `Win32ButtonHost` class definition, add the following code.

```
[DllImport("user32.dll", EntryPoint = "CreateWindowEx", CharSet = CharSet.Auto)]
internal static extern IntPtr CreateWindowEx(
    int dwExStyle,
    string lpszClassName,
    string lpszWindowName,
    int style,
    int x, int y,
    int width, int height,
    IntPtr hwndParent,
    IntPtr hMenu,
    IntPtr hInst,
    [MarshalAs(UnmanagedType.AsAny)] object pvParam);

protected override HandleRef BuildWindowCore(HandleRef hwndParent)
{
    hwndHost = CreateWindowEx(0, "static", "",
        WS_CHILD | WS_VISIBLE,
        0, 0,
        ButtonWidth, ButtonHeight,
        hwndParent.Handle,
        IntPtr.Zero,
        IntPtr.Zero,
        0);

    hwndButton = CreateWindowEx(0, "button", "Win32 Button",
        WS_CHILD | WS_VISIBLE | WS_BORDER,
        0, 0,
        ButtonWidth, ButtonHeight,
        hwndHost,
        IntPtr.Zero,
        IntPtr.Zero,
        0);

    return new HandleRef(this, hwndHost);
}
```

5. Include your `DestroyWindowCore` method override as well as the P/Invoke declaration to call the user32 function to `DestroyWindow`. Add the following code to your `HwndHost` implementation:

```
[DllImport("user32.dll", EntryPoint = "DestroyWindow", CharSet = CharSet.Auto)]
internal static extern bool DestroyWindow(IntPtr hwnd);

protected override void DestroyWindowCore(HandleRef hwnd)
{
    DestroyWindow(hwnd.Handle);
}
```

6. Add the WPF element to host your Win32 button. Replace the code in the Window1.xaml file with the following:

```
<Window x:Class="WPFwithWin32.Window1"
     xmlns="http://schemas.microsoft.com/winfx/2006/xaml/presentation"
     xmlns:x="http://schemas.microsoft.com/winfx/2006/xaml"
     Title="WPFwithWin32" Height="300" Width="300"
     >
     <Grid>
          <Border Name="HostElement"
               Width="200"
               Height="200"
               HorizontalAlignment="Left"
               VerticalAlignment="Top"
               BorderBrush="White"
               BorderThickness="3"
               DockPanel.Dock="Left"/>
     </Grid>
</Window>
```

7. Now all that is left is to instantiate your custom host and add it to your WPF window. Replace the Window1 class definition in the Window1.xaml.cs file with the following:

```
public partial class Window1 : Window
{
     Win32ButtonHost win32Button;

     public Window1()
     {
          this.Loaded += new RoutedEventHandler(Window1_Loaded);
          InitializeComponent();
     }

     void Window1_Loaded(object sender, RoutedEventArgs e)
     {
          win32Button = new Win32ButtonHost(100, 50);
          HostElement.Child = win32Button;
     }
}
```

8. Build the project in Debug to view the hosted control in WPF. Figure 10-2 shows the compiled result.

Figure 10-2

Using WPF in Win32 Applications

The HwndSource class was designed to provide interoperability between WPF and existing HWND based applications; therefore, it is the key component to hosting a WPF element in a Win32 application. The HwndSource instance gets a Win32 window and allows you to assign your WPF content into it through the RootVisual property. The process of including WPF elements into Win32-based applications can be summarized in a series of steps. We'll assume that you have already created your WPF content and you're ready to integrate.

1. First is the conversion of any unmanaged applications to managed code. Win32-based applications, like those created with MFC, are written as unmanaged C++.

Because WPF is a framework of managed code, it can't be called directly from an unmanaged program because it lives outside of the context of the CLR. Existing applications will need to become at least partly managed in order to access managed WPF resources.

2. Conveniently, existing C++ applications can be converted over to managed programs easily by modifying the configuration properties of the project. This simply involves accessing the project's property pages and selecting the Configuration Properties ⇨ General node. Under the Project Defaults section, change the Common Language Runtime Support property to Common Language Runtime Support (/clr). The project now becomes a managed C++ project. Figure 10-3 shows the property panel option in Visual Studio for modifying the /clr compiler option.

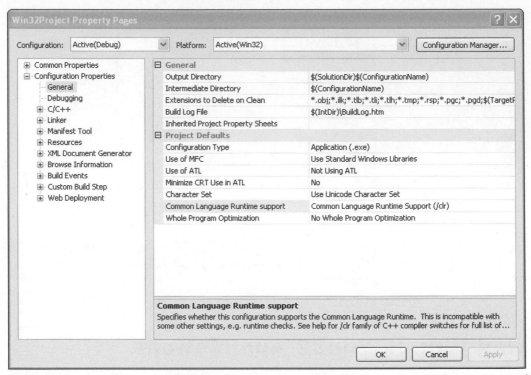

Figure 10-3

3. WPF uses a Single Threaded Apartment threading model so in order for the Win32 application to interact with WPF you need to set the application's threading model to STA. You can set the threading model to STA by including an attribute before the entry point of the application.

```
[System::STAThreadAttribute]
int APIENTRY _tWinMain(HINSTANCE hInstance,
    HINSTANCE hPrevInstance,
    LPTSTR    lpCmdLine,
    int       nCmdShow)
....
```

4. You will also need to handle the WM_CREATE notification in your windows message handling procedure to instantiate the HwndSource and assign your WPF element to it. The following code shows a rough and very basic implementation example of this. You will probably want to wrap the creation of the WPF element in some other function to handle any additional work when creating the HwndSource.

```
case WM_CREATE :
    System::Windows::UIElement^ wpfPage = gcnew CustomControlLibrary::Address();
    System::Windows::Interop::HwndSource^ source = gcnew
        System::Windows::Interop::HwndSource(
            0, // class style
            WS_VISIBLE | WS_CHILD, // window style
            0, // exstyle
```

```
                    x, y, width, height,
                    "Windows Presentation Framework Control", // NAME
                    System::IntPtr(parent) // parent window
          );

      source->RootVisual = wpfPage;
  break;
```

Adding Windows Forms Controls to WPF

There is a common pattern when trying to interop between WPF and Windows Forms. You must wrap the control or element in such a way that it can be introduced to the control tree of its framework. The WPF framework currently supports one out-of-the-box subclass of the HwndHost, which is the WindowsFormsHost.

Hosting Windows form controls is by far the easiest interop scenario. You don't have to worry about the conversion of unmanaged to managed code and you need only to instantiate a WindowsFormsHost object and assign the Windows Form control as its child in order to introduce it into our WPF element tree. You can still interact with the Windows Form control in code easily such as setting properties and assigning event handlers without any additional framework magic.

You can easily introduce a WindowsFormsHost into a WPF application either in code or through XAML.

Adding Your WIndowsFormsHost in Code

In this example, you complete the basic steps of adding a Windows Form control into a WPF window. The steps are as follows:

1. In Visual Studio, select File ➪ New Project from the menu. From the Project Types tree view, select the Visual C# ➪ Windows (WinFX) node, and then click the WinFX Windows Application icon from the list. Name your project **WPFwithWindowsForms** and click OK. This new project should create a Window1.xaml file, and a supporting partial class code-behind file.

2. Add a reference to the WindowsFormsIntegration.dll. The location for this assembly is %pro-gramfiles%\Reference Assemblies\Microsoft\WinFX\v3.0\. This will include the WindowsFormsHost class. Also add the System.Windows.Forms assembly.

3. Open the Window1.xaml file and select the Xaml view from the designer. Replace the code with the following segment:

```
<Window x:Class="WPFwithWindowsForms.Window1"
    xmlns="http://schemas.microsoft.com/winfx/2006/xaml/presentation"
    xmlns:x="http://schemas.microsoft.com/winfx/2006/xaml"
    Title="WPFwithWindowsForms" Height="337" Width="339"
    >
    <Grid Name="grid1">

    </Grid>
</Window>
```

4. Select the Source tab and replace the default code with the following:

```csharp
using System;
using System.Collections.Generic;
using System.Text;
using System.Windows;
using System.Windows.Controls;
using System.Windows.Data;
using System.Windows.Documents;
using WindowsForms = System.Windows.Forms;
using System.Windows.Forms.Integration;
using System.Windows.Input;
using System.Windows.Media;
using System.Windows.Media.Imaging;
using System.Windows.Shapes;

namespace WPFwithWindowsForms
{
    public partial class Window1 : Window
    {
        public Window1()
        {
            this.Loaded += new RoutedEventHandler(Window1_Loaded);
            InitializeComponent();
        }

        void Window1_Loaded(object sender, RoutedEventArgs e)
        {
            WindowsFormsHost host = new WindowsFormsHost();

            WindowsForms.Button button = new WindowsForms.Button();
            button.BackColor = System.Drawing.Color.LightGray;
            button.Text = "Windows Forms Button";
            button.Width = 150;
            button.Click += new EventHandler(button_Click);

            host.Child = button;
            host.VerticalAlignment = VerticalAlignment.Center;
            host.HorizontalAlignment = HorizontalAlignment.Center;

            grid1.Children.Add(host);
        }

        void button_Click(object sender, EventArgs e)
        {
            MessageBox.Show("Hello from Windows Forms!");
        }
    }
}
```

5. Compile and run the project in Debug mode to view the result. Figure 10-4 shows the compiled result.

Figure 10-4

Adding Your HwndHost in XAML

The previous example can also be implemented easily through XAML. The following is the XAML code required to achieve the same result.

```
<Window x:Class="WPFwithWindowsForms.Window1"
      xmlns="http://schemas.microsoft.com/winfx/2006/xaml/presentation"
      xmlns:x="http://schemas.microsoft.com/winfx/2006/xaml"
      xmlns:wf="clr-namespace:System.Windows.Forms;assembly=System.Windows.Forms"
      Title="WPFwithWindowsForms" Height="337" Width="339"
      >
<Grid>
        <WindowsFormsHost>
              <wf:Button
                    x:Name="wpfButton"
                    Text="Windows Forms Button"
                    Width="150"
                    Click="button_Click"/>
        </WindowsFormsHost>
    </Grid>
</Window>
```

Adding ActiveX Controls to WPF

To combine ActiveX components into WPF projects, you take a two-step approach. Because Visual Studio provides easy integration of COM components into Windows Forms or user control libraries, you can leverage that support by adding ActiveX components in WPF. Thus, the first step is to create a new C# user control library and add the desired COM object through the design time support of Visual Studio. The second step is to reference the control library in your WPF application and insert the object into the element tree by utilizing the `WindowsFormsHost`.

> Visual Studio .NET makes use of a command-line utility called Aximp.exe to generate an interop class that will allow you to use COM components in a managed way.
>
> You can learn more about the utility at http://msdn2.microsoft.com/en-us/8ccdh774.aspx.

Example of Adding ActiveX into a WPF Project

In this example you will add a ShockWave Flash COM component into a WPF windows application. This example assumes that you have the Macromedia Flash player installed on your machine. If you are uncertain if you have the component installed, you can download it at www.adobe.com/go/gntray_dl_getflashplayer.

1. In Visual Studio, create a new project. Select User Control Library from the Visual C# node and title the project **WindowsControlLibrary**. Rename the default file to **FlashControl.cs**.

2. In the Toolbox panel, select the COM Components section. Right-click on the section and select Choose Items from the context menu. Under the COM Components tab, select ShockwaveFlashObject and select OK (as shown in Figure 10-5). Once the component has been added, Visual Studio will automatically create references to the dynamically generated assemblies AxShockwaveObjects and ShockwaveObjects.

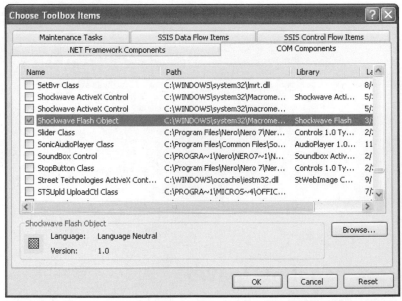

Figure 10-5

3. Drag and drop the Flash object onto the user control. Rename the control instance to **axShockwaveFlash** and set the Dock attribute in the Properties panel to Fill.

4. In the FlashControl.cs code file, replace the default code with the following:

```csharp
using System;
using System.Collections.Generic;
using System.ComponentModel;
using System.Drawing;
using System.Data;
using System.Text;
using System.Windows.Forms;

namespace WindowsControlLibrary
{
    public partial class FlashControl : UserControl
    {
        private string swfFilePath = "";
        public string SwfFilePath
        {
            get { return swfFilePath; }
            set { swfFilePath = value; }
        }

        public FlashControl()
        {
            InitializeComponent();
        }

        public void PlayMovie()
        {
            if (!String.IsNullOrEmpty(swfFilePath))
            {
                axShockwaveFlash.LoadMovie(0, swfFilePath);
                axShockwaveFlash.Play();
            }
            else
            {
                throw new ApplicationException(
                    "SWF file path not specified.");
            }
        }

        public void PlayMovie(string filePath)
        {
            swfFilePath = filePath;
            PlayMovie();
        }
    }
}
```

The code will expose a property for you to set the file path of the Flash file you would like to view and load as well as a method to play the movie once loaded.

5. Create a new WinFX window application in Visual Studio titled **WPFApplicationActiveX**. Rename the default form file to **MainWindow**.

6. As in the previous examples, include a reference to the `PresentationFramework`, `PresentationCore`, `System.Windows.Forms`, and `WindowsFormsIntegration` assemblies.

7. In the MainWindow.xaml file, replace the default code with the following code. This code will create your application window and supporting controls. You will include a grid control to load your ActiveX object into and a button to launch the Flash file playback.

```xml
<Window x:Class="WPFApplicationActiveX.MainWindow"
    xmlns="http://schemas.microsoft.com/winfx/2006/xaml/presentation"
    xmlns:x="http://schemas.microsoft.com/winfx/2006/xaml"
    Title="WindowsApplication1" Height="335" Width="402"
    >
    <Grid Name="grid1">
    <Grid Name="grid2" Margin="0,1,1,54"></Grid>
    <Button
        VerticalAlignment="Bottom"
        Grid.Column="0"
        Grid.ColumnSpan="1"
        Grid.Row="0"
        Grid.RowSpan="1"
        Margin="19,0,139,18.5"
        Height="23"
        Name="button1"
        Foreground="#FFFFFFFF">
        <Button.Background>
            <LinearGradientBrush StartPoint="0,0" EndPoint="1,1">
                <LinearGradientBrush.GradientStops>
                    <GradientStop Color="Red" Offset="0" />
                    <GradientStop Color="Blue" Offset="1" />
                </LinearGradientBrush.GradientStops>
            </LinearGradientBrush>
        </Button.Background>
        Play Flash Movie
    </Button>
    </Grid>
</Window>
```

8. In the MainWindow.xaml.cs code-behind file, replace the default code with the following code. As in the previous examples, you create `WindowsFormsHost` by declaring a new instance of the Host and assigning your Windows Form control as its child object:

```csharp
using System;
using System.Collections.Generic;
using System.Text;
using System.Windows;
using System.Windows.Controls;
using System.Windows.Data;
using System.Windows.Documents;
using System.Windows.Forms.Integration;
using System.Windows.Input;
using System.Windows.Media;
using System.Windows.Media.Imaging;
```

```
using System.Windows.Shapes;

namespace WPFApplicationActiveX
{
    public partial class MainWindow : Window
    {
        private WindowsControlLibrary.FlashControl axFlash;

        public MainWindow()
        {
            this.Loaded += new RoutedEventHandler(Window1_Loaded);
            InitializeComponent();
        }

        void Window1_Loaded(object sender, RoutedEventArgs e)
        {
            // Create the interop host control.
            WindowsFormsHost host = new WindowsFormsHost();

            // Create the ActiveX control.
            axFlash = new WindowsControlLibrary.FlashControl();

            // Assign the ActiveX control as the host control's child.
            host.Child = axFlash;

            // Add the interop host control to the Grid
            // control's collection of child controls.
            this.grid2.Children.Add(host);

            // Add the Handler
            this.button1.Click += new RoutedEventHandler(button1_Click);
        }

        void button1_Click(object sender, RoutedEventArgs e)
        {
            axFlash.SwfFilePath = @"C:\Animation.swf";
            axFlash.PlayMovie();
        }
    }
}
```

> **The example Flash file used for this project can be downloaded from** www.wrox.com.

9. Execute the project and click the button to load the Flash movie. Figure 10-6 illustrates the compiled output.

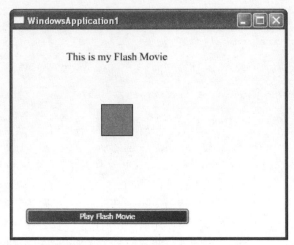

Figure 10-6

Adding the ActiveX Control in XAML

You can also leverage the power of declaratively adding your control through XAML. In this next example, you take advantage of the automatically generated assemblies from Visual Studio that wrap your COM component so that you can access it in your managed code.

The XAML code file references the generated managed COM assembly directly rather than referencing the control project you created. (The generated assemblies were really what you were after anyway.) Create a new xmlns attribute to declare the AxShockwaveFlashObjects namespace in addition to the XAML and Windows Forms namespaces that you used in the previous example.

```
<Window x:Class="WPFApplicationActiveX.MainWindow"
     xmlns="http://schemas.microsoft.com/winfx/2006/xaml/presentation"
     xmlns:x="http://schemas.microsoft.com/winfx/2006/xaml"
     xmlns:wf="clr-namespace:System.Windows.Forms;assembly=System.Windows.Forms"
     xmlns:ax="clr-namespace:AxShockwaveFlashObjects;assembly=
          AxInterop.ShockwaveFlashObjects"
     Title="WPFApplicationActiveX"
     Loaded="WindowLoaded"
     >
     <Grid Name="grid1">
          <WindowsFormsHost Name="host">
                <ax:AxShockwaveFlash x:Name="axShockwaveFlash "/>
          </WindowsFormsHost>
     </Grid>
</Window>
```

Now in your code-behind file, you handle when the window loads up to launch your SWF file into the player.

```
private void WindowLoaded(object sender, RoutedEventArgs e)
{
    // Get the AxHost wrapper from the WindowsFormsHost control.
    AxShockwaveFlashObjects.AxShockwaveFlash axFlashPlayer;
    axFlashPlayer = (AxShockwaveFlashObjects.AxShockwaveFlash) host.Child;

    // Play a .swf file with the ActiveX control.
    axShockwaveFlash.LoadMovie(0, @"C:\Animation.swf");
    axShockwaveFlash.Play();
}
```

Adding WPF Controls to Windows Forms

In order to introduce a WPF element into a Windows Form, you need a host that will wrap the WPF element in such a way that it can be added to the Controls collection of the Windows Form or control you would like to add the element to.

The ElementHost class in the System.Windows.Forms.Integration namespace is a class that derives from the System.Windows.Forms.Control class and is designed to host a WPF element. The WPF element can then be treated as a control.

The following code sample gives an example of how the host is created for a WPF control and added to the control tree of the Windows Form element:

```
private void Form1_Load(object sender, EventArgs e)
{
    // Create the ElementHost control for hosting the
    // WPF UserControl.
    ElementHost host = new ElementHost();
    host.Dock = DockStyle.Fill;

    // Create the WPF UserControl.
    WpfUserControl.WpfControl uc = new WpfUserControl.WpfControl();

    // Assign the WPF UserControl to the ElementHost control's
    // Child property.
    host.Child = uc;

    // Add the ElementHost control to the form's
    // collection of child controls.
    this.Controls.Add(host);
}
```

Adding a WPF control isn't a difficult process and can be handled with a few lines of code, which makes WinForms to WPF interop very easy.

Sample WPF in Windows Forms Application

To demonstrate how easy it is to integrate Windows Forms with WPF, you will create a new Windows Forms project and take advantage of some new functionality WPF has to offer out-of-the-box.

In this example, you dynamically load a WPF Button control that you have defined in a XAML file and use the new `XamlReader` object in the `System.Windows.Markup` namespace to create a concrete instance of it.

1. In Visual Studio, select File ⇨ New Project from the menu. From the Project Types tree view, select the Visual C# node, and then click the Windows Application icon from the list. Name your project **WindowsFormsApplication** and click OK. This new project should create a Form1.cs file, and a supporting partial class designer file.

2. Add a reference to the `PresentationCore` and `PresentationFramework` assemblies. This will import the new control classes available through WPF.

3. In order to interoperate Windows Forms with WPF, you will need to include a reference to the `System.Windows.Forms.Integration` namespace. Right-click on the References node in the Solution Explorer and add a new reference. Click Browse and navigate to the following folder in the filesystem: `%programfiles%\Reference Assemblies\Microsoft\ Framework\v3.0\ WindowsFormsIntegration.dll`. The References node in the Solution Explorer should match that shown in Figure 10-7.

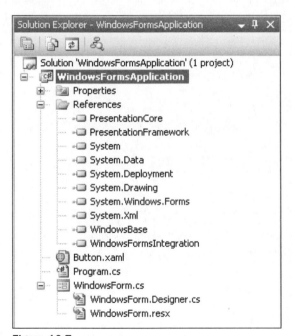

Figure 10-7

4. Include the references to the respective namespaces:

```
using System.Windows.Forms.Integration;
using System.Windows.Controls;
```

5. Rename the default form file to **WindowsForm**. In the code file for WindowsForm.cs, replace the existing code with the following code segment. This will include local references to a WPF button you will load up into your Win Form as well as the `ElementHost` to host the control.

```
using System;
using System.Collections.Generic;
using System.ComponentModel;
using System.Data;
using System.Drawing;
using System.IO;
using System.Text;
using WPFControls = System.Windows.Controls;
using System.Windows.Forms;
using System.Windows.Forms.Integration;
using System.Windows.Markup;

namespace WindowsFormsApplication
{
    public partial class WindowsForm : Form
    {
        private ElementHost ctrlHost;
        private WPFControls.Button wpfButton;

        public WindowsForm()
        {
            InitializeComponent();
        }
    }
}
```

6. In the designer, add a button control and assign it the label **Load Control**.

7. Add a Panel to the UI just below the button. This will be the container that you will add your WPF element to as a child control.

8. You will need to load up an external XAML file into our application, so add an OpenFileDialog control to the form.

9. Add a new text file to the project and rename it **Button.xaml** (make sure to change the file extension). Insert the following code segment into the file. This declares your WPF button that you are going to load into your Windows Form.

```
<Button
    xmlns="http://schemas.microsoft.com/winfx/2006/xaml/presentation"
    xmlns:x="http://schemas.microsoft.com/winfx/2006/xaml"
    VerticalAlignment="Bottom"
    Grid.Column="0"
    Grid.ColumnSpan="1"
    Grid.Row="0"
    Grid.RowSpan="1"
    Margin="19,0,139,18.5"
    Height="23"
    Name="button1"
    Foreground="#FFFFFFFF">
    <Button.Background>
```

```
        <LinearGradientBrush StartPoint="0,0" EndPoint="1,1">
            <LinearGradientBrush.GradientStops>
                <GradientStop Color="Red" Offset="0" />
                <GradientStop Color="Blue" Offset="1" />
            </LinearGradientBrush.GradientStops>
        </LinearGradientBrush>
    </Button.Background>
    WPF Button
</Button>
```

10. In the WindowForm.cs code file, add the following method declaration:

```
void LoadControlFromXAMLFile(string fileName)
{
    FileStream xamlFile = null;

    // Open the XAML with our control
    using (xamlFile = new FileStream(fileName, FileMode.Open, FileAccess.Read))
    {
        // Parse the XAML file to an object.
        object xamlObject = XamlReader.Load(xamlFile);
        if (xamlObject.GetType() == typeof(WPFControls.Button))
        {
            wpfButton = (WPFControls.Button)xamlObject;

            // Create the element host
            ctrlHost = new ElementHost();
            ctrlHost.Dock = DockStyle.Fill;

            // Add the host to the parent
            // control collection
            panel1.Controls.Add(ctrlHost);

            // Assign the document viewer to
            // the host
            ctrlHost.Child = wpfButton;
        }
    }
}
```

This method handles opening up an IO stream to a selected XAML file. The System.Windows.Markup namespace includes an object called XamlReader, which will parse a XAML document and return the object that is defined in it.

11. The last segment of code you need will handle the click event for the button you have defined in your Windows Form. When the Click event is fired, the OpenFileDialog will allow you to select the XAML file you wish to load.

```
private void button1_Click(object sender, EventArgs e)
{
    openFileDialog1.Filter = "xaml files (*.xaml)|*.xaml";
    if (openFileDialog1.ShowDialog() == DialogResult.OK)
        try
        {
            LoadControlFromXAMLFile(openFileDialog1.FileName);
```

```
                }
                catch (Exception ex)
                {
                        MessageBox.Show("Error loading file. " + ex.Message);
                }
        else
                MessageBox.Show("No file was chosen.");
}
```

12. Debug the project. Click the Load Control button and open the Button.xaml file you created earlier. You will see the WPF Button control loaded in to the panel area of the screen (see Figure 10-8).

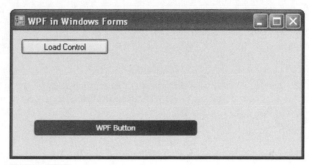

Figure 10-8

Affecting Control Properties

Property mappings allow for property changes within the `ElementHost` to be propagated to the child
UIElement control. The `PropertyMap` property of either the `ElementHost` or `WindowsFormsHost`
classes contains a dictionary of `PropertyTranslator` delegates mapped to the property key of the host
property.

The delegate definition is:

```
public delegate void PropertyTranslator (
        object host,
        string propertyName,
        object value
)
```

The parameters are as follows:

❑   `host` — The host control whose property is being mapped.

❑   `propertyName` — The name of the property that is being accessed.

❑   `value` — The value assigned to the host property.

Each `PropertyMap` entry allows you to define a `PropertyTranslator` delegate that coordinates the
property changes of the host child whenever the host property is changed.

Depending on how complex your WPF control is, you can create intricate property mappings that affect many different elements.

If there is no relationship between a host property change and a WPF element property change then WPF control properties and events can also be accessed in code directly and don't specifically require a property mapping to affect the control.

Let's modify the previous Windows Forms Application to include some new code that will demonstrate how to set up a property mapping as well as assign an event handler manually to your dynamically loaded WPF element. In the method definition for `LoadControlFromXAMLFile`, let's include a segment of code right below the point where you assign the wpfButton to the element host:

```
....
ctrlHost.Child = wpfButton;
ctrlHost.PropertyMap["Font"] = delegate(object host, string prop, object val)
{
      ElementHost eHost = (ElementHost)host;
      FrameworkElement element = (FrameworkElement)eHost.Child;
      WPFControls.Button button = (WPFControls.Button)element;
      button.FontSize = ((Font)val).Size;
};
```

The code segment defines an anonymous method that defines the property translation procedure. When the `Font` property of the `ElementHost` is modified, you make sure that the child WPF control that is being hosted also reflects the font size change. The property that defines the size of the font in WPF is `FontSize` whereas in Windows Forms it is the `Size` property of the `Font` object property.

Next, you will include some code that illustrates how you still have the ability to modify WPF control properties manually. Insert the following code in the `LoadControlFromXAMLFile` method declaration. This assigns an event handler to your button control to handle the click event of the button.

```
. . . .
wpfButton = (WPFControls.Button)xamlObject;
wpfButton.Click += new System.Windows.RoutedEventHandler(wpfButton_Click);
```

Next, you include the method definition for your event handler.

```
void wpfButton_Click(object sender, System.Windows.RoutedEventArgs e)
{
      MessageBox.Show("Hello from WPF!");
}
```

Last, you will include code that will change the font property of `ElementHost` so that you can see the work done by the `PropertyTranslator` delegate. In the Visual Studio designer for the Windows Form, drag and drop another button next to the XAML loading button. Change the text to read **Change Font** and double-click it to include an event handler in the code. Modify the default definition so that it is identical to the following code:

```
private void button2_Click(object sender, EventArgs e)
{
      Font myFont = new Font(FontFamily.GenericSansSerif, 14);
```

```
    ctrlHost.Font = myFont;

    wpfButton.Height += 25;
}
```

Now execute the project in Debug, load the control, and click the Change Font button. You will see the font change applied to the ElementHost is now propagated to the WPF Button. Click the loaded WPF Button to view the event handling procedure (displayed in Figure 10-9).

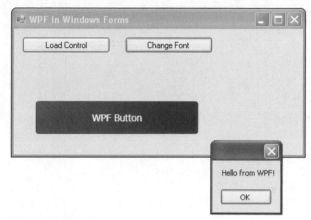

Figure 10-9

Summary

Even though interoperability with legacy applications may be a daunting task for any developer, we have discovered that hosting WPF elements in existing managed .NET applications can be done with relative ease. This chapter covered the basic interoperability points between Windows Forms and WPF and provided information on how to handle them effectively. The chapter included examples of the following:

❑   How WPF differs from HWND-based applications

❑   How to host WPF controls in Windows Forms applications

❑   How to host Windows Forms controls in WPF

❑   How to host WPF in HWND-based Win32 applications

❑   How to host ActiveX controls in WPF

❑   How to map property changes between the managed controls in WPF and Windows Forms

11

Advanced Development Concepts

In this chapter, we dig deeper into the details of the Windows Presentation Foundation (WPF) platform, as well as other new .NET 3.0 platforms, and we drill down below the surface of the concepts we have been using throughout this book. Understanding the inner workings of the WPF environment within .NET 3.0 will help you in writing professional next-generation applications using the platform. While some of the content in this chapter may repeat from earlier chapters, it is purely to set the stage for taking a deeper look at WPF architecture, framework, components, and concepts.

Architecturally, WPF consists of a managed visual system, an unmanaged composition system, and a communication channel between them called the message transport. These subsystems work together to provide presentation services, such as composing and painting pixels to the screen on behalf of WPF applications. WPF contains other important subsystems as well, such as the property system and input/event system, but at the core of the architecture, it is the visual system, composition system, and the communication between the two that provide the foundation for WPF. We will talk about each of these major subsystems in more detail throughout this chapter.

In addition to the subsystems that make up the WPF architecture, an extensive framework is at our disposal for developing applications. The WPF framework provides us with a toolset for taking advantage of all of the features that the platform provides. In this chapter, we examine the key components of the framework and how the classes in the framework build on each other to provide the services required to build feature-rich applications.

Also at your disposal is a new XML-based declarative language (XAML) for declaring objects and object properties using XML syntax. In this chapter, we take a deeper look at how XAML fits in with WPF applications as we deconstruct a simple application. We look at what happens to our XAML at compile time. We also look at the syntax of XAML and some of the more advanced XAML concepts, such as type converters, referencing custom classes, and markup extensions.

WPF introduces new classes for dealing with threads and multithreading in applications. We look at what makes multithreading in WPF different from multithreading in Windows Forms and Win32 applications. We take a detailed look at the Dispatcher object and its role in WPF. Finally, we walk through some sample code such as creating background threads and cross-thread synchronization.

WPF is not the only new platform in .NET 3.0. There are three other platforms that extend the .NET 2.0 Framework: Windows Communication Foundation (WCF), Windows Workflow Foundation (WF), and Windows CardSpace (WCS). You take a high-level look at what two of these platforms, WCF and WF, have to offer, what services they provide, and how you can leverage them in your WPF applications. You also build some simple applications using the WCF and WF platforms from within WPF.

WPF Architecture

The WPF architecture consists of two frameworks, one managed and one unmanaged. The managed API is referred to as the *presentation framework* and provides all of the functionality you need to build WPF applications, such as controls, layout, data binding, and visuals. The unmanaged API is referred to as the Media Integration Layer (MIL) and provides the low-level functionality of the WPF architecture, such as composition and rendering. Although the unmanaged functionality is not publicly exposed, it is the heart of the WPF presentation engine. All pixel rendering happens in the MIL.

This section covers the following:

❑ Architecture

❑ Core subsystems

❑ Threading model

Figure 11-1 illustrates the various components that make up the WPF architecture.

Taking a bottom-up approach, we can see that underlying WPF are DirectX, User32, display drivers (WDDM and XPDM), and the graphics card. All software rendering in WPF will ultimately end up being rendered by the graphics card. The WDDM and XPDM drivers work closely with your graphics card. If you are running Windows Vista then your system will use the new Windows Display Driver Model (WDDM) driver. If you are using XP, your system will use the XP Driver Model (XPDM). There is not necessarily a requirement when it comes to the graphics card you use; WPF will scale based on the amount of video memory your graphics card contains.

Sitting just above the display drivers are the DirectX and User32 libraries. DirectX is used to render 2D, 3D, text, or animation, utilizing the full power of the graphics processing unit (GPU). User32 manages the windows on the desktop. These components remain unchanged in WPF, but they provide the foundation upon which WPF builds.

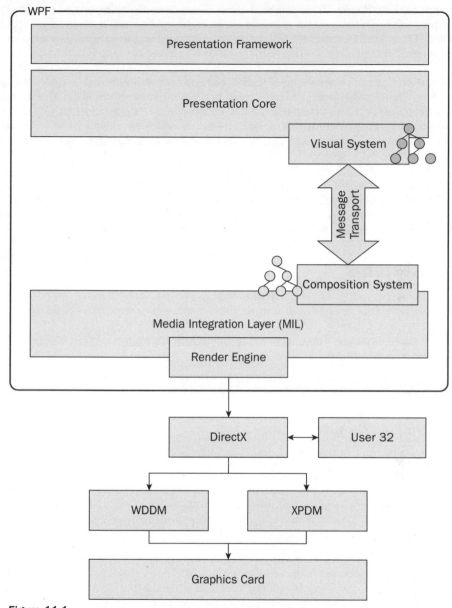

Figure 11-1

The Media Integration Layer (MIL) resides just above User32 and DirectX. The MIL consists of the WPF unmanaged composition system (don't confuse this with the composition model WPF uses in which elements contain other elements) and an unmanaged rendering engine, which talks to DirectX. The WPF composition and rendering engine are central components of the WPF architecture. The MIL analyzes an application's visual data in order to render the user interface and is ultimately responsible for painting pixels on the screen. The MIL doesn't work alone; it renders pixels with the help of DirectX. Because DirectX is a 3D rendering engine, the MIL translates the nodes on the composition tree into data that is consumable by DirectX.

The Presentation Core sits between the MIL and the presentation framework and is home to the WPF visual system. The visual system provides classes that represent visuals in WPF, which are the elements that make up an application's visual tree, ultimately representing the application's UI. The visual system communicates with the MIL through a message transport, which provides a two-way messaging system through which the visual system and MIL may communicate rendering data and instructions to ultimately get pixels on the screen.

The presentation framework sits at the top of the WPF architecture stack and is the primary API you will use to create WPF applications. The presentation framework provides application support, such as controls, layout, data binding, and styling to visuals located in the visual system. We discuss the components and classes that make up the presentation framework in the next section.

Core Subsystems

Let's review what we referred to in the introduction as the core subsystems of the WPF architecture: the visual system, message transport, and composition system, which were introduced in Chapter 1:

- ❑ The visual system is the subsystem through which applications access the core presentation services available through WPF.

- ❑ The visual system creates a visual tree, which contains all an application's visual elements and rendering instructions.

- ❑ The visual system communicates via the message transport with the underlying composition system to get pixels rendered to the screen.

- ❑ The composition system is an unmanaged subsystem that receives rendering instructions from the managed visual system, and turns those instructions into data consumable by DirectX.

- ❑ The message transport provides a two-way communication channel that supports messaging between the visual system and the composition system.

The Visual System

As you learned in Chapter 1, the visual system is the managed subsystem through which applications access the core presentation services available through WPF. The visual system is where an application's visual tree resides. The visual tree is a hierarchical data structure that represents all of an application's visual elements and drawing instructions for a given window or page. These drawing instructions are what the composition and rendering engine require in order to paint pixels to the screen. The visual tree is used by our application to manage its GUI. This tree allows for programmatic manipulation of visual elements. Many of the WPF subsystems, such as the input and event subsystems, use this tree.

The visual system does not actually render anything. It simply defines and manages what will be rendered. When an application needs to render its UI to the screen, or when an update to its UI needs to be made, it passes its visual data, one element at a time, down to the composition system via the message transport channel. The composition system will compose its own tree, called the composition tree, and then request rendering to be performed by the rendering engine. Because the visual system lives on a separate thread from the MIL systems, the application does not have to wait for rendering operations to complete in order to continue processing business logic. This is referred to as a *retained mode graphics model*.

The WPF retained mode graphics model (as shown in Figure 11-2) breaks from the traditional Win32 immediate mode graphics model, in which painting the screen is the responsibility of the application. With either model, when windows are moved or resized, the area behind the window that is exposed becomes invalid, requiring it to be repainted. Under Win32, when a region of the screen is invalidated, a WM_PAINT message is sent to the application from the Windows OS, and it is the responsibility of the application to repaint the invalidated surface. This often results in brief trails or blurriness of the screen while the re-painting takes place. The key concept in an immediate mode graphics system is that the application is itself responsible for managing its graphics data, rendering this data, and responding to system messages to refresh or repaint its client area.

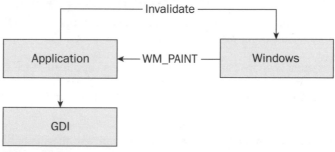

Figure 11-2

With the retained mode graphics model (as shown in Figure 11-3), WPF applications are no longer required to manage their own rendering. Applications merely manage their visual data and then pass this data along to the MIL. The MIL will handle the rest of the work, leaving an application free to continue processing input commands and executing code. Furthermore, the MIL can cache and optimize the graphical data it manages, allowing for greater performance on the desktop. The key concept in a retained mode graphic system is that the application merely defines and manages its graphics data, passes this data to the MIL essentially offloading the actual rendering work, and then only sends edits as necessary to the MIL when UI changes are required.

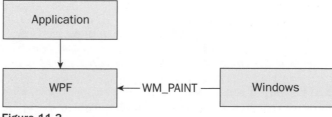

Figure 11-3

In addition to using a retained mode graphics model, WPF also implements a new painting algorithm. Objects that overlap each other are painted to the screen from back to front. This allows WPF to apply effects, such as transparency, to objects. The key concept here is that more than one object may affect any given pixel.

The Composition System

Before you explore the composition system, we need to point out that, although we have talked about the visual data being passed to the composition system for rendering, the composition tree used by the composition system is not the same visual tree used by the application. The primary differences between them are as follows:

- ❑ The visual tree is managed; the composition tree is unmanaged.

- ❑ The visual tree lives on the UI thread; the composition tree lives on the render thread.

- ❑ The visual tree is used by the application for managing its GUI and supporting subsystems, such as input and events; the composition tree is used strictly for rendering.

- ❑ The visual tree represents all elements that make up the application's UI; the composition tree contains only the elements that will be visible on the screen.

The composition system is responsible for composing all of an application's visible visual elements to the screen. The composition system manages an element tree, called the composition tree, for composing the application's GUI. The composition tree is an unmanaged tree containing only nodes representing elements that will be visible on the screen.

The composition system lives in the MIL on the render thread, and there is only one render thread per WPF process. The composition system runs on the render thread, in the background, waiting to receive visual data from the visual system via the message transport. Once the visual data is received, the composition system will modify its composition tree as necessary, process the drawing instructions for each element, and calculate pixels. Render data is then passed to the rendering engine of the MIL, where it is translated and communicated down to DirectX for painting pixels.

Once the composition system has prepared the visual data for rendering, it passes that data to the render engine of the MIL. The render engine uses DirectX to implement hardware-based rendering. This model takes full advantage of the power of the graphics card available in most modern computers. DirectX utilizes a computer's graphical processing unit (GPU) rather than the onboard CPU for rendering graphics. This decreases the load on the CPU, allowing it to focus on OS and application level commands, rather than on rendering pixels to the screen. The net effect is a rendering process handled through hardware rather than software.

> *DirectX does not know how to render shapes such as square, rectangle, or ellipse. DirectX understands rendering in terms of triangles. The render engine must translate shapes into triangles that DirectX can understand. The process of converting shapes to triangles is called tessellation.*

The WPF composition system is a vector-based composition engine. The vector-based composition system creates images on the screen composed from primitives. Primitives are defined as points, lines, polygons, and curves, which are all geometric shapes. This is different from Win32, which used fixed-size raster graphics. Raster graphics are composed from pixels, which are not scalable. Think about the effects of resizing a bitmap in an application. As the scale of the image increases, the quality degrades. Vectors, on the other hand, are highly scalable based on the fact they are constructed of primitives. What this means is that vector graphics can re-size without loss of graphic quality, regardless of screen resolution.

The Message Transport

The message transport provides a two-way communication channel across the threading boundaries of the visual system, which lives on the UI thread, and the composition system, which lives on the render thread. The message transport consists of two parts: a transport and a channel. The transport is a communication mechanism. The channel sits on top of the transport and allows an application to place resources, such as Brush or Rectangle, onto the transport.

Using this communication channel, visual data can be passed from the visual system to the composition system for rendering. When a change or edit occurs in the visual system, the visuals created, removed, or affected are passed individually across this channel to the composition system. This has a positive impact on performance, as the entire visual tree is not transferred every time an edit occurs.

> *In the two-way communication process, communication from the composition system to the visual system is limited and primarily involves simply reporting errors.*

When applications are running locally, this channel is really just a pipe accessing shared memory because the two threads are running in the same process. The composition system can access the memory and construct its own copy of the tree. In a remote scenario, such as Terminal Services, data is not shared; rather, it is passed along in a Terminal Services Envelope.

Now that you've reviewed the core systems, you can understand the following pseudo-logic example for how rendering occurs in WPF.

- ❑ An `Ellipse` is added to the application's UI, becoming part of the visual tree.
- ❑ The application sends a visual element (the `Ellipse`) across the message transport to the composition system (UI thread work is complete; render thread work starts).
- ❑ The composition system creates its own composition tree from the visual it receives.
- ❑ The composition system tells the rendering engine to "Draw an Ellipse."
- ❑ The rendering engine prepares the data for DirectX by tessellating the `Ellipse`.
- ❑ The rendering engine tells DirectX to render and passes along the tessellated data.
- ❑ DirectX issues the data to the display driver (WDDM or XPDM).
- ❑ The display driver works with the graphics card to render pixels on the screen.

WPF Threading Model

WPF applications are single-threaded applications (STA). An application may create one or many UI threads via the WPF `Dispatcher` object, but each UI thread, individually, is single-threaded. The visual system lives on the UI thread, and a WPF application essentially owns this thread. When the visual system needs to render its UI, it will pass visual elements to the composition system of the MIL, located on the render thread. There is only one render thread per WPF process.

Figure 11-4 illustrates the core components of WPF and their relationship to the UI and render threads.

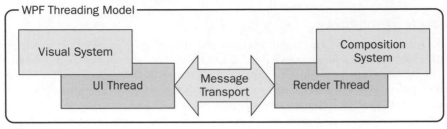

Figure 11-4

The threading model and separation of visual system and composition system responsibilities is an important concept in WPF architecture. Because a WPF application does not live on the same thread that performs rendering, the application does not have to wait for rendering to complete in order to continue processing.

The separation of responsibilities by thread provides for some unique functionality. In WPF, the separation of UI and render threads and the communication via the message transport provides a flexible model that applications, such as Terminal Services or Remote Desktop, can exploit. A remote server running an application will manage the UI thread. Using the message transport, the remote server application can simply send visual data to the client machine where the client's render thread can do the actual rendering. This requires far less bandwidth than sending bitmaps across the wire, providing for increased performance on the client machine.

Desktop Window Manager

The Desktop Window Manager (DWM) is new in Windows Vista. The DWM is the component responsible for providing the incredible new visual experience Vista provides. Why are we discussing the DWM in a book about WPF you ask? Well, because the DWM utilizes the same composition system of the MIL layer that our WPF applications utilize and, therefore, is a testament to the power of WPF.

The DWM presents a fundamental change in the way pixels are rendered to the screen from previous Windows display models. This fundamental change is rooted in a concept known as *desktop composition*, which is the process of composing the entire visible screen from all running application windows.

> *Under the hood, the DWM manages a visual tree just like WPF applications, but conceptually it's a higher level tree that represents all components that make up the visible desktop.*

Prior to WPF, Vista, and the DWM, applications managed the rendering of their window client areas directly. These applications would write directly to a buffer used by the video card to render UI. With WPF, applications are no longer required to do this. Rather, the WPF composition system writes the application's client area to an off-screen buffer and the DWM takes over from there. The DWM is responsible for composing off-screen buffers for all running applications and handing them off to the video card for rendering.

The division of rendering responsibilities between the application and DWM provides an opportunity for the DWM to transform windows before rendering. For instance, the DWM will apply Vista themes, such as the new Vista Aero or Glass themes. The DWM can also optimize pixel resolution, taking advantage of high resolution monitors when available.

Together, the WPF composition system and DWM provide a far richer user experience. Gone are the days of window trails when moving windows on the desktop, and here now are the days of transparent windows and thumbnail window viewing.

The WPF Framework

The WPF framework provides a rich programming model you can use to develop next-generation WPF applications. We have explored many of the classes that make up the framework throughout this book. The WPF framework provides classes for styling controls, layout, input, and event routing; using data binding; drawing 2D and 3D shapes; creating animations; accessing and manipulating the visual tree; and there's plenty more. All of this is exposed to you through a familiar programming model because WPF is built on top of the .NET 2.0 Framework.

The WPF framework is very extensive. There are many ways one can slice and dice the framework in an effort to describe it. One can look at each subsystem individually and the classes that support it, for instance the property system or event system. One can break it into presentation core and presentation framework layers and describe important classes in each. In this section, we explore the individual classes that make up the inheritance hierarchy and describe the subsystems supported at each step along the way.

Figure 11-5 illustrates the inheritance hierarchy of the core WPF framework classes.

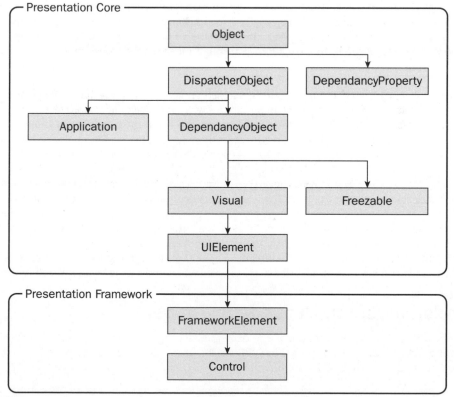

Figure 11-5

We refer to the classes in Figure 11-5 as core classes because they provide support for the major concepts in the WPF architecture. There are many other classes in the framework, most of which utilize the classes illustrated in Figure 11-5. Understanding these core classes will provide a solid foundation for working with the WPF framework in your applications — for instance, knowing which base class to inherit from when creating custom controls in WPF. In the following sections, we look at each of the classes illustrated in our diagram to understand what they offer and how they fit into the big WPF picture.

Before you begin exploring these classes, it's worth noting that the classes themselves are part of two separate framework layers:

❑ **Presentation core:** Provides base classes that support low-level functionality, such as threading, properties, rendering, and visuals.

❑ **Presentation framework (and the classes within):** Extend classes in the presentation core and add application-level support for layout and composition.

Dispatcher Object

WPF objects belong to the thread on which they are created and cannot be accessed directly by any other thread. In the context of WPF applications, this thread is called the *UI thread*. An object that participates in this single-threaded model is said to exhibit *thread affinity*, meaning they are tied to the thread on which they are created. Thread affinity is an important concept to understand when programming in WPF.

There is a class in WPF, called the `Dispatcher`, that manages all access to the thread on which it is created. There is only one `Dispatcher` object per thread. Objects created in WPF are actually tied directly to the `Dispatcher` rather than being tied directly to the UI thread itself; however, the net effect is the same. WPF objects are tied to the `Dispatcher` through inheritance because most objects in WPF derive directly or indirectly from `DispatcherObject`.

`Dispatcher` manages an event queue in WPF, which you can think of as the message loop in Win32. If a thread other than the one on which the `Dispatcher` was created wants to update an object on the thread owned by the `Dispatcher`, it must do so by placing a request in the `Dispatcher` queue. The `Dispatcher` will deliver the message in a thread-safe way to a specific target object. We talk about threading concepts in greater detail in a later section on WPF threading.

The `DispatcherObject` class represents an object that is associated with a `Dispatcher`. Therefore, objects that derive from `DispatcherObject` are associated with a single thread, the thread associated with the dispatcher instance to which their base class, `DispatcherObject`, is associated. For example, if you create a `Button` instance in a WPF application, the button can only be accessed directly on the UI thread because the button ultimately derives from `DispatcherObject`, which is associated with a dispatcher, which is associated with the UI thread. `DispatcherObject` is the lowest level class in the framework hierarchy, and because almost all objects inherit from it, most objects are inherently thread-safe.

DependencyObject/DependencyProperty

WPF introduces a new property system, the dependency property system (DPS). While typical `Get` and `Set` CLR properties are still supported in WPF, the DPS provides a new set of property types and property services to objects that derive from `DependencyObject`.

The DependencyObject class represents an object that participates in the WPF DPS. When an object derives from DependencyObject, it automatically has access to all of the services provided by the DPS. A dependency object may declare dependency properties. The DependencyProperty class represents a dependency property that is registered with the WPF dependency property system.

DPS concepts were covered in earlier chapters, so we'll just briefly recap here. The DPS offers many advantages over plain CLR type properties. For instance, through the use of a new type of properties called *dependency properties*, the DPS supports property-value inheritance, which allows elements to inherit property values from any of their containing elements. Dependency properties also provide the glue required for data binding and animation. Additionally, the DPS supports another new type of property, called an *attached property*, which is a dependency property with a twist. Attached properties are interesting in that they provide a mechanism by which one class can define a property that can be used by other classes, without the other classes knowing anything about the property or the class that defines it. Examples of these can be found in many of the built-in layout controls to provide a means for child controls to position themselves in their parent containers. One such example is the DockPanel.Dock attached property.

Additionally, the DPS provides a storage system for dependency property values and will notify objects when these values change. In doing so, each instance of a class that contains dependency properties does not have to provide storage for those properties. For instance, if you are defining number of labels on a form, chances are the background color property will be initialized to the default value and will rarely change. Without the DPS, if you had ten instances of the label class, all of which simply use the default background color property, you would be storing ten background color property values. The DPS, on the other hand, can manage this for you, storing only a single instance of the default value, assigning it to all instances of your class, and then storing separately only the instance properties that are different, minimizing the use of system resources.

Dependency properties are used most often when working with the DPS. Dependency properties are registered with the DPS when they are declared. You declare a dependency property in a class by defining a static field of type DependencyProperty, initialized with a call to the DependencyProperty.Register() or DependencyProperty.RegisterAttached() method.

```
public static DependencyProperty text = DependencyProperty.Register(...)
```

Once registered, your property is managed by the DPS and will provide all the services supplied by the DPS.

Application

Application is the primary class in the WPF application model. The Application class encapsulates your code and provides the interface between that code and the operating system. One could say that Application provides the glue that binds your XAML pages together into a unified application, and that would be correct, only it does much more than that.

Application exhibits three primary characteristics: It exists from startup until application shutdown (lifetime support), it is global, and it is local to the machine it is running on.

The Application class provides lifetime support services for your applications. Lifetime support refers to the stages an application goes through, such as startup, shutdown, and the events in between.

A number of events, including Startup, Activated, Deactivated, SessionEnding, and Exit, occur during the lifetime of an application. You can use these events to customize the behavior of your application. For instance, you can hook into the Startup event to add global properties for use throughout your application.

The Application class also provides a global Properties property for storing application state in a simple key/value dictionary collection. You can use this to store and manipulate data between windows; for instance, if you're familiar with ASP.NET, the Properties property will remind you of the session or application objects. The Properties property offers an opportunity to store data you want to share between all windows in your application, or to track state of various objects throughout the lifetime of your application.

Freezable

The Freezable class exists in the framework to increase application performance when using objects that do not require interactive behavior. A Freezable object has two states, frozen and unfrozen. An unfrozen Freezable object has all of the support offered by DependencyObject. When frozen, a Freezable object becomes read-only, and because it cannot be modified, it does not need the support of the dependency object, such as change notification. This is where the performance improvement happens. This benefits objects such as Brush and Pen. The Freezable class improves performance because the graphics system does not need to monitor frozen objects for changes.

Visual

The Visual class provides services and properties that are common to all visual objects. Visual provides core services such as rendering and hit-testing to elements that derive from it. If your control or element renders pixels, it derives from Visual.

Visual implements the IElement interface, which provides methods and properties, such as AddChild and RemoveChild, which allow elements to exist in a visual tree. IElement is not publicly exposed, but knowing a little about it helps you to understand some of what Visual provides. If you were to write your own implementation of a tree class and container it might look something like this:

```
public class tree
{
IList trees = new IList<treeItem>();
...
}

public class treeItem
{
bool hasParent;
treeItem parent;

bool hasChildren;
IList children = new IList<treeItem>();
...
}
```

While you can be absolutely certain the implementation of the `IElement` interface looks nothing like this, the code illustrates the concept of `IElement` and a visual tree. A visual tree is simply a collection of `Visual` objects. An application will usually contain many elements, and all elements inherit from `Visual`, so elements are by their definition readily equipped to be part of a visual tree, and that is exactly where they will end up.

The visual tree will eventually be passed to the composition system (remember the message transport?), which will traverse the elements of the tree, processing each element's drawing instructions, composing the UI, and ultimately rending pixels to the screen. Drawing instructions contain vector graphics data that tell the composition system how to render an element.

Now that you understand the visual tree in greater detail, let's recap. The visual tree contains a hierarchy of elements, each of which derives from `Visual`, which means it knows how to live in the visual tree, and each of which contains its rendering instructions, which tell the composition system how to render. The purpose of the visual system is now made clear; it offers support to elements through its base class `Visual`, and it manages a visual tree, which provides the elements needed by the composition system in order to render pixels to the screen.

`Visual` offers support for other features as well, such as transformations, clipping, and hit-testing. Notice, however, that `Visual` does not provide support beyond the single element that derives from it. Non-rendering features, such as event routing and handling, layout, style, and data binding, are not supported at this level. They are supported by either `UIElement` or `FrameworkElement`, which derive from `Visual`. You look at these classes in more detail shortly.

In addition to `Visual`, there are three additional visual classes in WPF: `ContainerVisual`, `DrawingVisual`, and `Viewport3DVisual`. We'll just discuss `DrawingVisual` briefly, as it is a lightweight class you can use for custom drawing. The `DrawingVisual` class provides a `DrawingContext` object, which is a drawing surface on which you can draw. `DrawingVisual` does not support layout, input, focus, or events. In order to get these services, a `DrawingVisual` instance must belong to a container that derives from `FrameworkElement`.

You now know that an application may contain many visual elements, and that these visual elements, along with their rendering instructions, compose the visual tree. Given this description, you might expect to see a visual tree representing a simple window, as illustrated in Figure 11-6.

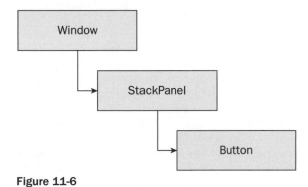

Figure 11-6

Figure 11-6 actually represents a logical tree rather than a visual tree. The logical tree is made up of the controls you place in your UI, such as Window, Button, or StackPanel. Remember, however, that in WPF, each control is composed of shapes, lines, rectangles, and so on. The following example should enforce the difference between logical and visual trees. So, if you go ahead and enumerate your element tree as a visual tree, you see the following:

```
-Trees.Window1
--System.Windows.Controls.Border
---System.Windows.Documents.AdornerDecorator
----System.Windows.Controls.ContentPresenter
-----System.Windows.Controls.StackPanel
------System.Windows.Controls.Button
-------Microsoft.Windows.Themes.ButtonChrome
--------System.Windows.Controls.ContentPresenter
---------System.Windows.Controls.TextBlock
----System.Windows.Documents.AdornerLayer
```

So what's going on here? Why does the visual tree contain so many elements? Figure 11-7 illustrates elements that make up the Button control.

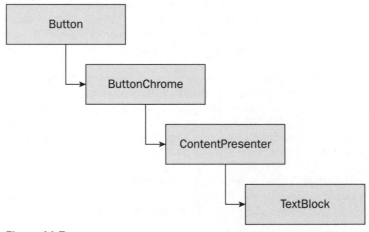

Figure 11-7

We declared a button, but we didn't declare any of the button's child elements that appear in the visual tree. Button is composed of various other elements that make up its visual appearance. This is achieved through the use of a control template. A control, such as our Button, is composed of one or more elements: shape, border, brush, and so on. In the case of the button illustrated in Figure 11-7, ButtonChrome, ContentPresenter, and TextBlock child elements are displayed. The visual tree contains all visual elements and instructions for rendering controls and, therefore, must contain the individual elements and instructions that make up the control. This is how the logical tree differs from the visual tree. When the button is rendered by WPF, WPF will render a collection of visual objects, such as shapes, borders, lines, ellipses, and so on. So *visually*, your button contains a collection of shapes to be rendered, but *logically* your UI simply contains a button.

Remember that a key concept in WPF, when it comes to controls, is the separation of presentation from logic. Controls are "lookless" in WPF. Controls provide functionality and, optionally, a default visual style.

In order to further illustrate the difference between the logical and visual tree, let's build a simple program. This program will enumerate and display the logical and visual tree of a specified element.

Open Visual Studio and create a new .NET Framework 3.0 application using the Windows Application (WPF) template and name the application **WPFTrees**. Modify the Window1.xaml file as follows:

```xml
<Window x:Class="WPFTrees.Window1"
  xmlns="http://schemas.microsoft.com/winfx/2006/xaml/presentation"
  xmlns:x="http://schemas.microsoft.com/winfx/2006/xaml"
  Title="WPFTrees" Height="304" Width="702" Name="MyWindow"
  >
  <DockPanel Name="DockPanel1">
    <StackPanel DockPanel.Dock="Right">
      <TextBlock>Logical Tree</TextBlock>
      <TextBox DockPanel.Dock="Right" Name="textbox2"
        Width="500" Height="115"
        TextWrapping="Wrap"></TextBox>
      <TextBlock>Visual Tree</TextBlock>
      <TextBox DockPanel.Dock="Right" Name="textbox1"
        Width="500" Height="115"
        TextWrapping="Wrap"></TextBox>
    </StackPanel>
    <StackPanel DockPanel.Dock="Left" Margin="6,4,4,4" >
      <Canvas Name="canvas1">
        <Button Name="button1">
          <Ellipse Name="ellipse1" Height="100"
            Width="100" Fill="Red"></Ellipse>
        </Button>
      </Canvas>
    </StackPanel>
    <Button DockPanel.Dock="Left" Height="20" Width="100"
      HorizontalAlignment="Left" Margin="1,4,4,4"
      Click="buttonPrint_Click">Print Trees</Button>
  </DockPanel>
</Window>
```

In the Window1.xaml file, you've defined a `DockPanel` as your element container. Within it, you've placed a `StackPanel` containing a couple of `Label` and `TextBox` elements for displaying your output, and a `StackPanel` that will contain a `Canvas`. The `Button` contained by `Canvas` is what you'll use as a root element for displaying your logical and visual trees.

Next, open up the Window1.xaml.cs code-behind file and modify as follows:

```csharp
using System;
using System.Collections.Generic;
using System.Text;
using System.Windows;
using System.Windows.Controls;
using System.Windows.Data;
using System.Windows.Documents;
using System.Windows.Input;
using System.Windows.Media;
using System.Windows.Media.Imaging;
```

```
using System.Windows.Shapes;

using System.Collections;

namespace WPFTrees
{

  public partial class Window1 : System.Windows.Window
  {

    public Window1()
    {
      InitializeComponent();

      // CANNOT PRINT TREES IN WINDOW1 CONSTRUCTOR
      // THE TREES AREN'T CREATED YET !!!!!
    }

    public void PrintVisualTree(int indent, ref string str, Visual visual)
    {
      string space = "";

      for (int count = 0; count < indent; count++)
      {
        space += " ";
      }
      str += space + visual.GetType().ToString() + Environment.NewLine;

      for (int i = 0; i < VisualTreeHelper.GetChildrenCount(visual); i++)
      {
        indent++;
        PrintVisualTree(indent, ref str,
          (Visual)VisualTreeHelper.GetChild(visual, i));
      }
    }
  }
```

First, create your method for printing your visual tree. This method will be called when the program's print button is clicked. This function accepts an object of type Visual because all elements ultimately derive from Visual, an indent level for display, and a reference parameter used to create your output text because this method uses recursion. This function uses the VisualTreeHelper class, which is a static WPF class available for working with the Visual tree.

> We stated that all elements ultimately derive from Visual, and this is true for typical applications. 3D elements, however, derive from Visual3D. Visual tree nodes derive from either the Visual or Visual3D WPF classes. You're not using 3D here, so you can get away with using a parameter of type Visual.

Now you need to create a method to print your logical tree.

```
public void PrintLogicalTree(int indent, ref string str, Object obj)
{
  if (obj is FrameworkElement)
  {
    FrameworkElement element = (FrameworkElement)obj;

    string space = "";
    for (int count = 0; count < indent; count++)
    {
      space += " ";
    }
    str += space + element.GetType().ToString() + Environment.NewLine;

    IEnumerable children = LogicalTreeHelper.GetChildren(element);
    foreach (Object child in children)
    {
      indent++;
      PrintLogicalTree(indent, ref str, child);
    }
  }
}
```

The PrintLogicalTree method is very similar to the PrintVisualTree method. What's different here is that you are using the LogicalTreeHelper class. This is a static class that provides methods for working with the logical tree. Note that the LogicalTreeClass also provides a GetChildren method, as opposed to the VisualTreeHelper class, which provides a GetChildrenCount method. This is why you can use IEnumerable to enumerate the collection.

Finally, you need to add your print button handler:

```
private void buttonPrint_Click(Object sender, RoutedEventArgs e)
{
  string lt = "";
  PrintLogicalTree(0, ref lt, this.button1);
  this.textbox2.Text = lt;

  string vt = "";
  PrintVisualTree(0, ref vt, this.button1);
  this.textbox1.Text = vt;
}
```

Here you simply call the methods you've defined, and pass the output to the appropriate TextBox element on your form. You are passing button1 to your methods as the element to enumerate. You can change this to be any element you like.

Press F5 to run the application. Figure 11-8 illustrates the results.

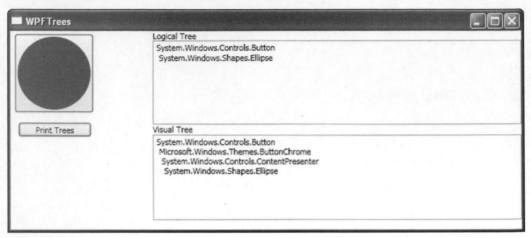

Figure 11-8

When you press the Print Trees button, our application enumerates the logical and visual trees and displays them. What is being enumerated is the Button, which contains an Ellipse as its content. As you can see, the logical tree displays only the Button and the Ellipse, but the visual tree shows two additional items, the ButtonChrome and ContentPresenter. These are graphical objects the visual system needs to know about in order to render the Button control.

UIElement

The UIElement class derives from Visual and marks the beginning of functionality that supports user interaction in WPF elements. In terms of elements, Visual represents a simple, non-interactive graphic. UIElement extends Visual by adding interactivity, such as, layout, input, focus, and events to an element. UIElement provides the definition for major interactive subsystems in WPF.

The layout system, covered earlier in this book, manages the size and position of an element through a two-step process of Measure (requesting desired size from child elements) and Arrange (telling an element what size it can be and where it should be located). UIElement provides two primary methods used in the WPF layout system, Measure and Arrange, and as such is the base class for elements that participate in the WPF layout system such as Panel. The final implementation of layout is defined by classes that derive from UIElement, such as FrameworkElement.

UIElement implements the IInputElement interface. The IInputElement interface defines the common events, properties, and methods for basic input processing in WPF. UIElement's implementation of the IInputElement interface is how UIElement provides support for input, events, and the WPF event routing subsystem. In a nutshell, UIElement knows how to respond to keyboard and mouse input and how to raise events.

UIElement also adds an OnRender method, which provides a DrawingContext for drawing text and graphics. When you want to perform custom drawing, UIElement provides OnRender, which you can use to draw to a specific rectangular region on the screen.

UIElement is an extremely functional class. We've only scraped the surface here and discussed some of the primary functionality provided. Understanding this class is important when developing WPF applications. For instance, in order to know why an element is positioned a certain way requires that you understand the layout system and UIElement's place in that system.

FrameworkElement

All the classes defined until now are part of the presentation core. Presentation framework is built on top of presentation core and defines a class called FrameworkElement, which derives from UIElement. The WPF presentation framework really just wraps and extends the presentation core. Any framework can implement a "FrameworkElement" class that derives from UIElement and get all of the functionality it provides. The WPF presentation framework is one such element implementation.

All elements in WPF derive, directly or indirectly, from FrameworkElement, which in turn derives from UIElement. FrameworkElement extends UIElement by adding the following characteristics: extended layout, styles, and data binding.

FrameworkElement extends the layout functionality provided by UIElement. Methods defined as in UIElement such as Measure, MeasureBase, Arrange, and ArrangeBase, are extended and implemented in FrameworkElement in order to specify WPF framework–specific features. FrameworkElement adds layout properties, such as Min/Max Width, Min/Max Height, Width, Height, AcutalWidth, ActualHeight, Margin, HorizontalAlignment, and VerticalAlignment to further control element layout.

FrameworkElement provides support for data binding. FrameworkElement offers the DataContext property, which provides a way in which you can define a data source for binding purposes. When the DataContext property is set on an element, all children of the element also inherit the data context. This provides for greater flexibility at design time.

FrameworkElement also provides a Resources property, which returns the associated resource dictionary. Resources are typically defined at the Window or Page level, but can also be defined at the element level, making the resource dictionary easy to find and access or bind to from an individual element.

Control

FrameworkElement provides all the functionality needed to build an element that fits neatly into the WPF programming model, such as layout, input, and event support. FrameworkElement's base classes provide support for drawing, thread affinity, and the WPF property system. WPF provides a control library that consists of the controls you would expect to find in a programming API, such as Button, TextBox, ListBox, and many more. Control provides the base class for all these controls.

Control derives from and extends FrameworkElement by adding support for additional features, such as context menus, tooltips, and control templates, and by providing additional properties such as Background and Foreground. Using the Control base class, you can define custom controls, should you need them.

Controls in WPF are referred to as *lookless*, meaning they provide behavior separate from appearance. The Control base class allows you to define behavior specific to a particular control. Button, for example, provides behavior through its Click event: A button is a clickable control.

A control's default appearance is defined in a Control Template and a developer should be free to supply his own template, should he want to change the default look-and-feel. For example, a Button provides a default Control Template for its appearance, which is a Rectangle with a Border. You can apply your own Control Template, which might have an Ellipse and no Border, to change the button control's appearance, but its behavior remains unchanged.

The following example illustrates the separation of a control's behavior from its appearance. Create a new WPF application, and modify the default window's XAML as follows:

```
<Window x:Class="ControlTemplate.Window1"
  xmlns="http://schemas.microsoft.com/winfx/2006/xaml/presentation"
  xmlns:x="http://schemas.microsoft.com/winfx/2006/xaml"
  Title="ControlTemplate" Height="300" Width="300"
  >
  <Window.Resources>
    <ControlTemplate x:Key="customizeButton" TargetType="{x:Type Button}">
      <Grid>
        <Ellipse Width="100" Height="100" Fill="Green"
          Stroke="Red" StrokeThickness="2"/>
        <ContentPresenter VerticalAlignment="Center"
          HorizontalAlignment="Center"></ContentPresenter>
      </Grid>
    </ControlTemplate>
  </Window.Resources>
  <Grid HorizontalAlignment="Center" VerticalAlignment="Center">
    <Button Name="button1" Template="{StaticResource customizeButton}"
      Foreground="White" Click="button1_Click">Press Me!</Button>
  </Grid>
</Window>
```

In the preceding XAML, we have simply created a ControlTemplate, set its TargetType to Button, and defined a new appearance in the form of an Ellipse with a green Fill and red Stroke. We've added a ContentPresenter so that our modified button will be able to participate in the WPF content model. We have also set our button's Template property to use our new Control Template. Finally, we define a Click event for our button, to demonstrate that although we've changed the button's appearance, the behavior remains unchanged.

Switch to the code-behind and add the following event handler.

```
private void button1_Click(object sender, RoutedEventArgs e)
{
  MessageBox.Show("Hello WPF!");
}
```

Press F5 to run the application. Clicking the button prompts a MessageBox to appear. You have effectively changed the appearance of the built-in WPF Button control using a Control Template. What's important here, is that your behavior did not change, illustrating the separation of a control's appearance from its behavior.

Probably the most functional control in the WPF framework is Window itself. Window derives from ContentControl, which derives from Control. Window represents a top-level control container and serves as the primary interface between a user and an application. We don't need to dive into the details of `Window` because we should all be intimately familiar with it. What's interesting to note is that in WPF it is, in essence, simply a control.

A Deeper Look at XAML

XAML is an XML-based language used to declare WPF objects, properties, and event handlers using XML elements and attributes. Objects and properties defined in XAML map directly to WPF objects and properties. You have seen many examples thus far of using XAML in your WPF applications. It is important to note that XAML is its own language and, as such, can be run independently of the WPF runtime. Standalone XAML is referred to as *loose XAML*. The PresentationHost.exe is responsible for hosting standalone XAML and essentially creates a Page object as the root container for XAML elements. You cannot use Window as a root object for standalone XAML. You can create a standalone XAML file and run it right in Internet Explorer. We mention "loose" XAML just to enforce the point that XAML is its own entity. What we are interested in here is how WPF utilizes XAML. When XAML is used with WPF, it allows you to define your UI in a declarative manner, separate from your procedural code.

In this section, you take a deeper look at XAML and how XAML integrates with WPF applications. You will look at the following:

- ❑ XAML under the hood
- ❑ Manipulating XAML on-the-fly
- ❑ Deconstruction Window1.xaml
- ❑ XAML markup extensions
- ❑ XAML and custom types

XAML Under the Hood

Raw XAML files are simply XML files that define an element hierarchy. In the WPF model, what you're typically doing is defining your UI objects and setting object properties, and you're doing this declaratively rather than programmatically. In Windows Forms, your objects and event handlers were defined in your Forms `InitializeComponent` method. The following shows a button declaration in a Windows Forms application:

```
private System.Windows.Forms.Button button1;
this.button1 = new System.Windows.Forms.Button();
this.button1.Location = new System.Drawing.Point(15, 35);
this.button1.Name = "button1";
this.button1.Size = new System.Drawing.Size(75, 23);
this.button1.TabIndex = 1;
this.button1.Text = "Press Me!";
this.button1.UseVisualStyleBackColor = true;
this.button1.Click += new System.EventHandler(this.button1_Click);
```

Because the button is defined in the Windows Forms class (partial class, actually), you have access to the button in your code-behind. A button field is created, properties populated, and events wired to handlers.

Here is the markup for the same button defined in XAML:

```
<Button Name="button1" Click="button1_Click">Press Me!</Button>
```

This declares the same button object, property values, and event handler in XAML, but your code-behind doesn't know it exists yet. How is it then that when you compile a WPF application, you are able to access and utilize the elements from your code-behind? To understand the answer to this question, you need to look at what happens to your XAML files when you compile your WPF application.

> **You do not have to compile XAML during the build process, but there are compelling reasons to do so. Alternatively, you can load your XAML files through code (more on this later), but you will incur a performance hit for this. Loading XAML at runtime involves parsing the XAML file, mapping CLR types, and validating properties, all of which affect performance at runtime.**

Typically, in your WPF applications, you will want to compile your XAML with your application code. When you compile, you are able to manipulate the XAML elements much easier than if you load your XAML dynamically.

WPF uses a markup compiler to process XAML code. When you compile your XAML files, the markup compiler performs a number of steps for you, including parsing and code generation, the output of which are some new files placed in your application's Obj\Release folder. The markup compiler performs the following steps:

❑ The markup compiler parses your XAML file.

❑ The markup compiler creates a binary representation of our object hierarchy (called BAML) and saves it with the file extension .baml.

❑ The markup compiler generates a language-specific code file and saves it with a file extension of .g.cs or .g.vb, depending on the language specified (g stands for "generated").

Figure 11-9 illustrates the relationship of XAML to the .NET objects and how you can move between the two dynamically or through compilation.

The BAML file created by the markup compiler is a binary representation of your XAML file. The BAML file is stored as an application resource in your assembly. The obvious reason for converting a text-based XAML file to binary is performance. BAML has already been parsed and is readily consumable by your application.

The partial class created by the markup compiler is a CodeDom representation of the XAML file. This file provides definitions similar to those created for you in Windows Forms applications, such as fields and names representing your objects. This file is responsible for loading your BAML resource for your application, resulting in a visual tree readily available to you in your code-behind. This file also hooks up event handlers.

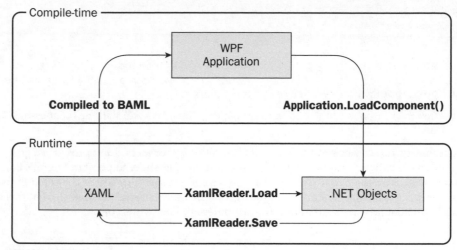

Figure 11-9

Let's look at an example:

1. Create a new WPF application and name it **HelloXAML**.

2. In the Window1 page, add the following XAML markup. You are declaring a window as a top-level container and adding to it a `StackPanel`, `TextBlock`, and `Button`. You are also declaring a name and an event for your button. This will enable you to see how XAML connects your UI elements to your C#.

```
<Window x:Class="HelloXAML.Window1"
  xmlns="http://schemas.microsoft.com/winfx/2006/xaml/presentation"
  xmlns:x="http://schemas.microsoft.com/winfx/2006/xaml"
  Title="Hello XAML" Height="100" Width="200"
  >
  <StackPanel Name="stackpanel1">
    <TextBlock>Welcome Message</TextBlock>
    <Button Name="button1" Click="button1_Click">Click Me!</Button>
  </StackPanel>
</Window>
```

3. Now open the Window1.xaml.cs class and add an event handler for your button.

```
public partial class Window1 : System.Windows.Window
{

  public Window1()
  {
    InitializeComponent();
  }

  private void button1_Click(object sender, RoutedEventArgs e)
```

```
    {
        MessageBox.Show("Hello XAML!");
    }

}
```

4. Run the application, and you see your simple form.

5. Click the button, and the button event handler fires, and you will see the message "Hello XAML!"

Although this is probably one of the simplest applications you can build, it provides a good example for looking at how XAML is compiled with your application. One thing to point out here is that inside the Window1 constructor is a call to the InitializeComponent method, which is located in the Window1.g.cs file that was generated for you at compile time. Let's take a look at what this method does for you. (For readability, we've removed the attributes applied by the compiler.)

```
public partial class Window1 : System.Windows.Window,
System.Windows.Markup.IComponentConnector
{

    internal System.Windows.Controls.StackPanel stackpanel1;
    internal System.Windows.Controls.Button button1;

    private bool _contentLoaded;

    public void InitializeComponent()
    {

        if (_contentLoaded)
        {
            return;
        }

        _contentLoaded = true;

        System.Uri resourceLocater = new
            System.Uri("/HelloXAML;component/window1.xaml", System.UriKind.Relative);

        System.Windows.Application.LoadComponent(this, resourceLocater);
    }

    void Connect(int connectionId, object target)
    {
        switch (connectionId)
        {
            case 1:
                this.stackpanel1 = ((System.Windows.Controls.StackPanel)(target));
                return;

            case 2:
                this.button1 = ((System.Windows.Controls.Button)(target));

                #line 9 "..\..\Window1.xaml"
```

```
      this.button1.Click += new System.Windows.RoutedEventHandler(this.button1_Click);

      #line default

      #line hidden

    return;
  }
    this._contentLoaded = true;
}
}
```

```
public partial class Window1 : System.Windows.Window,
System.Windows.Markup.IComponentConnector
```

The Window1.g.cs file is located in your application's Obj\Release or Obj\Debug folder depending on your compiler settings. The first thing to notice is that the partial class generated for you implements the IComponentConnector interface. This interface provides two methods: InitializeComponent and Connect. These methods essentially load and connect your XAML element tree to your code.

```
internal System.Windows.Controls.StackPanel stackpanel1;
internal System.Windows.Controls.Button button1;
```

Next, you see that fields have been defined for your XAML elements. Fields are only defined for elements that declare a Name attribute. The name you specify in your element is the name you use to reference the .NET object created for you in your code-behind. In the XAML declaration file, you declared names for the StackPanel and Button but not for TextBlock, and this is reflected here. You will not have access to the TextBlock element in your C# code because you did not define a name. These fields are what you will now use in your C# code to reference your controls.

```
public void InitializeComponent()
{
  if (_contentLoaded)
  {
    return;
  }
  _contentLoaded = true;

  System.Uri resourceLocater = new
     System.Uri("/HelloXAML;component/window1.xaml", System.UriKind.Relative);

  System.Windows.Application.LoadComponent(this, resourceLocater);
}
```

The InitializeComponent method that is called from the constructor in your Window class is defined here. Inside the InitializeComponent method, you see a call to the LoadComponent method of the Application object. Essentially, this method loads your XAML, which is now BAML stored as a resource embedded in your application, into our application object. Once loaded, LoadComponent converts it to an element tree and sets the target object to the root element, in this case Window1. Now you have access to your element tree from C#.

```
void Connect(int connectionId, object target)
{
```

```
    switch (connectionId)
    {
      case 1:
        this.stackpanel1 = ((System.Windows.Controls.StackPanel)(target));
        return;

      case 2:
        this.button1 = ((System.Windows.Controls.Button)(target));

        #line 9 "..\..\Window1.xaml"
    this.button1.Click += new System.Windows.RoutedEventHandler(this.button1_Click);

        #line default
        #line hidden
      return;
    }
      this._contentLoaded = true;
  }
```

The `Connect` method attaches events and element names to compiled content. In your XAML declaration file, you declared a `Click` event on your button. This event gets wired up here.

That is all there is to it. You can now code your application and utilize the elements defined in your XAML file through your C# code. The magic really happens in the Window1.g.cs file that the compiler generates for you.

Manipulating XAML On-the-Fly

As stated earlier, you do not have to compile XAML in order to load and access its element tree. Alternatively, you can parse it dynamically at runtime. We covered the benefits of compiling your XAML with your application, but in some situations you may prefer not to compile. For instance, you might want to parse XAML elements from an external source, such as from a file, or from a web service. While you will not get the benefit of a precompiled element tree or a generated code file, you can manipulate an application's visual tree and inject your external XAML elements dynamically.

You can use the `XAMLReader.Load` method to parse your source XAML into a WPF object tree. In the following example, you add a button, defined as an XAML string, to your window dynamically and have your button handle a `Click` event and show a `MessageBox`.

Let's create a new WPF project and give this a try.

1. Open Visual Studio and create a new WPF application named **DynamicXAML**.

2. Double-click the Window1.xaml file, and in the designer, modify the XAML window definition as follows:

```
<Window x:Class="DynamicXAML.Window1"
  xmlns="http://schemas.microsoft.com/winfx/2006/xaml/presentation"
  xmlns:x="http://schemas.microsoft.com/winfx/2006/xaml"
  Title="DynamicXAML" Height="300" Width="300"
  >
    <Grid Name="grid1" HorizontalAlignment="Center" VerticalAlignment="Center"/>
</Window>
```

You're simply giving your Grid a name so that you'll be able to access it from your code-behind, and declaring some alignment properties so your dynamic XAML elements can more easily be displayed.

3. Open the code-behind for your new window and add the following:

```csharp
using System.Windows;
using System.Windows.Controls;
using System.Windows.Media;
using System.Windows.Markup;
using System.Xml;
using System.IO;

namespace DynamicXAML
{

  public partial class Window1 : System.Windows.Window
  {

    public Window1()
    {

      InitializeComponent();

      StringReader sr = new StringReader(@"<Button
        xmlns='http://schemas.microsoft.com/winfx/2006/xaml/presentation'
        Foreground='BurlyWood' FontSize='20pt'>Click Me!</Button>");

      XmlReader reader = XmlReader.Create(sr);

      Button dynamicButton = (Button)XamlReader.Load(reader);

      this.grid1.Children.Add(dynamicButton);

      dynamicButton.Click += button1_Click;

    }

    private void button1_Click(object sender, RoutedEventArgs e)
    {
      MessageBox.Show("Dynamic Button Loaded From XAML String");
    }

  }
}
```

You initialize a StringReader with your button XAML string. There are two things to notice about your XAML. First, notice the use of the XAML namespace attribute, which is required to map the Button to a WPF Button type. Second, notice that no Click event is defined. Next you initialize an XMLReader, passing in your StringReader object. You then call the XamlReader.Load method, passing it your XmlReader object. This parses your XAML and returns the object tree. In this example, you know this object is a Button, so you can cast the results to type Button and then add the button to your window's StackPanel. Finally, you hook up the event handler for your button, which will ultimately show the MessageBox to the user.

Now, run the application. You'll see your window, which was nothing more than an empty `StackPanel` initially, now has a button, and clicking the button launches a `MessageBox` with the message "Dynamic Button Event Fired." Although the example is simple, it illustrates that you can, in fact, load XAML on-the-fly and hook it into your element tree dynamically.

In the previous example, you loaded your XAML based on a string, but this could have been any source that returns a well-formed XAML document. Create a XAML document and add the following markup:

```
<Button xmlns='http://schemas.microsoft.com/winfx/2006/xaml/presentation'
    Foreground='BurlyWood' FontSize='20pt'>
      Click Me!
</Button>
```

Changing the code as follows would load the button from an external file resource:

```
using System.Windows;
using System.Windows.Controls;
using System.Windows.Media;
using System.Windows.Markup;
using System.Xml;
using System.IO;

namespace DynamicXAML
{

  public partial class Window1 : System.Windows.Window
  {

    public Window1()
    {

      InitializeComponent();


      StreamReader sr = new StreamReader(@"C:\XamlButton.xaml");
      XmlReader reader = XmlReader.Create(sr);
      Button dynamicButton = (Button)XamlReader.Load(reader);

      this.grid1.Children.Add(dynamicButton);

      dynamicButton.Click += button1_Click;

    }

    private void button1_Click(object sender, RoutedEventArgs e)
    {
      MessageBox.Show("Dynamic Button Loaded From XAML File");
    }

  }
}
```

Because your XAML file is really just XML in structure, you simply load your external file into an XMLDocument object and pass the XMLDocument's OuterXML string to the StringReader. The rest of the code is the same as the previous example and yields the same results.

The XamlReader class has a complementary XamlWriter class you can use to create XAML from an object hierarchy. In the following example, you create a button in code and serialize it into XAML. Using the same XAML from the previous examples, modify the code-behind, as follows:

```
using System.Windows;
using System.Windows.Controls;
using System.Windows.Media;
using System.Windows.Markup;
using System.Xml;
using System.IO;

namespace DynamicXAML
{

  public partial class Window1 : System.Windows.Window
  {

    private string serializedButton = "";

    public Window1()
    {

      InitializeComponent();

      // Programmatically create the button
      Button button1 = new Button();
      button1.Height = 50;
      button1.Width = 100;
      button1.Background = Brushes.AliceBlue;
      button1.Content = "Click Me";
      button1.Click += button1_Click;
      this.grid1.Children.Add(button1);

      // Serialize the button and write for display
      serializedButton = XamlWriter.Save(button1);

    }

    private void button1_Click(object sender, RoutedEventArgs e)
    {
      MessageBox.Show(serializedButton);
    }

  }
}
```

Here you create a button programmatically and add it to your Windows Grid dynamically. You also wire up the event to show your MessageBox. You call XamlWriter.Save, pass in a reference to your button, and write the XAML out to the console. When you run the example, you'll see the following result in the console:

```
<Button Height="50" Width="100" Background="#FFF0F8FF"
xmlns="http://schemas.microsoft.com/winfx/2006/xaml/presentation">Click Me</Button>
```

As expected, you get back your button XAML element. What you do not see is a `Click` attribute for your event handler. This is by design. You define your event handler, but the code-behind is not visible to the serializer. The serializer has no way to preserve the event handler and, therefore, does not serialize the event attribute or its value.

Deconstructing Window1.xaml

Now that you have looked at how WPF uses XAML to create UI for your applications, let's examine the syntax in more detail. The WPF Window template in Visual Studio gives you the following XAML by default:

```
<Window
    x:Class="MyWPFApp.Window1"
    xmlns="http://schemas.microsoft.com/winfx/2006/xaml/presentation"
    xmlns:x="http://schemas.microsoft.com/winfx/2006/xaml"
    Title="DeeperXAML" Height="300" Width="300"
    >
    <Grid></Grid>
</Window>
```

Let's take a look at each element and attribute in detail.

XAML Root Element

A well-formed XML document has a single root element, and XAML is no different. The root element is the first element that appears in the file.

```
<Window
    x:Class="MyWPFApp.Window1"
    xmlns="http://schemas.microsoft.com/winfx/2006/xaml/presentation"
    xmlns:x="http://schemas.microsoft.com/winfx/2006/xaml"
    Title="DeeperXAML" Height="300" Width="300"
    >
    <Grid></Grid>
</Window>
```

By default, when you create a new XAML page, the Visual Studio template defines Window as the XAML root. The root element does not have to be Window: it can be any type of container or application model element, such as `Panel`, `DockPanel`, or `Page`.

Although not shown here, comments, whitespace, and processing instructions (PI) are allowed before the root element.

x:Class

You probably want to write code in addition to declaratively defining your UI. In order to write code, and make your XAML more than just a "loose" XAML document, you need to associate your Root Element with your application. When your WPF application is compiled, a `CodeDom` model of your XAML declaration is generated as part of your Window1 class. You must tell the compiler the class to which your XAML belongs.

```
<Window
    x:Class="MyWPFApp.Window1"
    xmlns="http://schemas.microsoft.com/winfx/2006/xaml/presentation"
    xmlns:x="http://schemas.microsoft.com/winfx/2006/xaml"
    Title="DeeperXAML" Height="300" Width="300"
    >
    <Grid></Grid>
</Window>
```

In order to associate your XAML with code, you need to add an `x:Class` attribute. The `x:Class` attribute links the XAML file with a procedural code file, the code-behind file. This attribute must be applied to a top-level `Page`, `Window`, or `Application` object. The `x:Class` attribute essentially tells the compiler to link the root element of your XAML file, in this case Window, to the `Window1` class defined in your application in the namespace `MyWPFApp`. As you saw earlier, when compiled, the markup compiler generates a partial class code file for you that will connect your XAML with your procedural code. The value of the `x:Class` attribute can be any string that identifies the name of a class in your application.

XAML Namespaces

Namespaces are logical containers that group similar or related objects. You should already be familiar with the namespace concept from the .NET Framework. The .NET Framework uses namespaces to uniquely identify and group a set of types. In XML, a namespace is a way to uniquely identify and group a set of elements. XAML maps each element to its corresponding type in the .NET Framework and, as such, identifies the types by the specified namespace.

```
<Window
    x:Class="MyWPFApp.Window1"
    xmlns="http://schemas.microsoft.com/winfx/2006/xaml/presentation"
    xmlns:x="http://schemas.microsoft.com/winfx/2006/xaml"
    Title="DeeperXAML" Height="300" Width="300"
    >
    <Grid></Grid>
</Window>
```

The first namespace declaration, considered the default namespace because no colon follows the "xmlns," defines types belonging to WPF. If no other namespace were to be specified, then all elements in the file would be considered WPF elements. The second namespace declaration defines XAML-specific elements, such as `x:Class`. It is not mandatory that you use the x prefix (you can use any prefix you like). It has become standard practice, however, to use the x prefix for XAML-specific elements.

A prefix is a name you give to a namespace that you can use throughout your XAML file to indicate an element or attribute belongs to a specific namespace. The XAML compiler will use this for locating the appropriate .NET type for mapping.

XAML Attributes and CLR Properties

You can set object properties by using XAML attributes in your elements. XAML attributes map to CLR properties.

```
<Window
    x:Class="MyWPFApp.Window1"
    xmlns="http://schemas.microsoft.com/winfx/2006/xaml/presentation"
    xmlns:x="http://schemas.microsoft.com/winfx/2006/xaml"
    Title="DeeperXAML" Height="300" Width="300"
    >
    <Grid></Grid>
</Window>
```

This is equivalent to the following procedural code:

```
Window1.Title = "DeeperXAML";
Window1.Height = 300;
Window1.Width = 300;
```

In this example, `Title`, `Height`, and `Width` are properties of the .NET `Window` object, represented by the `Window` element.

Child Elements

The WPF composition model defines objects as having other objects. XAML elements represent a hierarchical tree of elements that form the UI because XAML elements map to CLR objects. In the XAML file you get by default, a single child element is defined, `Grid`.

```
<Window
    x:Class="MyWPFApp.Window1"
    xmlns="http://schemas.microsoft.com/winfx/2006/xaml/presentation"
    xmlns:x="http://schemas.microsoft.com/winfx/2006/xaml"
    Title="DeeperXAML" Height="300" Width="300"
    >
    <Grid></Grid>
</Window>
```

This is equivalent to the following procedural code:

```
Grid grid = new Grid;
Window1.AddChild(grid);
```

`Grid` is a child object of `Window`. `Window` is special in that it may contain only one object. `Grid`, on the other hand, may contain unlimited children.

XAML Attributes

When you create an object in C# using the `new` keyword, you get an instance with all properties initialized to their default values. XAML is no different. Remember that XAML is a declarative language used to define WPF objects and object properties. The markup compiler creates an instance of a WPF object at compile time for each element in your XAML element tree. Each instance will have default property values unless you set otherwise. In the deconstruction of the default Window1 XAML file, you saw examples of basic property setting through XML attributes, such as `Title`, `Height`, and `Width` of `Window`.

```xml
<Window
    x:Class="MyWPFApp.Window1"
    xmlns="http://schemas.microsoft.com/winfx/2006/xaml/presentation"
    xmlns:x="http://schemas.microsoft.com/winfx/2006/xaml"
    Title="DeeperXAML" Height="300" Width="300"
    >
```

Attributes work well for simple properties. When the preceding `Window` element is parsed, the .NET runtime assigns the properties to the `Window` instance. To set the `Height` and `Width` properties, the .NET runtime will use a `TypeConverter` to cast the properties from strings to their correct types, which in the case of the Window class is `Double`. Type converters are not new to WPF: They have been around since .NET 1.0.

Often, a single text value will not suffice for setting an object's property value. For example, setting the `Background` property of a `Button` to a `GradientFill` requires a `LinearGradientObject`, which has its own set of properties. The following illustrates how you can accomplish setting a complex property:

```xml
<Button Foreground="White" FontWeight="Bold" FontSize="20pt">
  <Button.Background>
    <LinearGradientBrush>
      <GradientStop Color="Black" Offset="0"/>
      <GradientStop Color="Gray" Offset="0.5"/>
      <GradientStop Color="Black" Offset="1"/>
    </LinearGradientBrush>
  </Button.Background>
  Press Me!
</Button>
```

XAML provides property-element syntax as a way to set complex properties. Property-element syntax is expressed as `Object-Name.PropertyName`. Using property-element syntax, you can set properties whose type may be an object and, therefore, cannot be specified by a string.

XAML Markup Extensions

You have already seen and used markup extensions in this book, such as those used for applying resources and data binding. Markup extensions provide a mechanism through which property values can be set to objects, the value of which is determined at compile-time or runtime. A markup extension is implemented as a class that derives from `MarkupExtension`.

Markup extension syntax can be identified in XAML attributes by curly braces such as:

```xml
<Button Name="button1" Style="{StaticResource ButtonStyle}">
Press Me
</Button>
```

The first token immediately following the opening curly brace, in this case `StaticResource`, identifies the type of markup extension being used. The identifier `StaticResource` maps to the `StaticResourceExtension` class, which derives from `MarkupExtension`. This class will find the resource specified by searching the window's resource collection for the key `ButtonStyle`. In essence, it does the following:

```
Style style = (Style)this.FindResource("ButtonStyle");
this.button1.Style = style;
```

There would not be a way to declare the preceding procedural code in XAML were it not for markup extensions. This example also identifies another service markup extensions provide, which is the ability to determine a property value at compile time.

You can define custom markup extensions by simply creating a class that derives from `MarkupExtension` and implementing the `ProvideValue` method.

XAML and Custom Types

XAML allows you to use custom types you define in addition to the common types supplied by WPF. All you need to do is declare the namespace and assembly in your XAML, and you are ready to go. At the time of this writing there is one drawback, which is that you cannot use a type declared locally in your application. To work around this issue, simply create a separate class library project to hold your custom types. Probably the best way to explore using custom types in XAML is to jump right in with an example.

First, let's create a custom element. Create a new WPF class library project in Visual Studio and name it **MyCustomElements**. Add references to PresentationCore.dll and WindowsBase.dll. Then add the following class definition to your project:

```
using System;
using System.Collections.Generic;
using System.Text;

using System.Windows;
using System.Windows.Media;

namespace MyCustomElements
{
  public class MyCustomType : UIElement
  {
    protected override void OnRender(DrawingContext drawingContext)
    {

      Pen stroke = new Pen(Brushes.Black, 0.5);

      stroke.DashStyle = DashStyles.Dot;

      drawingContext.DrawRectangle(Brushes.Green, stroke,
        new Rect(14, 14, 200, 40));

      drawingContext.DrawEllipse(Brushes.Red, stroke,
        new Point(25, 25), 20, 20);

    }
  }
}
```

For this example, you simply define a class that derives from UIElement in order to get a DrawingContext so you can display something visual. This gives you a way to know that your sample is working.

Now you need to create a program to host your custom element. Create a new WPF application in Visual Studio and name it whatever you like. Add a reference in the new project to the MyCustomElements library you just built. In order to use your custom type in your XAML, simply add the MyCustomElements clr-namespace and assembly name to your XAML definition as follows:

```
<Window x:Class="UsingCustsomTypes.Window1"
  xmlns="http://schemas.microsoft.com/winfx/2006/xaml/presentation"
  xmlns:x="http://schemas.microsoft.com/winfx/2006/xaml"
  xmlns:local="clr-namespace:MyCustomElements;assembly=MyCustomElements"
  Title="UsingCustomTypes" Height="300" Width="300"
  >
  <DockPanel>
    <local:MyCustomType DockPanel.Dock="Left"/>
  </DockPanel>
</Window>
```

The key to using our own custom types is adding the xmlns declaration, which lets the XAML parser know where to find the CLR class(es) you've defined so it can map the XAML element <local:MyCustomType> from your custom library into the project.

Press F5 and you will see the shapes shown in Figure 11-10.

Figure 11-10

Adding custom types to your applications is easy. Obviously, you would not have a reason to map in this particular custom type because you can just define your Ellipse and Rectangle directly in XAML as content of a parent control. The key takeaway from this example is that mapping custom types for use in your XAML simply requires declaring the CLR namespace and assembly name that contains your custom type.

WPF Multithreading

Applications often have to perform long-running tasks. In a typical application, task processing happens synchronously, one task at a time. When one task completes, the next begins execution, and this continues in a sequential fashion. So, what happens to the UI while waiting for a long-running task to finish? Often the UI becomes unresponsive and may even freeze temporarily until a long-running task completes. This is referred to as *blocking* on a thread. For instance, executing a large batch process against a database in response to user interaction could render an application unresponsive until the database operation completes. Therefore, thread execution is essentially blocked until the process completes. An unresponsive application usually means an unhappy user. Conversely, an unhappy user will often be very responsive, which leads to an even unhappier developer.

When an application has to perform a long-running task, one solution to the problem of synchronous thread blocking is to create a separate background thread and allow it to run asynchronously. Running threads in parallel frees the application to accept more input from the user and start other tasks. The background thread can then alert the application when it completes, allowing the application to respond as appropriate—a process known as *thread synchronization*. Multithreading has been around for quite a while and works the same in WPF as it did in Windows Forms. Only the implementation details and underlying support are different, and that's what we will discuss in this section.

In this section, we will look at ways to schedule long-running processes in your WPF applications so that they run asynchronously rather than synchronously in order to avoid thread blocking and create a responsive UI. We'll also look at how you can synchronize multiple threads so that your UI can get updated when an asynchronous process returns. We will look at the following:

- ❑ Single-threaded application model
- ❑ Thread affinity and `DispatcherObject`
- ❑ WPF dispatcher
- ❑ Synchronous threading
- ❑ Asynchronous threading
- ❑ Background Worker object

Single-Threaded Application Model

WPF objects belong to the thread on which they are created and cannot be accessed by any other thread directly. When an object is tied to a single thread, it is said to be a single-threaded object and is said to exhibit thread affinity. Many objects in WPF exhibit thread affinity. For developers, this means you cannot directly modify UI objects from any thread other than the thread on which you create them. For example, a background thread cannot update the contents of a `TextBox` control that was created on an application's main UI thread. Of course, WPF supports a model for accomplishing this, but it is well defined to ensure thread safety.

In COM development, this threading model is called the Single Threaded Apartment (STA) model. Windows Forms also uses this same model. What is different about the WPF implementation is the extent to which this model is enforced and the way it is enforced through the use of the `DispatcherObject`.

You have probably noticed that in both WPF and Windows Forms applications the `Main()` application entry point is decorated with a `[STAThread]` attribute.

```
[STAThread]
static void Main()
{
}
```

The `[STAThread]` attribute defines the application as using a single-threaded apartment model. More specifically, it changes the state of the application thread to be single-threaded.

Thread Affinity and DispatcherObject

It is important to restate that an object with thread affinity can be accessed only on the thread that created it. It is the theme, if you will, of the WPF threading model. It is a simple concept, but how is this enforced by WPF?

WPF objects that participate in the threading model derive, directly or indirectly, from `DispatcherObject`. This includes objects such as `Application`, `Visual`, and `DependencyObject`. At first glance, this may seem like a small list, but we're talking about important base classes here, from which most framework classes derive. For instance, because `Visual` ultimately derives from `DispatcherObject`, then all UI elements have thread affinity as well. The rule of thumb is that when objects derive from `DispatcherObject`, they become objects that exhibit thread affinity.

`DispatcherObject` enforces thread affinity and, therefore, thread safety among WPF objects. WPF uses a `Dispatcher` object to route messages from Windows to your application. We talk about `Dispatcher` in a moment, but the reason we mention it here is to note that one and only one dispatcher is created for the UI thread. Only the thread that created the dispatcher may access a dispatcher object. Messages from Windows, such as input generated on other threads, can only access your application's UI thread through the dispatcher message loop. This enforces the thread affinity model.

`DispatcherObject` offers two methods you can use to determine if your object is on the correct thread: `VerifyAccess` and `CheckAccess`. Both methods basically return a `Boolean` value indicating whether you are on the correct thread. The following code snippet shows how you might use `VerifyAccess` in a program to ensure an element has access to the current UI thread:

```
try
{

  this.button1.VerifyAccess();

  MessageBox.Show("The Button Has Access");

  this.button1.Content = "I Belong";

}
catch (InvalidOperationException e)
{
  // Button does not have direct access, need to update through Dispatcher
}
```

One thing to notice is that the `VerifyAccess` method does not return a value. It will, however, throw an `InvalidOperationException` if access is denied. If access is denied, you need to use the dispatcher of the thread to which the target object belongs to perform an action on the target object. We look at an example of this shortly.

WPF Dispatcher

Applications need a mechanism to respond to user and system input: for example, mouse clicks, key presses, and system events. In Win32, this mechanism is called a message loop and it's an integral component of every Windows application. The message loop runs in the background of a Win32 application and routes messages to the application from Windows. For instance, when a mouse button is clicked, Windows sends a message to the message loop indicating that the mouse button was indeed clicked, and also, which mouse button was clicked, left or right. Windows places the messages in a prioritized queue for the window that generated the click. The message loop continually monitors this queue and dispatches messages to the application. In WPF, the message loop and queue are created and managed by the dispatcher. A dispatcher is an instance of the `Dispatcher` class. The dispatcher runs each task, one at a time, based on the task's priority level. `Dispatcher` is really a message dispatcher, hence its name.

In its simplest form, an application runs a single UI thread. One or many worker threads may be created, as well, to perform tasks in the background. In order for a worker thread to interact with the main UI thread, it must do so by passing messages to the UI thread's dispatcher. There is an important rule of thumb to understand about the dispatcher: only the thread that creates the dispatcher may access it. In other words, there is a one-to-one relationship between the dispatcher and the thread that creates it. WPF creates a dispatcher for your main UI thread so you do not have to declare one.

One thread cannot access another thread's objects directly. If a background thread does attempt to update the UI thread directly, an access violation in the form of an exception is thrown. `Dispatcher` provides the methods `Invoke` and `BeginInvoke`, which a background thread can use to schedule tasks on the UI thread and to specify delegates the dispatcher can use to modify the target object. Messages passed to the dispatcher are marked with a priority level and placed in a queue managed by the dispatcher. The dispatcher executes messages based on priority, not based on FIFO or LIFO methods. The following table details the different message priority levels in the `DispatcherPriority` enumeration.

Dispatcher Priority	Description
ApplicationIdle	Dispatcher will process when application is idle.
Background	Dispatcher will process after all other non-idle operations are complete.
ContextIdle	Dispatcher will process when the context is idle.
DataBind	Dispatcher will process at the same priority as data binding.
Inactive	Dispatcher will not process.
Input	Dispatcher will process at the same priority as input.
Invalid	Dispatcher will not process.
Loaded	Dispatcher will process when firing the Loaded event.
Normal	Dispatcher will process normally.

Dispatcher Priority	Description
Render	Dispatcher will process at the same priority as rendering.
Send	Dispatcher will process before other asynchronous operations.
SystemIdle	Dispatcher will process when the system is idle.

It is important to schedule your tasks on another thread with the correct priority. If you do not schedule correctly, the task may not be executed when expected.

Working with Single-Threaded Applications

When you perform long-running tasks synchronously on your UI thread you run the risk of your UI becoming unresponsive. When a method is called that executes a long-running process, your thread of execution waits for the method to return. This is referred to as "blocking," and occurs because you are processing in a synchronous fashion. You will explore using asynchronous multithreading to avoid blocking in the next example, but for now, let's write a simple example to illustrate how blocking affects our UI's responsiveness.

Let's create a quick example to see how blocking affects your application. Open Visual Studio and create a new project based on the WPF Windows Application template and name the project **WPFThreading**. You'll be adding a few windows to this application throughout the chapter, so rename the default Window1 to **BlockThread**. You'll use the same XAML in all of the examples in this section to illustrate the effects of your code on the UI, so you'll just display the XAML once. Refer to this XAML if you need to for examples that follow.

Modify the default window's XAML as follows:

```xaml
<Window x:Class="WPFThreading.BlockThread"
  xmlns="http://schemas.microsoft.com/winfx/2006/xaml/presentation"
  xmlns:x="http://schemas.microsoft.com/winfx/2006/xaml"
  Title="UI Thread Blocker" Height="275" Width="225"
  >
<Window.Resources>
  <Style TargetType="{x:Type Button}">
    <Setter Property="Height" Value="20" />
    <Setter Property="Background" Value="Beige"/>
    <Setter Property="Margin" Value="2" />
  </Style>
  <Style TargetType="{x:Type Label}">
    <Setter Property="FontWeight" Value="Bold" />
    <Setter Property="Margin" Value="2" />
  </Style>
  <Style TargetType="{x:Type TextBox}">
    <Setter Property="Margin" Value="2" />
  </Style>
</Window.Resources>
<Border Width="200" Height="225" BorderBrush="Black"
  BorderThickness="1" Margin="4">
```

```
        <StackPanel>

          <Label>Simulate Long-Running Process</Label>
          <Button Name="button1" Click="button1_click">Go to sleep</Button>

          <Label>Will I respond?</Label>
          <Button Name="button2" Click="button2_click">Try Me</Button>

          <Label>Output Messages</Label>
          <TextBox Name="textbox1"/>

          <Label/>

          <StackPanel Orientation="Horizontal">
            <Label>UI thread:</Label>
            <Label Name="UIThreadId"></Label>
          </StackPanel>

          <StackPanel Orientation="Horizontal">
            <Label>BG thread:</Label>
            <Label Name="BGThreadId"></Label>
          </StackPanel>

        </StackPanel>
      </Border>
  </Window>
```

You're simply defining a couple of buttons, a textbox to receive output messages, a couple of labels to display thread IDs, some additional labels, and a few styles.

Next, modify the code-behind as follows:

```
using System.Windows;

namespace WPFThreading
{

  public partial class BlockThread : System.Windows.Window
  {

    public BlockThread()
    {
      InitializeComponent();

      this.UIThreadId.Content = this.Dispatcher.Thread.ManagedThreadId;
      this.BGThreadId.Content = "N/A";
    }

    private void LongRunningProcess()
    {
      // simulate long running process
      System.Threading.Thread.Sleep(5000);
      this.textbox1.Text = "Done Sleeping...";
```

```
    }

    private void button1_click(object sender, RoutedEventArgs e)
    {
      // set up a block on this UI thread
      LongRunningProcess();
    }

    private void button2_click(object sender, RoutedEventArgs e)
    {
      this.textbox1.Text = "Hello WPF";
    }

  }
}
```

When you run the application, you are presented with two buttons. Pressing the first button labeled "Go to sleep" will put the thread to sleep for five seconds, simulating a long-running process. If you try to click the second button, labeled "Try Me," during the five-second sleep period, the UI will be unresponsive and the button event will not fire. You see how to remedy this in the next example.

Asynchronous Threading

In a previous example, you put together a window that blocked execution of your UI thread by putting it to sleep for five seconds, resulting in a UI that would not respond. You need to write some code now to handle the simulated long-running process in a manner that will keep your UI responsive. To do this, You'll process your long-running task asynchronously on a worker thread separate from your UI thread.

In order to start the thread asynchronously, you'll be using .NET delegates. If you're not familiar with delegates in .NET, delegates allow you to define the signature of a method you would like to call at runtime, without actually knowing the method you will call (of course, you must have some idea what method you will call because you have to define the signature). The event architecture in .NET makes good use of delegates. When you define an event handler, .NET is using delegates behind the scenes. For example, a button Click event in .NET expects a method with a specific signature, but you can declare the method implementation any way you wish and wire it up at runtime. Delegates can also be used to execute functions asynchronously. Although it might seem strange, behind the scenes, a delegate is actually a class that inherits from the `Delegate` or `MulticastDelegate` base class. When the compiler encounters a delegate in your code, it will generate `Invoke` and `BeginInvoke` methods for the delegate class. You can use `Invoke` to execute a method synchronously, or `BeginInvoke` to execute a delegate method on a separate thread in the background asynchronously.

Using delegates for asynchronous method execution is not new to WPF. What is new in WPF is how you can synchronize your UI thread when an asynchronous method returns. In WPF, thread synchronization is performed through the Dispatcher object.

Using your previous "WPFThreading" project, create a new Window and name it **UnblockThread**. You'll use the same window XAML as your previous Blocking example, so you can simply copy from the last example. Let's modify the code-behind for your new window, as follows:

```
using System.Windows;
using System.Windows.Threading;
using System.Threading;

namespace WPFThreading
{

  public partial class UnblockThread : System.Windows.Window
  {

    private delegate void SimpleDelegate();

    public UnblockThread()
    {
      InitializeComponent();

      this.UIThreadId.Content = this.Dispatcher.Thread.ManagedThreadId;
      this.BGThreadId.Content = "N/A";
    }

    private void LongRunningProcess()
    {
      int threadid = Thread.CurrentThread.ManagedThreadId;

      // Display this threads id
      SimpleDelegate del1 = delegate()
        { this.BGThreadId.Content = threadid; };
      this.Dispatcher.BeginInvoke(DispatcherPriority.Send, del1);

      Thread.Sleep(5000);

      // Schedule UpdateTextBox with the UI thread's Dispatcher
      SimpleDelegate del2 = delegate()
        {this.textbox1.Text = "Done Sleeping...";};
      this.Dispatcher.BeginInvoke(DispatcherPriority.Send, del2);
    }

    private void button1_click(object sender, RoutedEventArgs e)
    {
      // simulate long running process asynchronously
      SimpleDelegate del = new SimpleDelegate(LongRunningProcess);
      del.BeginInvoke(null, null);
    }

    private void button2_click(object sender, RoutedEventArgs e)
    {
      this.textbox1.Text = "Hello WPF";
    }

  }
}
```

When you run the application, you achieve the results you want: a responsive UI. Let's look at the details of how you accomplished this.

First, you declare a couple of namespaces, System.Windows.Threading and System.Threading. You need System.Windows.Threading to be able to schedule your delegate and set its priority with the Dispatcher. You need System.Threading to get access to the Sleep method for simulating your long-running process. You also declare a delegate, which takes no arguments to support the operations you'll perform later. This code is typical delegate boilerplate code.

Next, you modify your LongRunningProcess method. This method is going to be executing in a separate thread this time, so it cannot directly update the BGThreadId or the output message textbox1 target on the UI thread. What you need to do is to schedule the update to BGThreadId and textbox1 with the Dispatcher. To do this, you create a couple of delegate instances using anonymous delegate syntax and schedule them with the Dispatcher using a priority level of DispatcherPriority.Send through a call to BeginInvoke. In this case, BeginInvoke is being executed as a method of the Dispatcher (not the delegate). Dispatcher.BeginInvoke accepts a delegate and will execute the delegate's BeginInvoke method for you.

Finally, you need to execute your long-running process on a separate thread. To do this, you create a delegate and then call BeginInvoke on the delegate. Don't confuse calling BeginInvoke on the delegate with BeginInvoke on the Dispatcher. This will run your delegate code in a separate thread.

Note that for simplicity, you are not passing an AsyncCallback *argument in your delegate's call to* BeginInvoke; *rather, you are passing null. In a real-world scenario, you would want to specify a callback method so you could call* EndInvoke *on your delegate to free up system resources.*

Background Worker Object

As an alternative to using delegates to spin off worker threads, the BackgroundWorker class also allows you to perform long-running processes in a separate thread. The BackgroundWorker class is not new to WPF, but you can still use it in WPF. BackgroundWorker basically hides the implementation details of multithreading for you and provides some event mechanisms you can use to get messages back from the thread. Using this method, you no longer have to use the Dispatcher to synchronize threads.

Let's rewrite the previous non-blocking example you created, this time using BackgroundWorker. Add a new form to your project, and name it **UnblockThreadTwo**. Use the same XAML as before.

```
using System.Windows;
using System.ComponentModel;
using System.Threading;
using System.Windows.Threading;

namespace WPFThreading
{

  public partial class UnblockThreadTwo : System.Windows.Window
  {

    private BackgroundWorker worker;

    private delegate void SimpleDelegate();

    public UnblockThreadTwo()
    {
```

```
        InitializeComponent();

        this.UIThreadId.Content = this.Dispatcher.Thread.ManagedThreadId;
        this.BGThreadId.Content = "N/A";
    }

    private void button1_click(object sender, RoutedEventArgs e)
    {
      worker = new BackgroundWorker();

      worker.DoWork += new DoWorkEventHandler(RunOnBGThread);

      worker.RunWorkerCompleted += new
        RunWorkerCompletedEventHandler(BGThreadWorkDone);

      worker.RunWorkerAsync();
    }

    private void button2_click(object sender, RoutedEventArgs e)
    {
      this.textbox1.Text = "Hello WPF";
    }

    private void LongRunningProcess()
    {
      int threadid = Thread.CurrentThread.ManagedThreadId;

      // Display this threads id
      SimpleDelegate del1 = delegate()
        { this.BGThreadId.Content = threadid; };
      this.Dispatcher.BeginInvoke(DispatcherPriority.Send, del1);

      Thread.Sleep(5000);
    }

    private void RunOnBGThread(object sender, DoWorkEventArgs e)
    {
      LongRunningProcess();
    }

    private void BGThreadWorkDone(object sender,
      RunWorkerCompletedEventArgs e)
    {
        this.textbox1.Text = "Done Sleeping..";
    }

  }
}
```

Let's look at the code. First, you need to declare the `System.ComponentModel` namespace, which is where the `BackgroundWorker` class resides, and then define a `BackgroundWorker` instance.

In the button1_click event, you connect some event handlers to handle events raised by the `BackgroundWorker` instance. `BackgroundWorker` raises four events: `Disposed`, `DoWork`,

ProgressChanged, and RunWorkerCompleted. You are handling two of these events here. The last thing you do in this function is run your BackgroundWorker instance.

Finally, you define your event handler methods. When the thread starts, you receive the DoWork event. In your handler for this event you call your LongRunningProcess method. When the thread finishes, you handle the RunWorkerCompleted event by displaying a status message as before, only this time you are already back on the UI thread, so no special code is required.

The System.Windows.Threading namespace, delegate, and call to Dispatcher.BeginInvoke are used only to display the background thread ID to stay consistent with the other examples. The long-running process is managed by the BackgroundWorker instance.

The BackgroundWorker class provides a simple mechanism for creating and managing threads in your applications.

Windows Communication Foundation

WCF is all about services. A service is defined as an application that exposes an endpoint defined by an address through which a client may communicate. Notice the word "communicate" in our definition of service. In WCF, when you talk about communication, you are talking about communication between computer systems on a network. In other words, you're talking about how applications communicate. WCF services provide a mechanism that enables applications to communicate over the Internet or intranet via messages. Furthermore, these applications may be built on different technologies, as long as that technology supports the standards-based protocols for such communication, such as SOAP.

If you are thinking this all sounds familiar to the Web Service or Remoting programming models provided by .NET, you are correct. What WCF gives you is a unified model for system communication. Just as WPF unifies UI with varying media types, WCF unifies .NET Remoting, Web Services, Distributed Transactions, and Message Queues into a single, service-oriented programming model for distributed computing. In addition to unification, WCF offers extensive support for security, transactions, and reliability.

In this section, you take a high-level tour of WCF. You will look at why you might want to use WCF and how to use it. You will take a brief look at the WCF architecture and explore the fundamentals so you can get up and running creating WCF applications quickly. Specifically, you will look at the following:

❑   Service orientation

❑   WCF architecture

❑   WCF fundamentals

❑   Building a WCF service

Service Orientation

Service orientation (SO) is an architectural approach to designing and developing software solutions. SO promotes the idea that a solution's architecture should consist of autonomous, loosely coupled services, which integrate across different platforms.

Service orientation is based on four tenets:

- ❑   Boundaries are explicit.
- ❑   Services are autonomous.
- ❑   Services share schema and contract, not class.
- ❑   Service compatibility is based on policy.

Boundaries are explicit: In service orientation, every message sent between service and client crosses a service boundary. Boundaries represent the separation of a service's publicly exposed interface and its internal implementation. A client need not know any detail about a service's implementation. A boundary also refers to platform implementation and the geographical distance between services. Service orientation design recognizes that any boundary crossing is expensive in terms of performance. Service orientation methodology puts forth the notion that this cost should be respected, and as such, services should be used only when necessary.

Services are autonomous: Services are managed independently of one another. They are deployed, managed, and versioned independently. A change to any service should not affect any part of any other service or solution. The role played by a particular service in the big picture (for example, a solution, application, and so on) is not known or understood by the service. All the service needs to know about is the function it performs and that it needs to adhere to its contract in a reliable manner.

Services share schema and contract, not class: Services communicate based on schema and contract. Schemas are used to pass data, and contracts are used to define behavior. Services don't pass classes or types: These would be platform dependent, and services must be platform independent.

Service compatibility is based on policy: Every service provides a machine-readable description of its capabilities and requirements, called a policy. A policy separates a service's behavior from its accessibility. How you access the service should be configurable, possibly by system administrators rather than developers, and as such should be separate from behavior.

WCF Architecture

Figure 11-11 illustrates the high-level components that make up the WCF architecture.

At the top of the layer diagram are contracts. Contracts define services, what they do, what parameters they require, and what they return. A service must contain at least one Service Contract and may contain various other contracts as well, such as Data, Message, and Policy contracts. This is the layer in which you define your services.

Below the Contract layer is the Service Model layer. The Service Model layer provides the runtime services required by WCF. You can define service instance characteristics, such as message throttling, error handling, transaction behaviors, metadata presentation (how metadata is presented to service clients), and so on. Basically, this is your service configuration layer.

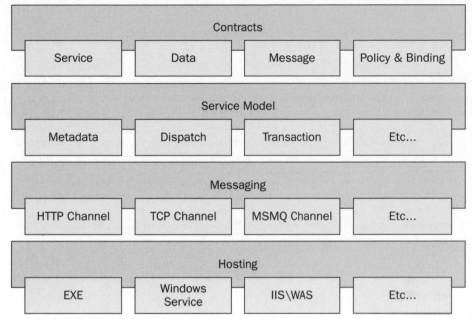

Contracts			
Service	Data	Message	Policy & Binding

Service Model			
Metadata	Dispatch	Transaction	Etc...

Messaging			
HTTP Channel	TCP Channel	MSMQ Channel	Etc...

Hosting			
EXE	Windows Service	IIS\WAS	Etc...

Figure 11-11

Below the Service Model layer is the Messaging layer. The Messaging layer is where message transports are defined. For instance, this is where you specify your message transport protocol, such as HTTP, TCP, MSMQ, WS Reliable Messaging, and so on.

At the bottom of the layer diagram is the Hosting layer. Services can be hosted in many environments, or they can host themselves. Common hosts include executables, IIS, windows services, and COM+ applications.

WCF Fundamentals

The following sections provide an overview of WCF fundamental concepts. Once you cover these fundamentals, you will jump into writing your first WCF service.

Service

Put simply, a WCF service allows clients and services to exchange messages. A WCF service is made up of three components: a service class that implements a service interface, a host environment to run the service, and one or more endpoints through which clients may communicate with the service. Programmatically, a service is a .NET class, which typically implements a .NET interface. Although the concept is similar, do not confuse a service contract with an interface contract: An interface is not required to create a service class; it's just good programming style to do so. Because it is good practice, we will assume the interface is used from here on out. The interface defines a set of methods your service will provide. A class that implements a service interface is referred to as a "Service Type" in WCF.

Client

A client communicates with service endpoints. Clients are the consumers of services and are responsible for initiating communication with the service.

Service Host

A service host provides runtime support to your services. WCF services may be run in any Windows process that supports managed code. For instance, a WCF service can be hosted by IIS for services that run over HTTP, or they can be run on the new Windows Activation Service (WAS) to take advantage of other transport protocols, such as TCP and Named Pipes. WCF services can even be hosted right inside of a console application or as a Windows Service. Because WCF unifies the distributed programming model, the hosting environment you choose will not affect how you code your service.

Endpoint

A WCF service exposes an endpoint. Endpoints allow services and clients to exchange messages. There are three key parts to a service endpoint:

❑   Address

❑   Binding

❑   Contract

Address

An address defines a service endpoint's location on the network. Service endpoints require a transport protocol, and therefore the address is specified as a protocol-specific address—for example, TCP or HTTP. An address also, optionally, specifies a port if necessary. The WCF framework provides an EndpointAddress class for defining an endpoint address. Syntactically, an address is defined as follows:

```
<protocol>://<Address>:<Port>/path
```

Binding

Service endpoints also define a binding. A binding is a set of properties that define how a client must communicate with the service. Bindings define transport protocols, such as TCP or HTTP; security credentials, such as SSL or SOAP message security; and a message encoding type, such as binary or text. The WCF framework provides the Binding class for creating service endpoint bindings. WCF provides several default bindings for use in your applications. These default bindings can be modified to fit your solution:

❑   BasicHttpBinding

❑   WSHttpBinding

❑   NetMsmqBinding

A BasicHttpBinding can be used for interoperability between platform-independent systems. This binding encodes SOAP messages in a text format. A WSHttpBinding supports advanced WS* features, such as transactions and reliable messaging. A NetMsmqBinding uses MSMQ as the transport protocol.

Contract

A key reason to create a service is to provide a communication channel between systems built on different platforms. A contract is what makes interoperability between disparate platforms possible. Service endpoints define a contract. A contract defines what services are provided by your service endpoint, in a platform-independent manner. Given this, service clients need only understand the contract, not the service implementation.

A contract is defined by a .NET interface and marked with a [ServiceContract] attribute. The interface defines your service contract. When you develop your service, you will define a service implementation as well. A service implementation is a .NET class that implements your contract interface. This is where you will place your service implementation code.

> *It is not required that you use a .NET interface to declare your contract: You could simply decorate your service implementation class with the appropriate attributes. Using an interface is referred to as contract-first programming and is considered good design, so we recommend that you follow this pattern for your service development.*

The methods you define in your interface are not included in the service contract by default. To include a method in the service contract, you add an [OperationContract] attribute to your method. The [OperationContract] attribute allows a method to be exposed through the service. If you do not decorate a method with this attribute, it will not be made available as part of the service. The WCF service attribute model controls how service WSDL will be generated.

> *When speaking "WCF," you'll encounter the term "operation" often. An operation is really just a method in your service class that will be exposed on the service endpoint. Operations are methods marked with the [OperationContract] attribute in your service class.*

Let's look at a simple contract definition and implementation.

```
[ServiceContract]
interface IServiceContract
{
[OperationContract]
string DoSomething(string value);

string DoSomethingElse(string value);
}

public class ServiceImplementation : IServiceContract
{
public string IServiceContract.DoSomething(string value)
{
// Do Something Here
}
}
```

In the preceding example, we have created our contract, IServiceContract, and defined one operation, DoSomething(), and one method, DoSomethingElse(). We refer to DoSomething() as an operation because it is marked with the [OperationContract] attribute, so it will be included in our contract. We refer to DoSomethingElse() as a method because it is not marked and, therefore, will not be an operation provided by our contract.

Following the contract definition, we add our contract implementation code in a class called `ServiceImplementation`, which implements `IServiceContract`. This is where you will put the code that actually does something.

WCF defines three types of contracts:

- ❑   Service Contract (WCF-to-WSDL)
- ❑   Data Contract (WCF-to-Schema)
- ❑   Message Contract (WCF-to-SOAP)

Contracts also define Message Exchange Patterns, referred to as either MEP or MEX, which describe how messages are exchanged between the client and the service endpoint. There are three types of message exchange patterns:

- ❑   Request/Reply
- ❑   One-Way
- ❑   Duplex

Request/Reply is the default message exchange pattern. In this pattern, the client receives a response and a return value. The client code processing the request will wait for a reply before proceeding. If the service does not define a return value, the client will still wait for an empty response before proceeding.

The One-Way message exchange pattern does not expect and will not wait for a response. Client processing will continue immediately as soon as its message is sent to the service.

The Duplex message exchange pattern is an asynchronous pattern, meaning both client and service may send messages to each other at-will, without waiting for a response. This pattern will use the Request/Reply or One-Way pattern, the difference being that a session is opened between client and server for asynchronous messaging.

The `ContractDescription` class defines the service contract.

Building a WCF Service

You now know enough to get your hands dirty and write a simple service. You will build a simple "Hello WCF" service and a client to communicate with the service. You will use the default Request/Reply message pattern.

Hello WCF Service

Let's get started. Open Visual Studio and create a new project using a C# Console Application template and name it **WCFHelloWorldService** (see Figure 11-12).

You need to add a reference to `System.ServiceModel` namespace. This namespace contains the classes that support the WCF framework.

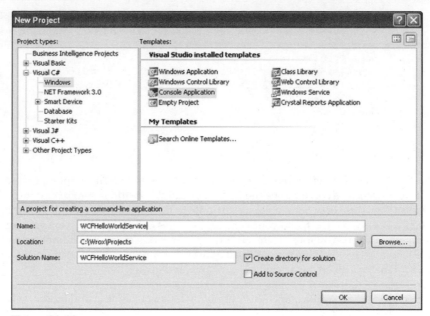

Figure 11-12

Next, open the Program.cs file and modify it as follows:

```csharp
using System;
using System.Collections.Generic;
using System.Text;

using System.ServiceModel;

namespace WCFHelloWorldService
{
    [ServiceContract]
    public interface IHelloWCF
    {
        [OperationContract]
        string SayHello();
    }

    public class HelloWCFService : IHelloWCF
    {
        string WCFHelloWorldService.IHelloWCF.SayHello()
        {
            return ("Hello WCF!");
        }
    }

    class Program
    {
        static void Main(string[] args)
```

```
            {
                ServiceHost host = new ServiceHost(typeof(WCFHelloWorldService
        .HelloWCFService));
                host.Open();
                Console.WriteLine("The HelloWCFService is running.");
                Console.WriteLine("Press <enter> to close host.");
                Console.ReadLine();
                host.Close();
            }
        }
    }
```

In the preceding code, you define your service contract. First, you create an interface and name it **IHelloWCF**. This interface contains one method, `SayHello`. You add a `[ServiceContract]` attribute to the interface and an `[OperationContract]` attribute to the `SayHello` method, indicating to WCF that this is, in fact, a service contract, and your contract provides one operation. Next you create your service contract implementation. You then create a `HelloWCFServices` class, which implements the `IHelloWCF` service contract interface. You implement the `SayHello` operation method, and simply return a string, "Hello WCF!" Finally, you create a new `ServiceHost` and open it.

Next, you need to add an Application Configuration File to your project and modify it as follows:

```xml
<?xml version="1.0" encoding="utf-8" ?>
<configuration>

  <system.serviceModel>

    <bindings></bindings>

    <services>
      <service name="WCFHelloWorldService.HelloWCFService"
        behaviorConfiguration="metadataSupport">
        <endpoint address="http://localhost:10001/Hello"
          binding="basicHttpBinding"
          contract="WCFHelloWorldService.IHelloWCF" />
      </service>
    </services>

    <behaviors>
      <serviceBehaviors>
        <behavior name="metadataSupport">
          <serviceMetadata httpGetEnabled="true"
            httpGetUrl="http://localhost:10001/Hello"/>
        </behavior>
      </serviceBehaviors>
    </behaviors>

  </system.serviceModel>

</configuration>
```

Here you are configuring the service and defining its endpoint. Go ahead and build and run the service to make sure your service compiles correctly. Next you will create your "HelloWCF" client application, which you'll use to consume the service you just created.

Hello WCF Client

Now you need to create a client to call your service. In Visual Studio, select File ⇨ Add ⇨ New Project, and create a new project using the Windows Application (WPF) template under .NET Framework 3.0 project type tree as shown in Figure 11-13. Name the project **WCFHelloWorldClient**, change the solution drop-down to Add to Solution, and click OK. For the purposes of this example, you want to have both projects in the same solution so you can more easily test your service.

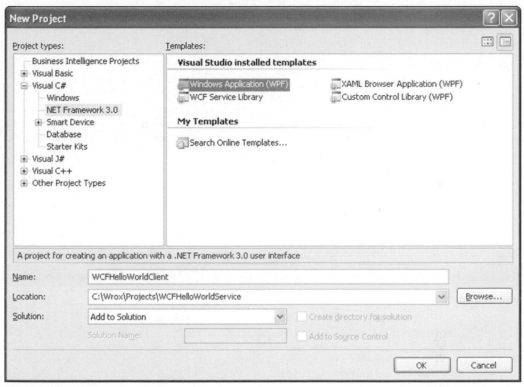

Figure 11-13

Add a `System.ServiceModel` reference to your project. You also want to add a project reference to your WCFHelloWorldService project.

Your form is going to be very simple: You're just adding a button. Modify your Window1 XAML as follows

```
<Window x:Class="WCFHelloWorldClient.Window1"
  xmlns="http://schemas.microsoft.com/winfx/2006/xaml/presentation"
  xmlns:x="http://schemas.microsoft.com/winfx/2006/xaml"
  Title="WCFHelloWorldClient" Height="300" Width="300"
  >
  <Grid VerticalAlignment="Center" HorizontalAlignment="Center">
    <Button Name="button1">Say Hello!</Button>
  </Grid>
</Window>
```

Now you need to generate a proxy class for your client. Open the properties dialog box for your solution (right-click solution, choose properties) and ensure that you have the "Single startup project" radio button selected. The WFCHelloWorldService should be selected as the startup project, as shown in Figure 11-14.

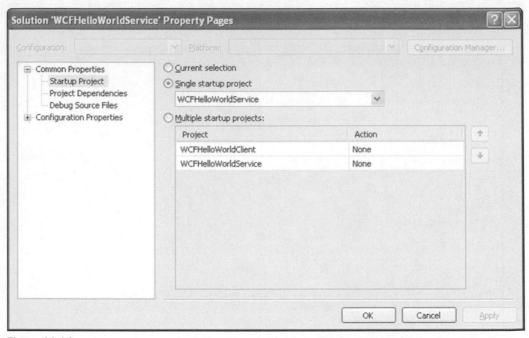

Figure 11-14

Press F5 to run the WCFHelloWorldService and make sure it compiles successfully. Leave it running for the next step. Now, you are going to add a service reference to your project. With your service running, right-click the client project and choose Add Service Reference. Then configure the dialog box, as shown in Figure 11-15.

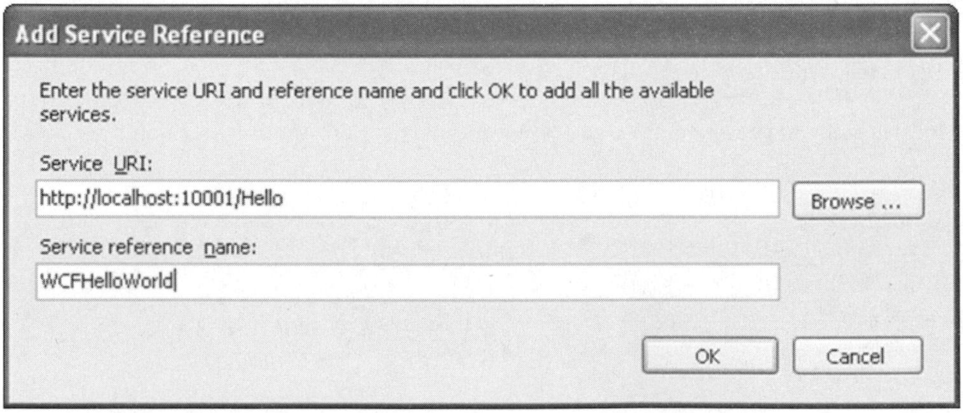

Add Service Reference

Enter the service URI and reference name and click OK to add all the available services.

Service URI:

http://localhost:10001/Hello   Browse ...

Service reference name:

WCFHelloWorld

OK   Cancel

Figure 11-15

Input the service URI and service reference name and Click OK. WCF generates your proxy classes for you. Now let's code your Window1.xaml.cs file

```csharp
using System;
using System.Collections.Generic;
using System.Text;
using System.Windows;
using System.Windows.Controls;
using System.Windows.Data;
using System.Windows.Documents;
using System.Windows.Input;
using System.Windows.Media;
using System.Windows.Media.Imaging;
using System.Windows.Shapes;

using System.ServiceModel;

namespace WCFHelloWorldClient
{

    public partial class Window1 : System.Windows.Window
    {
        WCFHelloWorldClient.lWCFHelloWorld.HelloWCFClient proxy;

        public Window1()
        {
            InitializeComponent();
            proxy = new WCFHelloWorldClient.lWCFHelloWorld.HelloWCFClient();
        }

        private void button1_Click(object sender, RoutedEventArgs e)
        {
            string response = "";
            response = proxy.SayHello();
            MessageBox.Show(response);
        }

    }
}
```

You are doing two things here. First, you are creating an instance of proxy class. Second, you are using that instance in the click handler for your button to call the service and display the results. Return to your Window1.xaml file, and add the following event handler declaration to the button1 element:

```xml
<Window x:Class="WCFHelloWorldClient.Window1"
   xmlns="http://schemas.microsoft.com/winfx/2006/xaml/presentation"
   xmlns:x="http://schemas.microsoft.com/winfx/2006/xaml"
   Title="WCFHelloWorldClient" Height="300" Width="300"
   >
   <Grid VerticalAlignment="Center" HorizontalAlignment="Center">
     <Button Name="button1" Click="button1_Click">Say Hello!</Button>
   </Grid>
</Window>
```

Now you need to add a configuration file to your client:

```xml
<?xml version="1.0" encoding="utf-8" ?>
<configuration>
  <system.serviceModel>
    <bindings>
      <basicHttpBinding>
        <binding name="BasicHttpBinding_IHelloWCF" closeTimeout="00:01:00"
            openTimeout="00:01:00" receiveTimeout="00:01:00"
            sendTimeout="00:01:00" allowCookies="false"
            bypassProxyOnLocal="false"
            hostNameComparisonMode="StrongWildcard"
            maxBufferSize="65536" maxBufferPoolSize="524288"
            maxReceivedMessageSize="65536" messageEncoding="Text"
            textEncoding="utf-8" transferMode="Buffered"
            useDefaultWebProxy="true">
          <readerQuotas maxDepth="32" maxStringContentLength="8192"
            maxArrayLength="16384" maxBytesPerRead="4096"
            maxNameTableCharCount="16384"/>
          <security mode="None">
            <transport clientCredentialType="None"
              proxyCredentialType="None" realm="" />
            <message clientCredentialType="UserName"
              algorithmSuite="Default"/>
          </security>
        </binding>
      </basicHttpBinding>
    </bindings>
    <client>
      <endpoint address="http://localhost:10001/Hello"
        binding="BasicHttpBinding"
        bindingConfiguration="BasicHttpBinding_IHelloWCF"
        contract="WCFHelloWorldClient.WCFHelloWorld.IHelloWCF"
        name="BasicHttpBinding_IHelloWCF" />
    </client>
  </system.serviceModel>
</configuration>
```

Here you are configuring your service on the client. You have one last step (as shown in Figure 11-16), which is to change your solution properties again so that both projects will run.

Press F5 and let the magic happen.

That's all there is to it. Although not the most exciting application, you now know how to create and define a service contract and how to run it in a host application. You saw how to create a client, and how to generate a proxy for your client. Creating services in WCF is really very easy and that ease is a testament to the team that built it.

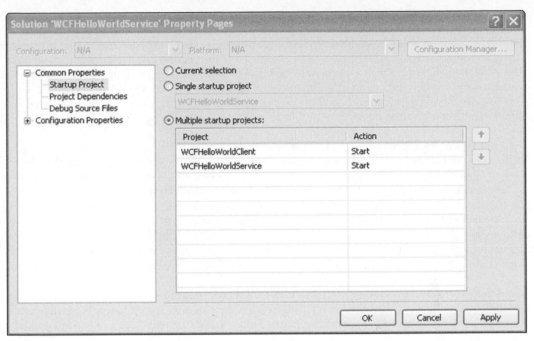

Figure 11-16

Windows Workflow Foundation

Software in the enterprise is created to support or automate business processes. A business process represents an activity or activities performed within a business, such as shipping products, approving documents, processing invoices, submitting timesheets, and so on. Business processes are either performed manually by people, automated by software, or more typically are a combination of the two. Business processes can be broken down into individual tasks and decisions. A business process has a start, a finish, and one or more tasks and decision points performed in between, constituting a process flow. Analysts and developers typically model business process flows as a flowchart diagram. Wouldn't it be nice if you could model your applications in the same manner using a designer?

Tasks within a business process may be short or long running. For instance, a task such as "Notify Bob in HR that a new employee, Stacy, has been hired" can be executed instantly, handled possibly by an e-mail. A task such as "Get approval for the purchase of a new workstation for Stacy" may take days. If these tasks were modeled in an HR application, for example, it would not be possible for the application to wait for approval for the new workstation to continue processing. A procedural application needs to continue processing when a long-running task is encountered. In addition, however it is handled, when a long-running process returns, the current business process typically must continue where it left off and the prior state of the process must be recovered.

Business process requirements often change. Suppose you were to model and implement a simple company expense reimbursement process. The process is as follows: Expense report is submitted by an employee; expense report is reviewed by manager; if approved, the expense report is sent to accounting and accounting writes the check. Now, let's assume "the powers that be" decide that management is dropping the ball and letting inappropriate expenses through the process, and this needs to be remedied immediately. The new process will still require manager approval, but will now also require executive approval. In a typical procedural application, it could take days or weeks to implement the change. To satisfy the business, we as developers should be able to make the change on-the-fly.

Business processes might also be supported by multiple applications, implemented using distributed application architecture. For instance, imagine a system that allows users to book roundtrip flights. The system is made up of three systems, the web interface through which customers make their reservations, a web service that handles the flight booking/scheduling, and a web service that processes payment for the flight. Now let's imagine a scenario where a customer books his roundtrip flight. The customer selects his flight and clicks a submit button. The application contacts the flight scheduling service and books the flight. Next the application contacts the payment processing service, but the customer has insufficient funds, and therefore this process fails. As in the database world, you need a way to "roll back" the flight booking. What is needed is a way to wrap two disparate services in a transaction.

Windows Workflow Foundation (WF) provides a solution to address these scenarios and more. In this section, you take a high-level tour of WF. You look at why you might want to use WF and how to use it. You take a brief look at the WF architecture and explore the fundamentals so you can get up and running creating WF applications quickly. Specifically, you look at the following:

❑ Workflow defined

❑ WF architecture

❑ WF fundamentals

❑ Building a workflow programmatically

❑ Building a workflow using the Workflow Designer

❑ Creating a custom workflow activity

Workflow Defined

A *workflow* is a model that defines the individual tasks, called activities, performed by people and software that constitute a business process.

Windows Workflow Foundation provides various components, tools, and a designer through which developers can model business processes and create workflow-enabled applications.

The Visual Designer provided by WF enables developers to create workflows by drawing them in a familiar flowchart-style diagram. Other developers can quickly come up-to-speed on what your application does and how it does it by reviewing the diagram. The Visual Designer also makes it possible for analysts to understand your application, as it closely resembles the flowcharts that they use in their day-to-day job function.

WF Architecture

The WF architecture consists of an activity model (workflow activities), a framework, a runtime, and runtime support services. Figure 11-17 illustrates the various components that make up the WF architecture:

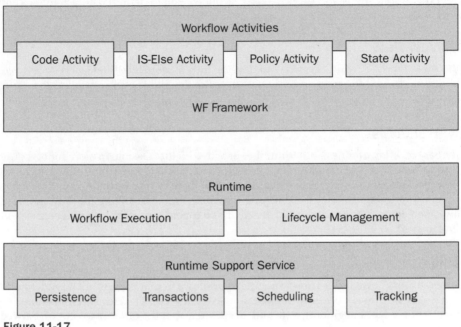

Figure 11-17

WF provides a set of canned workflow activities, such as Code and Policy, which you can use to model your workflows. These activities define specific units of work to be executed at specific points in a workflow. The WF framework provides common functionality used by workflow activities.

The WF runtime is responsible for managing the lifetime of a workflow instance. The runtime can support multiple workflow instances simultaneously. The WF runtime is an in-process engine that executes workflow instances within the context of a host application. The WF runtime requires a host application, such as a console or WPF application (a wide variety of applications can be host to workflows). A host application can support multiple instances of a workflow runtime simultaneously. The host application provides runtime support services, such as persistence and transaction management, required by the workflow runtime.

WF Fundamentals

This section covers the basic concepts of WF. It will provide you with enough information to get up and running fast with Windows Workflow Foundation.

Activities

A workflow consists of one or more activities. Activities represent discrete units of functionality within a workflow. WF offers many activities right out of the box that support control flow (for example, `IfThen`, `Case`, and `While`), rules and conditions, event handling, state management, and communication with other applications and services. WF also allows you to define custom activities and use them in your workflow.

Types of Workflow

There are three types of workflows you can develop in WF: sequential, state, and data-driven. Each workflow is modeled differently and has characteristics that may be more applicable to different business processes.

Sequential Workflows

A sequential workflow defines a finite number of activities that execute in a predefined order from beginning to end. This does not mean that workflow activities do not exhibit flow control and branching logic; they can and typically do. Sequential means that there is a single defined path through the workflow which is top-to-bottom, but there may be branching or looping along the way. In this scenario, the workflow itself controls the order in which activities happen; for example, an invoice is paid only after it has been received.

State Machine Workflows

State machine workflows differ from sequential workflows in that there is not a predefined order of execution. In a state machine workflow, the workflow contains a set of states and transitions. A state machine workflow has a beginning state and an end state, but the order of execution between has no fixed order. The order in which these transitions are executed is based on external forces, such as people, rather than the workflow itself.

For example, in a loan origination system, a loan document passes through various stages of state and transition. Status may change from created to processing to underwriting to closing and finally to funding. If during the underwriting process, a loan is found to be missing some critical information or is inaccurate, its state may be changed to a prior status of processing, and the workflow reverted to an earlier state. This type of process is simplified when defined as a collection of states and transitions and is therefore more manageable. Conversely, you would have to use a significant number of loops and branches to handle this in a sequential workflow, which would greatly increase complexity.

Data-Driven Workflows

In a data-driven workflow, activities are grouped together in a logical association, and the order in which they are executed is determined by external data or business rules. A data-driven workflow is essentially a sequential workflow whose execution path is determined by external business rules. Only activities or activity groups that meet certain criteria, implemented as rules, will be executed.

Using the earlier loan origination example, let's assume there are a set of business rules that govern when a loan is to be transitioned into a prior state. For instance, for a loan to be sent back to processing from underwriting, the loan must first be sent to quality control. But, if the loan has already been sent through quality control, the loan may be assigned back to processing. By using a data-driven workflow, you can define and build these types of rules into your system.

WF Runtime Support Services

Host applications provide services to the workflow runtime. WF provides many runtime service implementations out-of-the-box that support a number of different host types. Many services are available, and we strongly recommend you learn about all of them through the WF documentation. The workflow engine provides an `AddService` method you can use to add services to a runtime instance. I will discuss some of these services in this section.

Persistence Services

As I discussed in the introduction to WF, many activities within a business process may take a long period of time to execute, possibly days, weeks, months, or years. With a long-running process, it obviously would not be practical to leave the workflow instance in memory. If the process takes long enough, the server on which the application hosting the workflow runs may not even be the same machine, and if so, what are the chances the server will not be rebooted within a year? It's not hard to understand the need for persistence services.

By default, workflow instances are transient, meaning they live only as long as the runtime. In turn, the runtime lives only as long as the host. What a persistence service offers is a mechanism to store the state of a particular workflow instance in a data store for recovery at a later time.

A workflow runtime instance may contain only a single persistence service.

WF will use a persistence service made available by the workflow host to store the state of a workflow instance. This allows a workflow instance to live outside of an application boundary. As an application starts, stops, and starts again, the workflow can maintain its state independently of the application, by taking advantage of the persistence service. The application can then grab the stored workflow state and continue where the workflow left off. WF provides a persistence service out-of-the box that uses SQL Server to store workflow state data.

Transaction Services

As with typical application programming, data consistency is important. WF transaction services provide a mechanism through which an activity or set of activities can be grouped into a transaction for processing. Commitment of a transaction is ultimately the responsibility of the workflow runtime. However, WF allows you to hook into the transaction service so you may provide custom handling for failed transactions. It is important to note that you can only include activities that are part of the workflow and not code executed by the workflow host. Conceptually, you can think of WF transaction services the same way you think of transactions in SQL Server.

Tracking Services

WF tracking services allow hosts to monitor workflow instances during execution. Like any application, you will want to monitor the performance of your workflow and track statistics, such as frequency of activity use. WF supplies an out-of-the-box tracking service, which uses SQL Server to record and store tracking data. You can also write your own tracking service, which could use a custom data store for storing data captured. Unlike transaction services, you can run multiple different tracking services simultaneously. Like the other services we've explored, you add the service to the runtime using the `AddService` method. WF also allows you to specify what is tracked by defining a tracking profile, which is defined as an XML file. Additionally, WF provides a `SQLTrackingQuery` class you can use to query data stored while tracking.

Building a Workflow Programmatically

It's time to build something. You will create a very simple sequential workflow console application from scratch, without using one of the built-in Visual Studio workflow templates, so that you can better understand the internals of a WF application.

Fire up Visual Studio, create a new C# console application, and name it whatever you like. What you are really creating here is your workflow runtime host; in this case, your host will be a console application, as shown in Figure 11-18.

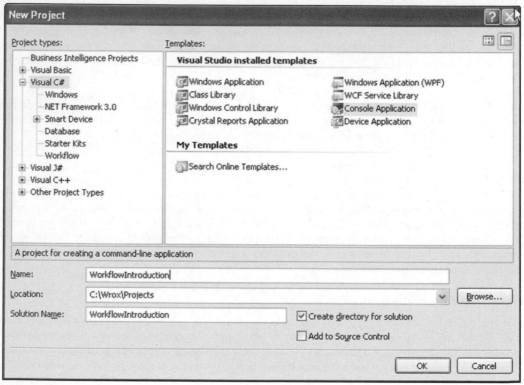

Figure 11-18

The first thing you need to do is to add references to your application for the following workflow libraries:

- ❑ `System.Workflow.Activities`
- ❑ `System.Workflow.ComponentModel`
- ❑ `System.Workflow.Runtime`

With your references in place, you can now define your workflow, create your runtime, and add an instance of your workflow to the runtime.

Modify your program.cs file as follows:

```csharp
using System;
using System.Collections.Generic;
using System.Text;

using System.Workflow.Runtime;
using System.Workflow.Activities;

namespace WorkflowIntroduction
{
  public class SimpleWorkflow : SequentialWorkflowActivity
  {
    public SimpleWorkflow()
    {
      CodeActivity ca = new CodeActivity();

      ca.ExecuteCode += delegate
      {
        Console.WriteLine("Code activity executed");
        Console.WriteLine("Press <enter> to stop the workflow");
        Console.ReadLine();
      };

      this.Activities.Add(ca);
    }
  }

  class Program
  {
    static void Main(string[] args)
    {
      WorkflowRuntime runtime = new WorkflowRuntime();

      runtime.StartRuntime();

      WorkflowInstance instance = runtime.CreateWorkflow(typeof(SimpleWorkflow));

      instance.Start();

      runtime.StopRuntime();

    }
  }
}
```

The first thing you add are your using declarations for the System.Workflow.Runtime and System.Workflow.Activities namespaces. You need these in order to write your WF code.

You create a public class called `SimpleWorkflow` and derive from `SequentialWorkflowActivity`, which is the base class for the Sequential Workflow model. In the class constructor, you first create a new code activity. You define an inline `delegate` that will execute when the activity is reached by your workflow. Your delegate simply writes a message to the console and then waits for input to continue. Finally, you add your code activity to the activities collection for this workflow. Your workflow definition code is basically defining a sequential workflow that will start, run a code activity, and then stop. You'll use the Workflow Designer in the next example so that you can see the visual model for your workflows.

With a workflow defined, the next thing you need is a runtime to host your workflow. In the console application's `Main` entry point, you define an instance of `WorkflowRuntime` and start it. The next thing you do is create an instance of our `SimpleWorkflow` class and hand it to the runtime engine in the `CreateWorkflow` method. You then start the workflow instance. When your workflow instance completes execution, the runtime is shut down with a call to `runtime.StopRuntime()`;

That's all there is to it. Press F5 to run the application.

Building a Workflow Using the Workflow Designer

Now let's create a workflow application using one of the Visual Studio workflow project templates. Unlike the last example, when you create a project from one of the templates supplied by Visual Studio, the boilerplate code that creates and manages the runtime will be generated for you. You need only define your workflow: An instance of your workflow is already created and passed to the runtime for you. This time you'll use the Workflow Designer to create your workflow rather than doing it in code.

Your workflow will model a simple bidding process in which a user bids on a new espresso machine. A user will be prompted to enter a bid. If the bid is higher than the current winning bid, the user will be prompted for whether or not to continue bidding. If the bid is too low, the user will be asked to bid again. When the user ends the bidding process, the winning bid will be displayed.

This example will show how you model a workflow using the Workflow Designer and WF Code and Control-Flow activities.

Fire up Visual Studio again, only this time create a new C# Sequential Workflow Console Application and name it whatever you like (as shown in Figure 11-19).

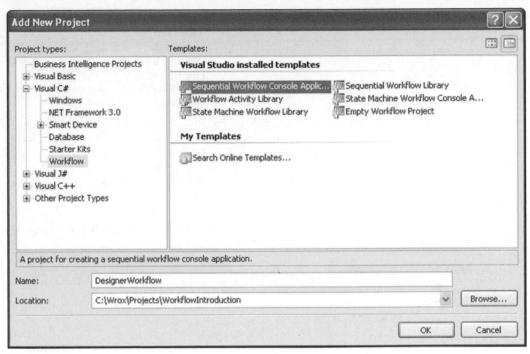

Figure 11-19

Visual Studio generates your project stubs for you and adds the necessary references. Let's take a look at the code that was generated. If you look at the Program.cs file, you will see the following:

```csharp
class Program
{
  static void Main(string[] args)
  {
    using(WorkflowRuntime workflowRuntime = new WorkflowRuntime())
    {
      AutoResetEvent waitHandle = new AutoResetEvent(false);

      workflowRuntime.WorkflowCompleted += delegate(object sender,
        WorkflowCompletedEventArgs e) {waitHandle.Set();};

      workflowRuntime.WorkflowTerminated += delegate(object sender,
        WorkflowTerminatedEventArgs e)
        {
          Console.WriteLine(e.Exception.Message);
          waitHandle.Set();
        };

      WorkflowInstance instance =
```

```
            workflowRuntime.CreateWorkflow(typeof(DesignerWorkflow.Workflow1));
        instance.Start();

        waitHandle.WaitOne();
    }
  }
}
```

Visual Studio has generated the code that will create an instance of the workflow runtime. Visual Studio has also added a few additional items that you did not create in the last example, such as delegate handlers for the WorkflowCompleted and WorkflowTerminated events. Visual Studio has also created an instance of your default Workflow1 class, handed it off to the runtime, and started the instance. You can add additional runtime or workflow instances in this method if you like, but you'll use the defaults in this example.

Let's take a look at the Workflow Designer by double-clicking the Workflow1.cs file. When the Workflow Designer opens, by default you see the graphic shown in Figure 11-20.

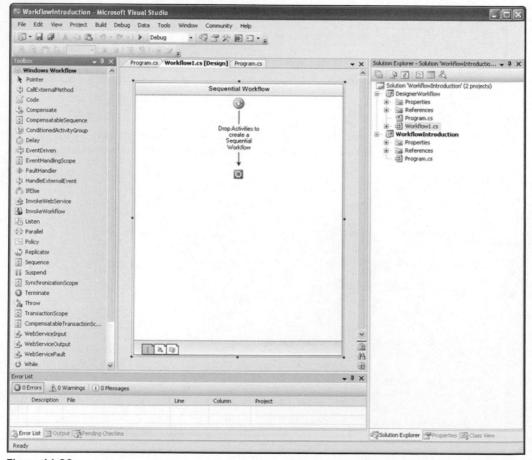

Figure 11-20

The Workflow Designer displays an empty model for your workflow, containing only a simple start and end point. You add your activities to the workflow by dragging them from the Toolbox onto the Workflow Designer and dropping them between the start and end point. On the left, in the Toolbox, you see the out-of-the-box activities supplied by WF. Also, at the bottom left of the Workflow Designer window are three tabs: These tabs show different views of the workflow in the Workflow Designer. The Workflow Designer views available are the Workflow view (which you are viewing now), the Cancel Handlers view, and the Fault Handler view.

Now, you need to start adding activities to your workflow to model the bidding process. Your end result will look like Figure 11-21.

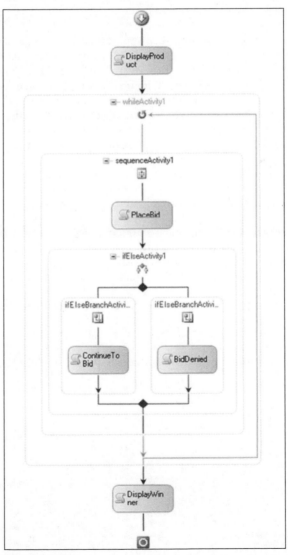

Figure 11-21

The first thing you need to do is to drag a `Code` activity onto the Workflow Designer and name it **DisplayProduct**. This activity displays the product details to the potential bidder.

Next, you need to set up the loop for accepting bids. In WF, you can accomplish this by adding a `While` activity to the Workflow Designer just below your `DisplayProduct` activity. Go ahead and add a `While` activity now. A `While` activity will loop based on a condition. We come back to setting the `While` activity condition in a moment.

Within your `While` activity, you will be adding a number of other activities. In order to do this, you will need to add a `Sequence` activity to your `While` activity. Inside the `Sequence` activity, the first thing you need is to add another `Code` activity to request the bid. Add a new `Code` activity and name it **PlaceBid**. This `Code` activity will ask for a bid and record it.

After a bid has been entered, you need to check to see if it is higher than the highest bid entered so far and then act accordingly. You will use an `ifElse` activity to get the branching logic you need. Drag an `ifElse` activity into your `Sequence` activity just below the `PlaceBid` activity. The `ifElse` activity gives you two branches by default (you could add more if you want, but you don't need to here). Next, you need to add a `Code` activity to each branch of your `ifElse` activity. These activities will execute based on whether the bid is higher than the current bid or not. On the left side of the `ifElse` activity, you place your condition, effectively making it the "if" branch. Name the `Code` activity **ContinueToBid**. On the right side, or in this case the "else" side of the `ifElse` activity, name the `Code` activity **BidDenied**.

Now that you have the control-flow defined, the last thing you need to do is to add one more `Code` activity to our workflow, which will display the winning bid. Place the final `Code` activity just above the endpoint of the workflow, outside of the `While` activity, and name it **DisplayWinner**.

Your workflow should now look like the one illustrated in Figure 11-21. You will not be able to run the workflow just yet because no code has been written for your `Code` activities and no conditions set in our `While` and `ifElse` activities. But before you can add conditions, you need to define the properties and fields of your workflow class that will hold the values the conditions will require.

Right-click on the Workflow Designer and choose View Code. Modify the Workflow1.cs file as follows:

```
namespace DesignerWorkflow
{
  public sealed partial class Workflow1: SequentialWorkflowActivity
  {

    private bool continueBidding;

    public bool ContinueBidding
    {
      get { return continueBidding; }
      set { continueBidding = value; }
    }

    private decimal bid = 0;
    private decimal highestBid = 0;
    private int totalBids = 0;

    public Workflow1()
```

```
    {
      InitializeComponent();

      ContinueBidding = true;
    }

    private void DisplayProduct_ExecuteCode(object sender, EventArgs e)
    {
      Console.WriteLine("You are bidding on a new expresso maker");
    }

    private void PlaceBid_ExecuteCode(object sender, EventArgs e)
    {
      totalBids++;
      Console.WriteLine("Current bid is {0}, total bids so far is {1}",
        this.highestBid, this.totalBids);
      Console.WriteLine("Enter your bid:");
      bid = decimal.Parse(Console.ReadLine());
    }

    private void ContinueToBid_ExecuteCode(object sender, EventArgs e)
    {
      highestBid = bid;
      Console.WriteLine("Do you want to bid again? [Y/N]");
      string response = Console.ReadLine();
      if (response.ToUpper() == "Y")
        ContinueBidding = true;
      else
        ContinueBidding = false;
    }

    private void BidDenied_ExecuteCode(object sender, EventArgs e)
    {
      Console.WriteLine("Your bid must be higher than the current bid, please try
        again");
    }

    private void DisplayWinner_ExecuteCode(object sender, EventArgs e)
    {
      Console.WriteLine("Final winnning bid is {0}", this.highestBid);
      Console.ReadLine();
    }
  }

}
```

You do not have to type the declaration for every ExecuteCode method; you can simply double-click the Code activity in the Workflow Designer.

You have added a couple of properties and fields to help you control your workflow. The ContinueLooping property is a simple Boolean value that will determine when bidding is complete and you should exit your While loop. The bid, highestBid, and totalBids fields are used for storing the state of your workflow locally. A number of ExecuteCode handlers have also been added, each one either printing or reading from the console.

Now that you have your code written, you need to jump back into the Workflow Designer and add your conditions to the While and ifElse activities. Right-click and choose View Designer. Highlight the While activity, right-click, and choose Properties. You need to add a condition to your loop. In the properties for your While activity, select the drop-down for the condition property, and select Declarative Rule Condition. Once selected, you can expand the condition property and you will see two additional properties are revealed: ConditionName and Expression. Set the values for these, as shown in Figure 11-22.

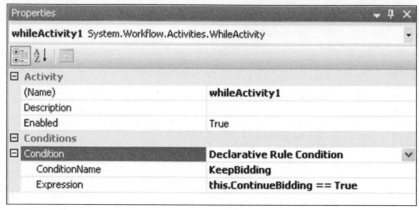

Figure 11-22

Now you need to add a condition to the first branch of your ifElse activity. Highlight the left branch of your ifElse activity, right-click, and select Properties. You'll see you have the same condition property available to you. Set the values for these, as shown in Figure 11-23.

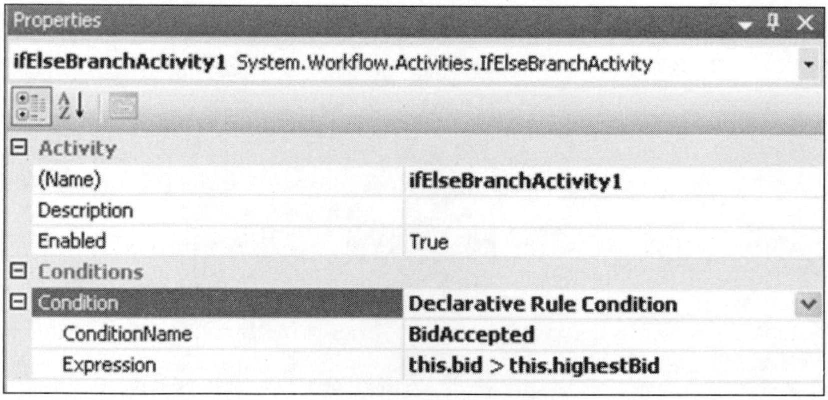

Figure 11-23

Now that you have your workflow and activities defined, you are ready to run the application. Press F5 to run the application.

Creating a Custom Activity

In the last example, you start with a Code activity that displays the product up for bid; then you enter the bidding process where bids are collected; and finally you display the winner. Say you decided to encapsulate the bidding process from the last example into an activity that could be used by any workflow. That workflow could then display a different product; run our custom activity that would model the bidding process; and display the winner. We can do this quite simply in WF.

We are going to create two projects: an Activity Library where you will create your custom bidding activity, and a new Sequential Workflow Console Application in which you create a streamlined workflow that uses your new custom activity.

Let's start with the custom Activity Library. Fire up Visual Studio and create a new project using the Workflow Activity Project template. Name the project **BidActivity**. Visual Studio generates the project and shows you the Workflow Designer for your new activity (as shown in Figure 11-24).

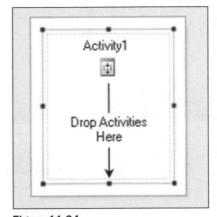

Figure 11-24

You can drag any activities you like into your custom activity. What you are going to do, however, is copy the While activity from the last example and drop it into the new activity. Open up the Workflow Designer for the last workflow you created, select the While activity, right-click, and select Copy. Now switch back to your custom activity, select Activity1, right-click, and select Past. Your custom activity should now look like Figure 11-25.

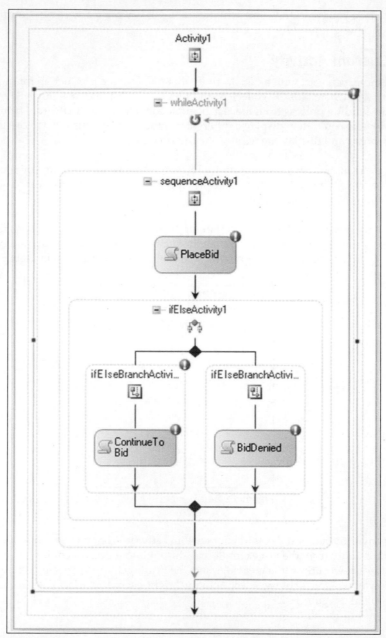

Figure 11-25

Now you are going to replicate many of the steps from the last example to add your activity handlers and conditional logic. Switch to the code-behind view, and modify your custom activity partial class as follows:

```csharp
namespace BidActivity
{
  public partial class Activity1: SequenceActivity
  {
    public Activity1()
    {
      InitializeComponent();
    }

    private bool continueBidding = true;
    public bool ContinueBidding
    {
      get { return continueBidding; }
      set { continueBidding = value; }
    }

    private decimal bid = 0;
    private int totalBids = 0;

    private decimal highestBid;

    public decimal HighestBid
    {
      get { return highestBid; }
      set { highestBid = value; }
    }

    private void PlaceBid_ExecuteCode(object sender, EventArgs e)
    {
      totalBids++;
      Console.WriteLine("Current bid is {0}, total bids so far is {1}",
        this.highestBid, this.totalBids);
      Console.WriteLine("Enter your bid:");
      bid = decimal.Parse(Console.ReadLine());
    }

    private void ContinueToBid_ExecuteCode(object sender, EventArgs e)
    {
      highestBid = bid;
      Console.WriteLine("Do you want to bid again? [Y/N]");
      string response = Console.ReadLine();
      if (response.ToUpper() == "Y")
        ContinueBidding = true;
      else
        ContinueBidding = false;
    }

    private void BidDenied_ExecuteCode(object sender, EventArgs e)
    {
      Console.WriteLine("Your bid must be higher than the current bid, please try
        again");
    }

  }
}
```

Now you have to add your `While` and `ifElse` conditional code (refer to the last example for details on how to do this).

That does it for the custom activity. Build the project to make sure there are no errors.

Now you are going to create a Workflow Console Application to host a new streamlined workflow. In Visual Studio, select File ⇨ Add ⇨ New Project. Select the Sequential Workflow Console Application template and name the project **Custom Activity Workflow**. Add a project reference to your BidActivity custom activity project. Now when you switch to design view and look at the Toolbox, you will see your BidActivity is listed under a new Toolbox Group called BidActivity Components.

Drag the following onto the Workflow Designer in this order: Code activity, Bid activity, Code activity. Name the first Code activity **DisplayProduct**, the Bid activity **CustomActivity**, and the last Code activity **DisplayWinner**. Your workflow should look like Figure 11-26.

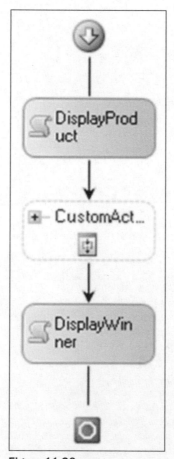

Figure 11-26

Now switch to the code-behind and modify as follows:

```
namespace CustomActivityWorkflow
{
  public sealed partial class Workflow1: SequentialWorkflowActivity
  {
    public Workflow1()
    {
      InitializeComponent();
    }

    private void DisplayProduct_ExecuteCode_1(object sender, EventArgs e)
    {
      Console.WriteLine("You are bidding on a new expresso maker");
    }

    private void DisplayWinner_ExecuteCode_1(object sender, EventArgs e)
    {
      Console.WriteLine("Final winnning bid is {0}",
        this.CustomActivity.HighestBid);
      Console.ReadLine();
    }
  }
}
```

That's it! Press F5 to run the application. The original example is now reduced to three activities, making your workflow model much more readable.

As you can see, creating a custom activity is really quite easy—it's just like creating a workflow. This is the simplest custom activity you can create. WF offers many other flavors of custom activities as well, and they are all highly customizable.

Summary

We've covered a lot of ground in this chapter. We dug a little deeper into the underpinnings of WPF and explored the components that support our applications, such as the visual system and composition system. We walked you through the core class hierarchy of the WPF framework and looked at how the various classes build on each other to provide a rich library for building WPF applications. We took a deeper look at XAML, uncovered how XAML is compiled and integrated within your applications, and explored XAML's relationship to CLR classes. We took a look at one of the more advanced concepts offered by the platform, Multithreading, and discussed how you can use threads in your applications to create a responsive UI. In addition, we looked at some of the other platforms .NET 3.0 has to offer. We explored the core concepts and fundamentals of Windows Communication Foundation and you built your first WCF service. This chapter explored the core concepts and fundamentals of Windows Workflow Foundation; you coded a WF application from scratch, another using the WF Workflow Designer in Visual Studio, and finally you created a custom activity and applied it to your samples.

Chapter 11: Advanced Development Concepts

After reading this chapter, you should now be able to:

❑ Describe the managed and unmanaged components that make up the WPF architecture and understand the interaction between them

❑ Describe the core classes of the WPF framework and know which base classes to use for custom development

❑ Understand XAML syntax in detail, how XAML fits within the WPF application model, and what happens at compile time and runtime

❑ Know when and how to use multithreading in your WPF applications

❑ Describe the basic concepts of the WCF platform and know how to create a simple WCF service

❑ Describe the basic concepts of the WF platform and know how to create WF workflow–enabled applications

Index

A

Activated **event, 33, 35**
Active Directory (AD), 306
ActiveX **controls, adding**
　example, 340–344
　overview, 339
　in XAML, 344–345
activities
　Code activity, 420, 423
　DisplayProduct activity, 420
　ifElse activity, 420, 422
　Sequence activity, 420
　SequentialWorkflowActivity class, 416
　While activity, 420, 422
Activity Library, 423
AD (Active Directory), 306
adaptive topology, 269, 278–286
Add and Remove Programs dialog box, Control Panel, 291
Add New Item dialog box, 91
Add Service Reference, 406
AddChild **method, 364**
Address **page function, 265, 266**
AddressData **class, 263, 265**
AddressData.cs **file, 262**
AddressInfo **object, 266**
AddressTaskController **class, 267**
Address.xaml.cs **file, 275**
AddService **method, 413**
Administrator account, 301
AdornerLayer **control, 9**
Advanced Security Settings dialog box, 320
Alignment **property, 99**
AllowPartiallyTrustedCallersAttribute
　　(APTCA) attribute, 314

alpha channel, 160
Angle **property, 186**
Angle slider, 188
AnimateFill( ) **method, 151, 152**
animation
　animation classes, 135
　creating controls
　　control inheritance, 109–110
　　editing, 110
　　overview, 108–109
　　styling, 110
　creating procedurally with code, 135–138
　importing audio/video media, 113
　keyframes, 105–106
　motion paths, 106–107
　of object's property, 106
　programmatic animation, 139–143
　states, 112–113
　styles, 111–112
　templates
　　common elements, 111
　　editing, 110
　Timeline sub-panel, 104–105
　triggers, 107–108
Animation API. *See also* **animation**
　animation classes, 135
　creating dynamic animation with code, 135–138
　programmatic animation, 139–143
Animation_Completed **method, 200, 202**
AnimationDurationProperty **property, 200**
App_Code directory, 242
App.config **file, 69**
AppDomain, **303, 306**
Appearance panel, 96, 97
Application **class, 254, 363–364**
.application extension, 296

application **models**
  browser-based applications
    overview, 238
    standalone or "loose" XAML, 239
    XAML browser applications, 239–246
  security considerations, 247–248
  standalone applications
    overview, 235–236
    windows, 236–237
    windows navigation, 237–238
Application **object**
  obtaining reference to, 31
  overview, 30–31, 248–250
  sharing information, 31–32
application trust, **323**
<Application> **element, 223**
ApplicationCommands **class, 47, 49, 50**
Application.Exit **event, 253**
ApplicationIdle **message priority, 390**
Application.OnExit **event handler, 251**
applications
  building, 292–293
  creating sample, 27–29
  enterprise application development
    application localization, 286–291
    application models, 234–248
    deployment models, 291–298
    navigation, 258–286
    overview, 233–234
    state management, 248–257
  express, 300
  .NET Framework 3.0 runtime, 296–298
  required installations for creating, 26
  single-threaded, 388–393
  standalone windows applications, 236–237, 294–295
  trusted, 300
  types of, 26–27
  using WPF in Win32 applications, 335–337
  XAML browser applications, 239–246, 295–296
Application.Startup **event, 251, 253**
Apply Resource command, Style context menu, 112
App.Manifest **file, 66**
AppState **class, 249, 253**
App.xaml **file, 223**
APTCA (AllowPartiallyTrustedCallers
  Attribute**) attribute, 314**
arc segment, 210
ArcSegment **class, 208–217**
artboard, 87–88
Artboard panel, Expression Blend **interface, 116, 135**
.asmx web service, 241
ASP.NET, 239
AssemblyInfo.cs **file, 66–67**
AsyncCallback **argument, 395**

asynchronous threading
  BackgroundWorker object, 395–397
  overview, 393–395
attached property, 363
attributes
  AllowPartiallyTrustedCallersAttribute
    (APTCA) attribute, 314
  BasedOn attribute, 225
  Binding attribute, 56
  BorderBrush attribute, 219
  CanResize attribute, Window class, 288
  Category attribute, 290
  Click attribute, 381
  ContentRendered attribute, 36
  declarative attributes, 73
  FontSize attribute, 223
  Ignore attribute, 290
  Inherit attribute, 290
  ItemTemplate attribute, 220
  Localization.Comments attribute, 291
  Modifiable attribute, 290
  NeverLocalize attribute, 290
  None attribute, 290
  [OperationContract] attribute, 401, 404
  Readable attribute, 290
  ResizeMode attribute, 288
  [SecurityCritical] attribute, 311
  SecurityCriticalAttribute attribute, 312
  [ServiceContract] attribute, 401, 404
  SizeToContent attribute, 288
  [STAThread] attribute, 389
  Style attribute, 46, 223
  SuppressUnmanagedCodeAttribute attribute, 312
  System.Security.SecurityCritical
    Attribute attribute, 311
  System.Security.SecurityTransparent
    Attribute attribute, 311
  TargetType attribute, 14, 223
  Value attribute, 227
  WidthAndHeight attribute, 288
  XAML namespace attribute, 379
  x:Class attribute
    child elements, 384
    CLR properties, 384
    namespaces, 383
    overview, 383
    XAML attributes, 384–385
  x:Key attribute, 14, 223, 224
  xmlns attribute, 30, 221, 344
  x:TypeArguments attribute, 259, 265
  x:TypeAttribute attribute, 266
audio/video media, importing, 113
authentication mechanism, of XBAP, 241
AuthenticationService directory, 246
automatic layout, 287

AutoReverse **property, 193**
AxShockwaveFlashObjects **namespace, 344**
AxShockwaveObjects **namespace, 340**

B

Background message priority, 390
Background **property, 166, 201**
BackgroundWorker **object, 395–397**
BAML file, 374
base classes, 205
Base Services, of Windows API, 2
BasedOn **attribute, 225**
BasicHttpBinding **default binding, 400**
Begin **method, 145**
BeginInvoke **method, 390, 393, 395**
BeginTime **property, 145**
BevelBitmapEffect **class, 171, 175**
BGThreadId, **395**
BidActivity **Components, 427**
Binding **attribute, 56**
Binding **class, 400**
Binding extension, 217, 218
binding modes
    data binding to List<T>, 218–219
    overview, 217–218
bitmap effects, 171–175
BitmapEffect **class, 171**
BitmapEffect **object, 171, 174**
BitmapEffectGroup **class, 171, 174**
blocking thread execution, 388
BlurBitmapEffect, **171**
Border **element, 103, 111, 219**
Border **objects, 192, 194, 199**
BorderBrush **attribute, 219**
bounding box, 94
browser-based applications
    overview, 238
    standalone or "loose" XAML, 239
    XAML browser applications, 239–246, 295–296
Brush **class, 157**
brush classes
    creating custom drawing and brush fill, 150–153
    overview, 149–150
Brush **object, 189**
brushes
    DrawingBrush, 167–169
    GradientBrush, 162–165
    ImageBrush, 165–167
    SolidColorBrush, 156–162
    VisualBrush, 169–171
Brushes panel
    applying fills, 96
    opacity masks, 96–97
    selecting colors, 95
    strokes, 96

bubbling events, 39, 47
Build Action **property, 197**
BuildWindowCore **method, 332, 333**
BulletPanel **element, layout panels, 103**
business processes, 409–410
Button **control, 14, 37, 366, 372**
button controls
    creating, 112–113
    styling, 112–113
<Button **opening tag, 28**
<Button> **control, 46**
button1 **element, 407**
button1_click **event, 396**
ButtonChrome **element, 366**

C

C# Console Application, 402, 414
caching technique, 10
CalcAngleFromPercentage **method, 213**
Calculate Permissions button, 319
CallingPage.xaml **file, 261**
CallingPage.xaml.cs **file, 277**
cancel_Click **event handler, 275**
CanMinimize **value,** ResizeMode **property, 287**
CanResize **attribute,** Window **class, 288**
CanResize **value,** ResizeMode **property, 288**
CanResizeWithGrip **value,** ResizeMode **property, 288**
Canvas **container control, 123–124**
Canvas panel, 100–101
Canvas.Loaded **event, 193**
Canvas.Triggers **object, 193**
CAS (Code Access Security)
    code groups, 306–307
    creating code groups for applications, 308–311
    evidence, 305–306
    overview, 303
    "partial trust," 316
    permissions, 304
    policy levels, 306
    verification process, 303–304
    zones, 305
CAS Full Trust zone, 247
Cascading Style Sheets (CSS), 111
Caspol.exe utility, 327
Category **attribute, 290**
Center **property, 162**
CenterX **property, 180, 186**
CenterX slider, 182, 188
CenterY **property, 180, 186**
CenterY slider, 182, 188
Cert2spc.exe utility, 327
Certificate Enrollment API, 302
Certmgr.exe utility, 327
change notification system, 11–13

CheckAccess **method,** DispatcherObject **class, 389**
child elements, 44, 101, 104, 123, 289, 384
Cider. *See* **Visual Designer**
class handlers, 11
Class1.cs **file, 75–78**
Click **attribute, 381**
Click **event, Events view, 119, 371, 378, 379**
ClickOnce
  and application deployment, 291, 294
  security
    overview, 323
    permission settings, 318
    personal certificate file, 324–326
    Trusted Publishers, 323
clients, 400
clipping regions
  creating with geometry, 146–149
  creating with shapes, 146–149
Closed **event, 33, 35**
Closing **event, 33, 35**
CLR (Common Language Runtime)
  properties and XAML attributes, 384
  security
    Code Access Security (CAS), 303–311
    critical code methodology, 311–312
    overview, 302
    verification, 313
CNG (Cryptography API: Next Generation), 302
code
  adding WindowsFormsHost in, 337–339
  creating, 308–311
  creating dynamic animation with, 135–138
  editing with Visual Studio 2005, 117–118
Code Access Security (CAS)
  code groups, 306–307
  creating code groups for applications, 308–311
  evidence, 305–306
  overview, 303
  "partial trust," 316
  permissions, 304
  policy levels, 306
  verification process, 303–304
  zones, 305
Code Access Security Policy Tool, 307
Code **activity, 420, 423**
code groups, CAS, 306–307
Code Groups folder, 308
code-behind file, 69
CodeDom **model, 374, 383**
Color **property, 157, 162, 164, 219**
color subpanel, 95
ColorAnimation **type, 135**
colors, selecting, 95
COM development, 388
combining special effects, 191–203
combo box template, 110
command class object, 50

CommandBinding **class, 48, 49**
commands, 47–51
Common Control Library, 2
Common Dialog Box Library, 2
Common Language Runtime (CLR)
  properties and XAML attributes, 384
  security
    Code Access Security (CAS), 303–311
    critical code methodology, 311–312
    overview, 302
    verification, 313
Common Language Runtime Support property, 335
communication channels, 14
compile time, 269
ComponentCommands **class, 47**
composite sites, 240
composition system, 9, 14–15, 356, 358–359
composition tree, 358
CompositionTarget **class, 129, 132, 139–143**
CompositionTarget.Rendering **event handler,**
  139, 148
compound paths, 93–94
Condition child elements, 226
ConditionName **property, 422**
.config file, 293
configuration utility, 69
configuring design environment, in Expression Blend,
  88–90
Connect **method, 377, 378**
Contact PageFunction, 272
ContactData.cs **file, 271**
content controls, 43, 109
Content **property, 43, 109**
ContentPresenter **element, 111, 366, 372**
ContentRendered **attribute, 36**
ContentRendered **event, 33, 35, 36**
ContextIdle **message priority, 390**
Continue behavior, HitTestFilterBehavior
  enumeration, 127
Continue value, HitTestResultCallback **delegate,**
  126
ContinueLooping **property, 421**
ContinueSkipChildren **behavior,** HitTestFilter
  Behavior **enumeration, 127**
ContinueSkipSelf **behavior,** HitTestFilter
  Behavior **enumeration, 127**
ContinueSkipSelfAndChildren **behavior,**
  HitTestFilterBehavior **enumeration, 127**
Contract layer, 398
ContractDescription **class, 402**
control base classes
  creating user control, 207–217
  UserControl **class, 207**
Control **class, 41, 371–373**
control properties, 156
control templates, 44–45, 228, 372
Controller.xaml.cs **file, 284**

controls
ActiveX controls, adding
  example, 340–344
  overview, 339
  in XAML, 344–345
adding Windows Forms controls
  adding ActiveX Controls, 339–344
  adding ActiveX Controls in XAML, 344–345
  adding WindowsFormsHost in code, 337–339
  adding WPF controls to Windows Forms, 345–349
  adding your HwndHost in XAML, 339
  affecting properties, 349–351
AdornerLayer control, 9
button, 112–113
Button control, 14, 37, 366, 372
button controls
  creating, 112–113
  styling, 112–113
Canvas container control, 123–124
commands, 47–51
Common Control Library, 2
composition, 44
content controls, 43, 109
control base classes
  creating user control, 207–217
  UserControl class, 207
Control class, 41, 371–373
Create Keyframe control, 106
creating
  control inheritance, 109–110
  editing, 110
  overview, 108–109
  styling, 110
custom
  control base classes, 207–217
  customizing with templates, 228–230
  data binding, 217–222
  overview, 205–206
  styles, 222–227
Custom Control Library, 79
default controls, 206
dependency property system, 43–44
Dock Panel control, Toolbox, 103
FlowDocumentScrollViewer text control, 99
gradient slider control, 96
Grid control, 14, 37
headered content controls, 43
headered items controls, 43, 110
Hyperlink control, 258
items controls, 43, 109
Label text control, 99
ListBox control, 180, 186, 218
lookless controls, 205, 371
nested controls, 40, 41
overview, 41–43
PasswordBox text control, 99
Presentation Framework control, 110

properties, 156
Rich Text Box text control, 99
ScrollViewer control, 109
Simple controls, 109
Slider control, 217
StackPanel control, 7, 49, 109, 198
steps to build it in Visual Studio, 211
styles, 44–46
System.Windows.Controls.Border control, 9
System.Windows.Controls.Button control, 7
System.Windows.Controls.Grid control, 9
System.Windows.Controls.Label control, 7
System.Windows.Controls.Primitives.Resize
    Grip control, 9
System.Windows.Controls.TextBox control, 7
System.Windows.Documents.AdornerDecorator
    control, 9
templates, 44–45, 228, 372
TextBlock text control, 99, 199
TextBox control, 37, 388
types, 43
User Control Library, 340
visual tree, 46–47
Windows Forms, adding controls, 337–351
  adding ActiveX Controls, 339–344
  adding ActiveX Controls in XAML, 344–345
  adding HwndHost in XAML, 339
  adding WindowsFormsHost in code, 337–339
  adding WPF controls to Windows Forms, 345–349
  affecting properties, 349–351
workspace zoom control, 89
WPF Custom Control Library, 78–82
conversions, data, 221–222
Converter **property, 221**
ConvertToRadians **method, 213**
Copy XAML command, 21
core operating system (OS), security
  Cryptography API: Next Generation (CNG), 302
  Least-Privilege User Access (LUA), 301
  overview, 300–301
  sandboxing, 301–302
  virtualization, 301
corner nodes, 94
create bindings task, 15
Create Keyframe **control, 106**
Create Test Certificate button, 325
CreatePointFromAngle **method, 213**
CreateWindow **function, 330**
CreateWorkflow **method, 416**
CreditCarad.xaml **file, 280**
CreditCardData **class, 281**
Cryptography API: Next Generation (CNG), 302
.cs **code-behind file, 137**
CSS (Cascading Style Sheets), 111
culture, 59
Current class member, 70
CurrentUICulture **property, 59**

Curves path, 93
Custom Control **class, 80**
Custom Control Library, 79

D

data binding
  conversions, 221–222
  markup extensions, 217
  modes, 217–219
  templates, 219–220
data triggers, 54–57
DataBind **method, 217**
DataContext **property, 218, 371**
DataSource **property, 217**
DataTemplate **element, 57**
Deactivated **event, 33, 35**
Debug This Application with the Selected Permission
    Set checkbox, Advanced tab, 321
DecimalToPercentageConverter **resource, 221**
declarative attributes, 73
Declarative Demands area, 320
declarative models, 15–16
declarative programming, XAML
  designer and developer collaboration, 18
  overview, 4
  XAML runtime support, 17–18
default controls, 206
Delegate **class, 393**
dependency properties, 12, 363
dependency property system (DPS), 43–44, 362
DependencyObject **class, 13, 362–363**
.deploy extension, 296
deployment
  building applications, 292–293
  .NET Framework 3.0 runtime, 296–298
  overview, 61
  project in Expression Blend, 91
  simplified, 4–5
  standalone windows applications, 294–295
  XAML browser applications, 295–296
design environment, 86
designer interface, 73
desktop composition, 360
Desktop Window Manager (DWM), 360–361
DestroyWindowCore **method, 332, 333**
detecting hit tests
  with geometry, 130–134
  to a point, 128–130
Direct3D, 4, 15
DirectX, 64, 330
Dispatcher **class, 353, 362, 389, 390–391**
DispatcherObject **class, 362, 388, 389–390**
DispatcherPriority **enumeration, 390**
DisplayProduct **activity, 420**
DLL (dynamic-link library), 26, 78

Dock **element, 111**
dock layout panel, 102
Dock panel, 102–103
Dock Panel **control, Toolbox, 103**
Dock **property, 199**
docking positions, 102
DockPanel.Dock **property, 199, 363**
document portability, 5
DoSomething( ) **method, 401**
DoSomethingElse( ) **method, 401**
DoubleAnimation **type, 135, 138**
DoWork **event, 397**
DPS (dependency property system), 43–44, 362
Drawing API
  brushes, 149–153
  geometry, 145–146
  shapes, 146–149
Drawing **object, 167**
DrawingBrush **class, 149, 156, 167–169**
DrawingContext **object, 365**
DrawingGroup **class, 167**
DrawingVisual **class, 365**
DrawPoint **method, 151**
DropShadowBitmapEffect, **171**
Duplex message exchange pattern, 402
DWM (Desktop Window Manager), 360–361
dynamic declarative model, 17
dynamic layout, 17
dynamic styling, 17
DynamicFill.xaml **file, 150**
dynamic-link library (DLL), 26, 78

E

ease-in value interpolation, 106
ease-out value interpolation, 106
Edit Style, context menu, 111
EditCommands **class, 47**
editing
  code with Visual Studio 2005, 117–118
  shapes, 92–93
  styles, custom controls, 222–227
  templates, 110
effects
  bitmap effects, 171–175
  brushes
    DrawingBrush, 167–169
    GradientBrush, 162–165
    ImageBrush, 165–167
    SolidColorBrush, 156–162
    VisualBrush, 169–171
  combining, 191–203
  overview, 155–156
  transformations
    opacity masks, 188–190
    overview, 175–177

RotateTransform, 186–188
ScaleTransform, 180–183
SkewTransform, 183–186
TranslateTransform, 178–180
Electric Rain ZAM 3D, 21–22
element system, 5–9, 10
element trees, 6–9
ElementHost **class, 345, 349, 350**
elements
  <Application> element, 223
  Border element, 103, 111, 219
  BulletPanel element, layout panels, 103
  button1 element, 407
  ButtonChrome element, 366
  child elements, 44, 101, 104, 123, 289, 384
  Condition child elements, 226
  ContentPresenter element, 111, 366, 372
  DataTemplate element, 57
  Dock element, 111
  element system, 5–9, 10
  element trees, 6–9
  ElementHost class, 345, 349, 350
  ElementTrees.Sample element, 7, 9
  Ellipse visual element, 359
  FocusVisualStyle element, 112
  FrameworkContentElement class, 118
  FrameworkElement class, 6, 34, 36, 41, 118, 207,
      288, 331, 365, 371
  Grid element, 111
  HeaderPanel element, 111
  IElement interface, 364
  IInputElement interface, 370
  interface elements, 85
  ItemContentStyle element, 112
  ItemsPresenter element, 111
  Label elements, 223, 367
  ListBox element, 220
  <local:MyCustomType> element, 387
  MultiTrigger element, 226
  MultiTrigger.Conditions XML element, 53
  nested child elements, 109
  nested elements, 11
  Page element, 239
  PageFunction element, 265
  parent elements, 11, 44
  Popup element, 103
  Pop-Up element, 111
  property-element syntax, 385
  Root Element, 383
  ScrollViewer element, 103, 111
  <Setter> XML element, 46, 52
  single-child elements, 109
  Stack element, 111
  Style element, 14, 112, 225
  <Style> XML element, 46
  <Style.Triggers> XML element, 52

  TextBlock element, 366, 377
  TextBox element, 367, 369
  ToolbarOverflowPanel element, 103
  UI element, 119
  UniformGrid element, 103
  UserControl element, 221
  Viewbox element, 103
  ViewPort3D element, 21
  visual elements, 85, 109, 116
  Window element, 16, 36, 192, 198, 385
  Window.Resources element, 14, 46, 228
  workflow elements, 102
ElementTrees.Sample **element, 7, 9**
Ellipse tool, 93, 121, 370
Ellipse vector shape, 92
Ellipse **visual element, 359**
EllipseGeometry **class, 168**
EmbossedBitmapEffect**, 171**
Empty **value,** VisualHit **property, 130**
EndInvoke **method, 395**
EndPoint **property, 164, 190**
EndpointAddress **class, 400**
endpoints, 400–402
enterprise application development
  application localization
    attributes, 290–291
    automatic layout guidelines, 287–289
    free-form comments, 290–291
    overview, 286–287
    using Grids for flexibility, 289–290
  application models
    browser-based applications, 238–246
    overview, 234–235
    security considerations, 247–248
    standalone applications, 235–238
  deployment models
    building applications, 292–293
    .NET Framework 3.0 runtime, 296–298
    overview, 291–292
    standalone windows applications, 294–295
    XAML browser applications, 295–296
  navigation
    elements of, 258
    overview, 258
    structured, 259–269
    topologies, 269–286
  overview, 233–235
  state management
    Application object, 248–250
    example, 252–257
    isolated storage, 250–252
    overview, 248
event handlers, 35, 36, 393
event listener, 35
event logic, 71
event routing, 41

event triggers, 155, 227, 228
EventLog, **247**
events
  Activated event, 31, 33, 35
  Application.Exit event, 253
  Application.OnExit event handler, 251
  Application.Startup event, 251, 253
  bubbling events, 39, 47
  button1_click event, 396
  Canvas.Loaded event, 193
  Click event, 119, 371, 378, 379
  Closed event, 33, 35
  Closing event, 33, 35
  ContentRendered event, 33, 35, 36
  Deactivated event, 31, 33, 35
  DoWork event, 397
  event handlers, 119–120
  EventTrigger event, 193
  Execute event, 48
  ExecuteEvent event, 47
  Exit event, 31, 251
  input/event system, 10–11
  IsolatedStorageFile event, 254
  LoadCompleted event, 34
  LocationChanged event, 33, 35
  MouseDown event, 151, 192
  MouseMove event, 192
  Navigated event, 34
  Navigating event, 34
  NavigationProgress event, 34
  OnInitialized event handler, 137, 141
  OnReturn events, 277, 286
  overview, 118
  PreviewExecute event, 48
  PreviewExecuteEvent event, 47
  PreviewMouseLeftButtonDown event, 39
  PropertyChanged event, 11–12, 218
  routed, 36–41
  routed events, 11, 36–41
  RunWorkerCompleted event, 397
  SessionEnding event, 31
  Startup event, 31, 364
  StateChanged event, 33, 35
  triggers, 58
  tunneling event models, 39
  tunneling events, 47
  window, 35–36
  window events, 35–36
  WorkflowCompleted event, 418
  WorkflowTerminated event, 418
Events view, property panel, 119
EventTrigger **event, 193**
evidence, 305–306
Evidence **object, 305**
.exe extension, 293, 295
Execute **event, 48**

Execute **method, 50**
ExecuteCode **method, 421**
ExecuteEvent **event, 47**
Exit **event, 251**
Expression Blend. See Microsoft Expression Blend
Expression **property, 422**
expressions, 13–14
eXtensible Application Markup Language. See XAML

F

FileDialogPermission.Open **permission set, 314**
FileIOPermission **permission set, 314**
files
  App.Manifest, 66
  AssemblyInfo.cs, 66–67
  Class1.cs, 75–78
  MyApp.xaml, 70–71
  Page1.xaml, 73–74
  personal certificate, 324–326
  Resources.resx, 68
  Settings.settings, 68–70
  UserControl1.xaml, 79–82
  Window1.xaml, 72–73
  XAML, 373–378
Fill **property, 190**
fills, applying, 96
filtering hit test, 127
fixed linear topology, 269–278
Flash Platform, 120
Flash player, 340
FlashControl.cs **code file, 341**
Flip tool, Transform panel, 94
FlowDocumentScrollViewer **text control, 99**
FlyInNewImage **method, 200**
FlyOutCurrentImage **method, 200, 202**
FocusVisualStyle **element, 112**
Font **property, 350**
font system, 10
FontSize **attribute, 223**
fps (frames-per-second) rate, 139
Frame **object, 34, 237**
frames-per-second (fps) rate, 139
FrameworkContentElement **class, 118**
FrameworkElement **class, 6, 34, 36, 41, 118, 207,
    288, 331, 365, 371**
free-form comments, 290–291
Freeform path, 93
Freezable **class, 364**
Front Page Extensions, 241
full demand, 312
Full-Trust environment, 250
FullyContains **value,** VisualHit **property, 130**
FullyInside **value,** VisualHit **property, 130**

G

GDI (Graphics Device Interface), 2, 330
GDI+ API, 146
geometry classes
    creating dynamic clipping region with, 146–149
    overview, 145–146
GeometryDrawing class, 167
GeometryHitTestResult class, 130, 133
GetBottom method, Canvas class, 124
GetChildren method, 46, 369
GetChildrenCount method, 369
GetLeft method, Canvas class, 124
GetParent method, 46
GetRight method, Canvas class, 124
GetTop method, Canvas class, 124
GetUserDefaultUILanguage method, 59
GetValue method, 13
Global Assembly Cache, 314
globalization, 59
GPU (graphics processing unit), 4, 354, 358
gradient opacity mask, 96
gradient slider control, Appearance panel, 96
GradientBrush, 162–165
GradientOrigin, 162
GradientStop object, 162
GradientStops, 190
graphic design view, 87
graphics, vector, 4
graphics card, 358
Graphics Device Interface (GDI), 2, 330
graphics processing unit (GPU), 4, 354, 358
grid cells, 101
Grid control, 14, 37
Grid element, 111
Grid panel, 101
grid pattern, 161

H

Handled property, 40
hardware-based rendering, 15
hash evidence, 306
Header property, 43, 109
headered content controls, 43
headered items controls, 43, 110
HeaderPanel element, 111
Height property, 385
Height value, SizeToContent property, 288
HelloWCFServices class, 404
history menu, 238
hit testing, 124–135
    detecting hit test to a point, 128–130
    detecting hit test with geometry, 130–134
    filtering hit test, 127

HitTestResultCallback delegate, 126–127
VisualTreeHelper class, 124–126
HitTest method, VisualTreeHelper class, 124, 125
HitTestFilterCallback method, VisualTree Helper class, 125
HitTestParameters method, VisualTreeHelper class, 125
HitTestParameters3D method, VisualTree Helper class, 125
HitTestResult class, 125, 130
HitTestResultCallback delegate, 126–127, 128, 130
HitTestResultCallback method, VisualTree Helper class, 125, 129
host parameter, 349
HTML forms, 240
HwndHost class, 331, 339
HwndHost WndProc method, 332
HWNDs
    hosting Win32 Button in WPF, 332–335
    how interoperate with WPF, 330–331
    using inside WPF, 331–335
HwndSource class, 331, 335, 336
hyperlink, 258
Hyperlink control, 258
Hyperlink object, 238

I

IComponentConnector interface, 377
IElement interface, 364
ifElse activity, 420, 422
Ignore attribute, 290
IHelloWCF service contract interface, 404
IInputElement interface, 370
IIS (Internet Information Services), 241, 295
Image object, 198
Image_MouseEnter event handler, 200
ImageBrush class, 149, 156, 165–167
imageCanvas, 200
imperative statements, 15
importing, audio/video media, 113
Inactive message priority, 390
Include code file checkbox, Add New Item dialog box, 117
Inherit attribute, 290
InitializeComponent( ) method, 148, 151, 373, 376, 377
INotifyPropertyChanged interface, 218
input gesture items, 49
input gesture types, 50
Input message priority, 390
input/event system, 10–11
InputGestureCollection class, 50
InputHitTest method, 124

installations, required for creating applications, 26
integration, 4
IntelliSense, 73, 118
Interaction workspace panel, 87
interface elements, 85
Internet domain address, 305
Internet Explorer, security
    overview, 313
    XAML Browser Application (XBAP), 314–322
    zone restrictions, 313–314
Internet Information Services (IIS), 241, 295
Internet Zone, 250, 318
interoperability, 118
interpolation, 106
Intersects value, VisualHit property, 130
Invalid message priority, 390
InvalidOperationException class, 390
Invoke method, Dispatcher class, 390, 393
I/O operations, 247, 250
IsEnabled property, 226
IServiceContract class, 402
IsFocused property, 53
IsInputComplete method, 275
IsLargeArc argument, 209
IsMouseOver property, 53, 225, 226, 229, 230
isolated storage, 233
IsolatedStorageFile event, 254
IsolatedStorageFilePermission permission set, 314
IsPressed property, 229
IsSharedSizeScope property, Grid panels, 289
ItemContentStyle element, 112
items controls, 43, 109
ItemSource property, 218
ItemsPresenter element, 111
ItemTemplate attribute, 220
IValueConverter interface, 221

K

Keyboard class, 118
keyframes, 104, 105–106
key/value dictionary collection, 364

L

Label elements, 223, 367
Label text control, 99
LabelStyle property, 223
language support
    globalization, 59
    localization, 60–61
    overview, 58–59
LastChildFill Boolean property, 102
layout model, 120
layout panels, 99–100
Layout UI task, 15

layouts
    nesting layout panels, 103–104
    other layout panels, 103
    overview, 99–100
    User Interface (UI) layout panels
        Canvas, 100–101
        Dock, 102–103
        Grid, 101
        overview, 100
        Stack, 101
        Wrap, 101–102
LayoutTransform object, 177, 180, 186
Least-Privilege User Access (LUA), 301
LeftToRightThenTopToBottom, FlowDirection
    property, 288
Library panel, 109
Line vector shape, 92
linear interpolation, 106
LinearGradientBrush class, 149, 156, 162, 163,
    190, 192, 199
line-by-line debugging, 118
LineSegment geometric segment, 208
link demand, 312
Link Demands area, 320
List<T>, data binding to, 218–219
ListBox control, 180, 186, 218
ListBox element, 220
ListBox object, 180
ListTemplate template, 220
LoadCompleted event, 34
LoadComponent method, 377
LoadControlFromXAMLFile method, 350
Loaded message priority, 390
local name address, 305
localization
    attributes, 290–291
    automatic layout guidelines, 287–289
    free-form comments, 290–291
    overview, 60–61, 286–287
    using Grids for flexibility, 289–290
Localization.Attributes property, 290, 291
Localization.Comments attribute, 291
<local:MyCustomType> element, 387
LocationChanged event, 33, 35
logical tree, 7, 36
LogicalTreeClass class, 369
LogicalTreeHelper class, 46, 369
LongRunningProcess method, 395, 397
lookless controls, 205, 371
loose XAML, 235, 373
LUA (Least-Privilege User Access), 301

M

machine policy configuration, 306
Macromedia Flash player, 340
MainAssembly value, 67

MainWindow **property,** Application **object, 33**
MainWindow.xaml **file, 342**
Makecert.exe utility, 327
Managed Certificate API, 302
Managed Cryptography API, 302
.manifest extension, 296
Manual **value,** SizeToContent **property, 288**
Margin **property, 99, 124**
margins, 124
markup compiler, 374
markup extensions, 217, 385–386
MarkupExtension **class, 385**
Math.Cos( ) **method, 142**
Math.Sin( ) **method, 142**
MatrixTransform **class, 176**
max point count, 151
Media Integration Layer (MIL), 354, 355
Media Time **property, 113**
MediaCommands **class, 47**
MediaPermissionhim **permission set, 314**
membership rules, 310
Message Exchange Patterns, 402
message loop, 390
message transport, 14, 356, 359
Messaging layer, 399
methods
  AddChild method, 364
  AddService method, 413
  AnimateFill( ) method, 151, 152
  Animation_Completed method, 200, 202
  Begin method, 145
  BeginInvoke method, 390, 393, 395
  BuildWindowCore method, 332, 333
  CalcAngleFromPercentage method, 213
  CheckAccess method, 389
  Connect method, 377, 378
  ConvertToRadians method, 213
  CreatePointFromAngle method, 213
  CreateWorkflow method, 416
  DataBind method, 217
  DestroyWindowCore method, 332, 333
  DoSomething( ) method, 401
  DoSomethingElse( ) method, 401
  DrawPoint method, 151
  EndInvoke method, 395
  Execute method, 50
  ExecuteCode method, 421
  FlyInNewImage method, 200
  FlyOutCurrentImage method, 200, 202
  GetBottom method, 124
  GetChildren method, 46, 369
  GetChildrenCount method, 369
  GetLeft method, Canvas class, 124
  GetParent method, 46
  GetRight method, 124
  GetTop method, 124
  GetUserDefaultUILanguage method, 59

GetValue method, 13
HitTest method, 124, 125
HitTestFilterCallback method, 125
HitTestParameters method, 125
HitTestParameters3D method, 125
HitTestResultCallback method, 125, 129
HwndHost WndProc method, 332
InitializeComponent( ) method, 148, 151, 373,
    376, 377
InputHitTest method, 124
Invoke method, 390, 393
IsInputComplete method, 275
LoadComponent method, 377
LoadControlFromXAMLFile method, 350
LongRunningProcess method, 395, 397
Math.Cos( ) method, 142
Math.Sin( ) method, 142
Mouse.GetPosition method, 120
MyHitTestResult method, 126
Navigate method, 34
non-static methods, 31
OnActivated method, 31
OnAddressReturned method, 277, 286
OnDeactivated method, 31
OnExit method, 31
OnRender method, 370
OnReturn method, 260, 265
OnSessionEnding method, 31
OnStartup method, 31
Pause method, 145
playback methods, 144–145
PrintLogicalTree method, 369
PrintVisualTree method, 369
ProvideValue method, 385
Register( ) method, 13, 363
RegisterAttached( ) method, 363
RemoveChild method, 364
RenderGraph method, 215
Resume method, 145
SayHello operation method, 404
SetBottom method, 124
SetKeepAlive method, 260
SetLeft method, 124
SetRight method, 124
SetTop method, 124
SetValue method, 13
Start method, 267
Stop method, 145
StopRuntime( ) method, 416
ToString( ) method, 122
VerifyAccess method, 389
virtual methods, 30
Visual method, 125
Visual3D method, 125
VisualTreeHelper.HitTest method, 126
XAMLReader.Load method, 378
XamlReader.Load method, 379

Microsoft DirectX, 64, 330
Microsoft Expression Blend
animation
creating controls, 108–110
importing audio/video media, 113
keyframes, 105–106
motion paths, 106–107
of object's property, 106
overview, 104
states, 112–113
styles, 111–112
templates, 110–111
Timeline sub-panel, 104–105
triggers, 107–108
Animation API
animation classes, 135
creating dynamic animation procedurally with code,
135–138
overview, 135
programmatic animation, 139–143
design environment
artboard, 87–88
configuring, 88–90
overview, 85–86
workspace panels, 86–87
Drawing API
brushes, 149–153
geometry, 145–146
overview, 145
shapes, 146–149
handling user input
events, 118–120
hit testing, 124–135
Keyboard class, 118
Mouse class, 118
overview, 118
positioning, 120–124
interacting with storyboards, 143–145
layouts
nesting layout panels, 103–104
other layout panels, 103
overview, 99–100
UI layout panels, 100–103
manipulating text, 98–99
overview, 19–20, 84
project structure
adding new file, 90–91
building, 91
deploying, 91
overview, 90
properties panel
Brushes panel, 95–97
opacity, 97–98
overview, 94
Transform panel, 94–95

transparency, 97–98
visibility, 97–98
vector objects
overview, 91–92
paths, 93–94
shapes, 92
workflow
code editing with Visual Studio 2005, 117–118
overview, 116–118
Microsoft Internet Explorer, security
overview, 313
XAML Browser Application (XBAP), 314–322
zone restrictions, 313–314
midpoint node, 94
Migpole.exe utility, 327
MIL (Media Integration Layer), 354, 355
MIME types, 295
Minimum Grant Set Determination Tool, 319–320
Mobiform Aurora, 22–23
`Modifiable` **attribute, 290**
motion paths, 106–107
`Mouse` **class, 118**
`MouseDown` **event, 151, 192**
`MouseEnter` **event handler, 201**
`Mouse.GetPosition` **method, 120**
`MouseMove` **event, 192**
`MousePosition.xaml.cs` **code-behind file, 122**
`MouseUp` **event handler, 137, 192**
`MovieClips`, **120**
MSBuild utility, 293
MSI (Windows Installer), 291, 292
MUI (Multilingual User Interface), 59
`MulticastDelegate` **class, 393**
multi-condition triggers, 53–54, 57
Multilingual User Interface (MUI), 59
multithreading
asynchronous threading, 393–397
`Dispatcher` class, 390–391
overview, 388
single-threaded applications, 388–393
thread affinity and `DispatcherObject`, 389–390
`MultiTrigger` **element, 226**
`MultiTrigger.Conditions` **XML element, 53**
`MyApplication` **object, 249**
`MyApp.xaml` **file, 70–71**
`MyHitTestResult` **method, 126**
`MyTextBox` **class, 13**
`MyWPFApp` **namespace, 383**

N

namespaces, 383
`AxShockwaveFlashObjects` namespace, 344
`AxShockwaveObjects` namespace, 340
`MyWPFApp` namespace, 383

`System.ComponentModel` namespace, 396

`System.Media.Input` namespace, 118

`System.ServiceModel` namespace, 402, 405

`System.Threading` namespace, 395

`System.Windows.Forms.Integration` name space, 329, 345, 346

`System.Windows.Interop` namespace, 329

`System.Windows.Markup` namespace, 346, 348

`System.Windows.Media` namespace, 124, 156, 176

`System.Windows.Media.Effects` namespace, 171

`System.Windows.Threading` namespace, 395, 397

`System.Workflow.Activities` namespace, 415

`System.Workflow.Runtime` namespace, 415

`Navigate` **method, 34**

`Navigated` **event, 34**

`Navigating` **event, 34**

navigation

  elements of, 258

  overview, 258

  structured, 259–269

  topologies

    adaptive, 278–286

    fixed linear, 269–278

    overview, 269

`NavigationProgress` **event, 34**

`NavigationService` **class, 34, 258**

`NavigationWindow` **class, 32–35, 237, 258**

nested child elements, 109

nested controls, 40, 41

nested elements, 11

nesting layout panels, 103–104

.NET 3.0 Common Language Runtime, 299

.NET classes, 29–30, 399

.NET Configuration tool, 306, 307

.NET Framework, 247

.NET Framework 2.0 Configuration tool, 306, 310

.NET Framework 3.0

  Custom Control Library Project, 26

  overview, 3

  runtime, 296–298

  security utilities, 327

  Service Library Project, 26

  Windows application, 71–73

  XAML Browser Application, 26

`NetMsmqBinding` **default binding, 400**

Network Services, 2

`NeverLocalize` **attribute, 290**

new keyword, 384

New Project Wizard, 216

`None` **attribute, 290**

non-static methods, 31

`NoResize` **value,** `ResizeMode` **property, 287**

Normal message priority, 390

O

Obj\Debug folder, 377

Object type, 249

objects

  manipulating with properties panel

    Brushes panel, 95–97

    opacity, 97–98

    overview, 94

    Transform panel, 94–95

    transparency, 97–98

    visibility, 97–98

  properties of, animating, 106

  vector, 91–94

Obj\Release folder, 377

`ObservableCollection` **class, 57**

`Offset` **property, 162, 164**

`OffsetX` **property, 178**

`OffsetY` **property, 178**

`OnActivated` **method, Activated event, 31**

`OnAddressReturned` **method, 277, 286**

`OnDeactivated` **method,** `Deactivated` **event, 31**

`OneTime` **mode, 218**

One-Way message exchange pattern, 402

`OneWay` **mode, 218**

`OneWayToSource` **mode, 218**

`OnExit` **method,** `Exit` **event, 31**

`OnInitialized` **event handler, 137, 141**

`OnRender` **method, 370**

`OnReturn` **event handler, 286**

`OnReturn` **events, 277**

`OnReturn` **method, 260, 265**

`OnSessionEnding` **method,** `SessionEnding` **event, 31**

`OnStartup` **method,** `Startup` **event, 31**

opacity, 96–98, 188–190

`Opacity` **property, 157**

opacity slider, 97

`OpacityMask` **property, 188**

`[OperationContract]` **attribute, 401, 404**

OS layer, 300

`OuterGlowBitmapEffect`, **171, 175**

P

`Padding` **property, 99**

Page and Table Service (PTS), 10

`Page` **class, 237, 258, 259, 260**

`Page` **element, 239**

`Page` **object, 32–35, 90**

`Page1.xaml` **file, 73–74, 262**

`PageFunction` **class, 258, 259–261, 267, 279**

`PageFunction` **element, 265**

painting algorithm, 358

`Panel. StackPanel` **class, 7**

parent elements, 11, 44

`PasswordBox` **text control, 99**

Path **class, 146**
Path **object, 150, 151, 208**
Path **variable, 57**
PathFigure **object, 208**
PathGeometry **class, 151, 152, 208, 215**
paths, compound, 93–94
PathSegment **object, 208**
Pause **method, 145**
People **class, 57**
Percentage **property,** PiePieceData **object, 227**
permissions, 304
Permview.exe utility, 327
personal certificate files, 324–326
Peverify.exe utility, 327
pfx **file, 325**
PI (processing instructions), 382
PieGraphControl **class, 213, 218**
PieGraphControl.xaml.cs **file, 211, 221**
PiePieceData **object, 219, 221**
pixel resolution, 360
playback methods, 144–145
Point **class, 122**
PointAnimation **type, 135**
policy levels, 306
policy statement, 307
Pop-Up **element, 111**
Popup **element, layout panels, 103**
portability, of documents, 5
Position tool, Transform panel, 94
positioning
  with Canvas container control, 123–124
  margins, 124
  overview, 120–123
presentation core, 356, 361, 362
presentation framework, 5, 354, 361, 362
Presentation Framework **control, 110**
PresentationFramework **assembly, 64, 346**
PresentationHost.exe, **238, 373**
PreviewExecute **event, 48**
PreviewExecuteEvent **event, 47**
PreviewMouseLeftButtonDown **event, 39**
PrintingPermission.Safeprinting **permission set, 314**
PrintLogicalTree **method, 369**
PrintVisualTree **method, 369**
private class declaration, 211
processing instructions (PI), 382
Product **class, 252**
program.cs **file, 415**
Project Properties dialog box, Security tab, 247
Project Types tree view, 243
Project workspace panel, 87
projects
  composition
    App.Manifest file, 66
    AssemblyInfo.cs file, 66–67

    MyApp.xaml file, 70–71
    overview, 63–65
    Resources.resx file, 68
    Settings.settings file, 68–70
  Microsoft Expression Blend
    adding new file, 90–91
    building, 91
    deploying, 91
    structure, 90–91
  .NET Framework 3.0 Windows Application
    overview, 71
    Window1.xaml file, 72–73
  Windows Communication Foundation (WCF) Service Library, 75–78
  WPF Custom Control Library
    overview, 78–79
    UserControl1.xaml file, 79–82
  XAML Browser Application (XBAP), 73–74
properties
  Alignment property, 99
  Angle property, 186
  AnimationDurationProperty property, 200
  AutoReverse property, 193
  Background property, 166, 201
  BeginTime property, 145
  Build Action property, 197
  CanMinimize value, ResizeMode property, 287
  CanResize value, ResizeMode property, 288
  CanResizeWithGrip value, ResizeMode property, 288
  Center property, 162
  CenterX property, 180, 186
  CenterY property, 180, 186
  Color property, 157, 162, 164, 219
  Common Language Runtime Support property, 335
  ConditionName property, 422
  Content property, 43, 109
  ContinueLooping property, 421
  Converter property, 221
  CurrentUICulture property, 59
  DataContext property, 218, 371
  DataSource property, 217
  dependency property system (DPS), 43–44, 362
  Dock property, 199
  DockPanel.Dock property, 199, 363
  DPS (dependency property system), 43–44, 362
  Empty value, VisualHit property, 130
  EndPoint property, 164, 190
  Expression property, 422
  Fill property, 190
  FlowDirection property, 288
  Font property, 350
  FullyContains value, VisualHit property, 130
  FullyInside value, VisualHit property, 130
  Handled property, 40

Header property, 43, 109
Height property, 385
Height value, SizeToContent property, 288
IsEnabled property, 226
IsFocused property, 53
IsMouseOver property, 53, 225, 226, 229, 230
IsPressed property, 229
IsSharedSizeScope property, 289
ItemSource property, 218
LabelStyle property, 223
LastChildFill Boolean property, 102
Localization.Attributes property, 290, 291
MainWindow property, Application object, 33
Margin property, 99, 124
Media Time property, 113
NoResize value, ResizeMode property, 287
Offset property, 162, 164
OffsetX property, 178
OffsetY property, 178
Opacity property, 157
OpacityMask property, 188
Padding property, 99
Percentage property, 227
Properties collection property, 31, 70, 248–249
Properties property, 250, 364
property animations, 143
property system
    change notification, 11–13
    expressions, 13–14
    overview, 11
    storage, 13
property triggers, 51–52, 228
PropertyChanged event, 11–12, 218
PropertyMap property, 349
propertyName parameter, 349
PropertyTranslator delegate, 350
PropertyTranslator dictionary, 349
Query property, 241
RemoveFromJournal property, 259, 260, 267
RenderTransformOrigin property, 186
RepeatBehavior property, 193
ResizeMode property, 287
Resources property, 223
RootVisual property, 331, 335
ScaleX property, 180
ScaleY property, 180
Segments property, 208
ShadowDepth property, 174
SizeToContent property, 288
Source property, 41
StartPoint property, 164, 190
StartupUri property, 262, 270
Stretch property, 166
Stroke property, 164
Style property, 46
Template property, 372

Text property, 13, 201, 217
TextBox.Text property, 174
Value property, 174, 179, 217
Visual property, 201
VisualBitmapEffect property, 171
VisualHit property, 130
Width property, 198, 385
Properties collection property, 31, 70, 248–249
Properties palette, 119–120
properties panel
    Brushes panel
        applying fills, 96
        opacity masks, 96–97
        overview, 95
        selecting colors, 95
        strokes, 96
    opacity, 97–98
    overview, 94
    Transform panel, 94–95
    transparency, 97–98
    visibility, 97–98
Properties property, 250, 364
Properties workspace panel, 87
property animations, 143
property system
    change notification, 11–13
    expressions, 13–14
    overview, 11
    storage, 13
property triggers, 51–52, 228
PropertyChanged event, 11–12, 218
property-element syntax, 385
PropertyMap property, 349
propertyName parameter, 349
PropertyTranslator delegate, 350
PropertyTranslator dictionary, 349
ProvideValue method, 385
PTS (Page and Table Service), 10
publisher signature evidence, 305

Q

Query property, 241

R

RadialButton style, 229
RadialGradientBrush class, 149, 156, 162, 163
raster graphics, 358
raster images, 92
ReachFramework assembly, 64
Readable attribute, 290
README file, 316
readme.txt file, 316
Rectangle vector shape, 92
redundancy, 47

Register( ) **method, 13, 363**
RegisterAttached( ) **method, 363**
RegistryPermission **permission set, 314**
RelationshipType **field, 58**
Remote Desktop, 360
Remoting programming models, 397
Remoting protocol, 14
RemoveChild **method, 364**
RemoveFromJournal **property, 259, 260, 267**
RenderGraph **method, 215**
rendering engine, 359
RenderTransform **object, 177, 186**
RenderTransformOrigin **property, 186**
RenderTransfrom **object, 179**
RepeatBehavior **property, 193**
Request/Reply message exchange pattern, 402
ResizeMode **attribute,** Window **class, 288**
ResizeMode **property, 287**
Resource Dictionary **object, 90**
resource files, 61
ResourceDictionary **file type, 117**
ResourceManager **class, 59, 60, 67**
resources, 60
Resources **collection, 144**
Resources **property, 223**
Resources workspace panel, 87
Resources.resx **file, 68**
Resume **method, 145**
retained mode graphics model, 357
ReturnEventArgs **argument, 260**
Rich Text Box **text control, 99**
Rights Management Services (RMS), 302
RightToLeftThenTopToBottom, FlowDirection
        property, 288
RMS (Rights Management Services), 302
Root Element, 383
root layout type, 104
RootVisual **property,** HwndSource **class, 331, 335**
rotAnimation **object, 202**
RotateTransform **class, 176, 177, 186–188, 200**
Rotation tool, Transform panel, 94
RotationAngle **argument, 209**
routed commands, 41
routed events, 11, 36–41
routed visual trees, 41
RoutedCommand **class, 47, 48**
RoutedEventArgs **parameter, 40, 41**
runtime, 269
runtime support, XAML, 17–18
RunWorkerCompleted **event, 397**

S

sandboxing, 301–302, 314–315
Satellite.MainAssembly **value, 67**

SayHello **operation method, 404**
Scale tool, Transform panel, 94
ScaleTransform **class, 176, 178, 180–183, 195, 200**
ScaleX **property, 180**
ScaleX slider, 182
ScaleY **property, 180**
screen design, 32
ScrollViewer **control, 109**
ScrollViewer **element, 103, 111**
security
  ClickOnce
    overview, 323
    personal certificate file, 324–326
    Trusted Publishers, 323
  Common Language Runtime (CLR)
    Code Access Security (CAS), 303–311
    critical code methodology, 311–312
    overview, 302
    verification, 313
  core operating system (OS)
    Cryptography API: Next Generation (CNG), 302
    Least-Privilege User Access (LUA), 301
    overview, 300–301
    sandboxing, 301–302
    virtualization, 301
  express applications, 300
  Microsoft Internet Explorer
    overview, 313
    XAML Browser Application (XBAP) security, 314–322
    zone restrictions, 313–314
  .NET 3.0 security utilities, 327
  overview, 247–248
  trusted applications, 300
  WPF security model, 299–300
security sandbox, 241, 247
[SecurityCritical] **attribute, 311**
SecurityCriticalAttribute **attribute, 312**
SecurityPermission.UnmanagedCode **permission**
        set, 314
Secutil.exe utility, 327
Segment classes, 208
Segments **property, 208**
Send message priority, 391
Sequence **activity, 420**
Sequential Workflow Console Application, 423
Sequential Workflow **model, 416**
SequentialWorkflowActivity **class, 416**
service boundary, 398
service hosts, 400
Service Library, 75
Service Model layer, 398
service orientation (SO), 397–398
[ServiceContract] **attribute, 401, 404**
ServiceImplementation **class, 402**

services
  building
    Hello WCF Client, 405–409
    Hello WCF Service, 402–404
    overview, 402
  overview, 399
  tracking, 413
  transaction, 413
SetBottom **method,** Canvas **class, 124**
SetKeepAlive **method, 260**
SetLeft **method,** Canvas **class, 124**
SetRight **method,** Canvas **class, 124**
<Setter> **XML element, 46, 52**
Settings.settings **file, 68–70**
SetTop **method,** Canvas **class, 124**
SetValue **method, 13**
ShadowDepth **property, 174**
shape classes, 146–149
shapes, 92–93
ShockWave Flash COM component, 340
ShockwaveFlashObject, **340**
SignTool.exe utility, 327
Simple **controls, 109**
SimpleWorkflow **class, 416**
simplified deployment, 4–5
Single Threaded Apartment (STA) model, 336, 359, 388
single-child elements, 109
singular content, 43
Size **argument, 209**
SizeToContent **attribute,** Window **class, 288**
SizeToContent **property, 288**
skew, 183
Skew tool, Transform panel, 94
SkewTransform **class, 176, 183–186**
Slider **control, 217**
Slider **object, 174, 180, 197, 198**
Sn.exe utility, 327
SO (service orientation), 397–398
SOAP message security, 400
software-based rendering, 15
SolidColorBrush **class, 149, 156–162**
Source **property, 41**
special effects
  bitmap effects, 171–175
  brushes
    DrawingBrush, 167–169
    GradientBrush, 162–165
    ImageBrush, 165–167
    overview, 156
    SolidColorBrush, 156–162
    VisualBrush, 169–171
  combining, 191–203
  overview, 155–156
  transformations
    opacity masks, 188–190

  overview, 175–177
    RotateTransform, 186–188
    ScaleTransform, 180–183
    SkewTransform, 183–186
    TranslateTransform, 178–180
SQLTrackingQuery **class, 413**
SSL message security, 400
STA (Single Threaded Apartment) model, 336, 359, 388
Stack **element, 111**
Stack panel, 101, 103
Stack Wall Modifiers area, 320
StackPanel **control, 7, 49, 109, 198**
standalone applications
  windows application, 236–237
  windows navigation application, 237–238
standalone windows applications
  deployment of, 236
  hosting of, 236
  installation of, 236
  offline use of, 236
  persistence, 236
  security for, 236
  updating of, 236
  user permission for, 236
Standard Accounts, **301**
Start **method, 267**
StartPoint **property, 164, 190**
Startup **event, 364**
StartupUri **property,** Application **object, 262, 270**
state management
  Application object, 248–250
  example, 252–257
  isolated storage, 250–252
  overview, 248
StateChanged **event, 33, 35**
states, 112–113
[STAThread] **attribute, 389**
static command object, 49
StaticResource **template, 220, 385**
StaticResourceExtension **class, 385**
Stop **behavior,** HitTestFilterBehavior **enumeration, 127**
Stop **method, 145**
Stop **value,** HitTestResultCallback **delegate, 126**
StopRuntime( ) **method, 416**
storage, 13, 250–252
Storeadm.exe utility, 327
storyboards, 104, 143–145
Straight Lines path, 93
Stretch **property, 166**
string key value, 31
StringReader **object, 379**
Stroke **property, 164**
strokes, 96
structure view, 105

structured hierarchical models, 46
structured navigation, 234, 258, 269
Style **attribute, 46, 223**
style definitions, 111
Style **element, 14, 112, 225**
Style **object, 198**
Style **property, 46**
style triggers, 226–227
<Style> **XML element, 46**
styles
  common, 112
  custom controls
    creating, 222–227
    editing, 222–227
    inheriting, 224–226
    overriding, 224–226
    specifying target type, 223–224
  overview, 111
  ways to extend to controls, 112
  working with, 111–112
<Style.Triggers> **XML element, 52**
subclassing, 207
sub-selection tool, 93
subsystems, 353
SuppressUnmanagedCodeAttribute **attribute, 312**
SweepDirection **argument, 209**
Swift3D, 21
System.ComponentModel **namespace, 396**
System.ComponentModel.INotifyProperty
  Changed **interface, 11**
System.Data **referenced assembly, 64**
SystemIdle **message priority, 391**
System.Media.Input **namespace, 118**
System.Printing **referenced assembly, 64**
System.Runtime.Serialization **referenced
  assembly, 64**
systems
  composition, 14–15, 358–359
  dependency property, 43–44
  element, 5–9
  font, 10
  input/event, 10–11
  message transport, 14
  property
    change notification, 11–13
    expressions, 13–14
    overview, 11
    storage, 13
  visual, 9, 356–358
System.Security.Authorization **referenced
  assembly, 64**
System.Security.Policy.Hash **class, 306**
System.Security.Policy.StrongName **class, 305**
System.Security.SecurityCriticalAttribute
  attribute, 311
System.Security.SecurityException, **247**

System.Security.SecurityTransparent
  Attribute **attribute, 311**
System.ServiceModel **namespace, 402, 405**
System.ServiceModel **referenced assembly, 64**
System.Threading **namespace, 395**
System.Windows.Controls.Border **control, 9**
System.Windows.Controls.Button **control, 7**
System.Windows.Controls.ContentControl
  class, 7
System.Windows.Controls.ContentPresenter, **9**
System.Windows.Controls.Grid **control, 9**
System.Windows.Controls.Label **control, 7**
System.Windows.Controls.Panel **class, 7**
System.Windows.Controls.Primitives.Resize
  Grip **control, 9**
System.Windows.Controls.StackPanel **class, 7**
System.Windows.Controls.TextBox **control, 7**
System.Windows.Controls.UserControl **class,
  207**
System.Windows.Documents.AdornerDecorator
  control, 9
System.Windows.Documents.AdornerLayer, **9**
System.Windows.Forms.Control **class, 345**
System.Windows.Forms.Integration **namespace,
  329, 345, 346**
System.Windows.FrameworkElement **class, 5**
System.Windows.Interop **namespace, 329**
System.Windows.Markup **namespace, 346, 348**
System.Windows.Media **namespace, 124, 156, 176**
System.Windows.Media.Effects **namespace, 171**
System.Windows.Navigation.JournalEntry **class,
  260**
System.Windows.Navigation.Navigation
  Service **class, 241**
System.Windows.Navigation.PageFunction **class,
  260**
System.Windows.Threading **namespace, 395, 397**
System.Windows.UIElement **class, 5**
System.Workflow.Activities **namespace, 415**
System.Workflow.Activities **workflow library, 414**
System.Workflow.ComponentModel **workflow library,
  414**
System.Workflow.Runtime **namespace, 415**
System.Xml **referenced assembly, 64**

T

TargetType **attribute, 14, 223**
task controller, 274
Template **property, 372**
templates
  common elements, 111
  customizing custom controls with, 228–230
  data, 219–220
  editing, 110
  overview, 110

Terminal Services, 360
text, manipulating, 98–99
Text property, 13, 201, 217
_text variable, 13
TextBlock element, 366, 377
TextBlock text control, 99, 199
TextBox control, 37, 388
TextBox element, 367, 369
textbox1 message, 395
TextBox.Text property, 174
TextProperty member, 13
ThemeInfo entry, 67
themes, 44
thread affinity, 362
thread execution, 388
thread synchronization, 388
Timeline panel, 105
Timeline Properties palette, 144
Timeline sub-panel, 104–105, 135
Timelines palette, 143
ToolbarOverflowPanel element, 103
Toolbox panel, 93
Toolbox workspace panel, 87
TopToBottomThenLeftToRight, FlowDirection
   property, 288
TopToBottomThenRightToLeft, FlowDirection
   property, 288
ToString( ) method, 122
Transform class, 176
Transform panel, 94–95
transformations
   opacity masks, 188–190
   overview, 175–177
   RotateTransform, 186–188
   ScaleTransform, 180–183
   SkewTransform, 183–186
   TranslateTransform, 178–180
TransformGroup class, 177, 200
TranslateTransform class, 176, 178–180, 182,
   193, 195
transparency, 97–98
Transparent value, 190
Trigger sub-panel, Interaction panel, 104
triggers
   creating, 108
   data triggers, 54–57
   event triggers, 58
   multi-condition triggers, 53–54, 57
   multiple triggers, 53
   overview, 51, 107–108
   property triggers, 51–52
   style, 226–227
Triggers panel, 112
Trusted Publishers, 323

Trusted Root Certificate Authorities Store, 326
Trusted Root Certification Authority Store, 323
tunneling event models, 39
tunneling events, 47
TwoWay mode, 218
type converters, 385
TypeConverter declaration, 159, 192, 195, 196
typographic properties of text, 99

U

UI element, 119
UIAutomationProvider referenced assembly, 64
UIAutomationTypes referenced assembly, 64
UICulture setting, 67
UIElement class, 6, 124, 186, 365, 370–371
UI-less page function, 269
UIPermission.SafeTopLevelWindows permission
   set, 314
UltimateResourceFallbackLocation
   enumeration, 67
UniformGrid element, 103
unstructured navigation, 234, 258
User Control Library, 340
User Experience (UX), 1
user input, handling
   events, 118–120
   hit testing, 124–135
   Keyboard class, 118
   Mouse class, 118
   positioning, 120–124
User Interface (UI)
   creating
      NavigationWindow object, 32–35
      overview, 32
      Page object, 32–35
      screen design, 32
      Window object, 32–35
   layout panels
      Canvas, 100–101
      Dock, 102–103
      Grid, 101
      overview, 100
      Stack, 101
      Wrap, 101–102
   Win32, 330
UserControl class, 207
UserControl element, 221
UserControl object, 90
UserControl1.xaml file, 79–82
UserData class, 263, 266, 268, 272, 281
using declarations, 415
using directives, 150, 332
UX (User Experience), 1

V

validation logic, 275
Value attribute, 227
value parameter, 349
Value property, 174, 179, 217
VB6 web community, 302
vector drawings, 91
vector graphics, 4, 92, 358–359
vector objects
  overview, 91–92
  paths, 93–94
  shapes, 92–93
verification
  Code Access Security (CAS), 303–304
  Common Language Runtime (CLR) security, 313
VerifyAccess method, DispatcherObject class, 389
Viewbox element, 103
ViewPort3D element, 21
virtual methods, 30
virtualization, 301
visibility, 97–98
Visibility drop-down list, Appearance subpanel, 97
Visual class, 364–370
visual design tools, 18–23
  Electric Rain ZAM 3D, 21–22
  Microsoft Expression Blend, 19–20
  Mobiform Aurora, 22–23
  visual designer for WPF, 20–21
  XamlPad, 18–19
Visual Designer, 4, 410
visual designer for WPF, 20–21
visual elements, 85, 109, 116
Visual function, 368
Visual method, VisualTreeHelper class, 125
Visual property, 201
Visual Studio 2005, 4, 117–118, 292
visual system, 9, 10, 356–358
visual tree, 46–47
visual trees, 36, 41, 356, 358, 365
Visual3D method, VisualTreeHelper class, 125
VisualBitmapEffect property, 171
VisualBrush, 169–171
VisualBrush class, 149, 155, 156, 197
VisualHit property, 130
VisualTreeHelper class, 124–126, 368
VisualTreeHelper.HitTest method, 126

W

WAS (Windows Activation Service), 400
WCF (Windows Communication Foundation)
  architecture, 398–399
  building services
    Hello WCF Client, 405–409
    Hello WCF Service, 402–404
    overview, 402
  fundamentals
    clients, 400
    endpoints, 400–402
    overview, 399
    service hosts, 400
    services, 399
  of .NET Framework 3.0, 3
  overview, 397
  service orientation (SO), 397–398
WCF (Windows Communication Foundation) Service Library, 75–78
WCS (Windows CardSpace), 353
WDDM (Windows Display Driver Model) driver, 354
Web Service, 397
WebBrowserAppSample_TemporaryKey.pfx file, 325
WebBrowserPermission permission set, 314
WebPermission permission set, 314
WF (Windows Workflow Foundation)
  architecture, 411
  fundamentals
    activities, 412
    building workflow programmatically, 414–416
    building workflow using the Workflow Designer, 416–423
    creating custom activity, 423–427
    overview, 411
    tracking services, 413
    transaction services, 413
    types of workflow, 412–413
  of .NET Framework 3.0, 3
  overview, 409–410
  workflow defined, 410
WFCHelloWorldService, 406
While activity, 420, 422
Width property, 198, 385
Width value, SizeToContent property, 288
WidthAndHeight attribute, Window class, 288
WidthAndHeight value, SizeToContent property, 288
Win16, 2
Win32, 2, 329–351
  adding Windows Forms controls to WPF, 337–351
    adding ActiveX Controls, 339–344
    adding ActiveX Controls in XAML, 344–345
    adding HwndHost in XAML, 339
    adding WindowsFormsHost in code, 337–339
    adding WPF controls to Windows Forms, 345–349
    affecting properties, 349–351
  HWNDs
    hosting Win32 Button in WPF, 332–335
    how interoperate with WPF, 330–331
    using inside WPF, 331–335
  User Interface (UI), 330
  using WPF in Win32 applications, 335–337

Win32 for 64-bit Windows, 2
Win32ButtonHost class, 333
Window class, 7, 32
Window element, 16, 192, 198, 385
window events, 35–36
Window file type, 117
Window object, 32–35, 72, 90
<window> element, 36
<Window> node, 45
Window1 constructor, 200
Window1.g.cs file, 376
Window1.xaml file, 71, 72–73, 367, 382, 407
Window1.xaml.cs class, 375
Window1.xaml.cs file, 199, 332
WindowForm.cs file, 348
Window.Resources element, 14, 228
<Window.Resources> XML element, 46
Windows Activation Service (WAS), 400
Windows Application (WPF) icon, 211
Windows CardSpace (WCS), 353
Windows Communication Foundation (WCF)
    architecture, 398–399
    building services
        Hello WCF Client, 405–409
        Hello WCF Service, 402–404
        overview, 402
    fundamentals
        clients, 400
        endpoints, 400–402
        overview, 399
        service hosts, 400
        services, 399
    of .NET Framework 3.0, 3
    overview, 397
    service orientation (SO), 397–398
Windows Communication Foundation (WCF) Service
    Library, 75–78
Windows Display Driver Model (WDDM) driver, 354
Windows Features dialog box, 241
Windows Forms, adding controls, 337–351
    adding ActiveX Controls, 339–344
    adding ActiveX Controls in XAML, 344–345
    adding HwndHost in XAML, 339
    adding WindowsFormsHost in code, 337–339
    adding WPF controls to Windows Forms, 345–349
    affecting properties, 349–351
Windows Forms Application, 350
Windows Installer (MSI), 291, 292
Windows Presentation Foundation (WPF)
    architecture
        composition system, 14–15
        core subsystems, 356–359
        Desktop Window Manager (DWM), 360–361
        element system, 5–9
        font system, 10
        input/event system, 10–11

message transport system, 14
        overview, 5
        property system, 11–14
        threading model, 359–360
        visual system, 9
    design principles
        declarative programming, 4
        document portability, 5
        integration, 4
        overview, 3–4
        simplified deployment, 4–5
        vector graphics, 4
    framework
        Application class, 363–364
        Control class, 371–373
        DependencyObject, 362–363
        DependencyProperty, 362–363
        Dispatcher object, 362
        FrameworkElement class, 371
        Freezable class, 364
        overview, 361–362
        UIElement class, 370–371
        Visual class, 364–370
    history, 2–3
    overview, 1
    visual design tools
        Electric Rain ZAM 3D, 21–22
        Microsoft Expression Blend, 19–20
        Mobiform Aurora, 22–23
        overview, 18
        visual designer for Windows Presentation Foundation,
            20–21
        XamlPad, 18–19
    XAML, 15–18
Windows Shell, 2
Windows Workflow Foundation (WF)
    architecture, 411
    fundamentals
        activities, 412
        building workflow programmatically, 414–416
        building workflow using the Workflow Designer,
            416–423
        creating custom activity, 423–427
        overview, 411
        tracking services, 413
        transaction services, 413
        types of workflow, 412–413
    of .NET Framework 3.0, 3
    overview, 409–410
    workflow defined, 410
WindowsBase referenced assembly, 64
WindowsFormsHost, adding in code, 337–339
WindowsFormsHost subclass, HwndSource class,
    337, 339, 342, 349
WinForms, 4, 236
WM_* messages, 10

`WM_CREATE` **notification, 336**
`WM_PAINT` **message, 357**
workflow
  building programmatically, 414–416
  building using Workflow Designer, 416–423
  defined, 410
  types of, 412–413
Workflow Activity Project template, 423
Workflow Designer, 416–423
workflow elements, 102
`WorkflowCompleted` **event, 418**
`WorkflowTerminated` **event, 418**
workspace panels, 86–87
workspace zoom control, 89
WPF (Windows Application) icon, 211
WPF (Windows Presentation Foundation)
  architecture
    composition system, 14–15
    core subsystems, 356–359
    Desktop Window Manager (DWM), 360–361
    element system, 5–9
    font system, 10
    input/event system, 10–11
    message transport system, 14
    overview, 5
    property system, 11–14
    threading model, 359–360
    visual system, 9
  design principles
    declarative programming, 4
    document portability, 5
    integration, 4
    overview, 3–4
    simplified deployment, 4–5
    vector graphics, 4
  framework
    `Application` class, 363–364
    `Control` class, 371–373
    `DependencyObject`, 362–363
    `DependencyProperty`, 362–363
    `Dispatcher` object, 362
    `FrameworkElement` class, 371
    `Freezable` class, 364
    overview, 361–362
    `UIElement` class, 370–371
    `Visual` class, 364–370
  history, 2–3
  overview, 1
  visual design tools
    Electric Rain ZAM 3D, 21–22
    Microsoft Expression Blend, 19–20
    Mobiform Aurora, 22–23
    overview, 18

    visual designer for Windows Presentation Foundation,
      20–21
    XamlPad, 18–19
    XAML, 15–18
WPF Custom Control Library, 78–82
Wrap panel, 101–102
`WSHttpBinding` **default binding, 400**
WYSIWYG interface, 115
WYSIWYG-style development environment, 116

X
XAML
  adding ActiveX Controls in, 344–345
  adding `HwndHost` in, 339
  browser applications, 239–246, 295–296
  custom types, 386–387
  declarative programming
    designer and developer collaboration, 18
    overview, 15–17
    XAML runtime support, 17–18
  files, 373–378
  manipulating, 378–382
  markup extensions, 385–386
  overview, 15, 29–30
  standalone or "loose," 239
  Window1.XAML, 382
  XAML root element, 382
  `x:Class` attribute
    attributes, 384–385
    child elements, 384
    CLR properties, 384
    namespaces, 383
    overview, 383
XAML Browser Application (XBAP)
  authentication mechanism, 241
  caching, 240
  deployment, 240
  features, 239–240
  hosting, 240
  installing, 240
  offline use, 240
  `Page1.xaml` file, 73–74
  security, 240, 314–322
  user permission for, 240
.xaml extension, 296
XAML namespace attribute, 379
`XamlPad`, **18–19**
`XamlReader` **class, 381**
`XamlReader` **object, 346, 348**
`XAMLReader.Load` **method, 378**
`XamlReader.Load` **method, 379**
`XamlWriter` **class, 381**

XamlWriter.Save **class, 381**
XBAP. *See* XAML Browser Application
.xbap extension, 295, 296
XbapApplication project, 246
x:Class **attribute**
  child elements, 384
  CLR properties, 384
  namespaces, 383
  overview, 383
  XAML attributes, 384–385
XCopy, 291, 296
x:Key **attribute, 14, 223, 224**
XML Paper Specification (XPS), 5
XML-based declarative language. *See* XAML
XMLDataProvider, **198**
XMLDocument **object, 381**
xmlns **attribute, 30, 221, 344**
XmlReader **object, 379**
XPDM (XP Driver Model) driver, 354
XPS (XML Paper Specification), 5
.xps extension, 296
x:TypeArguments **attribute, 259, 265**
x:TypeAttribute **attribute, 266**

Z

ZIndex, **101**
z-index, 126
zones
  Code Access Security (CAS), 305
  Microsoft Internet Explorer, 313–314
zooming, 88, 105

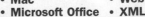